Y0-ASQ-704

A HISTORY OF THE THIRD REICH

VOLUME 3: PERSONALITIES

by Jeff T. Hay
Christopher R. Browning, *Consulting Editor*

Daniel Leone, *President*
Bonnie Szumski, *Publisher*
Scott Barbour, *Managing Editor*

GREENHAVEN PRESS®

THOMSON
GALE

THOMSON
GALE

Acknowledgments

The author wishes to thank Professor Christopher R. Browning of the University of North Carolina, Chapel Hill, a Holocaust expert and early mentor, for his contribution to the selection of entries for these volumes. He would also like to thank the staff of Greenhaven Press, notably editor Viqi Wagner, whose hard work and resourcefulness were a great help in completing the project.

© 2003 by Greenhaven Press. Greenhaven Press is an imprint of The Gale Group, Inc., a division of Thomson Learning, Inc.

Greenhaven Press® and Thomson Learning™ are trademarks used herein under license.

For more information, contact
Greenhaven Press
27500 Drake Rd.
Farmington Hills, MI 48331-3535
Or you can visit our Internet site at http://www.gale.com

ALL RIGHTS RESERVED.
No part of this work covered by the copyright hereon may be reproduced or used in any form or by any means—graphic, electronic, or mechanical, including photocopying, recording, taping, Web distribution or information storage retrieval systems—without the written permission of the publisher.

LIBRARY OF CONGRESS CATALOGING-IN-PUBLICATION DATA

A history of the Third Reich / Jeff T. Hay, book author.
   p. cm.
Includes bibliographical references and index.
  ISBN 0-7377-1116-7 (v. 1 : alk. paper)
  ISBN 0-7377-1118-3 (v. 2 : alk. paper)
  ISBN 0-7377-1478-6 (v. 1 and v. 2 set : alk. paper)
  ISBN 0-7377-1120-5 (v. 3 : alk. paper)
  ISBN 0-7377-1477-8 (v. 4 : alk. paper)
  1. Germany—History—1933–1945. 2. National socialism—History. I. Hay, Jeff T.
DD256.5 .H529 2003
943.086—dc21

2002033900

Printed in the United States of America

CONTENTS

A
Abetz, Otto, 7
Amann, Max, 7
Axis Sally (Mildred Gillars), 8

B
Bach-Zelewski, Erich von dem, 9
Badoglio, Pietro, 10
Baeck, Leo, 10
Barbie, Klaus, 11
Barth, Karl, 11
Beck, Ludwig, 12
Benes, Edouard, 13
Bernadotte, Folke, 14
Best, Werner, 14
Bismarck, Otto von, 15
Blomberg, Werner von, 16
Bock, Fedor von, 18
Bonhoeffer, Dietrich, 18
Bormann, Martin, 19
Bouhler, Philip, 22
Brauchitsch, Walther von, 23
Braun, Eva, 24
Braun, Wernher von, 25
Brüning, Heinrich, 26

C
Canaris, Wilhelm, 28
Chamberlain, Houston Stewart, 28
Chamberlain, Neville, 29
Churchill, Winston, 30
Ciano, Galeazzo, 32
Clauberg, Karl, 33

D
Daladier, Edouard, 34
Daluege, Kurt, 34
Darré, Walther, 35
de Gaulle, Charles, 36
Dietrich, Josef (Sepp), 38
Dietrich, Otto, 39
Dohnanyi, Hans von, 40
Dönitz, Karl, 40
Drexler, Anton, 42

E
Ebert, Friedrich, 44
Eckart, Dietrich, 44
Eichmann, Adolf, 45
Eicke, Theodor, 48
Einstein, Albert, 49
Epp, Franz Xaver Ritter von, 50
Esser, Hermann, 51

F
Falkenhorst, Nikolaus von, 53
Faulhaber, Michael von, 53
Feder, Gottfried, 54
Fegelein, Hermann, 55
Flick, Friedrich, 56
Forster, Albert, 56
Franco, Francisco, 57
Frank, Anne, 58
Frank, Hans, 59
Frank, Karl-Hermann, 60
Freisler, Roland, 60
Frick, Wilhelm, 61
Fritsch, Werner Freiherr von, 63
Fritzsche, Hans, 65
Fromm, Friedrich, 66
Funk, Walther, 67
Furtwängler, Wilhelm, 68

G
Galen, Clemens August Graf von, 70
Galland, Adolf, 71
Gerstein, Kurt, 71
Gisevius, Hans Bernd, 72
Globke, Hans, 73
Globocnik, Odilo, 74
Gluecks, Richard, 75
Gobineau, Artur Comte de, 75
Goebbels, Joseph, 76
Goerdeler, Carl, 79
Göring, Emmy Sonnemann, 80
Göring, Hermann, 80
Göring, Karin von Kantzow, 84

Greiser, Arthur, 85
Groener, Wilhelm, 85
Grynszpan, Herschel, 86
Guderian, Heinz, 87

H

Hacha, Emil, 89
Halder, Franz, 89
Hanfstaengl, Ernst (Putzi), 90
Hassell, Ulrich von, 91
Heinkel, Ernst, 92
Heisenberg, Werner, 93
Helldorf, Wolf Heinrich Graf von, 93
Henlein, Konrad, 94
Hess, Rudolf, 95
Heydrich, Reinhard, 97
Himmler, Heinrich, 99
Hindenburg, Oskar von, 105
Hindenburg, Paul von, 105
Hitler, Adolf, 108
Hitler, Alois, 118
Hitler, Klara Poelzl, 119
Hoffman, Heinrich, 120
Horthy, Miklos, 121
Höss, Rudolf, 121
Hossbach, Friedrich, 123
Huber, Kurt, 123
Hugenberg, Alfred, 124

J

Jeschonnek, Hans, 126
Jodl, Alfred, 126

K

Kaltenbrunner, Ernst, 128
Keitel, Wilhelm, 129
Keppler, Wilhelm, 130
Kerrl, Hans, 131
Kesselring, Albert, 131
Kirdorf, Emil, 132
Kleist, Ewald von, 133
Kluge, Günter Hans, 134
Koch, Erich, 134
Koch, Ilse, 135
Kramer, Josef, 136
Krupp von Bohlen und Halbach, Alfred, 136
Krupp von Bohlen und Halbach, Gustav, 137
Kube, Wilhelm, 139

Kubizek, August, 139

L

Lammers, Hans, 141
Laval, Pierre, 142
Leeb, Wilhelm Ritter von, 142
Ley, Robert, 143
Liebenfels, Jörg Lanz von, 145
List, Wilhelm, 145
Lohse, Heinrich, 146
Lord Haw Haw (William Joyce), 146
Lorenz, Werner, 147
Ludendorff, Erich, 147
Lueger, Karl, 149
Luther, Martin, 150
Lutze, Victor, 150

M

Mannerheim, Karl Gustav, 151
Manstein, Friedrich Erich von, 151
Maurice, Emil, 153
Mayer, Helene, 153
Meissner, Otto, 154
Mengele, Josef, 154
Milch, Erhard, 155
Model, Walther von, 156
Molotov, Vyacheslav, 157
Moltke, Helmuth James Graf von, 158
Morell, Theodor, 159
Müller, Friedrich Max, 159
Müller, Heinrich, 160
Müller, Ludwig, 161
Mussert, Anton, 162
Mussolini, Benito, 162

N

Naujocks, Alfred, 166
Nebe, Arthur, 167
Neurath, Constantin Freiherr von, 167
Niemöller, Martin, 168
Nietzsche, Friedrich, 169

O

Oberg, Karl, 171
Ohlendorf, Otto, 171
Olbricht, Friedrich, 173
Oster, Hans, 173

P

Papen, Franz von, 175
Paulus, Friedrich, 178
Pétain, Philippe, 179
Pius XI, 180
Pius XII, 180
Pohl, Oswald, 181

Q

Quisling, Vidkun, 182

R

Rademacher, Franz, 183
Raeder, Erich, 183
Raubal, Geli, 185
Rauschning, Hermann, 186
Reichenau, Walther von, 186
Reitsch, Hanna, 187
Remer, Otto, 188
Ribbentrop, Joachim von, 189
Riefenstahl, Leni, 191
Röhm, Ernst, 192
Rommel, Erwin, 194
Roosevelt, Franklin D., 196
Rosenberg, Alfred, 198
Rudel, Hans-Ulrich, 201
Rundstedt, Gerd von, 201
Rust, Bernhard, 202

S

Sauckel, Fritz, 204
Sauerbruch, Ferdinand, 205
Schacht, Hjalmar, 205
Schellenburg, Walter, 207
Schindler, Oskar, 208
Schirach, Baldur von, 210
Schlageter, Albert Leo, 212
Schleicher, Kurt von, 212
Schmeling, Max, 213
Schoerner, Ferdinand, 215
Scholl, Hans and Scholl, Sophie, 215
Scholtz-Klink, Gertrude, 216
Schröder, Kurt Freiherr von, 218
Schuschnigg, Kurt von, 218
Schwerin von Krosigk, Lutz Graf, 220
Seeckt, Hans von, 220
Seldte, Franz, 221

Seydlitz, Walter von, 221
Seyss-Inquart, Artur von, 222
Skorzeny, Otto, 223
Smigly-Rydz, Edward, 224
Speer, Albert, 224
Speidel, Hans, 227
Sperrle, Hugo, 227
Stalin, Joseph, 228
Stangl, Franz, 230
Stark, Johannes, 231
Stauffenberg, Claus Schenk Graf von, 232
Stieff, Helmuth, 234
Stinnes, Hugo, 234
Strasser, Gregor, 234
Strasser, Otto, 236
Streicher, Julius, 237
Stroop, Jürgen, 239
Stuckart, Wilhelm, 239
Stuelpnagel, Karl Heinrich von, 240
Stuelpnagel, Otto von, 241

T

Terboven, Josef, 242
Thälmann, Ernst, 242
Thierack, Otto Georg, 244
Thyssen, Fritz, 244
Todt, Fritz, 245
Tojo, Hideki, 246
Tresckow, Henning von, 247
Troost, Paul Ludwig, 247
Trott zu Solz, Adam von, 248
Truman, Harry S., 249

V

van der Lubbe, Marinus, 251

W

Wagner, Richard, 252
Wagner, Winifred, 253
Wallenberg, Raoul, 254
Warlimont, Walther, 255
Weizsäcker, Ernst Freiherr von, 255
Wessel, Horst, 256
Wiedemann, Fritz, 256
Wiesel, Elie, 257
Wiesenthal, Simon, 257
Wilhelm II, 257

Wirth, Christian, 258
Wisliceny, Dieter, 259
Witzleben, Erwin von, 259
Wolff, Karl, 260

Y

Yorck von Wartenburg,
 Peter Graf, 262

Z

Zeitzler, Kurt, 263

Index, 264
Picture Credits, 271
About the Author, 272
About the Consulting Editor, 272

A

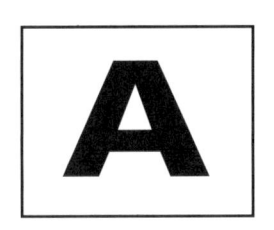

Abetz, Otto (1903–1958)

An SS lieutenant colonel and the Third Reich's ambassador to Vichy France. A former art teacher, he joined the Nazi foreign service in 1935 and was assigned to Paris, where he stayed until 1939, when he was thrown out of France because of his excessive pro-German activities. He returned to France, however, in 1940 after the Third Reich conquered and occupied the country. Nazi foreign minister Joachim von Ribbentrop had decided to reward him by naming him ambassador to the collaborationist Vichy regime.

As ambassador Abetz was an active anti-Semite, thinking that attacks on French Jews would encourage support for Germany among the French general public. He took an active role in gathering Jews for deportation to Poland. After World War II a French court sentenced him to twenty years at hard labor, but he was released after only five years, in 1954. Four years later he died in a mysterious auto accident in Germany. *See also* collaboration, Vol. 1; Vichy France, Vol. 2.

Amann, Max (1891–1957)

The chief of Eher Verlag, the Nazi Party's publishing house, and the head of the Reich Press Chamber under Joseph Goebbels's Propaganda Ministry. Born in Munich on November 24, 1891, Amann was an early comrade of Adolf Hitler: He was a sergeant in the same Bavarian infantry unit that Hitler served in as a corporal during World War I. Enjoying Hitler's full trust, he became the business manager of the Nazi Party in 1921, and in 1922 took control of Eher Verlag, whose main publication at the time was the *Völkischer Beobachter*, the Nazi newspaper. In later years he served as a Nazi Party official in the German Reichstag.

Amann also was Adolf Hitler's personal banker, and in that capacity he did a great deal to ensure that the Nazi leader had, first, a steady income, and later, substantial personal wealth. Most of this came from royalties from Hitler's *Mein Kampf*, published by Eher Verlag. Indeed, it was Amann who gave Hitler's book its title; he convinced the Nazi leader that the original title, *Four and a Half Years of Struggle Against Lies, Stupidity, and Cowardice*, would render it unsellable. To further boost Hitler's income Amann also arranged for the Führer to receive large fees whenever he issued statements to the German press. Hitler rewarded him for these services, and for his loyalty, by assigning him to a number of posts. Amann became head of the Reich Association of German Newspaper Publishers, chief of the Reich Press Chamber, and even a Reichsleiter, an executive title highly regarded in the Nazi administrative hierarchy. Using his numerous skills, which ranged from buyouts to intimidation, Amann managed to acquire a near-monopoly of German newspapers and substantial personal wealth of his own. Indeed he was one of the richest Nazis, and for several years Eher Verlag was the world's largest publishing house.

Amann survived World War II. He tried to hide his past by posing as a simple businessman with no political ties. Nevertheless, German denazification procedures revealed the truth, which was that he had profited more than any other man by being a Nazi Party member. The denazification courts labeled him a major offender, and sentenced him to ten years in a labor camp as well as the loss of his property and wealth. He returned to Munich after his release and died there, ruined and destitute, on March 30, 1957. *See also* Eher Verlag, journalism in the Third Reich, Vol. 1; *Mein Kampf*, Reich Press Chamber, Vol. 2.

Axis Sally (Mildred Gillars) (1901–1988)

An American woman who broadcast anti-Allied propaganda from Berlin during World War II. Mildred Elizabeth Gillars was born in Ohio in 1901, and early on demonstrated an individualist streak; she was, for example, the first woman to wear pants at Ohio Wesleyan University, then a very conservative institution. She dropped out in 1920, and left for Germany to study music. She stayed on after Adolf Hitler took power and gravitated toward radio broadcasting, where officials such as Propaganda Minister Joseph Goebbels realized the public relations value of an American woman who, for whatever reason, preferred to live in the Third Reich. During World War II she maintained a radio program on which she alternately played jazz, which was officially frowned on by top Nazis but which they knew Americans liked, and broadcast propaganda by recommending that Americans simply go home and give up a useless fight. American soldiers tuned in for the music and ignored or ridiculed the propaganda, dubbing her Axis Sally after the enemy alliance.

After the war Gillars was arrested by American officials and later sentenced to a twelve-year term in a federal prison. After her release in 1961 she was a teacher at a Roman Catholic school in Columbus, Ohio. She returned to Ohio Wesleyan in 1973 to complete her degree, and died in Columbus on June 25, 1988. *See also* Lord Haw Haw, Vol. 3.

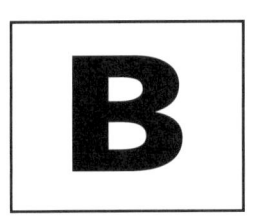

Bach-Zelewski, Erich von dem (1899–1972)

A Waffen-SS general responsible for numerous atrocities and tens of thousands of deaths on the eastern front during World War II. He was born in eastern Germany on March 1, 1899, into a traditional Junker family from East Prussia, and he fell easily into his family's military tradition. He served briefly in World War I and then as a member of the right-wing Freikorps in the aftermath of the war. During the period of the Weimar Republic he was a Reichswehr officer. Like a number of young aristocrats, Bach-Zelewski was both ambitious and strongly nationalist, and he made his decision to join the Nazi movement in 1932, naturally gravitating toward the SS as the best potential opportunity for action and advancement. During the 1930s he served as an SS officer in East Prussia, where he oversaw certain Gestapo activities. In 1939 he was promoted to general of the SS, and within two years to a post as general of the Waffen-SS, the organization's military arm. His promotion coincided with the Nazi invasion of the Soviet Union, and Bach-Zelewski served as an officer in one of the special task forces, or Einsatzgruppen, that had allegedly received verbal orders to massacre millions of Soviet Jews in the wake of the German offensive. Between July 1941 and the end of 1942 Bach-Zelewski was involved in a number of mass murder operations in the Baltic states as well as at Minsk and Mogilev in Belarus. He later denied his involvement in the Einsatzgruppen massacres.

Over the next years Bach-Zelewski served as chief of Heinrich Himmler's antipartisan operations, and in that capacity was involved in actions against Polish and Soviet civilian populations. After German occupation forces left Warsaw in the summer of 1944 ahead of approaching Soviet forces, Bach-Zelewski was given the task of assembling a force to devastate the city. He picked SS criminals, desperate young men from occupied territories, and rootless freebooters and set them loose in a dayslong orgy of destruction and plunder in central Warsaw. Adolf Hitler awarded him the Knight's Cross for this action. At war's end Bach-Zelewski was a regular army commander.

Bach-Zelewski was never called to account for either the Einsatzgruppen massacres or his involvement in the destruction of Warsaw, although he spent most of the rest of his life in German prisons. He made a deal with the International Military Tribunal at the Nuremberg war crimes trials to testify for the prosecution, in exchange for immunity from both personal charges and extradition to Poland or the Soviet Union. During his testimony he was highly critical of Himmler and other SS leaders and even denounced his own role in wartime atrocities. In 1951 a German denazification court sentenced him to ten years' confinement as a Nazi fellow traveler, and in 1961 he was put on trial for his involvement in the 1934 Blood Purge. He was tried again in 1962 for the murder of six Communists in 1933 and given a life sentence. Bach-Zelewski died in a Munich prison on March 8, 1972. *See also* Einsatzgruppen, Vol. 1; Waffen-SS; Warsaw, destruction of, Vol. 2; Graebe, The Einsatzgruppen in Action, Vol. 4.

Badoglio, Pietro (1871–1956)

Italian soldier and politician who replaced Benito Mussolini as head of state after Mussolini was forced out of office in July 1943. Badoglio first rose to prominence as an army officer in World War I, when he commanded Italian troops on the Austrian front. After the war he served as the Italian army's chief of staff. He also served as colonial governor in Libya from 1928 to 1933 and, after commanding the army that conquered Ethiopia, served as viceroy there. He was recalled as chief of staff when World War II began but resigned over the Italian failure to capture Greece in December 1940. An Italian patriot and nationalist rather than a Fascist, Badoglio was a strong opponent of Mussolini, and he helped devise the plot that overthrew the Fascist dictator. Afterward, as prime minister, he surrendered Italy to the Allies, although at that point Allied armies occupied only the southern part of the country. German forces still occupied the north and, after rescuing Mussolini from Badoglio's guards, propped him up as, in effect, the Nazi Gauleiter of occupied northern Italy. Badoglio, meanwhile, resigned as prime minister in June 1944 and retired to his family home, where he died on November 1, 1956. *See also* fascism, Vol. 1; Mussolini, Benito, Vol. 3.

Baeck, Leo (1873–1956)

A leading figure among German Jews during the era of the Third Reich. He was born in Prussia in May 1873 and earned his diploma as a rabbi in Berlin in 1897. In the early years of his career he established himself as a theologian, teacher, and writer, publishing his first book, *The Essence of Judaism*, in 1905. In 1912 he took a position as head of the leading Jewish synagogue in Berlin. During World War I he served the German army as a chaplain.

After World War I Baeck became active in Jewish organizations ranging from the Union of German Rabbis, of which he became president in 1922, and the Welfare

Jewish religious leader and rabbi Leo Baeck remained in Germany to assist Jews suffering from Nazi persecution.

Center for Jews. He was accepted by various different Jewish interest groups, and proved himself able to navigate effectively among orthodox Jews, liberal Jews, and Zionists. Although he was not a Zionist himself, he was sympathetic to the interest among younger Jews in reviving Jewish culture and a sense of national identity, a position that sometimes put him at odds with both conservative and highly assimilated Jews.

After the Nazis took power, and especially after 1935, when the Nazi state began to aggressively enact and enforce measures against all German Jews, Baeck found himself in a powerful leadership role. He was president of the Reich Central Representation of German Jews, an organization whose many missions included trying to mitigate the worst effects of Nazi oppression, seeking ways to retrain Jews for trades after they were locked out of their established jobs or professions, raising funds for Jewish emigration, and searching the world for places where German Jews could go. Baeck's position, which involved frequent contact with Nazi officials, was certainly a very difficult one. He took the position in 1933, the same year that Adolf Hitler took power, and he realized that the Jews of Germany were in great danger. Nevertheless he personally was unwilling to leave Germany, unlike many other prominent Jews. He chose to stay to be able to minister to his people in their time of need.

In 1939 the Nazi regime closed the Central Representation and replaced it with the Reich Organization of Jews in Germany. Baeck was appointed to head the body, and he was continually reminded by the Gestapo that a large part of his responsibility was to ensure that Jews in Germany (the Nazi mind could no longer conceive of a German Jew) both obeyed Nazi edicts and asked nothing of the state. He was arrested several times and finally, in 1943, sent to the concentration camp at Theresienstadt, the so-called model ghetto where the Nazis interned a number of prominent people. In the camp Baeck continued to teach and lead a congregation. He was also the leader of the camp's council of Jewish elders.

Baeck survived the deportations, the death camps, and in the end, World War II. In the next years he moved to London, where he continued to be a community leader, writer, and teacher, heading numerous international Jewish organizations. He also helped found the Leo Baeck Institute, which dedicated itself to maintaining the memory of the now-decimated German Jewish community of central Europe. He died in London in November 1956. *See also* anti-Semitism, Vol. 1; Reich Central Representation of German Jews, Theresienstadt, Vol. 2.

Barbie, Klaus (1913–1991)

Gestapo officer known as the Butcher of Lyon for his various brutalities in occupied France during World War II. Barbie was born in Bad Godesberg in 1913. He was a member of the Hitler Youth as a student and joined the SS in 1934 after leaving school. He became a member of the Nazi Party in 1937. Heinrich Himmler, head of the SS, approved of Barbie's zeal and enthusiasm for police work, and Barbie was tagged as a future leading officer. After the fall of western Europe in 1940 he was assigned to occupation forces there. Barbie was assigned to RSHA (Reich Central Security Office) Section IV, the Gestapo, which dealt with "Jewish affairs," and he proved to be dedicated and creative in rooting out and deporting Jewish communities in both France and the Netherlands. He used torture as a matter of course to gain information. Barbie is thought to have been personally responsible for the deaths of up to twenty-six thousand people. His greatest notoriety, however, stems from the arrest and death of Jean Moulin, a high ranking officer in the French resistance. Moulin died under torture during Barbie's interrogation.

After the war Barbie was sentenced to death in absentia by French authorities. According to some accounts, however, he was protected for a number of years by intelligence groups in the West who saw him as a valuable resource in the new fight against communism. In the mid-1950s Barbie escaped to Bolivia with his wife and children, obtaining citizenship in 1957 and living under the name Klaus Altmann. He was identified by Nazi hunters as early as 1971, but various Bolivian governments protected him until 1983, when he was finally extradited to France. In 1987 Barbie was tried for war crimes in Lyon in a highly publicized event. He was sentenced to life in prison (France did not use the death penalty) and died in prison on September 25, 1991. *See also* Gestapo, Vol. 1.

Barth, Karl (1886–1968)

A leading Protestant theologian of the twentieth century who was forced to leave the Third Reich when he refused to swear an oath of allegiance to Adolf Hitler. Barth was born in Basel, Switzerland, in 1886 and served as a minister in a local church until the 1920s, when he took up a professorship at the University of Göttingen in Germany. He was later a professor of theology at the Universities of Münster and Bonn, also in Germany. In 1918 Barth published *The Letter from Rome*, a book that both made his reputation and became one of the most important works of Protestant theology of the era. After he was forced out of Hitler's Germany he wrote a larger work, *Churchly Dogma*. He was also the editor of two German theological journals, *Between the Eras* and *Theological Existence Today*. Barth was concerned that Christian thinking was taking too scientific an approach in the urge to find ways in which Christianity could remain relevant and meaningful in the modern, industrialized, scientific era. He argued that the attempt to reconcile theology with science was misleading; true revelation could come only through the grace of God and was the product of something closer to intuition than science. He also argued that the Protestant churches had grown too worldly, too committed to German nationalism and earthly concerns. In fact, Barth considered the leaders of the church in Germany to be corrupt. After Hitler and the Nazis took power in 1933, Barth spoke out against the new regime's attempt to coordinate the German Protestant churches into the Nazi state in the form of the German Christian movement. In 1935, when he refused to take the oath of loyalty then required of all state employees, Barth lost his professorship at the University of Bonn. He returned to Switzerland to continue his teaching and theological writing. He died in Basel in 1968. *See also* exiles and refugees from the Third Reich, German Christians, Vol. 1; religion in the Third Reich, Vol. 2.

Beck, Ludwig (1880–1944)

One of the leaders of the German resistance movement that wanted to overthrow Adolf Hitler and the Nazi regime but was never able to carry out an effective coup. In fact, Beck was among the earliest and most powerful Germans to speak out against Hitler, and was considered by his fellow conspirators the best candidate to be future head of state should Hitler be removed.

Beck was born in the Rhineland in 1880 and joined the German army as a young man, where he marked himself out for rapid promotion. In 1911 he joined the General Staff, and during World War I he served with distinction in Alsace-Lorraine on the western front. During the era of the Weimar Republic he held numerous posts in the Reichswehr. On October 1, 1933, after the Nazis took power, Beck was appointed adjutant general in the Ministry of the Reichswehr, a post of some political as well as military importance. Skilled in planning and logistics, Beck succeeded in the ministry as he had elsewhere. In 1935 he rose to the position of chief of the General Staff of the army, in charge of planning and operations, and his only army superiors were Generals Werner von Blomberg and Werner Freiherr von Fritsch. In this post he came into increasing conflict with Adolf Hitler, whom he had never admired and whom he never supported by joining the Nazi Party. Presumably, however, Beck took the oath of loyalty that all military officers were required to swear beginning in 1935, pledging themselves to Adolf Hitler personally rather than to the German nation or people. Nevertheless, Beck was a traditionalist as a military officer. Warfare, he thought, should be avoided if possible. If not, it should be limited and guided by both specific, realistic objectives and by the customs of honorable warfare. He was opposed to political revolutions and to wars of conquest, and he suspected that Hitler's unrealistic ambitions might bring Germany to ruin.

By 1938 Hitler was ready to begin Germany's eastward expansion. Beck, whose post required him to be present at all high-level army planning sessions, expressed surprise when he learned of Hitler's plan to invade Czechoslovakia. He also disapproved of Hitler's tendency to base his military planning on racial philosophy rather than on practical limitations and objectives. After trying to persuade other generals to follow him in preventing Hitler from moving forward, Beck resigned from his post on August 18, 1938. The move worked, ironically, in Hitler's favor rather than Beck's. Blomberg and Fritsch, who were also concerned about Hitler's territorial goals, had been removed as the result of personal scandals in early 1938, leaving Beck the only top officer willing to stand in Hitler's way. Beck's resignation allowed Hitler to complete his takeover of what was left of Germany's traditional officer corps and take control of the German military himself.

After leaving his post, and ostensibly in retirement, Beck remained a focal point of the German resistance movement. He played key planning roles in plots undertaken in late 1939 and July 1944 to remove Hitler from power. During the planning for the July plot, moreover, Beck was named as the head of state in the interim government that, in the wake of the removal of the Nazis from power, would stabilize Germany and seek peace with the Allies. When the plot failed, however, Beck elected to commit suicide, suspecting that he would be certainly humiliated, perhaps tortured, and probably executed if Hitler's men captured him alive. After two unsuccessful attempts to shoot himself, he asked a German army sergeant to finish the task. He died in the evening of July 20, 1944. *See also* July 1944 Plot, Vol. 1; Hitler, Hitler Promises Revenge for the July 1944 Plot, Vol. 4.

Benes, Edouard (1884–1948)

Czechoslovakian politician who was one of the founders of the nation in 1918 and served as president in 1938, when the Czechs were forced to surrender much of their territory to the Third Reich. Benes was born in Kozlany in Bohemia on May 28, 1884. After embarking on an academic career as a lecturer in economics and sociology at the University of Prague, Benes spent World War I in Paris. There, along with Tomas Masaryk, he made plans to organize a Czechoslovakian republic. The two were able to enact the plan when, at the end of the war, the Austro-Hungarian Empire was dismantled. Benes served as the nation's first foreign minister from 1918 to 1935, when he succeeded Masaryk as president.

Benes became one of the first victims of Adolf Hitler's territorial ambitions in 1938, when ethnic Germans living in the Sudeten area of Czechoslovakia demanded autonomy from the Prague government. When Benes proved hesitant to partition his own nation, Hitler accused him of oppressing and terrorizing Germans. Hitler's charges grew even more shrill when Benes approved the use of military force to defend his nation against the Third Reich. In September 1938, Benes tried to save his country by joining British and French leaders in negotiations with Hitler in order to prevent a large-scale war. But at the Munich Conference of September 30, when Czechoslovakia's fate was decided, Benes was not even allowed to speak, and his representatives were kept away from negotiations. After the so-called Munich sellout of the Czechs, which resulted in the loss of the Sudetenland, Benes resigned as president.

After spending some time as a professor in Chicago, Benes moved to London when World War II began. He took up the presidency of the Czech government in exile, and strove mightily to get the British to recognize him as the legitimate leader of his nation. They finally did so in July 1941 and repudiated the Munich Agreement in August 1942. Beyond his political activities he helped organize units of Czech exiles to serve in the British armed forces, and it was Benes who gave the order for Czech commandos to assassinate Reinhard Heydrich, the Nazi occupation governor, in the spring of 1942. At war's end Benes returned to Prague as president, but found himself forced to negotiate with the nation's large Communist Party, which was backed up by the guns and diplomacy of the Soviet Union. After the Communists took power in 1948, Benes resigned. One of his lasting accomplishments, however, was the expulsion of tens of thousands of ethnic Germans from Czechoslovakia, which helped to stabilize his nation but proved a lasting bone of contention among the Germans who were forced to move. Most of them ended up in Bavaria. Benes died in a Bohemian village on September 3, 1948. *See also* Munich Conference, Vol. 2; Hitler, Hitler Threatens Czechoslovakia, Vol. 4.

Bernadotte, Folke (1895–1948)

Swedish diplomat and Red Cross official. Bernadotte was born in Stockholm on January 2, 1895. His background was aristocratic, and one of his uncles was the Swedish king Gustavus V. In 1943 Bernadotte became the vice chairman of the Swedish Red Cross; in that position he actively arranged exchanges of prisoners between the Third Reich and the western Allies via the Swedish city of Göteborg. He also arranged for the return of Norwegian and Danish political prisoners. In February 1945, Bernadotte met with Reichsführer-SS Heinrich Himmler, who was pursuing peace negotiations behind the back of Adolf Hitler. The two had four meetings altogether, which Bernadotte later described in his book *The Curtain Falls*. Himmler promised the further release of prisoners from Nazi camps, including Jews and also women from the Ravensbrück concentration camp, in hopes that he might protect himself from Allied retribution. Himmler hoped also that Bernadotte might act as an intermediary between Himmler and Dwight D. Eisenhower, supreme commander of Allied forces. Bernadotte delivered Himmler's proposals, which were rejected by the Allies; meanwhile Hitler, hearing of the meetings, removed Himmler from all his posts as a traitor to the Third Reich.

Bernadotte went on to become the president of the Swedish Red Cross and a UN mediator in the postwar partition of Palestine. He was assassinated by Jewish extremists in Jerusalem in 1948. *See also* Office of Strategic Services, Vol. 2; Himmler, Heinrich, Vol. 3.

Best, Werner (1903–1989)

An officer in the RSHA (Reichssicherheitshauptamt), or Reich Central Security Office of the SS, who became the top Nazi official in occupied Denmark, holding the post of Reich commissioner. He was also one of the leading legal thinkers in the Third Reich, finding ways for the Gestapo and other branches of the SS police to rid Germany of political and racial opponents without due process of law.

Best was born in Darmstadt in western Germany and grew up mostly in the nearby city of Mainz. His father was killed in France during World War I. He demonstrated an early interest in politics and, from 1921 to 1927, was a student of law. He received his doctorate in law from the University of Heidelberg in 1927. During those same years he became involved in rightwing, German nationalist political movements. He was also imprisoned, twice, by French authorities in the occupied areas of the Ruhr for nationalist activities. In 1927 he was appointed to a judgeship in Hesse, where he developed an interest in the Nazi movement. At one point he helped to draw up plans for a Nazi takeover with comrades at an estate near the city of Worms; discovery of these plans forced Best to resign his judgeship in 1931.

The Nazi takeover of power revived Best's career, and he had prepared for this possibility by joining the SS as an officer. Best, indeed, was just the type sought out by SS chiefs Heinrich Himmler and Reinhard Heydrich: He was intelligent, university educated, loyal, and ruthless. In March 1933 he became police commissioner for Hesse and then was appointed governor. Soon after he became the top legal adviser to the Gestapo and a protégé of Heydrich.

Heydrich, it appears, wanted Best to find ways to justify the arrests and "disappearances" of political and racial opponents to the German Reich. Best complied by using legal explanations based on racial ideology, claiming that the Germans were a people "organically" united by blood. The job of the SS police was to protect that organic unity. Therefore the police had the right to root out any perceived threat to the Germanic racial body. Heydrich grew to rely on Best's abilities, and Best is often considered second only to his chief in building up the SS security and police divisions, which in 1939 were combined under the umbrella of the RSHA.

Soon after World War II broke out Best was promoted to SS-Obergruppenführer (SS general) and served the RSHA in occupied Poland, where he is thought to have been involved in the murders of thousands of Polish Jews and intellectuals in the period from October 1939 to June 1940; postwar trials were never conclusive on the matter. Best then moved from occupied Poland to occupied France, where he served as chief of civil administration, a Nazi Party post rather than an SS one, although in the occupied territories those lines were often blurred. In November 1942 he was appointed Reich commissioner for occupied Denmark. The Nazis considered Denmark to be a potential ally, a racial "little brother," and Best accordingly ruled Denmark with some tolerance. Evidence suggests, in fact, that Best helped to prevent the deportation of most of Denmark's Jews to the Polish death camps in 1943.

After the war Best was tried by a Danish court for complicity in the murders of Danish political prisoners and resistance fighters. He was sentenced to death, but the sentence was commuted and he was released in 1951. Thereafter he returned to Germany to work as a lawyer, but his past as an SS officer continued to haunt him. In 1958 he was fined seventy thousand marks by a German denazification court. In 1969 he was arrested over concerns about his involvement in mass atrocities in Poland during his RSHA days. He was eventually released on medical grounds, however, without having been convicted, and died in 1989. *See also* RSHA, Vol. 2.

Bismarck, Otto von (1815–1898)

Prussian statesman who was the true founder of the Second German Reich (1871–1918). Bismarck worked to unify Germany along the Prussian model of hierarchy, paternalism, and militarism, and he claimed that "blood and iron" rather than diplomacy and ideas were what made a nation strong. The pattern that Bismarck set was thought to have given Germans an appetite for arrogant militarism, strong political leadership, and hierarchical order that the Nazis would exploit.

Bismarck was born into an aristocratic family in Schönhausen, Prussia. He studied law at the Universities of Göttingen and Berlin and passed the Prussian bar in 1835. Afterward he served as an officer in the Prussian army before entering politics as a member of the Prussian Diet, or parliament, in 1847. In 1849 he took a strong stand against liberal revolutionaries who wanted to unite Germany under a republican government, an action that brought him to the attention of the Prussian king Frederick William IV. The king made Bismarck a Prussian representative in the German Confederation that was considering national unification as well as Prussian ambassador to France and Russia. In 1862 Bismarck returned to Prussia as prime minister, where he set about the task of unifying Germany under Prussian guidance.

Bismarck accomplished German unification through a combination of warfare and cunning diplomacy. In 1864 he instigated a successful war against Denmark, which gained him some territory and also demonstrated that he was willing to use overwhelming force. In 1866 Prussian forces

German chancellor Otto von Bismarck (center) in 1871. Bismarck unified the militaristic German empire through a policy of "blood and iron."

defeated the Austro-Hungarian Empire, thereby ensuring that powerful Austria would not play a role in any future German confederation. Finally, in 1870 he started a war with France using a diplomatic trick. The Prussians defeated the French in six weeks, signaling to the hesitant southern German states, such as Bavaria, that their proper future lay in Berlin, not Vienna, and also demonstrating to Europe that there was now a major new power in central Europe, a Second German Reich. The new Prussian king, Kaiser Wilhelm I, was crowned emperor of Germany in the Hall of Mirrors at Versailles in January 1871. Bismarck, meanwhile, was named chancellor, the head of the government. Europe soon knew him as the Iron Chancellor.

Until he was forced into retirement in 1890 by Kaiser Wilhelm II, who was jealous of Bismarck's competence and fame, the Iron Chancellor proceeded to solidify the Second German Reich's place among the great world powers. He concocted a number of treaties both offensive and defensive, helped to begin a massive arms buildup, and acted to create a German overseas empire. He also treated the German people with great paternalism, choosing not to give them any true political power while ensuring they were well cared for through steady employment as well as Europe's first true state-sponsored social welfare measures. After his dismissal by the kaiser, Bismarck retired to his estates at Friedrichsruh, were he died in 1898. *See also* Junkers, Vol. 1; Prussia, Second German Reich, Vol. 2.

Blomberg, Werner von (1878–1946)

A German army officer who was instrumental in helping Adolf Hitler consolidate power in Germany in 1934 but was later forced to resign after expressing concerns about the Nazi dictator's plans for territorial expansion. Born in Pomerania in 1878 into a traditional officer's family in the Prussian style, Blomberg served in the German army during World War I and then joined the Reichswehr in 1919. In the late 1920s he served the Reichswehr in a political post, the head of conscription in the War Office. In that capacity he made a number of visits to the Soviet Union, where by secret arrangement the Germans were training both officers and pilots. He first met Adolf Hitler in 1931, when he was in a command post in East Prussia. Blomberg was very impressed by the Nazi leader, and the meeting ended what had been a short flirtation with communism. Shortly before Hitler took office as chancellor on January 30, 1933, Blomberg was appointed minister of defense and general of infantry.

In the early spring of 1934 Blomberg pledged his support to Hitler at a crucial moment in the Nazi era. At this time Hitler wanted both to integrate the traditional German officer corps into his plans and to combine the offices of German chancellor and president to create a single executive, a single German Führer. He was already chancellor and wanted to assume the office of president when its current holder, the aged Field Marshal Paul von Hindenburg, died, an event likely at any time. The army, for its part, wanted to control the Nazi SA, the millions of storm troopers whom SA leader Ernst Röhm saw as the core of a new and revolutionary German army. Hitler, in a meeting with Blomberg and other top military officials, agreed to contain Röhm and the SA. In return, he asked that the generals support him in combining the two executive offices on the death of Hindenburg. Blomberg enthusiastically agreed, and the other officers soon followed suit, although generally with less enthusiasm. With the help of the German army as well as the SS, Hitler had Röhm and other SA leaders killed in the event known as the Blood Purge of June 30, 1944. In the days before and after the purge Blomberg publicly congratulated Hitler for having spared Germany from the ravages of a potential SA revolution; among the places where these congratulations appeared was in the pages of the *Völkischer Beobachter*, the Nazi newspaper. He also proclaimed that the army would remain loyal to Hitler. In August, after Hindenburg died, Blomberg fulfilled the remainder of his agreement by supporting Hitler's takeover of Hindenburg's position. He also supported the transformation of the Reichswehr into the Wehrmacht, an administrative move that involved, among other changes, an oath of loyalty to Hitler personally taken by all members of the armed forces. Blomberg was among the first, as it happened, to take the oath, and few officers could fail to follow the minister of war's example.

Hitler certainly rewarded him for his loyalty. In May 1935 Blomberg was named commander in chief of the Wehrmacht and, in the aftermath of the successful German reoccupation of the Rhineland in 1936, raised to the level of the first general field marshal of the Wehrmacht. At this point Blomberg seemed not to realize that, since the arrangements of the spring of 1934, Hitler had been taking steps to remove the independence of the officer corps and bring the military under the domination of the Nazi state. Other officers, however, understood, and many thought Blomberg was far too ready to give in to Hitler.

In November 1937, Hitler announced to Blomberg and other top military and diplomatic officials that it was time for Germany to start planning for territorial expansion in eastern Europe. Blomberg expressed some surprise and dismay, concerned that Germany was not ready for such moves. Soon after, he found his favored status was reversed. Not only was he less than enthusiastic in support of Hitler's expansion plans, but both Hermann Göring and Heinrich Himmler were jealous of his power. The pretext for his removal was a scandal connected with Blomberg's marriage to his second wife, a young secretary named Eva

Grühn, who was many years his junior. The wedding took place on January 12, 1938, a discreet affair attended by both Hitler and Himmler. Soon after, Göring released a file on Grühn that had been compiled by Berlin police chief Wolf Heinrich Graf von Helldorf and which, apparently, Göring knew of before the wedding. The file reported that the young woman had a criminal past and had posed for pornographic pictures in earlier years. Many German officers and other leaders were already discomfited by Blomberg's marriage to a young girl far beneath him in terms of social class. When the rumors of her unsavory past spread, Blomberg's fall was inevitable. He was forced to resign as minister of war and commander in chief, and to give up his field marshal's baton, on February 4, 1938. Soon after, General Werner Freiherr von Fritsch, who also expressed concern over Hitler's expansionist goals, was himself forced to resign as the result of a personal scandal, and the Nazi dictator was able nearly to complete his domination of the German armed forces; he named himself both minister of defense and supreme commander of the Wehrmacht. Blomberg spent World War II in anonymity with his young wife in a Bavarian village. After the war ended he was confined in an American detention center, where he died on March 14, 1946. *See also* Blomberg-Fritsch crisis, Vol. 1; Pact of the *Deutschland,* Vol. 2.

Bock, Fedor von (1880–1945)

General field marshal in the Wehrmacht and a Prussian officer of the old school who frequently disagreed with Adolf Hitler's strategies. Bock was born in Küstrin, Prussia, on December 3, 1880, to an aristocratic and military family. He joined the German Imperial Army as a junior officer on 1898 and served during World War I as a staff officer and infantry commander, earning one of Germany's most prized honors, the Pour le Mérite. In the interwar period he served in a variety of staff and regimental posts, rising to the rank of lieutenant general by 1931. In 1938, as a general of infantry, he led the German Eighth Army into Austria during the Anschluss.

When World War II began Bock was a full general and third in seniority as a Wehrmacht officer. He led major army groups during the Third Reich's military campaigns from 1939 to 1941. As commander of Army Group North, Bock was a key figure in the rapid conquest of Poland. From May to September 1940 he was the commander of the Second Army Group on the western front. In July 1940, after the fall of France, Bock was one of twelve top Wehrmacht and Luftwaffe generals promoted by Hitler to the rank of general field marshal. In the Soviet invasion of summer 1941, Bock led Army Group Center, taking it to the outskirts of Moscow before, his supply lines badly strung out and his troops widely dispersed and freezing, he was badly beaten in December. Hitler removed him from his command only to recall him to take over Army Group South in January 1942, a command he held until July 1942. Afterward, Bock served as a staff officer until Hitler again forced him to resign after the Nazis lost at Stalingrad in early 1943. Bock was killed in an Allied air raid on May 4, 1945. *See also* Barbarossa, Battle of Stalingrad, Vol. 1; Operation Typhoon, Vol. 2.

Bonhoeffer, Dietrich (1906–1945)

A Protestant thinker and pastor who became a vocal opponent of the Nazi regime and a leader of the German resistance movement. He was shot at the Flossenbürg concentration camp in the last weeks of World War II for his alleged involvement in the July Plot of 1944 against Adolf Hitler's life.

Dietrich Bonhoeffer was born in Breslau in 1906. His parents were both highly educated, one a psychiatrist and the other a university professor. He took theology degrees at both the University of Tübingen in Germany and the Union Theological Seminary in New York City. He returned to Germany to work as both a teacher and pastor. After Hitler took power in 1933, Bonhoeffer joined the Confessing Church, a body of Protestant pastors who rejected the nazified German Christian movement, which attempted to reconcile the racial and leadership doctrines of the Nazi Party with Protestant Christianity. Bonhoeffer argued, with others, that the church must remain true to its beliefs and that it should remain free of interference from the Nazis or any other state.

Unlike other leading Protestants, however, Bonhoeffer claimed that the church should take an activist role in seeking to prevent social injustices, practicing, as he called it, a "religionless Christianity," where Christians would seek to live according to the teachings of Jesus rather than confuse them with church ritual, history, and doctrine. During the era of the Third Reich this attitude brought Bonhoeffer to such actions as assisting Jews to leave Germany and helping other Christians to resist Hitler, even if it endangered their lives. It also brought him into contact with others in the German resistance movement, notably those in the German army and in the Abwehr, the army's intelligence section.

A fluent English speaker with many foreign contacts, Bonhoeffer made numerous trips to England in the late 1930s, hoping to find some way to forestall the coming war as well as foment sympathy for his theology. In addition, he made one trip to the United States. He also began to work as an intelligence agent under Admiral Wilhelm Canaris, chief of the Abwehr and a central figure in the resistance movement. After the Gestapo closed his seminary in 1940, he was forbidden to speak, publish, or work as a pastor. The onset of war, however, had made him more willing to take risks, and Bonhoeffer maintained useful contacts in both Sweden and Switzerland. On one trip, to neutral Sweden in 1942, Bonhoeffer delivered proposed peace terms organized by General Hans Oster of the Abwehr and General Ludwig Beck, formerly of the Wehrmacht, hoping for British support in the event the resistance movement ousted Hitler from power. The British refused, however, to consider the terms.

In 1943 Bonhoeffer was arrested on the charge of attempting to subvert the armed forces. He remained in Tegel Prison in Berlin until the days following the July 1944 attempt on Hitler's life. He was then removed to a Gestapo interrogation center. He was moved to Buchenwald in January 1945 and then to Flossenbürg, where on April 9 he was shot along with Canaris and Oster. Thanks to both his theological stance and his dignity and sacrifice in the face of Nazi terror, Bonhoeffer is considered by many to be a twentieth-century martyr comparable to Mahatma Gandhi and Dr. Martin Luther King Jr. *See also* Confessing Church, Vol. 1; religion in the Third Reich, Vol. 2; Bormann, Christianity and Nazism Are Incompatible; Hitler, The State Must Dominate the Churches, Vol. 4.

Bormann, Martin (1900–1945?)

A leading Nazi Party official and, according to observers within the Third Reich and later historians, the power behind Adolf Hitler's throne from 1942 until 1945. Bormann was able to achieve this status because of his close proximity to the Führer and because of his skill at political and personal manipulation and intrigue; the post he held, the head of the Party Chancellery, was actually a relatively minor one. Nazi Party insiders referred to him as "the Brown Eminence," a man able to outmaneuver other top Nazis including Hermann Göring, Joseph Goebbels, Albert Speer, and even Heinrich Himmler. In the last months of the Third Reich, in fact, Bormann was likely the true leader of Germany as Hitler, thanks partly to Bormann's manipulations, retreated further and further from reality.

Martin Bormann was born in Halberstadt, Prussia, on June 17, 1900. His background

Nazi Party leader Martin Bormann rose to become one of Hitler's closest and most influential advisers.

was lower-middle-class Prussian: His father was a regimental sergeant who later worked in a minor civil service post. Bormann himself was a high school dropout who served briefly as an artilleryman in World War I; he was too young to have seen much action. After the war Bormann joined the Rossbach Freikorps regiment active in Mecklenburg in Prussia while also serving as an agricultural inspector. During the early 1920s he maintained his activities as a right-wing political agitator and, in other regards, as a common criminal. He was connected, apparently, with several murders. The most noteworthy of these was the killing of Walther Kadow, a schoolteacher whose betrayal had supposedly led to the death of Albert Leo Schlageter, one of the first National Socialist martyrs. Kadow's convicted killer was Rudolf Höss, later to achieve notoriety as the commandant of Auschwitz. Bormann was convicted of being his accomplice, and sentenced in March 1924 to one year's imprisonment in Leipzig. He joined the Nazi Party officially after his release from prison.

The late 1920s was the era of the Nazi Party's rise to the status of a truly national political movement, and Bormann took full advantage of the opportunity to grow powerful along with the party. He first served as the press director for the party in Thuringia, then rose to both Gauleiter and party business manager in the same region. Meanwhile he joined the supreme command of the SA. He married Gerda Buch in 1929. Buch, the daughter of a politician, had come to Hitler's attention, and the Nazi leader was fond of her. Bormann certainly considered the marriage a propitious one for his personal ambitions, and invited Hitler to serve as a witness at their wedding. Gerda Bormann remained an uncritical devotee of Adolf Hitler throughout the era of the Third Reich and named the first of her ten children Adolf after his godfather.

Bormann's rise continued after Hitler and the Nazis took power in 1933. In July Hitler appointed him the chief of staff to Rudolf Hess, the deputy Führer. The position gave Bormann access to the inner circles of Nazi Party decision making. He remained active in other ways as well. He administered the Adolf Hitler Fund, a huge fund fed by contributions from German industrialists, who were encouraged to donate in exchange for patronage. Bormann then used the fund to provide gifts to top party officials to help secure his own influence. In addition he took over the administration of Adolf Hitler's personal finances from the publisher Max Amann and convinced Hitler of the importance of acquiring property. Thanks to Bormann's conniving, in fact, Hitler agreed to the purchase of his childhood home in Braunau am Inn, Austria; his parents' home in Leonding, Austria; and a huge area in the Obersalzburg along the German-Austrian border, where Hitler's massive mountain getaway, the Berghof, was built. He also served as a deputy in the Reichstag and in October 1933 was named a Reichsleiter, one of the top Nazi Party officials.

Bormann's opportunity to become a true Nazi leader came after Rudolf Hess, his superior at the Office of the Deputy Führer, took his strange solo flight to Great Britain in May 1941 and retired from the Nazi stage. On May 12, Hitler abolished the office of the deputy Führer and named Bormann the head of the Party Chancellery. The Party Chancellery was one of several Berlin Party bureaucracies—the Reichs Chancellery and Führer Chancellery were others—that competed to control personal access to Adolf Hitler and as such, its top officials served as the Führer's chiefs of staff. Bormann's skill at political infighting, his large network of patronage, and his single-mindedness and ruthlessness enabled him to outmaneuver his rivals in the other chancelleries and to build up a sort of wall around Hitler that only he could penetrate. One of his main tasks, now that World War II was under way, was to protect the influence of the party against that of the armed forces and the SS, which in the context of war were growing more important. He also took on the role of the Nazi Party's main spokesman for racial and cultural policy. He argued that the power of the Christian churches, for instance, should be broken; Bormann saw the church as incompatible with Nazi ideology and dictatorial rule. Indeed, Bormann was the most active anti-Christian among Nazi leaders, even more so than Heinrich Himmler.

Bormann was also ruthless in his attitudes toward Jews and Slavs, at least after other branches of the Nazi state adopted a general policy of ruthlessness toward those groups. In October 1942, for instance, he issued a decree that the remaining Jews in the German Reich be subjected to deportation to the labor and extermination camps in eastern Europe. In 1943 he also granted Adolf Eichmann, in the Führer's name, total power over the Jews of occupied Europe, a move that allowed Bormann to bypass Himmler, Eichmann's ostensible superior. With regard to Poles and Russians, Bormann was hardly more generous and adhered strictly to the orthodox Nazi line that Slavs should be forced to work as slaves for the Third Reich and that they should be discouraged or prevented from having children. In these areas, in fact, Bormann was not an initiator of policy but rather a dedicated implementer, provided the policy could be manipulated in a way that would increase his own power.

By the beginning of 1943 Bormann had begun to encourage Hitler's tendency to withdraw from the public eye, and from that point until Hitler's suicide on April 30, 1945, Bormann very nearly ruled the Third Reich in the Führer's name. He proved himself willing to carry out the dull administrative tasks that Hitler, never a hard worker, hated to do, and he developed such an understanding of Hitler's personality that he was able to manipulate him into authorizing Bormann's own measures. He also oversaw Hitler's correspondence and schedule of appointments. For instance, in 1943 Himmler was named minister of the interior in place of Hans Frick, an appointment that seemed to increase his power even beyond SS leadership. Bormann knew that Himmler, his potential opponent, was largely preoccupied with events in the occupied countries rather than Germany proper and, moreover, Bormann was able to determine whether and when Himmler would have personal access to Hitler. This left the interior minister's office effectively empty, and aside from police functions, which were under Himmler's purview anyway, Bormann was able to step into the void. In similar ways Bormann was able to outmaneuver Göring, ostensibly second in command in the Reich; Goebbels, who tried mightily to maintain his position as an insider; and Speer, who considered himself a personal friend of Hitler's but whom Bormann managed to largely shunt aside. Bormann's critics compared him to a worm or a mole, always anonymously digging and tunneling in darkness in the attempt to create a network of influence. They also noted that his physical appearance—short, squat, squint-eyed, and unkempt—even resembled a mole. Adolf Hitler, meanwhile, grew to rely more and more on Bormann, considering him his most loyal associate and his main connection to the world outside his increasingly narrow sphere.

After January 1945, when Hitler and his entourage moved into their massive underground bunker in Berlin, Bormann continued his intrigues. He managed to convince Hitler to dismiss both Göring and Himmler, and he took over a quasimilitary post when Hitler named him the chief of the Volkssturm, the last-ditch force created as a final defense against an Allied invasion. When Hitler married Eva Braun on April 29, 1945, Bormann returned the favor, from 1929, of witnessing the wedding. He also signed Hitler's last will and political testament and promised to take it to the nation rather than commit suicide, as Hitler himself did on April 30. Allegedly, and also upon Hitler's orders, it was also under Bormann's authority that the bodies of the Führer and his wife were taken to the Reichs Chancellery gardens and burned so that they would not be found by the onrushing forces of the Soviet Union.

Bormann's fate was never conclusively determined. He escaped from the Führerbunker, but accounts of what happened after that differ greatly. Two others who escaped the bunker, Artur Axmann and Erich Kempka, both claimed to have seen Bormann's dead body. Axmann argued that he commited suicide on May 2 while Kempka said he was killed by a Russian shell. Others claimed, in later years, to have spotted him as a monk in northern Italy and as a businessman in Brazil or Chile. In 1973, after a skeleton was uncovered about a half-mile from the Reichs Chancellery, Bormann was declared officially dead by a West German court, although even then some doubted the evidence. One verdict of history on Martin Bormann came at the postwar Nuremberg trials of surviving top Nazis: He was sentenced to death in absentia for his numerous crimes. *See also* Committee of Three, Vol. 1; Bormann, Christianity and Nazism Are Incompatible; Goebbels, Goebbels and Göring Comment on Their Rivals, Vol. 4.

Bouhler, Philip (1899–1945)

The head of the Führer Chancellery, a top Nazi Party bureaucracy in Berlin, and the leading figure behind the euthanasia program that put to death approximately one hundred thousand Germans between 1938 and 1942. Bouhler was born in Munich on September 2, 1899, to a military family. During World War I he served in the Royal Bavarian Cadet Corps and in regular army service, where he was wounded. After the war Bouhler embarked on a literary and academic career, seeking work with publishing companies and pursuing a degree in philosophy at the University of Munich. In 1922, however, he dropped these efforts to join the Nazi Party, where he took a staff position with the *Völkischer Beobachter*, the Nazi newspaper. He also served as the business manager of the party until 1925. Bouhler, like Heinrich Himmler, was among the relatively few younger Germans attracted to the Nazi movement during its early days.

After the Nazis rose to power in 1933 Bouhler became an SS lieutenant general, a Reichsleiter, a member of the Nazi Reichstag, and in 1934 president of the Munich police. He also enjoyed reasonably close access to Adolf Hitler, who assigned him to a staff position within his offices and, in time, named him head of the Führer Chancellery. There, Bouhler helped to oversee Hitler's memos and statements and, perhaps taking advantage of his brief career in publishing, oversaw groups concerned with the censorship of German books and with the production of nazified historical and educational publications. He also wrote a book of his own—*Napoleon, the Comet-Path of a Genius*—which Hitler much admired.

The Führer Chancellery, like several other branches of the Nazi bureaucracy in Berlin, vied to control Hitler's attention. One way in which Bouhler sought to do this was by overseeing the Führer's personal correspondence, of which there were hundreds of pieces daily. Part of Bouhler's job was to choose which letters to take directly to Hitler for response or action. In late 1938 Bouhler intercepted a letter sent by a German family asking for Hitler's help in "putting down" their young son, who apparently suffered from a variety of physical and mental handicaps. Bouhler forwarded the letter to Hitler, who shortly afterward selected Bouhler to oversee the Nazi regime's euthanasia program. First, several thousand children who suffered from physical or mental problems were killed either by injection or by allowing disease to develop through neglect. Beginning in 1939, however, Bouhler received authorization to expand the program to include Germany's mentally ill adults. He used his connections within both the German medical community and the SS police to set up what was known as the T-4 Program. Before it was shut down, largely in response to a public outcry, an estimated seventy thousand people were gassed to death and their bodies then cremated. Even after the gassing facilities were shut down for this operation, the program returned to the use of lethal injections. Bouhler, along with his wife, committed suicide in May 1945 at Hermann Göring's headquarters in northern Germany, just prior to the arrival of American military police. *See also* Führer Chancellery, Vol. 1; T-4 Program, Vol. 2; The First Gas Chambers, Vol. 4.

Brauchitsch, Walther von (1881–1948)

One of many German army officers of the traditional school who enjoyed a rapid rise in fortunes under Adolf Hitler but experienced a likewise rapid fall. He served as commander in chief of the army from 1938 to 1941.

Brauchitsch was born in October 1881 in Berlin to a family of Prussian aristocrats and officers. He took his first command in the German army in 1900 and served as a captain of artillery during World War I, earning the Iron Cross, First Class, Germany's top military honor. During the Weimar years Brauchitsch held numerous staff appointments and enjoyed a steady rise in rank and responsibility. His star continued to rise after Hitler started to assert his control of the German military. In 1936 he was named general of infantry and in 1937 commander of the fourth Army Group, Leipzig. After General Werner von Blomberg was forced to resign as commander in chief of the army on February 4, 1938, Brauchitsch was named to take his place.

Brauchitsch, unlike even the mostly pliant Blomberg, was never able to stand up to Adolf Hitler, a quality the Führer certainly appreciated in his top commanders. Part of Brauchitsch's deference was due to a personal debt; Hitler had helped him divorce his first wife so that he could marry his second, Charlotte Schmidt, a dedicated Nazi. Although Brauchitsch was aware of the doubts about Hitler's military plans expressed by Blomberg and others, and although he was approached by General Ludwig Beck to join the resistance movement among the officer corps, Brauchitsch was unable to go against the desires of his wife and his Führer, claiming that he was bound by the oath of personal loyalty all military men had to take from 1935 on.

Brauchitsch helped in the planning and execution of all the Third Reich's major military endeavors between 1938 and 1941, including the annexation of Austria, the military occupation of Czechoslovakia, and the blitzkrieg attacks on Poland, the Netherlands, Belgium, and France. Since those operations all succeeded, Brauchitsch's prestige rose, as did his esteem in Hitler's eyes, who named him a general field marshal. The

Führer began to turn against Brauchitsch, however, when the attack on the Soviet Union bogged down in the fall of 1941. The field marshal was forced to resign on December 19, 1941, ostensibly for reasons of poor health. Hitler himself replaced him. After the war Brauchitsch was arrested by the British, who planned to try him along with other officers in 1949. He died of heart failure, however, in a British military hospital in October 1948.

Braun, Eva (1912–1945)

Adolf Hitler's mistress after 1932, and for one day in 1945, his wife. Eva Braun was born in Munich to a middle-class Catholic family. She was an active girl, interested in outdoor activities, gymnastics, and dancing, interests she was to maintain throughout her life. She first met Adolf Hitler in 1929 when she was only seventeen; she was an assistant in the photography studio of Heinrich Hoffman, then Hitler's official photographer. She was considered an attractive girl —healthy, even-featured, good-natured— but not a beautiful one. Hitler, whose interest in women was minimal, was at the time much attached to his young niece, Angela (Geli) Raubal. Shortly after Raubal committed suicide in 1931, Hitler took Eva Braun as his mistress.

The young woman had little interest in politics, and indeed her father opposed the relationship for political as well as personal reasons, since the Nazi leader was twenty-three years older than Eva Braun. Nevertheless, she remained devoted to Hitler for the rest of her life, content to fill what probably amounted to a small, part-time role in his life. The main exceptions to what appeared

Hitler leaves the Berghof with his longtime mistress, Eva Braun. Braun and Hitler were married on April 29, 1945, and committed suicide the next day.

from the outside to be a fairly smooth relationship were several suicide attempts. After the first one, in 1935, Hitler bought her a house near Munich and supplied her with a car and driver. Hitler was certainly fond of his mistress; he was very concerned about her health and ensured that she would be financially secure by signing over to her most of the fees and royalties earned from his photographs. He also named her as a chief beneficiary in his will. Moreover, the Nazi leader preferred her simplicity, lack of ambition, and middle-class background to the more glamorous lives of a number of the women who moved in his social circles.

In 1936 Eva Braun moved more or less permanently to the Berghof, Hitler's massive retreat in the Alps along the Austrian-German border. There she served as official hostess, although she was expected to remain in the background. The servants, in fact, were not allowed to speak of her and she was asked to leave any room where important political, diplomatic, or social matters were discussed. She spent a great deal of time on her own, especially since Hitler limited her travel and he himself spent a great deal of time traveling or in Berlin. He did not allow her to go to Berlin until 1943, and apparently very few Germans were aware that Hitler even had a mistress, much less knew who she was. She passed the time at the Berghof by exercising, reading romantic novels, writing in her diary, and watching movies.

Eva Braun went to Berlin on April 15, 1945, to join Hitler in the massive underground Führerbunker. Hitler wanted her to remain in Munich, but she claimed that she did not want to live on in a Germany where there was no Adolf Hitler. On April 29, Hitler granted her fondest wish for years: marriage. The two were wed in a simple ceremony in which both certified that they were racially pure. The wedding was witnessed by Martin Bormann. The next day at about 3:00 P.M., she committed suicide by swallowing poison. A few minutes later her husband of a few hours followed suit. Then, according to Hitler's orders, the bodies were taken to the gardens of the Reichs Chancellery and burned. Russian soldiers, reportedly, later found her remains. *See also* Berghof, Führerbunker, Vol. 1; Hitler, Adolf, Vol. 3; Braun, Diary Entries, Vol. 4.

Braun, Wernher von (1912–1977)

A German aeronautical engineer who, in different historical eras, helped both the Third Reich and the United States develop effective rockets. He was born in March 1912 to an aristocratic Berlin family and was a brilliant student of physics and astronomy at the Charlottenburg Technological Institute in Berlin. He took up a research post with the German Army Ordnance Office at the age of twenty; his job was to help develop rockets for the long-distance delivery of explosives. In 1937, at only twenty-five, Braun was appointed technical director of the Third Reich's major rocket research project, which was built on the Baltic island of Peenemünde. The project quickly produced a prototype of what was later called the V-2 rocket, a self-guided device capable of supersonic, high-altitude flight. Nazi authorities, however, shifted funding, expertise, and attention away from Peenemünde and toward the Luftwaffe and the pilotless "flying bomb" known as the V-1 in the early years of World War II.

By 1943, however, Hitler had begun the search for military miracles, and Braun's continual lobbying for more resources paid off. Braun was given the authorization to put the V-2 rocket into production. Between September 1944 and March 1945, by which time the launch bases had been captured by Allied forces, the Germans launched some thirty-five hundred V-2 rockets against England. Many of them were assembled at a huge slave labor complex in southern Germany known as Dora-Mittelbau, under Braun's watchful eye. At one point Heinrich Himmler tried to take control of the

V-2 project and had Braun and others arrested on the suspicion that they were squandering the Reich's resources by planning space travel rather than offensive weaponry. Through the machinations of Nazi insider politics, however, Braun and his associates were freed on the authorization of Minister of Armaments and War Production Albert Speer.

Rather than be taken by the Russians, Braun left Peenemünde in March 1945 and surrendered to the Americans, as did much of his research staff. Braun and his associates formed much of the core of what later became the American space program; after being questioned by investigators in London in 1946, Braun, who was never a Nazi Party member, was allowed to go to the United States to continue his research. He became an American citizen in 1955, and in 1960 was appointed director of the Marshall Space Flight Center in Huntsville, Alabama. Braun is credited with, among other things, the design of the *Redstone* rocket, which put the first American astronaut into orbit in 1961, and the *Saturn 5* rocket, which took Americans to the moon in 1969. He was appointed deputy assistant director of the National Aeronautics and Space Administration (NASA) in 1970. He died in Alexandria, Virginia, in 1977. *See also* Dora-Mittelbau, Vol. 1; Peenemünde, V-1 and V-2 rockets, Vol. 2.

Brüning, Heinrich (1885–1970)

The leader of the Weimar-era Catholic Center Party and one of the last chancellors of Germany before Adolf Hitler took power. He was born in Münster in western Germany in 1885 to an upper-middle-class Catholic family. He showed a great deal of early academic promise, earning a Ph.D. from the University of Bonn in politics, history, and philosophy, but was distracted from his academic pursuits by service in World War I. After the war he entered politics, first as the business manager of the League of German Christian Trade Unions and then as a Reichstag deputy. He belonged to the conservative wing of the Catholic Center Party, believing in both moral and fiscal probity. He also remained a devout Catholic.

In March 1930, after responses to the Great Depression had splintered the "Great Coalition" of center parties that ruled Weimar, Brüning was appointed the chancellor of a new cabinet and therefore the German head of state. He remained chancellor until May 1932. From June 1930, when he dissolved his cabinet for not supporting his policy of economic austerity, Brüning ruled by decree. According to Article 48 of the Weimar Constitution, the president of Germany had the right to rule by decree in times of emergency. At this point the president was the aged, and somewhat detached, Field Marshal Paul von Hindenburg. Brüning issued most of the decrees, then had Hindenburg sign off on them.

One of Brüning's major challenges, and the main reason why he was unable to build a new coalition cabinet and stop ruling by decree, was the polarization of German politics caused by the effects of the depression and by the chancellor's own economic policies, which kept thousands of Germans unemployed and lowered standards of living. Large numbers of people left the center parties to join either the Communists or the Nazis, and the representation of these two parties in the Reichstag swelled. Both strongly criticized Brüning's economic policies, and considered the chancellor to be of the same sort who paralyzed Germany in 1918 and 1919 and forced the nation to accept a humiliating peace settlement to end World War I. Street fights, meanwhile, inspired Brüning to declare a ban on both the SA and the SS in April 1932. Brüning's greatest political success, as Germany descended further into unemployment, poverty, chaos, and political intrigue, was to bring about major revisions to the Treaty of Versailles. At a conference in Lausanne, Switzerland, in 1932 he negotiated the end of war reparations, and he was on the way to reducing other treaty restrictions.

By this time, however, largely due to the effects of his economic policies, Brüning had lost the support of both Hindenburg and the Prussian officer and aristocrat class, as well as radicals from the right and left. Under the influence of General Kurt von Schleicher, Hindenburg asked Brüning to leave the government on May 10, 1932. His replacement as chancellor was Franz von Papen, and the way was open to the entrance of Adolf Hitler and the Nazis into the government.

By July 1933 Hitler had either declared all political parties except the Nazis illegal or inspired them to disband "voluntarily." Brüning, who still held his Reichstag seat, gave it up as well as the leadership of the Catholic Center Party. The next year he went into exile in Switzerland, and shortly after moved to the United States. There he took up a professorship in political science at Harvard University, where he stayed until 1951. He died in Norwich, Vermont, on March 20, 1970. *See also* Article 48 of the Weimar Constitution, Catholic Center Party, Vol. 1; Machtergreifung, Vol. 2; Hindenburg, Paul von, Vol. 3.

C

Canaris, Wilhelm (1887–1945)

Naval officer, head of the Abwehr, the intelligence section of the High Command of the armed forces (OKW), as well as a leading figure in the German resistance movement despite his indecision at crucial moments. Canaris was born in western Germany on January 1, 1887, to a family of partially Greek background. He joined the German navy in 1905, and during World War I he served as an intelligence agent in Spain and Italy as well as a U-boat commander. After the war he continued to rise in rank, becoming ultimately a battleship commander. Canaris also began to display a split personality politically. He was a strong German nationalist and anticommunist who took part in the Kapp Putsch of 1920. On the other hand he disapproved of the low-class brutality, vulgarity, and violence of the Nazi movement.

By this time promoted to admiral, Canaris was named head of the Abwehr on January 1, 1935. In this position he had close access to accounts of SS police activities, and was well aware of Gestapo and other abuses within Germany and, after World War II began, in the occupied territories. Although he objected to certain events, such as the murder of the Polish intelligentsia, he continued to cooperate with the SS Security Service (SD). He also maintained an outwardly cordial relationship with Reinhard Heydrich, the commander of the SD and a man who had served directly under Canaris as a young naval officer. Beneath the surface, however, Canaris hated Heydrich, and compiled a dossier on him that purported to show that Heydrich had Jewish ancestry. In other regards, neither the leaders of the Wehrmacht nor Adolf Hitler were very pleased with the work of the Abwehr under Canaris, and the organization was increasingly marginalized.

From at least 1938 on Canaris maintained contacts with the German resistance movement, and due to his high rank and powerful position was considered by the conspirators to be an important ally. Yet Canaris remained on the fence, unwilling to commit himself to the resistance and objecting to almost any attempt to assassinate Adolf Hitler. He was pleased by Germany's military successes and greatly feared either a German surrender or another humiliating peace such as the Treaty of Versailles. Only in 1944, after he was removed from his post with the Abwehr and assigned to the Office for Commercial and Economic Warfare (in effect a demotion), did Canaris throw in his lot with the resistance. He helped plan the July 1944 plot on Hitler's life and was prepared to take a role in any postcoup government. After the plot failed Canaris was arrested (the Gestapo had long suspected him of anti-Hitler sympathies) and sent first to Buchenwald, then to the Flossenbürg concentration camp. He was hanged there, along with other resisters including Hans Oster and Dietrich Bonhoeffer, on April 9, 1945. *See also* Abwehr, Vol. 1; resistance movements, Germany, Vol. 2; Oster, Hans, Vol. 3.

Chamberlain, Houston Stewart (1855–1927)

English-German writer whose works were an important influence on Nazism. Chamberlain was born in Southsea, England, on

September 9, 1855, to a respected English family. After falling under the spell of the music and ideas of Richard Wagner and studying at the University of Dresden as a young man, he became a member of the inner circle of the composer's family. He married Wagner's daughter Eva and, in 1908, moved to Bayreuth, the Bavarian village that had become a sort of shrine to Wagnerism thanks to an annual opera festival. By this time Chamberlain had decided that the German way of life was preferable to the English one, and he became a fanatical Germanist. During World War I, in fact, he wrote anti-British propaganda and was considered a turncoat at home.

A prolific writer, Chamberlain published his major work in 1899, a book published in English in 1910 under the title *The Foundations of the Nineteenth Century*. The book was thought to have been a profound influence on Nazi ideology. It characterized European history as a struggle among the races. After the fall of the Roman Empire, according to Chamberlain, Europe fell into a "chaos of peoples," and over time the "Teutons" and the "Jews" emerged as the two dominant forces in European civilization. But, he maintained, while the Teutons (Germans) were a positive, creative force, responsible for innumerable innovations in politics, science, economics, and the arts, the Jews were a constant disruptive influence. The Teutons, to Chamberlain's mind, were strong, manly, fresh, and pure; the Jews were dark and deceitful. Moreover, the Teutons had truly provided the "foundation of the nineteenth century" because of their contributions to the Italian Renaissance, their creation of the concept of human liberty, and their master of science, industry, and empire. The Jews, meanwhile, had raised themselves to an undue level of influence in the nineteenth century through deceit, and they threatened to return Europe to the "chaos of peoples" that characterized the centuries after the fall of Rome. It was important, Chamberlain argued, for European leaders to recognize the Jewish threat, as had all important men of the past, and find ways to counter it. Moreover, and in contrast to all historical evidence and traditional belief, Chamberlain argued that Jesus was not a Jew but rather a racial precursor of the Teutons who himself denied Jewish law and tradition.

Chamberlain's book was very popular in the years before World War I. Kaiser Wilhelm II, emperor of Germany until 1918, considered it a work of brilliance, and even before its English translation appeared the book had sold out eight German editions. It was also praised outside Germany by those who felt that the uniquely creative "Nordic" race was under threat by a new "chaos of peoples" in the forms of intermarriage and immigration. Others, however, noted that the book was a confused mishmash built on a false reading of history, and that Chamberlain simply called those he liked "Teutons" while relegating those he did not like to the "chaos of peoples" or to Jewry.

Adolf Hitler probably never read Chamberlain, but other Nazi thinkers, such as Alfred Rosenberg or Rudolf Hess, almost certainly did, and his work provided Nazism with what appeared to the Nazi mind to be a serious philosophical and historical foundation. The phrase "chaos of peoples," for instance, frequently appears in Nazi writings as well as in the rhetoric of World War II, where it was used to describe the conquered, devastated lands of eastern Europe. Moreover, the Nazis had no doubt of the racial superiority of the "Teutons" as well as the need to protect, they thought, their racial purity and creativity. Chamberlain died in Bayreuth on January 9, 1927, but not before he grew aware of and praised the Nazi leader. *See also* anti-Semitism, Aryans, Vol. 1; racial science, Social Darwinism, Vol. 2; Wagner, Winifred, Vol. 3.

Chamberlain, Neville (1869–1940)

Prime minister of Great Britain from May 1937 to May 1940, Chamberlain was the primary architect of the policy of appeasement, which helped give Adolf Hitler the confidence to aggressively seek territorial gains. Chamberlain was born in Birmingham, England, in 1869. His family was one of the great political families of the British Empire and included several parliamentarians and cabinet ministers, such as his father, Colonial Secretary Joseph Chamberlain, and his half-brother, Foreign Secretary Austen Chamberlain. All three were members of Britain's Conservative Party, known popularly as the Tories.

After serving as a member of Parliament, Chamberlain, now head of the Conservative Party, became prime minister in May 1937. Although most of his experience was in domestic affairs, the European situation required him to devote most of his energies to foreign affairs. Concerned that Great Britain was not ready to fight a major war, Chamberlain adopted the policy of appeasement to avoid war. He was concerned also that the costs of another major war might be too high—in particular, that Britain might lose its vast overseas empire. Finally, he wanted to do anything within reason to prevent another devastating conflict like World War I. Therefore, and like almost every other world leader ready to still consider Adolf Hitler a reasonable man, Chamberlain grew willing to accede to some of the Führer's demands, hoping he would be satisfied. His most famous example of appeasement was during the Czech crisis of 1938. He did not want Britain to go to war over Czechoslovakia, which was, in his words, "a far-off country of which we know little" (Shirer, 1960), and he considered German domination of Czechoslovakia, as well as annexation of the German-speaking Sudetenland, to be inevitable. Consequently, Chamberlain met with Hitler twice in September 1938, the first times he had ever flown in an airplane. At the second meeting, in Munich on September 30, with Mussolini of Italy in attendance as well as Daladier of France (as well as two minor Czech officials who were not allowed to take part in important negotiations), Chamberlain acquiesced to Hitler's demands over the Sudetenland. He returned to a frightened London famously announcing that he had preserved "peace in our time." Simultaneously, however, Chamberlain had begun a massive program of war preparation, including rearmament and conscription.

By 1939 Chamberlain was no longer willing to consider Hitler's promises or grant him accommodations and, to Hitler's surprise, he brought Britain into World War II on September 3, 1939, in support of Poland. The rapid defeat of Poland, as well as his reputation as an appeaser and British military inaction, undermined him as a war leader. His position was further weakened with the beginning of the German onslaught on western Europe in April 1940, which involved the defeat of the British Expeditionary Force in northern Norway. Criticism of Chamberlain was wide and vicious in Parliament and in the British press, and on May 10 he was replaced by Winston Churchill. Chamberlain remained a part of Britain's war cabinet but died, broken and humiliated, in November 1940. *See also* appeasement, Vol. 1; Munich Conference, Vol. 2; Daladier, Edouard, Vol. 3.

Churchill, Winston (1874–1965)

Prime minister of Great Britain from May 1940 to July 1945 and, along with President Franklin D. Roosevelt of the United States and Premier Joseph Stalin of the Soviet Union, one of the "Big Three" world leaders who defeated the Third Reich in World War II. Churchill was born on November 30, 1874, in Oxford, England. His father was Lord Randolph Churchill, a politician of aristocratic background, and his mother, Lady Churchill, was the former Jennie Jones, daughter of an American businessman. Churchill graduated from the British Military Academy at Sandhurst in 1895, and began a career in the military. Prior to ac-

British prime minister Winston Churchill led his country through World War II, one of the darkest periods in modern history.

tive duty, however, he traveled to Cuba as a reporter and became renowned as a political and military correspondent. Returning to the army, he served in India (1897), the Sudan (1898), and in South Africa, where in 1899 he made a dramatic escape from a Pretoria prison camp during the Boer War. He entered politics as a member of Parliament in 1901 and took his first cabinet appointment, as president of the Board of Trade, in 1910. In 1911 he was appointed first lord of the admiralty, the equivalent of naval minister, and was serving in that capacity when World War I began. Although Churchill had foreseen the war and built up the navy, he resigned his post after designing the disastrous British campaign against the German-allied Turks at Gallipoli in 1915. Afterward, he served as a frontline officer before returning to the cabinet as minister of munitions.

After the war Churchill remained in the government in a variety of cabinet posts until 1929 and as a member of Parliament until 1940. He also spent a great deal of time writing, an avocation he had practiced since his experience in Africa as a young officer. One of his major writings from this era was *World Crisis*, a four-volume history of World War I. During the 1930s Churchill was also one of the few to perceive the dangers of Adolf Hitler and the Nazi regime in Germany, often raising the subject in his speeches and writings and encouraging the British to build a strong navy and air force to counter the Third Reich's military buildup. Few, however, paid attention.

When World War II began on September 1, 1939, Churchill was again appointed first lord of the admiralty in the government of Neville Chamberlain. Over the next months he encouraged strong action, particularly in the North Sea off the coast of Norway, but he was neither fast enough nor convincing enough to accomplish a British occupation of Norway, a country that wanted to remain neutral in any conflict. When Hitler invaded Norway on April 9, 1940, the British rapidly sent a defending British Expeditionary Force, but it was defeated. In the ensuing scandal, Chamberlain was forced to resign and, on May 10, King George VI asked Churchill to form a new government. The same day the Nazis invaded France.

Churchill proved to be a stellar wartime leader. He refused to consider surrender, but neither did he promise the British people more over the next years than "blood, sweat, tears, and toil" (Shirer, 1960). His solid charisma and moving rhetoric played a key role in bolstering the morale of the British people, while he proved to be a creative and innovative military thinker, always ready to listen to new ideas and new men. Churchill also cultivated a strong friendship with Roosevelt, whom he had known for years and who shared a keen interest in naval affairs. The two remained in frequent contact long before the American entrance into the war, and Roosevelt clearly planned to support the British war effort through measures like the Lend-Lease Act of March 1941. During face-to-face conferences such as that held off the coast of Newfoundland in August 1941, Churchill and Roosevelt reiterated common goals, such as the need to defeat Hitler as the first priority of war and their mutual renunciation of territorial gains. Far more than Roosevelt, however, Churchill maintained a cynical grasp of real-world politics, and while Roosevelt was prone to think that Stalin could be trusted, Churchill did not agree. On the issue of opening a second front to remove pressure from the Soviets, Churchill argued for launching it in the Balkans and Mediterranean region in order to protect eastern Europe and prevent Russian expansion. He was forced to defer, however, to the American desire to open the second front in France.

Always a controversial figure, facing two votes of no confidence even during the war (both were soundly defeated in Parliament), Churchill lost his prime ministership in early July 1945. The British electorate, who blamed the Conservative Party for failing to prepare their nation for war in 1938 and 1939 and who wanted a new course for the country, elected a Labor Party government. The leader of the Labor Party, Clement Attlee, therefore stepped into Churchill's post and attended the last of the Big Three conferences, held later that month in Potsdam, Germany. There Attlee was joined by another new figure, President Harry S. Truman, who had replaced the deceased Roosevelt in April.

After the war Churchill remained the leader of the Conservative Party and up to his old tricks of warning of new world dangers and of the need for preparedness, noted for his "iron curtain" speech marking the beginning of the Cold War. He became prime minister once again, from 1951 until his retirement in 1955. Churchill also remained active as an author; his six-volume history of World War II, *The Second World War*, was published from 1948 to 1953 and he finished a massive *History of the English-Speaking Peoples* in 1958. In 1953 he was awarded the Nobel Prize in literature, in 1955 he was knighted by Queen Elizabeth II, and in 1963 he was granted honorary U.S. citizenship. Churchill died in London on January 24, 1965, at the age of ninety. *See also* Atlantic Charter, Battle of Britain, Vol. 1; Tehran Conference, Yalta Conference, Vol. 2.

Ciano, Galeazzo (1903–1944)

Foreign minister of Fascist Italy from 1936 to 1943. Ciano was born in the port city of Livorno on March 18, 1903; his father was a naval officer who served with great distinction during World War I, rising to the rank of admiral. Ciano entered the Italian Foreign Office in 1925 and served in diplomatic posts in China, Argentina, and Brazil. In 1933 he married Edda, the daughter of Italian Fascist dictator Benito Mussolini.

The dynamic and charismatic Ciano, who now had access to the highest circles of power in Fascist Italy, served as a bomber pilot during the Italian conquest of Ethiopia in 1936, and Fascist propaganda later claimed that he was the first Italian to enter Addis Ababa, the capital, to secure the conquest. Later that year Mussolini named him foreign minister though he was only thirty-three years old. Over the next years he was a key figure in putting together the alliance between Italy and the Third Reich, and his *Diaries*, published after his death, are a primary source of information on not only diplomatic history but the inner workings of the Nazi regime as well as the character and behavior of leading Nazis. In 1939 he and his Nazi counterpart, Joachim von Ribbentrop, concluded the so-called Pact of Steel, which tied the destinies of their two nations together.

Ciano remained unsure, however, whether Italy could succeed in a massive European war, and he tried to convince Mussolini to delay entrance into World War II, not entirely trusting either Ribbentrop or Adolf Hitler. Mussolini only entered the war on June 10, 1940, ready to mop up his share of French territory. Ciano, meanwhile, turned enthusiastic about Italy's war efforts until after defeats in Greece and North Africa, when his doubts returned. He resigned from his post as foreign minister in February 1943, having experienced too many disagreements with his increasingly desperate father-in-law. He remained, however, a top official as a member of the Fascist Grand Council. Along with others, such as General Pietro Badoglio, he voted to remove Mussolini as head of state on July 25, 1943. After the fall of the Fascist government, when Italy was split by the Allies and the Germans, Ciano and his family made their way to Germany, from where they hoped to escape to Spain. The diplomat found, however, that he was now supported by no one, and because of German tricks he was sent back to Italy. With the approval of Mussolini, who was now little more than the Nazi occupation governor of northern Italy, Ciano was put on trial for high treason in Verona. He was found guilty and executed by firing squad on January 11, 1944. *See also* allies of the Third Reich, fascism, Vol. 1; Pact of Steel, Vol. 2; Mussolini, Benito, Vol. 3.

Clauberg, Karl (1898–1957)

One of the notorious SS doctors who performed medical experiments on concentration camp and death camp inmates during World War II. Clauberg served in the German infantry during World War I, then studied at Kiel and Hamburg Universities in Germany and the University of Graz in Austria, where he took his medical degree in 1925. He joined the Nazi Party in 1933, when he was a physician at a women's hospital in Kiel. His field of specialty was female reproduction and fertility, and he published two books on the subject. He also rose to a position of high status within the Nazi state as an SS-Brigadeführer and professor of gynecology and obstetrics at the University of Königsberg.

In 1940 Clauberg asked Heinrich Himmler, head of the SS, whether he might be allowed to conduct sterilization experiments on women in concentration camps. He wanted to research ways to sterilize patients without surgery. He conducted his first experiments at Ravensbrück, the women's concentration camp, in 1942. These first efforts consisted of introducing chemicals into the uterus. Soon, however, he was transferred to Auschwitz, where there was a large complex of clinics and laboratories. At Auschwitz Clauberg had a huge staff of doctors, nurses, and guards. He continued his work on sterilization by injection, usually given without anaesthetic and without cleaning instruments, which resulted in a huge number of painful infections and, not infrequently, the death of the research subjects. Clauberg performed these experiments on Jewish women, mostly, but he also expanded his interests to include Gypsies and others. He was very proud of his ability to sterilize large numbers of women quickly, and boasted to Himmler that one day a single doctor and his assistants might be able to sterilize hundreds of women per day.

Not among the Nazi doctors tried in Nuremberg after World War II, Clauberg was captured by the Russians, who sentenced him to twenty-five years in prison for crimes against the Soviet people. Released after ten years, he returned to Kiel in West Germany. Upon learning of his return, German Jews demanded that he be prosecuted for war crimes, and he was arrested by the police in Kiel. He died there in prison on August 9, 1957, while waiting for his trial to begin. *See also* medical experiments, Vol. 2.

D

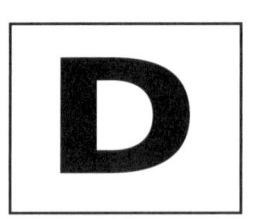

Daladier, Edouard (1884–1970)

Prime minister of France from April 1938 to March 1940. Daladier was born in Carpentras in southern France on June 18, 1884. He became a schoolteacher and served with distinction in World War I, entering politics after the war as a member of the Radical Socialist Party. During the interwar period, in France's constantly shifting political firmament, he served in a variety of cabinet posts as well as in the prime minister's office in 1933. As leader of the Radical Socialists, he helped form the Popular Front, a coalition of left and center parties that governed France from 1935 until 1938. When he returned as prime minister in April 1938, he proved completely unready or unwilling to oppose the now obvious aggressions of the Third Reich, and he joined with British prime minister Neville Chamberlain in pursuing a policy of appeasement. He was one of the signers of the Munich Agreement of September 1938, which gave Adolf Hitler a free hand in Czechoslovakia. Daladier's weakness in this regard led to the breakup of the Popular Front, although he remained prime minister until March 1940. By that time France was at war, and Daladier was dismissed and quickly replaced by Paul Reynaud, who promised a more aggressive approach to the Nazis. He remained, however, in the cabinet. After France collapsed in the face of a German onslaught in May, Reynaud, too, was forced out of office, to be replaced ultimately by Marshal Philippe Pétain, the founder of the collaborationist Vichy regime. Daladier, for his part, escaped to French North Africa hoping to take part in continued resistance, but he was arrested by Vichy authorities. They brought him back to France, where he was put on trial for failing to prepare the nation for war. After keeping Daladier in prison from September 1940 until February 1942, Vichy officials turned him over to the Germans. He survived the rest of the war in the Buchenwald and Dachau concentration camps, which were liberated in April 1945. The consummate political survivor, evidently, Daladier returned to the French Parliament in 1946 and served as mayor of Avignon from 1953 to 1958. He died in Paris on October 10, 1970. *See also* appeasement, Vol. 1; Munich Conference, Vol. 2. Chamberlain, Neville, Vol. 3.

Daluege, Kurt (1897–1946)

SS officer who was the chief of all German police during the era of the Third Reich and, after the death of Reinhard Heydrich in the spring of 1942, the deputy protector of Bohemia-Moravia. Indeed, after Heydrich's death Daluege became effectively the number two man in the SS under Heinrich Himmler, and therefore one of the most powerful men in the Third Reich.

Kurt Daluege was born in eastern Prussia on September 15, 1897. After World War I service, he trained as an engineer and worked for a short time in an engineering company. He quickly turned his energies, however, toward right-wing, nationalist activism by taking part in the Freikorps movement of the post–World War I period. He joined the Nazi Party in 1922, where he gravitated toward the SA. There, he displayed leadership ability, organizational efficiency, and a skill in developing attack tactics. In March 1926 Daluege became the leader of the Berlin SA, the first SA organization in northern Germany. In 1928 he shifted to the SS, where he commanded contingents in East Prussia.

By 1933 Daluege's various talents had come to the attention of top Nazis. Hermann Göring, for one, recognized that he could be useful in reforming the Prussian police, which had fallen under Göring's authority. Consequently, Daluege was named head of all Prussian police forces, where he took up the responsibility of ridding the force of political opponents. He also made efforts to connect the Prussian police with the larger SS organization, and in so doing greatly helped to expand the jurisdiction of the SS. As part of this larger process, Daluege sought to staff the police with SS men and, at the same time, encourage police officers to join the SS.

Daluege's star continued to rise throughout the 1930s. In 1933 he became a Prussian state councillor and, in 1934, an SS Obergruppenführer. In 1936 he was named commander in chief of the Order Police, a new national organization whose responsibilities paralleled those of regular police forces in free countries: public order, investigation of crimes, and police administration. The Order Police remained, however, under the larger purview of the SS, and in this manner the German police grew increasingly nazified and ideological in orientation. Daluege's other primary role was as head of the Security Police in Heydrich's SD. There his main responsibilities included the protection of Adolf Hitler and other top Nazis as well as internal political security within the German Reich.

These responsibilities continued, and in some areas expanded, after World War II began. Both the Order Police and the Security Police became increasingly military in their activities, and played a large role in the atrocities committed in the occupied territories. After the war Daluege was arrested by the Czechs, who executed him on October 24, 1946, for various war crimes committed while he was deputy protector of Bohemia-Moravia. Notable among these was the destruction of the village of Lidice and the massacre or deportation of its inhabitants in reprisal for the assassination of Heydrich. *See also* Bohemia and Moravia, Protectorate of; Lidice massacre, Vol. 1; Order Police, Security Police, Vol. 2.

Darré, Walther (1895–1953)

The Nazi Party's chief agricultural official as Reich farmers' leader (Reichsbauernführer) and Reich minister of food and agriculture (Reichsernährungs minister), as well as a racial theorist. Darré was born to a German family in Buenos Aires, Argentina, in July 1895. He was educated, however, in Germany and at King's College in London. He eventually took a degree as an agronomist, or agricultural scientist. During World War I he served as an artillery officer.

Darré's interest in right wing political activity emerged in the immediate postwar period, when he served in the Berlin Freikorps. He also maintained a friendship with Heinrich Himmler, who shared with him a strong interest in agriculture. Darré did not join the Nazi movement until the late 1920s, but he quickly emerged as the main force behind Nazism in the German countryside. He tried to bring farmers into the Nazi Party, for instance, and worked at developing an ideology built around the notion of the unity of "blood and soil." He published his thoughts in three books that appeared in the late 1920s: *Das Bauerntum als Lebensquell der Nordischen Rasse (The Farmer as the Lifespring of the Nordic Race)*, *Blut und Boden (Blood and Soil)*, and *Neuadel aus Blut und Boden (Redefining Blood and Soil)*. These books brought him to the attention of Adolf Hitler, who found much that was congenial in Darré's odd philosophy. Darré claimed, for example, that the rural people of Germany were the true source not only of all German greatness but of European civilization as a whole. The peasantry, therefore, should be nurtured and cared for, since they were the "bloodspring" of the German race. Darré contrasted the German peasantry with the Jews, whom he referred to as a nomadic and parasitical race. During the early 1930s, when the Nazi Party was trying to expand its base of voters to include the rural population, Darré's ideas received a wide hearing from Adolf Hitler, and Darré was given free rein to try to bring farmers into the Nazi movement by spreading his ideas about the essential greatness of the German peasant as well as the notion that farmers might one day form part of the ruling class of the new Nazi Reich.

In April 1933 Darré was named Reich farmers' leader, a post he held for the duration of the Third Reich. Soon after, he was named to Hitler's cabinet as Reich minister of food and agriculture. He also attained the mostly honorary posts, in his case, of Reichsleiter and SS colonel general, although he served with more impact as the head of the SS Race and Resettlement Office, which was responsible for, among other things, the population shifts that Nazi leaders envisioned. Meanwhile, he continued his writing; Darré was at heart more an intellectual than a soldier, policeman, or politician. He wrote books on ancient Germanic mythology and folklore, the "soul" of the German peasant, and, in a reflection of his true origins, on the importance of pig farming.

Darré's policies as Reich minister of food and agriculture were largely failures, based as they were on ideology rather than practical circumstances. He wanted to take strong measures to not only preserve the German peasantry but single them out as an honored group. To these ends he required all German peasants whose farms were less than 360 acres in size to stay on the land. Moreover, the farms could not be subdivided or mortgaged. These policies flew in the face of the free market economic measures favored by German economic officials, and they ignored the larger trends of farmers either altering the size of their holdings to remain competitive or moving to the cities to find work. Perhaps even more importantly in the eyes of top Nazis, Darré's policies failed to increase German food production. By the beginning of World War II he had squandered most of his prestige and had little influence on affairs, although he retained his various posts until 1942, when he was replaced by Himmler as head of the SS Race and Resettlement Office.

After World War II Darré was captured by the Americans, who sentenced him to five years in prison for crimes including the theft of property from Poles and Jews as well as deliberately starving Jews. He died in Munich in September 1953. *See also* blood and soil, Vol. 1; Reich Food Estate, Reich Hereditary Farm Law, Vol. 2.

de Gaulle, Charles (1890–1970)

The leader of the French National Committee of Liberation, known popularly as the Free French, during World War II as well as one of the top European statesmen of the twentieth century. De Gaulle was born in Lille on November 22, 1890, into an upper-class family of soldiers and literary figures. He graduated from the French Military Academy at Saint-Cyr in 1911 and served with great distinction as a field officer during World War I before being captured by the Germans at Verdun in 1916. After the war he served as a French military adviser in Poland before returning to teach at Saint-Cyr. In the years prior to World War II he continued to serve as an active duty officer and an instructor. He also wrote two books, *The Edge of the Sword* in 1932 and *The Army of the Future* in 1934. The latter book predicted that, in future wars, armored divisions dominated by tanks and able to move quickly would play a decisive role. French strategists largely ignored the work but it was studied closely by the Germans, who used it to help develop the blitzkrieg strategy that would serve them so well in the early years of World War II.

Free French leader Charles de Gaulle addresses his countrymen during the German occupation of France.

After the Germans invaded France in May 1940, de Gaulle, now a general, was given the opportunity to test his theories when he was placed in charge of one of France's four armored divisions. He had some success attacking German flanks, but was ultimately forced to retreat. Raised briefly to undersecretary of war, de Gaulle attended the last cabinet meetings before the French surrender. He escaped to England on June 17, the day after Marshal Philippe Pétain, the founder of the collaborationist Vichy regime, contacted the Germans to offer them terms of surrender. De Gaulle, however, refused to accept Pétain's authority and pledged to continue the fight for France from the nation's African and Middle Eastern colonies. The Vichy government in turn condemned him as a traitor and sentenced him to death in absentia.

Over the next months de Gaulle emerged as the leader of the exiled French forces in Britain, although he had a difficult time getting British authorities to recognize him as a legitimate leader. He also failed, for the most part, to establish effective bases in French colonies in West Africa and the Middle East, where occupation forces remained loyal to Vichy. Only after the successful Allied landings in French North Africa in 1942, and only after it was clear that Vichy authorities were actively collaborating with the Nazis, did the British and Americans fully accept de Gaulle as leader of the Free French. Even then, they hesitated to lend their full support to the aloof, recalcitrant, and physically imposing general, preferring instead to deal with the more malleable Henri Giraud.

De Gaulle returned to France for the first time on June 13, 1944, shortly after the Allied landings on the Normandy beaches on D-Day. In August, he ignored Allied plans to bypass Paris on their way to the German border, suspecting that if the Allies passed Paris by, the city might be left open to destruction by the Germans or a takeover by Communists among the French resistance. In any case, de Gaulle did not want to be denied his triumphal return to the French capital, and he presented Allied military commanders with a fait accompli by mustering forces and entering Paris under his own authority on August 26. He was welcomed as a returning hero by the local people, and early in September he took his place at the head of a provisional government prepared to create a postwar French state, which came to be known as the Fourth Republic. De Gaulle remained bitter, however, that the Allies still chose not to view him as their equal.

De Gaulle remained the dominant figure in French politics from the end of the war until his final retirement in 1969. He retired from the presidency, however, in January 1946, in response to a lack of support from left-wing parties, and he watched with dismay as the Fourth Republic devised a constitution that left France without a strong leader and descended into doomed colonial wars in Vietnam and Algeria. He was recalled as president in 1958 when the Algerian crisis threatened to tear the nation apart, but he insisted that a new constitution be drawn up that granted the president extensive powers. The result was the French Fifth Republic, of which de Gaulle was president until 1969. In addition to restoring order and structure to French politics, de Gaulle strongly promoted European unification, especially in the form of agreements between France and Germany. He died in Paris shortly after leaving office, on November 9, 1970. *See also* French National Committee of Liberation, Vol. 1; resistance movements, occupied countries, Vol. 2.

Dietrich, Josef (Sepp) (1892–1966)

SS officer who served as the head of Adolf Hitler's personal bodyguard contingents. He was also one of the guiding lights behind the militarized Waffen-SS, and served as a Waffen-SS army commander during World War II.

Sepp Dietrich was born in Bavaria on May 28, 1892. He came from a poor peasant background, and until the outbreak of World War I worked as a common laborer. During World War I he served as a sergeant in the German Imperial Army. After the war he drifted toward Munich, where he became an early member of the Nazi Party and a powerful contributor to SA violence and strong-arm tactics. He took part in the Beer Hall Putsch of November 1923 and therefore qualified as one of the Nazi Party's "Old Fighters."

In 1928 Hitler named Dietrich to be the head of his personal bodyguard, and early photographs and propaganda films show him almost constantly in the Nazi leader's presence. Dietrich often worked, in fact, as Hitler's chauffeur in his trips across Germany, and was given the affectionate nickname of "chauffereska." After the Nazis took power, Dietrich was appointed the head of the Leibstandarte-SS Adolf Hitler, the unit of the SS responsible for protecting the Führer. In this capacity he took charge of the SS contingents who arrested and murdered Ernst Röhm and others in the Blood Purge of June 30, 1934. In recognition of his accomplishments in "protecting" the German Reich from Röhm, Dietrich was raised to the rank of SS general.

During World War II Dietrich was one of the Third Reich's most accomplished military officers, and both Nazi propaganda and Hitler's frequent praise of him raised his reputation even further. He served as a Waffen-SS commander across Europe, and his ruthlessness, skill, and leadership ability were acknowledged even by competitors in the Wehrmacht. He participated in a number of wartime atrocities, including the killings of civilians and prisoners of war. One area where he is alleged to have been involved in the killing of civilians was in the Kharkiv district of the Soviet Union, where he was the commander of an SS Panzer corps between 1941 and 1943. On the eastern front, as it happened, killing of civilians was a relatively common practice of German military contingents. In 1944 Dietrich transferred to the western front; by this period of the war Hitler was rapidly losing faith in the commanders of the regular army, and pinned his hopes on the Waffen-SS. On D-Day, June 6, 1944, Dietrich's 1st SS Panzer Corps failed to prevent Allied landings on the beaches of Normandy. During the so-called Battle of the Bulge, Germany's last offensive of World War II in December 1944, Dietrich commanded the Sixth SS Panzer Army despite his personal realization that Germany had lost the war. On December 17, troops under Dietrich's command executed without cause seventy-seven American prisoners of war, an event known as the Malmedy massacre.

Dietrich was captured by American forces in May 1945, after continued futile fighting in Hungary and Austria. He was eventually put on trial for his involvement in the killings at Malmedy and sentenced to twenty-five years in prison for the crime. He was released, however, in 1955, despite the general sentiment that he was a top Nazi war criminal. A year later, in 1956, a German court placed him on trial for the murder of Ernst Röhm and others during the Blood Purge. He was convicted of being an accessory to premeditated murder and sentenced to nineteen months' imprisonment, although yet again he was released early, this time because of ill health. He died in Ludwigsburg, near Stuttgart, on April 21, 1966. *See also* Blood Purge, Leibstandarte-SS, Vol. 1; Malmedy massacre, Old Fighters, Waffen-SS, Vol. 2.

Dietrich, Otto (1897–1952)

The main public relations officer for both the Nazi Party and Adolf Hitler and, along with Joseph Goebbels, one of the Third Reich's great propagandists. Otto Dietrich was born in Essen in the Rhineland on August 31, 1897. His service in World War I earned him the Iron Cross, First Class, one of Germany's highest military honors. After the war he embarked on an academic career, receiving a Ph.D. in political science from the University of Freiburg in 1921. Rather than teach, however, Dietrich took a job with the Essen Chamber of Commerce before turning to journalism. He served as deputy editor of the *Essen National News* and business manager of the *Augsburg News*, a national evening paper. He also established a network of contacts and influence among important Rhineland industrialists, thanks to his marriage to the daughter of an important newspaper publisher. Numbered among his contacts was Emil Kirdorf, an early industrial supporter of Nazism.

Dietrich joined the Nazi Party in August 1931 and was appointed press chief to take advantage of his contacts and his skills. He served as Hitler's top publicist during the elections of 1932, when the Nazi leader crisscrossed the country seeking to increase his electoral support. He also served as a liaison between Hitler and the workers and industrialists of the Ruhr, Germany's main industrial center. He tried, with some success, to turn the workers away from Gregor Strasser, who led a branch of the Nazi Party that took socialism seriously and literally. Meanwhile, he also helped make Nazism a viable option to such industrial magnates as Fritz Thyssen.

After the Nazis took power in 1933, Dietrich continued his public relations work in both official and less formal ways. One of his more noteworthy accomplishments was to accompany the police contingents involved in the Blood Purge of June 30, 1934. He later issued a detailed and dramatized version of the events to the German press, noting both the ruthlessness of the arrests and executions and Hitler's supposed shock at the alleged homosexual behavior of Ernst Röhm, the chief target of the purge. Dietrich was appointed in 1937 to be state secretary in the Ministry of Public Enlightenment and

Propaganda under Goebbels. There and as head of the Reich Association of the German Press he helped to enforce the Third Reich's censorship of newspapers and radio broadcasters as well as ensure that much of the content that ended up in the German media was favorable to Hitler's regime. Meanwhile, he wrote a number of books extolling Adolf Hitler the man as well as Hitler's accomplishments and ideas. These included *With Hitler Toward Power*, which sold over 250,000 copies, *The Philosophical Foundation of National Socialism*, *The Philosophy of Teamwork in the Third Reich*, and as war approached, *On the Road to Victory: With Hitler in Poland*. During World War II Dietrich continued along similar lines, taking special pains to ensure that German newspapers printed positive news about the Third Reich's war effort. In fact, he sent daily "press releases" to German editors detailing how war news should be reported. Although he was somewhat prone to rash statements, such as claiming prematurely (and incorrectly) that the war in the east was over, Dietrich enjoyed the loyalty of Adolf Hitler until 1945.

Dietrich was imprisoned by the British in 1945, and in 1949 he was put on trial for crimes against humanity. He was sentenced to seven years' imprisonment in Landsberg Prison in Munich but was released after only one. During his earlier imprisonment Dietrich wrote an apologetic work known as *Twelve Years with Hitler.* It was published in 1955, three years after Dietrich died in Düsseldorf in the Rhineland. *See also* Ministry of Public Enlightenment and Propaganda, propaganda in the Third Reich, Vol. 2.

Dohnanyi, Hans von (1902–1945)

A prominent member of the German resistance movement. Dohnanyi was born in Vienna, Austria, on January 1, 1902, of part-Hungarian and part-Jewish heritage. After taking a law degree in 1929, he worked in Germany for the Reich Ministry of Justice, where he remained until 1938 and during his last year was raised to the position of supreme court justice. Thanks to a special order from Adolf Hitler, Dohnanyi's Jewish heritage was "Aryanized" away and he was able to work for the government of the Third Reich, although he was never allowed to join the Nazi Party. He had a number of contacts with the German resistance movement. His wife was the sister of Dietrich Bonhoeffer, the noted theologian and opponent of Nazism. In 1938 Dohnanyi took a staff position with the Abwehr, the intelligence section of the High Command of the German armed forces, where his superior officer was Major General Hans Oster, a leader of the resistance. Over the next years Dohnanyi worked with Oster, as well as other Abwehr officials such as Admiral Wilhelm Canaris, in building contacts and making vague plans to oust Hitler. He was arrested twice. The first time, in April 1943, the Gestapo took him in based on their suspicion that he was involved in plots against the Führer. He was released, however, due to a lack of evidence. He was arrested a second time after the July Plot of 1944, when the Gestapo and SS swept up nearly everyone conceivably connected to the German resistance. Dohnanyi was held in the Sachsenhausen concentration camp near Berlin, where he was apparently tortured and, on April 8, 1945, killed. *See also* resistance movements, Germany, Vol. 2.

Dönitz, Karl (1891–1980)

Grand admiral of the navy of the Third Reich and the man Adolf Hitler chose to be his successor; as such, Dönitz presided over the end of the Third Reich in May 1945.

Karl Dönitz was born in a suburb of Berlin on September 16, 1891, and belonged to an upper-middle-class family. He joined the German Imperial Navy in 1910, and during World War I he served as an officer in naval aircraft squadrons and on U-boats. When a U-boat he was serving on in 1918 sank in the Mediterranean Sea, he was captured by Allied forces but soon released.

After World War I, Dönitz joined the now greatly reduced navy of the Weimar Republic; since the Treaty of Versailles forbade Germany from building or using submarines, Dönitz served instead on surface ships.

In 1935, when Hitler felt confident enough to ignore the treaty's military restrictions, Dönitz was chosen to be the commander of the new U-boat wing of the Third Reich's navy. By this time he had joined the Nazi Party and, unlike many other high-level military officers, was an enthusiastic supporter of Hitler. He was promoted to admiral in 1940 and to grand admiral in 1942. Under Dönitz's leadership the U-boat wing of the German navy became a significant force and, in the opinion of British prime minister Winston Churchill and many others, came close to winning World War II for Germany. U-boats were used mostly in the Atlantic Ocean and around the British Isles, where their purpose was to contain the British fleet while interfering with the shipping of supplies and men from North America. From 1940 to 1943 Dönitz's U-boats sank dozens of Allied ships and threatened to cut off Britain from its vital supply lines from the United States and Canada. Dönitz developed the "wolf pack" strategy in order to concentrate his power and prevent detection by Allied surface ships. The strategy involved the placement of a number of U-boats in a V-shape parallel to the surface of the ocean. The "wolf" would not strike until Allied supply convoys entered the V, at which point it was too late for them to take evasive action. The strategy was so successful that Dönitz was able to persuade both Hitler and Grand Admiral Erich Raeder, his superior in the navy until 1943, to devote a great deal of resources to the U-boat fleet. By 1943 Dönitz had over two hundred ships at his disposal, supplied and repaired by a network of submarine pens strung out along the Atlantic coasts of Germany, the Netherlands, Belgium, and France. Only the development of sophisticated listening equipment allowed the Allies, after 1943, to avoid the "wolf packs" and keep the supply lines open across the Atlantic.

On January 30, 1943, Dönitz replaced Raeder, whose surface ships had failed to impress Hitler, as chief of the German navy. He was also awarded some of the highest honors available to military men and Nazi Party members, including the Knight's Cross with Oak Leaves and the Blood Order. His loyalty to Hitler, his accomplishments as U-boat commander, and his relative invisibility as naval chief freed Dönitz from many of the ongoing demands Hitler imposed on army officers. In April 1945, after Hitler denounced both Hermann Göring and Heinrich Himmler for betraying him, and after Joseph Goebbels decided to kill himself, the Nazi leader named Dönitz to succeed him as Führer of the Reich. He made the

Grand Admiral Karl Dönitz (pictured) succeeded Hitler as leader of the collapsing Third Reich and oversaw the German surrender.

appointment in his last will and political testament. Dönitz received the word at his base in northern Germany, and was fairly surprised.

From May 1 to May 23, 1945, Dönitz attempted to govern a collapsing German nation from his base in Flensburg near the Danish border. His main priority was to stop the fighting between Germany and the western Allies. Briefly, he tried to convince Allied leaders to join Germany in fighting the Soviet Union and the spread of communism. Failing that, the new leader of the Reich tried to stall the official German surrender, hoping that the bulk of his armed forces, as well as a number of important individuals, could escape to the West and thereby avoid capture by the Soviets. On May 8, however, Dönitz authorized all German military commanders to surrender unconditionally (a number of them had already done so) and World War II in Europe was over.

Dönitz managed to elude Allied capture until May 23, when he was taken prisoner by the British, who were then in command of northern Germany. He was put on trial, along with twenty other surviving top Nazis, in Nuremberg in the autumn of 1945, surprised to be counted among such obvious war criminals as Göring, Hans Frank, Ernst Kaltenbrunner, and Julius Streicher. Also to his surprise, Dönitz was found guilty on two of the four charges: war crimes and crimes against peace. He was sentenced to ten years in Spandau Prison in Berlin and served his entire term. He published his memoirs in 1959 and died near Hamburg on December 24, 1980. *See also* Battle of the Atlantic, Vol. 1; U-boats, Vol. 2; Hitler, Hitler's Last Will and Political Testament, Vol. 4.

Drexler, Anton (1884–1942)

One of the founders of the German Workers' Party, the precursor of the National Socialist German Workers', or Nazi, Party. For a short time he also served as Adolf Hitler's superior as chairman of the Nazi Party.

Anton Drexler was born in Munich on June 13, 1884, to a working-class family. He apprenticed as a pipe fitter in Berlin but was unable to maintain his job there because of his political views: He rejected the social democracy that many Berlin laborers favored. He took work instead as an independent locksmith, first in Berlin and later in Munich.

Drexler was declared physically unfit to fight in World War I. Perhaps in compensation he became active politically. He joined the Munich branch of the Fatherland Party during the war, where he developed the ideology that was later to be the basis of the German Workers' Party. This way of thinking combined advocacy of leftist economic measures, such as the abolition of profiteering and speculation, with an intense German nationalism. In 1918 Drexler organized a political action group known as the Committee of Independent Workmen, where he continued to develop these ideas. He wanted to liberate workers from the chains placed on them by the extremely rich, but he also rejected both social democracy and communism. He also claimed that it was impossible for workers to be both truly free and truly German unless Jews and foreigners were excluded from legal citizenship and from the German national community.

On January 5, 1919, when he was working as a locksmith at the Munich railway yards, Drexler formed the German Workers' Party along with a second man, Karl Harrer. Like the Committee of Independent Workmen, the new party was based on a combination of prolaborer ideas and a vehement German nationalism. In the Munich of the day, the formation of the party was hardly newsworthy, since new political movements came and went with great frequency. The German Workers' Party, however, proved to have staying power, and attracted the interest of members of the Thule Society, an organization founded on German nationalism and anticommunism. The party met infrequently in Munich's beer halls, and its early gatherings were as much occasions for drinking and celebration as opportunities for political discussion. In September 1919 Adolf Hitler, then working as an intelligence gatherer for the German army, visited a meeting of the German Workers' Party. He was not impressed, having already seen numerous right-wing nationalist groups. Nevertheless, Hitler had decided on a political career and figured that joining forces with Drexler was as good an opportunity as any other. He joined, apparently, as member number 555 of the party, not number 7, as he was to claim in *Mein Kampf*.

For some months after Hitler joined the party, Drexler remained its leading theorist and certainly in some ways an influence on the future Führer. Drexler produced a pamphlet entitled *My Political Awakening* in which he honed his version of Germanic socialism, claiming that German workers were being held back by a combination of profiteering and Jewish economic manipulation. Drexler was drawing fine distinctions that Hitler was to pick up on; he was opposed to both socialism and communism, but favored the workers and hoped to create a classless society. What might free German workers, Drexler argued, was a national resurgence based on racial unity and anti-Semitism. These ideas were further described, with Hitler's help, in a twenty-five-point program announced by Hitler at a meeting in February 1920. Although the so-called Twenty-Five Points make up a rather muddled political program, Hitler never repudiated them and in them are the seeds of measures later pursued vigorously by the Third Reich, notably expansion to the east and rejection of the Jews from the German national community.

Anton Drexler, meanwhile, was increasingly shouldered aside in the party's leadership councils by the more aggressive and determined Hitler, limited also because he continued to work a full-time job while Hitler, having quit the army, was able to devote all of his time to politics. The German Workers' Party became the Nazi Party in the spring of 1920, and while Drexler was the chairman, Hitler's stature grew. In the summer of 1921, when Hitler insisted on complete control, Drexler stepped aside. Two years later he quit the organization he had helped to found, and for a time he served on the Bavarian legislature as the representative of another nationalist party.

In later years Drexler never rejoined the Nazi Party, and was thus never considered one of the "old fighters" whom Hitler claimed to revere so much. In fact, on the rare occasions his opinion was sought, Drexler often criticized Hitler's tactics, if not his ideas. He died in Munich on February 24, 1942. *See also* German Workers' Party, Vol. 1; The Twenty-Five Points of the German Workers' Party, Vol. 4.

E

Ebert, Friedrich (1871–1925)

One of the founders and the first president of the Weimar Republic. Ebert ranked high on Adolf Hitler's list of the "November criminals" who betrayed Germany at the end of World War I. Ebert was born on February 4, 1871, in Heidelberg and came from a working-class background. In the 1890s he entered politics as a member of the Social Democratic Party (SPD). Rising quickly to a position of authority, he became the leader of the SPD in 1913. He played a major role in keeping the so-called Majority Socialists unified when, during World War I, the SPD split over Germany's war policy. At the end of the war, when the SPD was the strongest political party in Germany, he was instrumental in forming the uneasy coalition between the SPD and the traditional officer corps which allowed the Weimar Republic to take hold. On February 11, 1919, he was named provisional president of the republic; soon after, he was granted the office until 1925 so that potentially divisive elections could be avoided in these critical times.

As president, Ebert strove to maintain a middle course despite constant criticism from conservatives, uncertain loyalty from the army, and a French occupation army in the west. He put down threats of uprisings from both Communists and extreme nationalists, including the Kapp Putsch of 1920 and Hitler's Beer Hall Putsch of 1923. To maintain order he invoked, when necessary, Article 48 of the Weimar Constitution, which allowed the president to rule by decree. Ebert died on February 28, 1925, before his term was up. He was replaced as president by Field Marshal Paul von Hindenburg. *See also* November criminals, Weimar Republic, Vol. 2.

Eckart, Dietrich (1868–1923)

German nationalist poet and an early influence on Adolf Hitler and the Nazi movement. Eckart was born in the Rhineland on March 23, 1868. After initially aiming at a career in journalism he turned to poetry and drama. He had little success in either field and blamed his failures on Jews and Communists rather than his own shortcomings. In 1915 he moved to Munich, where after World War I he displayed an interest in nationalist politics. In 1919 he founded a newspaper, *Auf Gut Deutsch (In Good German)*, in which he blamed Germany's defeat in World War I on, again, Jews and Communists. The paper was also highly critical of the Versailles Treaty, profiteering, and the Social Democratic orientation of the new Weimar regime. Alfred Rosenberg, later the Nazi Party's philosopher, was a frequent contributor to the paper, as was Gottfried Feder, another early Nazi. Meanwhile, Eckart kept up his poetic efforts. The title of one poem, "Deutschland Erwache!" ("Germany Awake!") was to become one of the frequent rallying cries of the Nazis.

Hitler himself acknowledged that Eckart was a major influence on him; the two got to know each other in late 1919 or early 1920. Eckart served as a sort of spiritual mentor and father figure to Hitler, who admired Eckart's poetic sensibilities, crude anti-Semitism, and strong nationalism. Hitler remembered Eckart so fondly, in fact, that he dedicated *Mein Kampf* to him and, when Eckart died in 1923, arranged his burial in the village of Berchtesgaden in the Alpine border region that Hitler so loved. Beyond personal affection, Eckart provided practical assistance to the rising Nazi leader. He introduced him to influential and wealthy people in Munich and, in 1920, arranged the funding that made it possible for the Nazi Party to purchase the *Völkischer Beobachter (People's Observer)*, the official newspaper of the Nazi movement. Eckart also served as the first editor of the paper, ultimately replaced by Rosenberg. He died on December 23, 1923, after a long illness, his health already threatened by alcoholism and morphine addiction. *See also Auf Gut Deutsch*, Vol. 1; Thule Society, Vol. 2.

Eichmann, Adolf (1906–1962)

SS lieutenant colonel and one of the men most deeply involved in the mass extermination of Jews by the Third Reich during World War II. He was the chief of the Jewish Office of the Gestapo, Section IV-B-4 of the Reich Central Security Office (RSHA), the police and security branch of the SS. In his role as an expert in both "Jewish affairs" and transportation logistics, Eichmann organized the transports that took millions of Jews to their deaths in the extermination camps in Poland, and meanwhile devised ways for the SS to steal their property. He was also one of the few top Nazi war criminals to survive World War II and, for a time, avoid capture and prosecution for his actions.

Adolf Eichmann was born in Solingen, Germany, on March 19, 1906, to a middle-class, Protestant family. He grew up mostly in Linz, a city in western Austria where his father operated a mining company. An indifferent if intelligent student, Eichmann dropped out of engineering college as a young man, and worked for a short time as a laborer and then as a salesman. While living in Vienna he conceived a strong dislike for Jews, whom he blamed for both his personal misfortunes and the general poverty and strife of post–World War I Austria. He joined the Austrian Nazi Party in April 1932 with the encouragement of a friend, Ernst Kaltenbrunner, later the chief of the RSHA. He moved back to Germany in July 1933, leaving a sales job with an oil company, to join a group of fellow Austrian Nazi exiles in Bavaria and undergo extensive military training.

Eichmann's first major professional break came in September 1934 when he joined the SD, the Security Service of the SS and the precursor of the RSHA. After working for six months as a file clerk, Eichmann's administrative and bureaucratic abilities became clear to his superiors, and he took over the Jewish Office at SD headquarters in Berlin. There he specialized in Zionism, and dallied with the idea that it was proper for Jews to seek repatriation to Palestine; it would get them out of Europe. He even studied both Yiddish and Hebrew in order to enhance his expertise, and made a trip to Palestine in 1937. There he tried to meet with Arab leaders to discuss Jewish emigration, but the British, who were trying to keep the peace in Palestine at that time, ordered him out of the country, concerned that he might stir up trouble between Arabs and Jews.

Having worked since 1933 in support of the Anschluss, the annexation of Austria to the Greater German Reich, Eichmann was happy when the union was finally accomplished in March 1938. He was posted to Vienna as the assistant to the local SD chief. Within months Eichmann had largely set up and become the director of the Vienna Office for Jewish Emigration. There he truly began to come to the notice of top SS leaders. By 1938, the SS had largely seized control of "Jewish matters" within the Nazi bureaucracy, and its main efforts in cleansing the Third Reich of Jews were focused on getting them to leave the country. By the time World War II began, and thanks largely to Eichmann's diligence, creativity, and ruthlessness, the jurisdiction of the Office for Jewish Emigration had expanded from Vienna and Austria to both Czechoslovakia and Germany. Eichmann, in the same period, found ways for nearly 150,000 Jews to leave the Reich while at the same time forcing them to sign over most of their wealth and property. These were impressive, if evil, achievements, requiring the coordination of transport schedules, the arrangement of assembly points, and interaction with various bureaucratic, financial, and aid associations. Thanks to his clear abilities in these areas Eichmann became the man the SS turned to on matters of forced emigration or deportation. In the aftermath of the German conquest of Poland in the fall of 1939, when the Germans appeared to have made the decision to concentrate Jews in Poland for purposes of forced labor and later evacuation, Eichmann was working as a special adviser on "evacuations." He was transferred to the Gestapo in December 1939, and at that point took up his position as chief of Section IV-B-4 of the RSHA. The Gestapo itself was Section IV of the RSHA; office B-4 dealt with Jewish affairs. His immediate superior was Heinrich Müller, chief of the Gestapo, and his ultimate superiors were Reinhard Heydrich, head of the RSHA, and Heinrich Himmler.

Eichmann's responsibilities expanded along with the developing Nazi policies toward Jews. For most of 1940 and into 1941 these policies involved forcing Jews into ghettos in Poland. The first to go were Poland's millions of Jews, but they were soon followed by Jews from the western European nations Germany defeated and occupied in the spring and fall of 1940. While short-term plans involved using the ghettoized Jews as forced laborers, the long-term plan, at this point, was to send them all to a reservation of some kind, either in eastern Europe or on the Indian Ocean island of Madagascar. Eichmann was consulted on all of these plans, and Reinhard Heydrich increasingly relied on his abilities. When in the summer and fall of 1941 the SS, with Hitler's approval, embarked upon mass extermination as the "Final So-

SS lieutenant colonel Adolf Eichmann organized the transport of millions of Jews to extermination camps.

lution to the Jewish Question," Eichmann's expertise was again necessary. He was an important participant at the Wannsee Conference of January 20, 1942, when the Final Solution was announced to the appropriate Nazi functionaries and where he served as Heydrich's right-hand man, at least on Jewish matters. Eichmann had taken the initiative in determining that there were 11 million Jews across Europe for the SS to deal with, and he assumed the responsibility of transport and logistics expert, prepared to address such issues as the use of railway cars or the kind and quantity of goods deported Jews would be allowed to carry. He was also in charge of the official minutes of the conference. By this time he had been promoted to SS lieutenant colonel, a relatively low rank given the circles he moved in. But his power and influence in his special fields of expertise were rarely questioned.

After Heydrich died of wounds sustained in an assassination attempt in the spring of

1942 Eichmann truly came into his own. By this period the Final Solution was fully under way. Often with the help of local collaborators, Eichmann organized the roundup and deportations of Jews from the Polish ghettos, the occupied countries of western Europe, and finally from the allies of the Third Reich, although he was frustrated in his efforts in some areas. The Italians and Finns in particular were less than enthusiastic in their cooperation, while in Denmark local resistance movements managed to spirit most of the country's small Jewish population across to neutral Sweden before they could be assembled. Eichmann's last roundups were in Hungary, by 1944 a reluctant ally of Nazi Germany that had managed to preserve most of its population of seven hundred thousand Jews from Eichmann's transports. In the spring and early summer of 1944, Eichmann personally went to Budapest, the Hungarian capital, to ensure that the deportations proceeded. He wheeled and dealed with Hungarian officials, German bureaucrats, and even foreign agencies and diplomats, such as Sweden's Raoul Wallenberg, who were trying frantically to save the country's Jews. In the end nearly four hundred thousand were sent to Auschwitz. By August 1944 Eichmann, the devoted bureaucrat, was able to report to Himmler that SS killing programs had murdered some 6 million Jews in eastern Europe, the number that has been associated with the Holocaust ever since although the true total can probably never be known. Eichmann claimed that 2 million were killed in the Einsatzgruppen operations in 1941 and 4 million died in the six death camps.

After World War II Eichmann was arrested by American forces and placed in an internment camp. He escaped from the camp under disguise and managed to live in Germany under assumed names, working as a farm laborer, for several years. In 1950 he escaped to Argentina using ODESSA, the organization that secretly helped numerous Nazi war criminals escape to South America via Italy or Spain. In Argentina he joined the substantial local German community and took the name of Richard Klement. As was the case during the Nazi years, Eichmann's hard work and administrative abilities, displayed in jobs with a water company and an automobile company, made it difficult for him to escape notice. By the mid-1950s Eichmann was under suspicion by Nazi hunters, who considered him a prime target. After Simon Wiesenthal conclusively identified Eichmann in 1959, he informed the Israeli government, which sent a team of agents and commandos to kidnap the former SS killer. On the evening of April 11, 1960, on his way home from work, carrying a briefcase and wearing a shabby suit, Eichmann was grabbed by the Israeli team and taken back to Israel to stand trial for crimes against humanity and crimes against the Jewish people.

The Eichmann trial, held in Jerusalem, lasted from April 2 to August 14, 1961. The Israelis used the proceeding as a forum to remind a world whose memory was beginning to fade of the crimes that men like Eichmann committed during World War II. Prosecutors called witnesses from around the globe and assembled mountains of documentation, photographs, films, and other evidence. Meanwhile reporters from dozens of countries covered the trial in detail. For his own protection, Eichmann was kept in a bulletproof glass box in the courtroom. One conclusion reached by a number of observers, notably the philosopher and German Jewish refugee Hannah Arendt, was that Eichmann seemed completely ordinary. Despite his enthusiastic participation in mass murder as a Nazi bureaucrat in earlier years, Eichmann seemed to be no more than a clerk or a midlevel civil servant. Arendt later published a book, *Eichmann in Jerusalem*, which examined the "banality of evil," the capacity of completely nondescript men for cold-blooded atrocities.

Eichmann was found guilty on December 2, 1961. He was executed by hanging in

Israel's Ramleh Prison on May 11, 1962. *See also* Eichmann trial, Vol. 1; Office for Jewish Emigration, Vol. 2; Eichmann and Less, Eichmann Remembers, Vol. 4.

Eicke, Theodor (1892–1943)

SS officer, concentration camp official, and founder of the Death's Head–SS formations who guarded the camps. He was the inspector of concentration camps from 1934. Eicke was largely responsible for developing the procedures by which camp prisoners were progressively dehumanized through both systematic and selective brutality.

Theodor Eicke was born in Alsace-Lorraine along the French-German border on October 17, 1892. His father was a civil servant. Eicke served in behind-the-lines functions for the German army during World War I and eventually rose to the level of subpaymaster. After the war Eicke gave up the army for police work in Thuringia, although by 1923 he had been let go from several police jobs because of right-wing political activities. He then joined the IG Farben conglomerate as a security officer concerned with industrial espionage.

Eicke joined the Nazi Party in 1928 and the SS in 1930, where he rose quickly to a position of leadership. By 1931 he was an SS colonel and the chief of a regiment in the Rhineland. In 1932 he was sentenced to two years in prison for his involvement in bomb plots but Heinrich Himmler, who apparently had come to appreciate Eicke's ruthlessness and devotion, asked him to leave for Italy, where he stayed as a free man until February 1933. In an early example of the conflict between the Nazi Party and the increasingly important SS, Eicke was cashiered out of the SS and placed into a psychiatric clinic by the Nazi Gauleiter of the Rhineland-Palatinate, Josef Bürckel, who considered him to be insane. Eicke was rescued, again, by Himmler, who on June 26, 1933, named him to be the commandant of the new concentration camp at Dachau, near Munich.

At Dachau, Eicke developed techniques such as making all prisoners look the same with shaved heads and drab uniforms, setting prisoners to forced labor, referring to them as numbers rather than people with names, and, more drastically, subjecting inmates to solitary confinement and random beatings. He also realized the usefulness of a divide-and-conquer strategy and found ways to set groups of prisoners—Communists and Socialists, for instance—against one another. Prisoners who refused to obey instructions or who might be considered "dangerous" to the "harmony" of the camp were shot, on Eicke's authorization. To standardize and instill these practices among SS administrators and guards, Eicke turned Dachau into a training center for the concentration camp network. Among his "graduates" were members of the Death's Head–SS, a special contingent Eicke organized to guard the perimeters of the camps. The Death's Head tended to attract the most brutal and amoral of SS recruits, and by 1937 its membership had reached four thousand and enjoyed paramilitary capabilities. Meanwhile, Eicke cemented his loyalty to Himmler and Hitler by taking an important role in the Blood Purge of June 30, 1934. Eicke himself killed Ernst Röhm, SA chief and the main target of the purge.

Perhaps as a reward for his role in the purge, but also certainly because of his success at Dachau, Eicke was promoted to SS lieutenant general and inspector of concentration camps, as well as head of the Death's Head, in July 1934. In his new position he could expand his ideas about concentration camp management and bring them to bear throughout the growing camp network. Eicke continually reminded his men that they had to be hard and ruthless: Anyone who could not sustain such a state, Eicke wrote, should retire to a monastery.

During World War II Eicke transferred to a combat command with the SS. His first contingent was a division of Death's Head men that saw action in Poland in the fall of

1939. Thereafter Eicke remained on the eastern front, replaced as inspector of concentration camps in 1940 by Richard Gluecks. Eicke enjoyed continued professional success and was promoted by 1943 to general of the Waffen-SS. He was killed in an airplane crash on February 16, 1943. *See also* Dachau, Inspectorate of Concentration Camps, Vol. 1.

Einstein, Albert (1879–1955)

One of the great scientific minds of the twentieth century and a Jewish exile from Adolf Hitler's Third Reich. He was awarded the Nobel Prize in physics in 1921 for his formulation of the photoelectric theory of light, but is more famous for his development of the general and special theories of relativity, hypotheses that helped transform humankind's understanding of the operation of the universe. In 1933, after Hitler took power and began to target prominent Jews, Einstein, then in a visiting academic post in the United States, chose to give up his German university position even as the new Nazi authorities were taking it away.

Albert Einstein was born in Ulm in southwestern Germany on March 14, 1879, into a Jewish family. His father was a scientist and small businessman. Einstein showed early promise as a student, but did not fit in the regimented German educational system of his time. Instead, he learned much of his mathematics and rudimentary physics at home. In 1896 he moved to Switzerland to study at the Polytechnic Institute in Zürich, from which he graduated in 1900. By then a Swiss citizen, Einstein took a job in a Bern patent office since he could not find an academic position. At night he continued to work on advanced mathematics and physics, and he published his first scientific papers in 1905. These were four articles published in the *Annalen der Physik*, one of the main learned journals in the field in the German language. The four articles, on the transformation of light, Brownian movement, molecular dimensions, and the electrodynamics of motion, were major contributions to an ongoing revolution in physics which included the work of Max Planck, Edward Rutherford, and a number of other distinguished names. Einstein, meanwhile, took up a post at the University of Zürich in 1909, transferred to Prague in 1911, and became director of the Kaiser Wilhelm Institute for Physics in Berlin, where he was also a full professor at the Prussian Academy of Science.

Einstein published his general and special theories of relativity in 1916, and thereby transformed the unified gravitational dynamics of Isaac Newton, which scientists had held to be fundamental since the late 1600s. According to Einstein, $E=mc^2$ where E is energy, m is mass, and c is the speed of light. The notion, once it was verified by experts in England and elsewhere, changed scientists' understanding of space and time; they now realized that these concepts were relative and that matter was eminently changeable.

By the 1920s Einstein was one of the most famous people in the world, known as much for his thoughtful comments on politics and religion as for his brilliant scientific theories. In Germany, however, Einstein faced oppression not only because of his Jewish heritage but also because he espoused pacifist political ideals and was sympathetic to the idea of supranational government. He was an active supporter of both the Zionist movement and the League of Nations.

Einstein traveled in Europe after Hitler took power in 1933, but never returned to Germany. The official Nazi stance on Einstein was that his personal politics and scientific work were "un-German" and that he himself, as a Jew, would never be welcome in a Nazi Reich. There his work was viciously attacked by pro-Nazi Nobel Prize–winning physicists Johannes Stark and Philipp Lenard. The scientist was stripped of his academic posts, his property was confiscated, his books were burned, and a few Nazis pledged to kill him if he returned to Germany. After living for a while in England

Einstein moved to Princeton, New Jersey, where he accepted a permanent position at the Institute for Advanced Study. He became an American citizen in 1940 (retaining Swiss citizenship as well), and throughout World War II he remained a vocal critic of Hitler and Nazi Germany. He also took steps to make Allied leaders aware of the advanced state of physics in Germany, signing a letter to American president Franklin D. Roosevelt in 1939 warning him that German scientists were developing the capability to build an atomic bomb. The letter, allegedly, was a contributing factor in Roosevelt's decision to try to beat the Germans to it.

In 1952, thanks to his global prestige as well as his lifelong devotion to Jewish causes, Einstein was offered the presidency of Israel. He declined it, however, knowing he was no politician. He remained a scientific celebrity, and an active participant in research and discussion, until his death in Princeton on April 18, 1955. *See also* exiles and refugees from the Third Reich, Law for the Restoration of the Civil Service, Vol. 1; Stark, Johannes, Vol. 3.

Epp, Franz Xaver Ritter von (1868–1947)

One of the earliest and most influential supporters of Nazism among the conservative German aristocracy and Reich governor of Bavaria from 1933 to 1945. Epp was born in Munich in October 1868 and became a professional soldier as a young man, serving in a variety of posts in Germany and in Germany's colonial territories in China and Africa. He fought with distinction as an officer during World War I, earning several decorations including the Iron Cross, First Class. After the war he took up right-wing political activism, founding his own Freikorps unit in Munich and even acting as the dictator of Bavaria for a short time in the chaotic year of 1919.

Epp's military contacts in Munich included a Reichswehr officer named Ernst Röhm, who told him of a young enlisted man

The support of conservative aristocrat Franz Xaver Ritter von Epp, Reich governor of Bavaria from 1933 to 1945, lent respectability to the Nazi movement.

named Adolf Hitler who appeared interested in nationalist activism. Epp used Hitler as a sort of liaison between the army and various right-wing political groups in Munich in 1919. It was while engaged in this activity that Hitler joined the German Workers' Party, later the Nazi Party. After Hitler quit the army and emerged as the leader of the Nazis, Epp maintained contact with him, often through Röhm. It was a mutually advantageous relationship; Epp appreciated Hitler's ability as a rabble-rouser while Hitler came to rely on Epp as one of several individuals who helped him look respectable among Munich's monied, cultural, and aristocratic classes. In addition, Epp's help was essential in finding the funding that allowed the Nazi Party to buy the *Völkischer Beobachter*, the party's official newspaper, in 1921. Epp chose not to support the Beer Hall Putsch of 1923 but committed himself to the Nazi cause in the late 1920s. In 1926 he was named head of the SA in Bavaria; in 1928 he officially joined the party and was elected to the German parliament, the Reichstag, as a representative of Upper Bavaria. Epp hoped to turn the SA into a viable military force, using both his experience and contacts and a Nazi organization known as the Defense Political Office, which was later disbanded. Despite Epp's best efforts, however, the SA never turned into much more than a band of street fighters.

After Hitler took power in 1933, Epp filled a variety of impressive-sounding but largely powerless posts. In March 1933, on Hitler's orders, he forcefully disbanded the government of Bavaria and set himself up as Reich governor. He was also named master of the hunt in Bavaria, a Nazi Party Reichsleiter, and chief of the Colonial Office. He also held the honorary title of general of infantry. Nevertheless, after many years dedicated to the Nazi movement, Epp's background among the conservative German aristocracy reasserted itself when he spoke out against the construction of the SS terror network, which he claimed was dangerous because it operated outside the law. For most of the period of the Third Reich Epp remained a sort of aristocratic figurehead with little actual authority. After World War II he was captured by the Americans and he died, on January 31, 1947, in an internment camp. *See also* Epp Freikorps, Vol. 1.

Esser, Hermann (1900–1981)

One of the cofounders of the Nazi Party and one of Adolf Hitler's early political associates, although over the years Hitler as well as other top Nazis learned to keep him at a distance because of his extreme views, boorish personality, and crude behavior.

Hermann Esser was born near Munich on July 29, 1900, to a lower-middle-class family. He attended local schools and served in the German army as a teenager during World War I, an experience that left him with an interest in radical politics. Immediately after the war Esser was a left-wing Socialist, but he soon discovered a way to combine his opposition to profiteering with German nationalism and anti-Semitism. In 1919 he formed the German Workers' Party, the precursor of the Nazi Party, with Anton Drexler and Karl Harrer. At first the German Workers' Party was little more than a drinking club where men met to air their unhappiness with the Weimar Republic and the Treaty of Versailles; indeed, when Hitler went to his first party meeting, in September 1919, the organization had the equivalent of two dollars in its treasury.

Early in 1920 Esser met Adolf Hitler. Both were working for the German army in Munich as speakers in its press office, and both were proud of their abilities as rabble-rousing orators. Soon they discovered other common ground: anti-Semitism, hatred for the greed of war profiteers and Jews, bitterness toward Weimar and the Versailles Treaty, and a desire for direct political action. Esser supported Hitler's moves to become the leader of the German Workers' Party, after the spring of 1921 the Nazi Party, and was the first to refer to Hitler as the Führer. He was also a skilled propagandist and recruiter who attracted many disaffected young men to the Nazi movement. His loyalties were not unconditional, as Hitler recognized almost from the first, when at one point Esser threatened to join the Communists if he was not paid promptly. Nevertheless the Nazi leader appreciated Esser's devotion and ruthlessness.

During the early years of the Nazi movement Esser filled various posts, including editor of the Nazi newspaper *Völkischer Beobachter* and chief propagandist. After failing to take part in the Beer Hall Putsch of 1923, citing illness, Hitler accused him of cowardice. Esser was able to reestablish himself in Hitler's affections, however, by making frequent visits to the future Führer during his stay in Landsberg Prison in Munich. He remained a Nazi insider for a number of years afterward, surviving conflicts with, among others, Gregor Strasser, the northern

German leader of the "Socialist" branch of the Nazi Party, and Julius Streicher. Whenever he was in danger of losing his place at Hitler's side, Esser threatened to give away secrets to political opponents and to Weimar and Bavarian authorities. Hitler, in response, mollified Esser with various posts. From 1926 to 1932 he was editor in chief of the *Illustrierter Beobachter*, the illustrated companion publication to the *Völkischer Beobachter*. During the early 1930s Esser served on the Munich City Council and kept his hand in as a Brownshirt (SA) leader and rabble-rouser. After Hitler took power in 1933 he appointed Esser to be the Bavarian minister of economics. Esser also became a member of the Nazi Reichstag in Berlin.

Esser's scandalous personal life and rude behavior continued to work against him, however. Strasser, among others, had long argued that Esser was an immoral coward, and even from his "safe" positions in Bavaria Esser allegedly continued to assault women and intimidate businessmen. Hitler released him from his positions in 1935, but even then hesitated to go so far as to repudiate him entirely. In 1939 Hitler named Esser vice president of the Reichstag and, soon after, secretary of state for tourist traffic, a largely symbolic post given the fact that much of Europe was at war.

Esser remained the prototypical gruff, unrefined Nazi Old Fighter, a type Hitler appreciated but had little use for after he became the leader of Germany. Esser published a pamphlet known as the *Jewish World Pest* to maintain his anti-Semitic credentials. He also continued to speak on occasion at gatherings of other Old Fighters, for example, at the annual commemoration of the Beer Hall Putsch on November 9. Hitler, however, ignored him, and Esser never again managed to regain his place as a Nazi insider.

After the war Esser was determined insignificant by American war crimes tribunals, although he was arrested and spent over a year in an internment camp. A German denazification court, however, convicted him of spreading anti-Semitic and Nazi propaganda and sentenced him to five years' imprisonment at hard labor. He was released for reasons of ill health in 1952, and lived on, largely unnoticed, until his death in 1981. ***See also*** German Workers' Party, Vol. 1; SA, Vol. 2.

F

Falkenhorst, Nikolaus von (1885–1968)

German army general and commander in chief of German forces in occupied Norway from 1940 to 1944. Falkenhorst was born on January 17, 1885, to a traditional military family in eastern Germany. He began his army service in 1907, and during World War I he served in a variety of posts as a junior officer. He joined the right-wing Freikorps at the end of the war, but as Germany settled down in 1919 he reentered the army. During the 1920s he was steadily promoted and enjoyed political connections; he served in the War Ministry from 1925 to 1927 and, after the Nazis took power in 1933, was the military attaché to the German embassies in Prague, Belgrade, and Bucharest.

From 1935 to 1940 Falkenhorst served in combat commands. He was promoted to lieutenant general and served as the chief of staff of the Third Army, based in Dresden. During the invasion of Poland in the fall of 1939 he commanded the Twenty-first Army Corps and was promoted again, to general of infantry. His combined political and military background suited him well as an occupation commander in Norway, although he often clashed with SS officer Josef Terboven, the Reich commissioner for Norway. Terboven, in fact, had him dismissed in December 1944.

After the war Falkenhorst was sentenced to death by the British for his ruthless treatment of prisoners of war; he had British captives, for instance, summarily executed. Though the sentence was ultimately reduced to twenty years, Falkenhorst was released in 1953 for health reasons. He died in 1968. *See also* Terboven, Josef, Vol. 3.

Faulhaber, Michael von (1869–1952)

German official of the Roman Catholic Church during the era of the Third Reich. Faulhaber was born in the town of Klosterheidenfeld in Franconia on March 5, 1869. He became a priest in 1892 and taught at the University of Strasbourg. In 1911 he became bishop of Speyer and in 1917 bishop of Munich-Freising. He was appointed cardinal in 1921. As the leading Roman Catholic official in Bavaria, the largest Catholic state in Germany, Faulhaber was an extremely influential man.

Faulhaber was a dedicated German nationalist with aristocratic sympathies as well as a high church official whose superiors, and ultimately loyalties, were in Rome. Therefore he tried to maintain a moderate course in politics, seeking to reflect his conservative and nationalist stance but not offend either church tradition or Roman Catholic belief. During World War I he was a strong supporter of the German effort and argued that the German cause was just. He had little faith in the legitimacy of the Weimar Republic, arguing that it was born of decisions that were traitorous to Germany and that he disapproved of the republic's openness toward all religions.

After Adolf Hitler and the Nazis took power Faulhaber tried to keep to the middle road. He reported to the pope, Pius XI, that the church likely had little to fear from the new regime, and he was happy when the

Concordat of 1933 was announced. The concordat, an agreement between Hitler and the pope, guaranteed German Catholics the right to freedom of worship without interference from the state. Faulhaber rarely objected even when Hitler failed to observe the terms of the concordat. In meetings between the two, furthermore, Faulhaber was impressed by Hitler as a leader.

On the other hand, Faulhaber carefully pointed out that Hitler's regime was wrong to persecute Jews. In 1934 he gave a number of sermons on the matter at St. Michael's Church in Munich. In them he pointed out that the extreme nationalism of the Nazi movement was no justification for anti-Semitic measures. He also spoke out against the Nazi attempt to "Aryanize" Christianity by, among other things, denying the Jewish authority of the Old Testament. During the Kristallnacht pogrom of November 1938 Faulhaber made a vehicle available to the chief rabbi of Munich so that the sacred texts, relics, and other items from his synagogue could be saved. He did not, however, issue a public statement against the attack.

Faulhaber was one of the authors of the papal encyclical "Mit Brenneder Sorge" ("With Burning Sorrow"), issued in 1937. In it, Faulhaber and other church officials under the pope's authority officially objected to the fact that, by now, the Nazi state was violating the Concordat of 1933. Elsewhere, however, Faulhaber continued to sit on the fence. He was supportive, for instance, of Nazi foreign policy when, in 1938 and 1939, the Third Reich annexed Austria and Czechoslovakia. He also remained publicly loyal to Hitler; after the Führer survived an attempt on his life in Munich in November 1939 Faulhaber staged a great thanksgiving mass. During World War II Faulhaber held to this middle course and did not involve himself with the German resistance movement, even though one of its leaders, Carl Goerdeler, personally asked the cardinal to commit himself to the July 1944 Plot. In the aftermath of the plot Faulhaber was questioned by the Gestapo, and although he admitted to a meeting with Goerdeler, he reiterated his loyalty to Hitler and denounced the resistance movement. Throughout, it seems, Faulhaber remained a dedicated church official, trying to steer it successfully through difficult and challenging times, and was therefore neither a devoted Nazi nor a committed opponent of the Third Reich. He stayed in his post until he died in Munich in 1952. *See also* Concordat of 1933, Vol. 1; "Mit Brennender Sorge," religion in the Third Reich, Vol. 2; Pius XI, Pius XII, Vol. 3.

Feder, Gottfried (1883–1941)

One of the leading figures of the Nazi Party in its early days, and the producer of its original economic policies. Feder was born in Würzburg on January 27, 1883. He was originally an engineer but, during World War I, turned himself into an economic theorist. He developed the notion that the cause of Germany's failure in the war was what he referred to as "interest slavery." By this he meant that Germany's industrialists and financiers, and therefore the German economy as a whole, were victimized by interest payments on loans and debt, payments that to his mind created no value but instead simply drained the country of wealth. After the war he became increasingly obsessed with the idea and formed an organization known as the German Society for the Abolition of Interest Slavery to make the idea known to political figures. He argued that to prevent interest slavery Germany should structure its economy around small farmers, small businessmen, and craftsmen rather than large estates, corporations and department stores, and labor unions.

Failing to convince other politicians, including Communists, of the merit of his ideas, Feder joined the German Workers' Party in 1919. His membership predated even Adolf Hitler's. But after Hitler became a member late that year Feder's ideas became a major influence on the future party leader. Feder, Hitler suspected, offered a sort of middle way between communism and unbridled international capitalism, and moreover, offered practical suggestions to strengthen the national economy of Germany. It was, in other words, National Socialism. Feder's influence was apparent in the German Workers' Party platform of Twenty-Five Points, announced by Hitler early in 1920. The influence went both ways, however, as Feder began to add elements of Hitler's political philosophy to his own speeches such as denunciations of the Weimar Republic and the Treaty of Versailles and attacks on Jewish financiers and businessmen. During the early 1920s, he went on to become one of the leading Nazi intellectuals: editor of the *National Socialist Library* as well as Nazi newspapers in several towns. He published several books including *What Does Adolf Hitler Want?* in 1931 and *The Struggle Against High Finance* in 1933. Feder was also one of the first Nazi Party members elected, in 1924, to the German Reichstag, or national legislature, where little attention was paid to his ongoing attempts to control interest payments and establish small farms side by side in preference to large estates.

By the early 1930s Hitler had turned away from Feder. The Nazi leader was growing more powerful politically, and his strong anticommunist and nationalist stance had begun to attract the attention of some of Germany's powerful economists and industrialists. Hitler realized that Feder's policies as head of the Nazi Party's Economic Council could undermine his relationships with such figures. In addition, respected economists such as Hjalmar Schacht warned Hitler that Feder's economic policies made little sense and would likely drive the German economy to ruin. After Hitler took power in 1933 Feder became a marginalized figure. He was made an undersecretary in the Nazi Ministry of Economic Affairs, where his ultimate superior was Schacht. In December 1934 he was forced out of the post. Afterward, Feder remained disappointed that Hitler had chosen another path rather than freeing Germany from interest slavery and high finance, but he no longer sought to put his ideas into practice. He lived a quiet life until his death in Murnau in Bavaria in January 1941. *See also* Days of Struggle, German Workers' Party, Vol. 1.

Fegelein, Hermann (1906–1945)

Waffen-SS officer, brother-in-law of Adolf Hitler's mistress, Eva Braun, and the liaison between Adolf Hitler and Heinrich Himmler from 1943 to 1945. Fegelein was born in Franconia on October 30, 1906. While working as a jockey he met Christian Weber, one of the Nazi Party's "Old Fighters" and a man who grew wealthy and influential during the 1930s through his contacts within the Nazi regime. Weber helped Fegelein find a post with the SS as head of its first mounted squadron, and Weber's continued influence helped Fegelein rise high within the ranks of the SS. By the end of 1942 Fegelein was a brigadier general in the Waffen-SS. After he was wounded in action on the eastern front in late 1943 Fegelein's luck continued to hold, and Heinrich Himmler sent him to Berlin to be his personal representative to the Führer. In this position he married Eva Braun's sister Gretl and was promoted to SS lieutenant general.

Fegelein was ultimately the victim of the chaos and uncertainty among Hitler's entourage during its final weeks in the Berlin Führerbunker from January to April 1945. He was one of a number of SS officers in Hitler's company, and his family relationship with Eva Braun, who refused to leave Hitler even though the Führer encouraged her to, made him even more a part of the inner circle. However, when Fegelein left the bunker on April 26 to ensure his own survival, Hitler ordered that a squad be sent to bring him back. Because of this attempted "escape" Hitler grew suspicious that Fegelein was conspiring with his SS superior, Himmler, to replace the Führer. When, on April 28, news reached the bunker that Himmler had indeed tried to establish contact with the Allies via Swedish intermediaries, Hitler's paranoia was reinforced. Though Fegelein protested that he knew nothing of Himmler's plans or intentions, Hitler ordered his execution for desertion and treason. Eva Braun did not try to save her brother-in-law, preoccupied as she may have been with her impending marriage to Hitler and, soon after, her own death. Fegelein was taken up to the garden of the Reichs Chancellery building and shot by SS men. *See also* Führerbunker, Vol. 1; Braun, Eva, Vol. 3.

Flick, Friedrich (1883–1972)

German industrialist who greatly enriched himself through his support of Adolf Hitler and the Nazi regime. He was also an unrepentant user of slave labor during World War II; up to his death in 1972 he refused to accept any responsibility for his use of slaves.

Friedrich Flick was born in Westphalia on June 10, 1883. He began to work in the metal industry in the Ruhr, Germany's industrial heartland, in 1913, and rose to become one of the directors of the German United Steel Works, the nation's largest steel company. One of his duties, evidently, was currying political favor and financial support. In 1932 he provided nearly a million marks for President Paul von Hindenburg's reelection in addition to large sums for the Nazi Party. After Hitler took power in 1933 Flick raised the sums his company donated to the Nazi movement. Before the end of the Third Reich, in fact, Flick had donated a total of 7 million marks. He also made separate contributions to Heinrich Himmler and the SS at the sum of one hundred thousand marks per year. He joined the Nazi Party in 1937 and was named a Leader of the War Economy, an honorific title the Nazis devised for influential industrialists.

Meanwhile, he maintained posts on the boards of directors of a number of German companies involved in iron, steel, and coal production. During World War II Flick's enterprises made extensive use of slave labor. An estimated forty-eight thousand slaves worked in his factories, among them Jewish concentration camp inmates marched westward during the so-called death marches of late 1944 and early 1945. The slaves were apparently not well cared for: Some 80 percent of them died.

In 1947 Flick was convicted of war crimes along with several other major industrialists. He was sentenced to seven years in prison, although he was released, along with the other industrialists, in 1951 thanks to a clemency order from John McCloy, the American high commissioner. Though Flick and his concerns were supposedly stripped of their assets after the war, by 1955 Flick was once again one of Germany's most influential businessmen, controlling more than one hundred different companies, including Daimler-Benz. Indeed, Flick became one of the richest men in the world. He vigorously resisted, however, any attempt by victims' groups to make reparations claims against him, and he refused to accept any guilt for his widespread use of slave labor. Flick died in Constance, Germany, on July 20, 1972. *See also* business in the Third Reich, Vol. 1; slave labor, Vol. 2; Thyssen, Fritz, Vol. 3.

Forster, Albert (1902–1952)

Reich governor of Danzig. Forster was born on August 26, 1902, and worked in a bank before involving himself in Nazi activities in and around Danzig, the free port city under nominal Polish control that was heavily populated by ethnic Germans. He was named Gauleiter of Danzig in 1930 as well as a member of the German Reichstag for Franconia. During the 1930s Forster slowly and steadily established Nazi control of Danzig in preparation for the Third Reich's annexation of the free city. For his efforts he was named Reich regent of Danzig. He remained in that post during World War II, taking in addition to his other honors the rank of SS lieutenant general. One of his tasks was supervising, the "Aryanization" of the area, which meant reducing the population of ethnic Poles and Jews and replacing them with people deemed to be German. Forster proved extremely strict, moreover, in his definition of which Poles might be judged suitably "German" and therefore allowed full Reich citizenship rights. For non-Germans he had only contempt, and his record toward them is full of atrocities.

After World War II Forster was arrested by the Allies, who extradited him to Poland in 1947. The Poles tried him for war crimes in Danzig and sentenced him to death. The sentence was later reduced to life imprisonment; he died in prison in 1952. *See also* Danzig, Vol. 1; Wathegau, Vol. 2.

Franco, Francisco (1892–1975)

Authoritarian dictator of Spain from 1939 to 1975 and a man who was often compared to Adolf Hitler or Benito Mussolini, though such comparisons were in truth very limited. Franco was born in La Caruna in 1892 to a military family. After attending a military academy in 1912 Franco joined the Spanish armed forces, serving from 1912 to 1929 in increasingly responsible posts in Spanish Morocco. He was promoted to general in 1926.

Franco's rise to power took place within the context of dramatic political upheaval in Spain. In 1931 its monarchy was replaced by a republican government, opening the door to widespread conflict between leftists and conservative forces in the aristocracy and army. Franco, not surprisingly, allied himself with the conservatives. He tried at first to stay out of politics and in 1935 became army chief of staff, but he found himself increasingly targeted by other conservatives as a potential political chief. In 1936 military conspirators instigated the Spanish Civil War, which devastated Spain until 1939. Franco, after some bargaining, took command of what became known as the Nationalists though the faction was, in fact, rebelling against a legitimate government. On the other side were the so-called Loyalists or Republicans, an uneasy coalition of center and left forces. The Nationalists, who enjoyed the vast support of Fascist Italy and Nazi Germany, both of which sent massive military aid, won the war and took over Spain on April 1, 1939.

Franco then transformed himself into an authoritarian dictator, assuming the title "El Caudillo" ("the Leader"). In certain ways Franco's regime resembled those of Hitler and Mussolini. He combined the offices of head of state, prime minister, and commander in chief of the armed forces. Moreover, he was the head of the Falange, the only legal political party, and he proved harsh in the face of political dissent. Unlike his counterparts, however, Franco had no territorial ambitions. Nor did he share the ethnic prejudices and apocalyptic sense of destiny of Adolf Hitler, or Hitler's readiness to commit mass murder to prove a point. During World War II Spain was officially neutral, and Franco and Hitler remained in a state of mutual distrust. Franco allowed, however, forces of Spanish "volunteers" to fight for the Germans.

After the war, Franco's Spain became a Cold War ally of the United States, Britain, and the other western powers, thanks to Franco's strong opposition to communism. Moreover, Franco eased his political, economic, and press restrictions as the years passed, and although Spain remained, in comparison with such nations as France or Britain, an intolerant dictatorship, it enjoyed fairly steady economic growth. Franco did not want his dictatorship to continue after his death, predicting that Spain would have a king once more. Indeed, following Franco's death in November 1975, King Juan Carlos took the throne and watched while Spain transformed itself into a liberal democracy. *See also* fascism, Vol. 1; Spanish Civil War, Vol. 2.

Frank, Anne (1929–1945)

German Jewish girl who was deported from her family's Amsterdam hideaway to the Bergen-Belsen concentration camp, where she died in March 1945. Her record of her months in hiding, published worldwide after the war as *Anne Frank: The Diary of a Young Girl*, became the most well known account of Nazi oppression toward Jews in the world.

Anne Frank was born in Frankfurt on June 12, 1929. Her father, Otto Frank, was an established and affluent Jewish businessman. Soon after the Nazis took power in 1933 the Franks left for Amsterdam in the Netherlands, where Otto Frank established a wholesale food business. The family continued to thrive until May 1940, when the Netherlands was defeated and occupied by Nazi Germany. In February 1941 Nazi authorities began rounding up Jews in Amsterdam and shipping them to German concentration camps. With the help of some of Otto Frank's Dutch business associates, the Franks arranged a hiding place at the back of a warehouse. There they were joined by a family of Dutch Jews, the Van Daans, as well as an elderly dentist Anne wrote of as Mr. Dussel. The Van Daans had a son, Peter, who was near Anne in age. Provided with food and news from the outside, the Franks, Van Daans, and Dussel managed to hide safely for more than two years. On August 4, 1944, however, they were given up by a Dutch informant and arrested by Gestapo officers. As had been the fate of thousands of European families, the Franks were separated. Anne and her sister were sent to Bergen-Belsen, where both died of typhus; the others were sent to Auschwitz. Otto Frank was the only one to survive.

In 1946 Otto Frank returned to the hiding place in Amsterdam. There, lying on the floor where a Gestapo man had tossed it, was Anne Frank's diary. Otto edited it and had it published in 1947 as *The Diary of a Young Girl*. The book was an immediate best-seller and was translated into dozens of languages, becoming one of the most popular memoirs in history. Not only was it an account of Nazi oppression, Anne Frank's diary told a very human story of people trying to live peacefully together, facing boredom, deprivation, and fear under extremely difficult circumstances. Moreover, it was a coming-of-age story, the observations of a young girl passing through a stage of adolescence and examining her emotions and thoughts. Throughout, Anne's positive outlook and insight into the importance of reminding herself of the bright side of human life was remarkable. The diary has continued to appear in new editions, and was adapted into popular stage and screen versions. The Anne Frank House, meanwhile, the annex on the Prinsengracht Canal in Amsterdam where the young girl and her companions hid, has become a shrine to Holocaust remembrance. ***See also*** deporta-

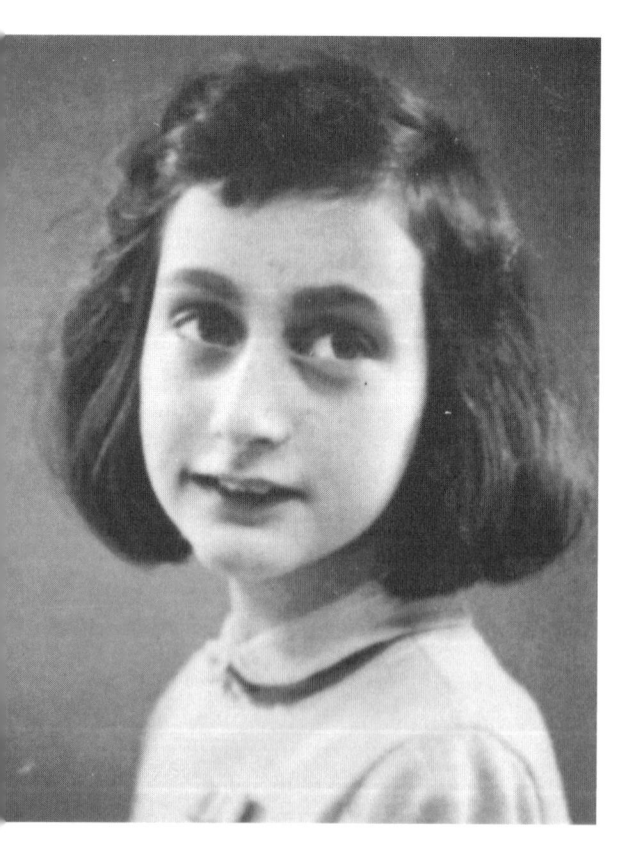

Anne Frank's diary, written during her years in hiding, has become one of the most popular memoirs in history.

tion, Final Solution, Vol. 1; Frank, Final Diary Entries, Vol. 4.

Frank, Hans (1900–1946)

The top legal official in the Nazi Party, Adolf Hitler's personal lawyer, and from 1939 to 1945, governor-general of occupied Poland. He was involved in the deprivation, forced slavery, and mass murder of hundreds of thousands of Poles and Jews during World War II.

Hans Frank was born into a middle-class family in Karlsruhe on May 23, 1900. His father was a lawyer who had been disbarred for corrupt activities. The young Frank served briefly in World War I, then settled in 1919 in Munich. There he participated in Freikorps attacks on Communists and joined the German Workers' Party and, soon after, the Nazi Party. He was originally an SA man who took part in the Beer Hall Putsch as well as smaller street actions. He became a lawyer in Bavaria in 1926 and devoted his entire attention to defending other storm troopers in their frequent appearances in court and to his position as head of the Nazi Party legal division. He also defended Adolf Hitler personally at least 150 times, and by 1929 the Nazi leader had retained Frank as his personal attorney. Although Hitler never particularly liked Frank or allowed him entrance into his inner circle, the Führer appreciated Frank's devotion to Nazism as well as his legal skill. Frank was entrusted, incidentally, with the task of proving conclusively that Hitler's heritage was completely Aryan. After the Nazis took power Frank's responsibilities expanded to include Bavarian minister of justice, Reich minister of justice, and president of the Academy of German Law. In 1934 he was named minister without portfolio in the Reich cabinet.

Frank's influence with Hitler began to wane after he made the mistake of criticizing the Blood Purge of June 1934. His criticism was perhaps a reflection of Frank's fundamental misunderstanding of the inner workings of the Nazi terror state. Expert in law though he may have been, he was unskilled in the political manipulations and ideological ruthlessness displayed to varying degrees by such men as Hermann Göring, Heinrich Himmler, and Reinhard Heydrich, and like Wilhelm Frick, another important early Nazi, Frank found himself increasingly ignored by Nazi decision makers at the highest levels.

After the German conquest and occupation of Poland in the fall of 1939, Hitler named Frank governor-general of Poland, a small rump area of central and southern Poland that remained after the Third Reich and its temporary ally, the Soviet Union, had gobbled up other territories. Hitler made the appointment, apparently, as a way to appease Frank with a high title while keeping him busy with unappealing tasks. Frank embarked on his new role with gusto. He ruled from a castle in the city of Krakow, chosen by the Germans in order to diminish the importance of the prewar capital of Warsaw. He also took steps to destroy Polish culture and nationhood by murdering or arresting intellectuals, declaring German to be the official language of the region, and taking personal control of Poland's agricultural wealth and artistic treasure and deporting much of it to Germany. Meanwhile he declared that the Polish people, following the standard Nazi line, were to be turned into slave laborers for the German Reich. He stuffed his castle in Krakow with art treasures, the finest food and wine, and a huge retinue of servants.

As governor-general, however, Frank was outflanked by the SS, which increasingly considered itself the sole authority in occupied Poland, the location of one of its most important projects: the "Final Solution to the Jewish Question." When in the summer or fall of 1941 the SS, with Hitler's approval, decided that Europe's Jews would be gassed to death in camps located mostly in occupied Poland, Frank was not consulted, even though the camps lay within his jurisdiction. He did not object to the policy when he found out about it, however. Instead he responded enthusiastically, claiming that all Jews "must be done away with in one way or another." Though it would be difficult to "shoot or poison the . . . Jews . . . we shall be able to take measures which will lead, somehow, to their annihilation" (Shirer, 1960). While the SS largely carried out the deportations and exterminations, Frank as occupation governor undoubtedly assisted in the process, even as he found his own responsibilities increasingly diminished. In July 1942 Frank made the unusual decision to present a series of lectures in Germany on the subject of reducing the power of the Nazi regime and returning to the rule of law. Hitler promptly removed him from all of his offices except governor-general of Poland. Although he remained in the post until the end of World War II, he was almost entirely irrelevant; the SS police were the true occupation government of Poland.

Arrested by the Allies at the end of the war, Frank was one of twenty-one high-ranking Nazis brought to trial in Nuremberg by the International Military Tribunal in November 1945. A convert to Roman Catholicism, Frank was one of the few defendants to publicly denounce Hitler and the Nazi regime and admit his own guilt. Nevertheless, the tribunal found him guilty of war crimes and crimes against humanity. He was hanged at the Nuremberg prison on October 16, 1946. *See also* General Government, Vol. 1; Nuremberg trials, Vol. 2; International Military Tribunal, The Charges Against the Surviving Nazi Leaders, Vol. 4.

Frank, Karl-Hermann (1898–1946)

One of the top Nazis in occupied Czechoslovakia. Frank was born on January 24, 1898, in the town of Karlsbad, which was at that time within the Austro-Hungarian Empire. During World War I he fought in the Austrian army. After the war he ran a bookstore before joining the Sudeten Nazi Party in the new nation of Czechoslovakia. The Sudetenland, where Frank grew up, was a part of the country largely populated by ethnic Germans, many of whom clamored to be allowed to join Adolf Hitler's Greater German Reich, and Hitler himself helped support the Sudeten Nazis. Frank emerged as one of the group's leaders, second only to Konrad Henlein. After the Third Reich absorbed the Sudetenland in October 1938, Frank was appointed deputy Gauleiter of the region. When the Nazis occupied the entire nation of Czechoslovakia months later Frank was given a number of new responsibilities including chief of police, secretary of state, and the honorary rank of SS-Gruppenführer, or lieutenant general. Over the next years he loyally and enthusiastically served his German superiors within the new Protectorate of Bohemia and Moravia, based in the former Czech capital of Prague. These superiors included, notably, Reinhard Heydrich and Kurt Daluege, SS police officials who operated a terror state. After the war Frank was captured by American forces, who turned him over to the revived Czech government. A war crimes tribunal in Prague sentenced him to death for his actions under the Germans, and he was hanged on May 22, 1946. *See also* Bohemia and Moravia, Protectorate of, Vol. 1; Sudetenland, Vol. 2.

Freisler, Roland (1893–1945)

President of the People's Court in Berlin from 1942 to 1945, and one of the most brutal and ruthless of Nazi judges. Freisler was born to a peasant family in Hesse on October 30, 1893. As a German soldier fighting on the eastern front during World War I he was captured by the Russians, who sent him to a camp in Siberia for five years. There he learned to speak fluent Russian and, according to some reports, after the 1917 revolution became both a dedicated Communist and a Bolshevik official. He escaped and returned to Germany in 1920, where he took a law degree from the University of Jena.

He opened him own law office in Kassel in 1923, where he also briefly served in the city government on the Socialist ticket.

Apparently changing his stripes, Freisler joined the Nazi Party in 1925 and joined the SA. In the early 1930s he was elected on the Nazi ticket to both the Prussian state legislature and the national Reichstag. He joined the Prussian Ministry of Justice in 1933 and in 1934 the Reich Ministry of Justice, where he served until 1942 as a state secretary concerned with preventing attacks on Nazi officials. He also concerned himself with the question of reforming the German criminal code so that it would reflect the goals and practices of the Nazi regime. In January 1942 Freisler represented the Ministry of Justice at the Wannsee Conference, where Reinhard Heydrich of the SS made it clear to Nazi bureaucrats that mass extermination would be the "Final Solution to the Jewish Question." Freisler, apparently, made no objections or qualifications to the plan on legal grounds.

In August 1942, after Otto Georg Thierack was appointed to replace Hans Frank as Reich minister of justice, Freisler replaced Thierack as the president of the Berlin People's Court. The People's Court was a special court where show trials of Germans who had displayed disloyalty to the Nazi regime were conducted. While Freisler was its chief officer, the other members of the court included officials representing the Nazi Party, the armed forces, and the SS. Freisler proved himself a truly dedicated Nazi terrorist in his new position, showering defendants with insults and sarcastic comments in hopes of humiliating them before they received their sentences. Among those Freisler tried personally were the defendants from the White Rose, the resistance movement established by German university students in 1942. He was also the presiding officer at the hundreds of People's Court trials conducted to condemn those involved, or suspected of involvement, in the July 1944 Plot on Hitler's life. A number of the trials were filmed, and the surviving films are clear evidence that Freisler spared no effort in trying to humiliate and dehumanize the defendants, many of whom were hanged with piano wire at Berlin's Plötzensee Prison. While Freisler was conducting yet another trial of alleged conspirators on February 3, 1945, the building where the People's Court sessions were held was struck by an Allied bomb and the so-called hanging judge was killed. *See also* judicial system in the Third Reich, Vol. 1; People's Court, Vol. 2; The Verdict of the People's Court on Rebels, Vol. 4.

Frick, Wilhelm (1877–1946)

One of Adolf Hitler's closest political associates in the early years of the Nazi struggle and minister of the interior from 1933 to 1943. Frick, more than any other top Nazi, provided Hitler with the legal framework that justified his system of state terror and allowed him to target groups who failed to fit into the Nazi conception of the German nation.

Wilhelm Frick was born in the Rhineland on March 12, 1877, to a petit bourgeois family. His father was a schoolteacher. After secondary school he studied law at the Universities of Munich, Göttingen, Berlin, and Heidelberg, taking his juris doctor degree in 1912. He did not fight in World War I because he was judged to be physically unfit. Instead, he became a government bureaucrat, working in the Munich police department. His section was known as the political police, and one of its responsibilities was dealing with rabble-rousers and fringe political parties. He got to know Adolf Hitler when the Nazi leader came to his office to apply for permission to stage rallies and marches. Quickly Frick became a Nazi himself, and for several years acted as Hitler's contact inside Munich police headquarters. From this insider position Frick was able to ensure that Hitler was rarely formally charged when he was arrested; Frick also found ways for right-wing murderers and criminals of all sorts to escape capture or prosecution. Hitler, in *Mein*

Kampf, remembered Frick fondly from this era as a man who was willing to put his devotion to Germany ahead of his duties as a government official. Frick took an active part in the Beer Hall Putsch of 1923, despite the fact that it required him to betray his office; indeed, Hitler had wanted Frick to take over Munich police headquarters as part of the putsch. He was arrested and sentenced to a prison term, but the sentence was suspended and, strangely, Frick was allowed to return to an important position with the Munich police: head of the criminal division. Meanwhile, he became one of the first Nazis to be elected to the national German parliament, the Reichstag, where he became the head of the Nazi political caucus.

Frick emerged as an important politician even before the Nazis took power. In 1930 he was appointed to the post of minister of the interior for the German state of Thuringia, the highest office any Nazi had achieved to that point. Many argue that Frick took advantage of the posting to provide a preview in Thuringia of what life would be like under a Nazi regime. He tried to staff the provincial police force, for instance, with loyal Nazis, and encouraged opposition to non-Nazi political parties. He actively supported Nazi candidates for office rather than act as an objective cabinet member. He helped to find funds for a special university position, a chair in racial science at the University of Jena. Claiming that certain measures were necessary for public order, he banned jazz music and forbade the showing of the antimilitaristic film of *All Quiet on the Western Front*. Finally, since his post gave him responsibility over education, he was able to force schools to accept a so-called German freedom prayer for students to recite. The prayer extolled the Fatherland and the unlimited power of Germans to unite and triumph.

After the Nazis took power in January 1933 Frick was appointed Reich minister of the interior. From this position Frick both initiated and implemented many of the measures that allowed Hitler and his followers to consolidate their hold over Germany in the coming years. Soon after the passage of the March 1933 Enabling Act, for instance, Frick used it to dissolve all of the provincial legislatures in Germany, such as the one he worked for in Thuringia, except for the Prussian state legislature. Then he reorganized them so that they would be dominated by Nazis just like the Reichstag. In April 1933 Frick enthusiastically supported the Law for the Restoration of the Civil Service, a measure that allowed the Nazis to purge the German bureaucracy of people they did not approve of, mostly Jews, Social Democrats, and Communists, and replace them with loyal Nazi Party members so that the civil service would be largely Nazi. In June 1933 he abolished the Social Democratic Party on the grounds that it was a threat to public order.

In later years Frick continued to use his political clout and bureaucratic skill to extend the Nazis' hold over Germany. After the Blood Purge of June 30, 1934, Frick rushed into the Reichstag with a new law that declared that the murders and arbitrary arrests carried out by Hitler's henchmen, with the knowledge and support of much of the German military, were legal and necessary. The Reichstag, now almost entirely Nazi, gave it the rubber stamp of approval. Then in 1935 Frick took the responsibility of framing the two so-called Nuremberg Laws, which removed the citizenship rights of German Jews. He also had a hand in the various "improvements" on the Nuremberg Laws that steadily deprived Jews of their other rights. His ministry simply observed quietly when, in 1938, Jews across Germany were attacked during the Kristallnacht pogrom.

Throughout, Frick's laws and bureaucratic maneuverings resulted in the internment of tens of thousands of Germans in concentration camps. After 1935, however, the branches of the Nazi state that ran concentration camps, the SS and Gestapo, had largely begun to ignore Frick. Frick was

Nazi interior minister Wilhelm Frick addresses the Reichstag in Berlin during World War II.

technically the superior of Heinrich Himmler, head of the SS, but Himmler easily outflanked Frick in the Nazi councils of leadership and particularly in police matters. Thus Frick's importance dropped in the late 1930s, and his influence continued to decline into the years of World War II. The colorless legalist and bureaucrat was no match for his rivals in the SS, the military, and the Ministries of Propaganda and War Production in terms of political manipulation in a time of war. In 1943 Frick was replaced as minister of the interior by Himmler himself; perhaps as consolation Hitler appointed Frick the protector of Bohemia and Moravia. Even there, however, true power lay in the hands of Deputy Protector Kurt Daluege and Secretary of State Karl-Hermann Frank, both of whom were ruthless SS men.

After the war Frick was one of the twenty-one top Nazis brought before the International Military Tribunal at Nuremberg in the fall of 1945. He refused to testify. The tribunal found him guilty on three of the four charges brought against the defendants: crimes against peace, war crimes, and crimes against humanity. The court also noted that he was more responsible than almost any other Nazi for bringing Germany under Hitler's control. The tribunal sentenced him to death, and he was hanged at the Nuremberg prison on October 19, 1946. *See also* Gleichschaltung, Vol. 1; Ministry of the Interior, Nuremberg trials, Vol. 2.

Fritsch, Werner Freiherr von (1880–1939)

Chief of the High Command of the German army from 1934 to 1938, commander in chief of the German army from 1935 to 1938, and an opponent of Adolf Hitler's military and territorial ambitions. Fritsch was born near Düsseldorf on August 4, 1880. He came from a family of traditional Prussian aristocrats and military officers, and Fritsch saw himself as carrying on that tradition. He joined the German Imperial

Army at age eighteen and at twenty-one was invited to attend the German War Academy, the traditional training ground for high-level military officers. During World War I he served on the General Staff, rising from 1914 to 1918 in both rank and responsibility.

After World War I Fritsch continued to serve the German army, known during the era of the Weimar Republic as the Reichswehr. In 1922 he was promoted to lieutenant colonel and four years later he took a staff position in the War Ministry. In 1930 he took command of a cavalry division in eastern Germany and was promoted to the rank of major general. Having now gained the friendship and patronage of German president Paul von Hindenburg, as well as the admiration of many of his fellow officers, Fritsch was promoted to lieutenant general and made commander of the Berlin military district in 1932. After the Nazis took power Fritsch continued his rise, again with Hindenburg's help. In February 1934 he was named chief of the High Command of the German army and in May 1935, as Hitler reformed the Reichswehr into the Nazi Wehrmacht, Fritsch was named Wehrmacht commander in chief.

Fritsch, in many ways the prototype of the traditional Prussian officer, was never a devoted Nazi. He was uneasy about the Blood Purge of June 1934, which he knew about beforehand and which a close colleague, General Werner von Blomberg, supported wholeheartedly. Moreover, he felt the Nazis were low-class and vulgar, unfit to run a civilized country for more than a short time or for anything but limited purposes. Later he vaguely identified these purposes as the defeat of the working class, Catholics, and Jews. Fritsch remained, however, a loyal soldier and took an enthusiastic role in Hitler's plan to defy the Treaty of Versailles by enlarging the German armed forces and equipping them with the most advanced armament.

When, in November 1937, Hitler announced his plan to begin Germany's military expansion into eastern Europe, Fritsch was alarmed. He knew that such moves would bring about a new Europe-wide war, which he also suspected Germany would lose. He expressed his objections to the strategy to Hitler at the so-called Hossbach Conference, where the Führer first laid out his plans. Knowing he had to tread softly, Fritsch claimed that Germany was not yet ready for such ambitious moves, militarily or economically. Blomberg, present in his capacity of minister of war, also expressed reservations to the plan. Both ended up paying the price for outspokenness.

In early 1938 Fritsch found himself the victim of a complicated plot devised by Hermann Göring and Heinrich Himmler. Göring wanted to replace him as commander in chief; Himmler wanted to weaken the Wehrmacht and increase the power of the SS. Both, moreover, knew that he was not an enthusiastic Nazi and that the Wehrmacht remained the only potential obstacle to Hitler's ambitions. Using the SD, the Security Service of the SS under Reinhard Heydrich, the two accused Fritsch of being an active homosexual who had tried to prevent exposure of his sexual identity with blackmail payments since 1935. Göring and Himmler reminded Hitler that Fritsch was unmarried, was completely devoted to his military career, and had rarely shown an interest in women. Hitler confronted Fritsch with the accusations on January 28, 1938. When the general denied the charges strongly, Göring and Himmler brought forward the alleged blackmailer, Hans Schmidt, who claimed to have witnessed Fritsch's activities. Fritsch continued to protest his innocence, and he demanded that he be brought before a military tribunal to defend his honor. On February 4, however, he was forced to resign as commander in chief and was replaced by General Walther von Brauchitsch, an unquestioning supporter of Hitler. Meanwhile, Blomberg was also made the victim of a personal scandal, this time involving the reputation of a young woman he had recently married, and he was forced to resign. The timing of the two scandals seemed hardly coincidental; in any case it allowed Hitler to rid himself of the two generals who questioned his plans for the German Reich and put himself in firm control of the armed forces.

Fritsch was acquitted by a military court of honor on March 18, 1938, but by then it was too late for him to regain his high position in the Wehrmacht. Suggesting to a friend that perhaps Hitler was Germany's destiny, Fritsch settled for retirement. He refused to become involved in the plots beginning to be concocted by German officers to overthrow Hitler, even though one of the motives behind the plots was the shocking treatment of Blomberg and himself. Fritsch was recalled to the Wehrmacht just prior to the invasion of Poland and given the honorary position of colonel in chief of his old regiment. On September 22, 1939, while his regiment was in battle outside Warsaw, Fritsch, some said deliberately, walked into a stream of Polish machine-gun fire and was killed. *See also* Blomberg-Fritsch crisis, Vol. 1; Pact of the *Deutschland*, Vol. 2.

Fritsche, Hans (1900–1953)

Nazi propaganda officer and chief of radio broadcasting in Joseph Goebbels's Ministry of Public Enlightenment and Propaganda. His voice was one of the most familiar in Germany during World War II. Fritzsche was born in the Rhineland on April 21, 1900. After serving briefly in World War I he went to the Universities of Berlin and Greifswald. There he studied languages, history, and philosophy, but he did not take an academic degree and embarked instead on a career in the media. In 1924 he became editor of the monthly journal *Prussian Yearbooks*. In 1924 he went to work for the German media magnate and nationalist politician Alfred Hugenberg, who ran both the Telegraph Union and the International Press Service, where Fritzsche worked until 1932. That year he began to turn his skills to radio broadcasting as head of the Rundfunk, Germany's radio news network. A conservative nationalist like Hugenberg, Fritzsche joined the German Nationalist People's Party in 1924.

After the Nazis took power the new minister of propaganda, Joseph Goebbels, sought Fritzsche out, figuring that his expertise in mass media could be useful. Fritzsche took the opportunity and decided to join the Nazi Party. Goebbels named him head of the press section of the Propaganda Ministry. There his work included previewing and approving news items for German newspaper editors as well as responsibility for wire services and foreign correspondents. In this position he played a fundamental role in ensuring that the German press was supportive of the Nazi regime and that foreign reporters heard only the news that Hitler's regime wanted them to hear. He began radio broadcasts in 1937, and proved very popular among the general public.

In November 1942 Fritzsche left the press section to become the Propaganda Ministry's head of radio broadcasting. His official title was Plenipotentiary for the Political Organization for the Greater German Radio, and he made hundreds of broadcasts himself. German radio listeners got used to hearing his deep voice proclaim, "This is Hans Fritzsche" (*"Hier spricht Hans Fritzsche"*), followed by the latest official war news. Although Fritzsche toed the Nazi line during his broadcasts—consistently reporting that the Third Reich was winning the war, that Hitler had revived Germany's position in the world, that German expansion was justified in order to prevent the domination of Bolshevism or world Jewry—many Germans preferred Fritzsche to any other broadcaster, including Goebbels. Not only did he have a pleasant, authoritative voice, Fritzsche used thoughtful explanations and reasonable arguments instead of the emotional rants typical of other Nazi speakers. As the war entered its final months Fritzsche continued to broadcast. Now his task was to maintain German morale and offer various forms of justification and consolation to German listeners, many of whose menfolk were dead on the war's battlefields and who suffered greatly from Allied bombings.

Fritzsche was one of the twenty-one top Nazis brought before the Nuremberg war crimes tribunal in the fall of 1945. Some observers wondered why he was there, since his rank and importance were relatively low compared with such defendants as Hermann Göring, Wilhelm Keitel, and Albert Speer. Some observers suggested that his fame and familiarity among Germans made him sufficiently notable; others considered him a sort of stand-in for Goebbels, who had committed suicide at the end of April 1945. Along with Speer and Hans Frank, Fritzsche was one of the few defendants at Nuremberg who expressed remorse both for the actions of Hitler's regime and for his own role in it. The tribunal found him not guilty on all four counts brought at the trial and set him free on October 1, 1946, noting that while Fritzsche was a dedicated propagandist he could not be considered guilty of either participation in war crimes or the incitement of atro-cities. Soon after, on February 4, 1947, Fritzsche was indicted by a German denazification court on charges that he had fomented anti-Semitism and misled the German people. He was finally released from detention in September 1950. He had earlier published a memoir, *This Is Hans Fritzsche*, in which he asserted that he was innocent of charges against him and that he had acted as a good German. He died in Cologne on September 27, 1953. *See also* Nuremberg trials, propaganda in the Third Reich, radio in the Third Reich, Vol. 2; Fritzsche, The Legacy of the Nuremberg Trials, Vol. 4.

Fromm, Friedrich (1888–1945)

Commander in chief of the German Reserve Army, chief of armaments for the War Ministry, and a man whose actions on July 20, 1944, helped doom the plot devised by the German resistance movement to toss Adolf Hitler from power. Fromm was born in Berlin on October 8, 1888, and embarked on a military career as a young man. He served as a junior officer during World War I and held a number of staff positions during the Weimar years. In February 1933 he was posted to the Ministry of War and promoted to colonel. In September 1939, instead of taking a combat command, he was named chief of armaments as well as commander in chief of the Reserve Army, the forces stationed in Germany for both garrison purposes and to replenish combat forces.

The planners of the July 1944 Plot, Friedrich Olbricht and Claus Schenk Graf von Stauffenberg, were both officers in the Reserve Army, which they assigned a vital role in their attempted takeover of power after assassinating Hitler. They hoped to enlist Fromm, now a general, in their cause, but he was noncommittal whenever they approached him. He knew of the plot but hesitated to throw in his lot with it until he knew it would succeed. As soon as he learned that Stauffenberg's bomb had gone off on July 20 but had failed to kill Hitler, Fromm decided that his best course would be to stop the conspiracy in its tracks and thereby prove that he was a loyal Nazi. Although the plotters, under Olbricht, arrested him, he was soon released, and when Stauffenberg returned from Hitler's eastern headquarters at Rastenburg, where the bomb had gone off just hours earlier, Fromm confronted him. He told Stauffenberg that the bomb plot had failed and that he should shoot himself. When Stauffenberg refused, Fromm hauled him as well as Olbricht and two others before a summary court-martial. After declaring the plotters guilty, Fromm had them taken into a garden outside the War Ministry and shot to death. He also was responsible for the death of Ludwig Beck, the former general who was to be head of state in Germany's new government. Fromm tried to get Beck to commit suicide, but the rebellious former general failed to successfully shoot himself; an army sergeant finally delivered the killing shot. All of these actions failed, however, to save Fromm. Hitler and the Gestapo considered him too close to the conspirators and had him arrested and tried by Roland Freisler's People's Court. He was executed in March 1945. *See also* Home Army, July 1944 Plot, Vol. 1.

Funk, Walther (1890–1960)

Third Reich minister of economic affairs and head of the Reichsbank, the German national bank. Funk was born in East Prussia on August 18, 1890, into a middle-class family. He studied economics, philosophy, and law at the University of Berlin, where he also evinced an interest in literature and the arts. He did not serve in World War I, though he was drafted into the army, because of ill health. In 1916 he took a job with Berlin's *Börsenzeitung*, the stock exchange newspaper, where he rose steadily to positions of increasing responsibility. He was editor of the paper's business section from 1920 until 1922, then editor in chief from 1922 until 1932. The position gave him access to Germany's top industrialists and financiers, contacts that would serve him, and the Nazi movement, well in later years.

Funk met Adolf Hitler in 1931 and soon joined the Nazi Party, satisfied that it reflected his conservative, nationalist outlook and was the strongest anticommunist force in German politics. He quickly replaced Gottfried Feder as Hitler's chief adviser on economic matters and was named head of the Nazi Office for Economic Policy. During the two years prior to Hitler's rise to power Funk greatly helped the Nazi leader become more respectable among leading businessmen such as Fritz Thyssen, Friedrich Flick, and the directors of the IG Farben cartel. He provided a conduit by which businessmen could funnel money toward the Nazi Party and, in turn, these business leaders considered Funk a moderating influence on Hitler's racial and ideological extremism. Funk indeed helped convince Hitler of the importance of a free market economy as opposed to the vague "national socialist economics" that the Führer had earlier espoused. He also proposed practical measures that would lessen the effects of the depression on German workers while making the Nazi movement look like a beneficial, paternal force. These included public works projects and proposals to make both agriculture and industry more productive.

After the Nazis took power Funk returned, briefly, to positions in journalism. He was named press chief of the Reich and an undersecretary in Joseph Goebbels's Ministry of Public Enlightenment and Propaganda. He was also named chairman of the board of directors of the Reich Broadcasting Corporation. In a reflection of his wide interests outside economics and journalism he helped Goebbels create the Reich Chamber of Culture, a supervisory body that exercised broad authority over almost all the arts and media in the Third Reich, and became vice president of the chamber. He returned to economics, however, in 1937. He was named to succeed Hjalmar Schacht, a rival who considered Funk a useless drunk and homosexual, as minister of economics. Soon afterward he also became plenipotentiary for the war economy and president of the Reichsbank.

Despite these impressive titles, however, Funk exercised little power over the German economy during World War II. He faced a major rival in Hermann Göring, who was head of the so-called Four-Year Plan for the recovery of the German economy, an organization that lasted well beyond its designated four years. Moreover, the need for the German economy to emphasize war production left much planning and implementation in the hands of Fritz Todt and Albert Speer, sequential heads of the Ministry of Armaments and War Production. Indeed, in 1944 almost all of Funk's duties were turned over to the more assertive and efficient Speer, and few top Nazis paid much heed to his opinions.

In 1942 Funk arranged with Heinrich Himmler to create a special account known as the Max Heiliger Fund in the Reichsbank. Its purpose was to launder the wealth stolen from Jews deported to the death and labor camps in Poland, in the process creating ways the wealth could be credited to the SS. The wealth was substantial; Jews frequently smuggled with them precious stones, pieces of gold and silver, and cash. These were invariably confiscated by SS functionaries, who were even known to remove gold and silver fillings and teeth from dead bodies as well as search for swallowed valuables. By the end of the war the Max Heiliger Fund had filled the vaults of the Reichsbank, and the SS took to storing these ill-gotten gains in caves.

Funk was one of the twenty-one top Nazis put on trial in the fall of 1945 by the International Military Tribunal in Nuremberg. Although Funk continually denied that he was guilty of any war crimes, the tribunal decided that Funk was well aware of the source of the valuables in the Max Heiliger account. He was found guilty of war crimes, crimes against peace, and crimes against humanity, and the tribunal sentenced him to life in prison. He was released, however, from Spandau Prison in Berlin because of ill health. Funk died in Düsseldorf in 1960. *See also* Max Heiliger Fund, Nuremberg trials, Reichsbank, Vol. 2; Schacht, Hjalmar, Vol. 3.

Furtwängler, Wilhelm (1886–1954)

Renowned orchestral and operatic conductor who remained in Germany for the duration of the Third Reich. Furtwängler was born in Berlin on January 26, 1886, and studied music in Munich. After serving assistantships in several cities, he was named director of opera in Mannheim, one of western Germany's largest cities, in 1915. In 1922 he became director of the Berlin Philharmonic Orchestra, where he remained until 1945, and in the nomadic way of top musicians he

German conductor Wilhelm Furtwängler directed the Berlin Philharmonic, one of the world's premier orchestras, throughout the Nazi era.

also served for several years as the chief conductor of the Vienna Philharmonic.

Furtwängler was mostly nonpolitical, although he was a conservative on musical issues. He disliked the modernism and atonalism of contemporary composers such as Arnold Schoenberg, whom the Nazis also disapproved of. He did, however, defend the work of Paul Hindemith, a composer who was forced to leave Germany after the Nazis declared him "degenerate." Nonetheless, Furtwängler concentrated on music and turned a blind eye to the developing Nazi terror state as well as the tragedies of World War II. Nazi authorities, for their part, were content to tolerate some of the conductor's cultural heresies because of the prestige that he afforded their regime. Indeed, the Berlin Philharmonic Orchestra together with the Berlin State Opera made up one of the centers of classical music performance during the Nazi era, attracting hundreds of foreign visitors as well as Germans and providing visiting diplomats and correspondents with a welcome break from the constant bad news and stonewalling from Nazi officials. To ensure, meanwhile, that Furtwängler's reputation and activities remained "coordinated" with the regime, officials named the conductor to the state council of Prussia and director of the Bayreuth Wagner festival.

Unlike many other artists and cultural figures, but like most German musicians, Furtwängler chose to stay in Germany during World War II. For this he was much criticized in other countries. After the war he claimed that he had misunderstood the true nature of the Nazi regime and that he was opposed to its racial and social measures. He was cleared by a denazification court in 1946. From 1950 to 1954 he was again director of the Berlin Philharmonic. He died in Baden-Baden in western Germany on November 30, 1954. *See also* music in the Third Reich, Vol. 2; Furtwängler and Goebbels, The Purpose of Art, Vol. 4.

Galen, Clemens August Graf von (1878–1946)

German official of the Roman Catholic Church and one of the most outspoken critics of Nazi policies. Galen was born in Dinklage on March 16, 1878, to an aristocratic family. He began his career in the church at the age of twenty-six, when he served as a bishop's assistant in Münster in western Germany. He was ordained as a priest in 1919 and served initially in Berlin before returning to parishes in Münster. He was named bishop of Münster in 1933. A German nationalist, Galen was happy when Hitler and the Nazis took power. He adopted the stance that church officials should not attempt to interfere in politics and he declared an oath of allegiance to the Nazi regime. He also publicly praised Hitler when, in 1936, German troops marched into the Rhineland in violation of the Treaty of Versailles, a document Galen considered insulting and unfair to Germany. Even when Hitler led Germany into World War II Galen continued his public praise, and he urged his flock to be ready to defend Germany.

However, Galen developed strong misgivings over certain policies of the Third Reich. He objected strongly, for instance, to the attempt on the part of the Nazi state to control the Christian churches, and was outspoken in his criticism of anti-Catholic propaganda. In addition he objected to Nazi racial doctrines. In 1941 Galen was driven to fury and almost active rebellion by the T-4 Program, a euthanasia project developed by Nazi officials and the SS to murder Germany's mentally ill patients in gas chambers and then burn their bodies in crematoria. The gassing facilities were located not far from residential centers, and they were no secret to Germans. Galen, for his part, began to speak against the program from his pulpit, referring to it as unlawful murder and denouncing Hitler's secretive and brutal police state. His criticisms were so vehement, and in 1941 so unusual, that people began to refer to the bishop as the "lion of Münster." On August 3, 1941, he delivered a sermon in which he promised to sue the people involved in the T-4 Program on the grounds that they were committing murder, a charge that was undeniably true even under the laws of the Third Reich.

Galen's protests drew attention to the T-4 Program across Germany and even in much of the rest of Europe. Although top Nazis wanted to either arrest or execute him, Joseph Goebbels pointed out that he was too powerful and influential a figure, and that the issue was too sensitive. Hitler himself promised to have his vengeance on Galen, but only after the war was over. In the short term Galen's protests were stilled when the T-4 Program suspended the gassings (patients were killed with lethal injections for several more months).

Galen then continued to serve as bishop of Münster, although his activities were closely watched by the Gestapo. He was arrested in the aftermath of the July 1944 Plot on Hitler's life, when the Führer's desire for vengeance swept up almost every prominent figure who had ever opposed Nazi measures. Galen was confined to the Sachsenhausen concentration camp near Berlin, where he survived till the end of the war. He was elevated to cardinal in February 1946 and died in Münster on March 22, 1946. *See also* "Mit Brennender Sorge," religion in the Third Reich, Vol. 2; Galen, A Bishop Calls for an End to Euthanasia, Vol. 4.

Galland, Adolf (1912–1996)

Fighter pilot and commander in chief of the fighter arm of the Luftwaffe, the German air force, from 1941 to 1945. Galland was born in East Prussia in 1912 and became a glider pilot at the age of nineteen. In 1932 he went to work for Lufthansa, the German civil airline that was in certain ways a cover organization for military aviation. He joined the Luftwaffe in 1935, when Hitler no longer cared whether Germany's rearmament violated the terms of the Treaty of Versailles (which forbade Germany from having an air force at all). He first came to the attention of top German military officials when he flew with the Condor Legion during the Spanish Civil War. Indeed, Galland flew more than three hundred missions in Spain, and his experiences and observations played a vital role in developing the aviation aspects of the blitzkrieg strategy that was to serve the Germans so effectively during World War II. During the invasion of France in 1940 he led fighter squadrons and was one of the chief Luftwaffe squadron leaders during the Battle of Britain in August and September 1940. Altogether he recorded over one hundred kills of enemy aircraft and was one of the most highly decorated German fliers of the war.

In November 1941 Galland was named commander in chief of the fighter arm of the Luftwaffe and soon after, at thirty, became the youngest general in the German armed forces. He proved to be an extremely capable commander, keeping his planes in the air and the morale of his pilots reasonably high despite increasing hardships, Allied bombings, and shortages of vital supplies and equipment. Nevertheless, Adolf Hitler as well as Hermann Göring, in his capacity as head of the entire Luftwaffe, used Galland as a scapegoat for the failure of the fighter arm to defend Germany from Allied bombs. Göring, in fact, sent him on forced leave in January 1945, effectively firing him from his post. He was, however, allowed to return to a combat post flying the new jet fighters that Germany had developed. The jets proved to be largely useless, however; the Allies were able to destroy many of them on the ground and as the war dragged on Germany was no longer able to produce the special fuel the jet fighters needed. On April 26, 1945, Galland was shot down in combat with an American fighter, but survived the experience.

Galland later turned up as an air force adviser with the quasi-Fascist regime of Juan Perón in Argentina, where he stayed for six years. After returning to Germany he worked as a technical adviser to German industry and was even considered as a possible chief of the air force of the Federal Republic of Germany, although those plans came to nothing. He also published his memoirs, in which he claimed that what doomed the Luftwaffe in the Battle of Britain was British use of radar combined with poor strategy on the part of German planners and officers. He also lamented the heavy loss on the German side of pilots during the Battle of Britain, asserting that these future leaders had been sacrificed uselessly, and therefore the fighter arm of the Luftwaffe had few capable commanders in later years. Galland died at his Oberwinter home near Bonn in February 1996. *See also* Battle of Britain, Luftwaffe, Vol. 1; Göring, Hermann, Vol. 3.

Gerstein, Kurt (1905–1945)

An SS officer who tried, largely in vain, to bring the news of the mass extermination of Europe's Jews to the outside world. Gerstein was born in Münster in western Germany on August 11, 1905. He remained a devout Christian throughout his life, despite the official discouragement of religious faith by SS chieftains. He joined the Nazi Party in 1933 but also maintained ties with the Confessing Church, a body organized by thousands of Protestant pastors to defy Adolf Hitler's efforts to nazify Protestantism. Indeed, Gerstein was arrested at one point by the Gestapo for promoting religion. He was tossed out of the Nazi Party and sent to a concentration camp.

In 1941 Gerstein, whose background and education were in engineering rather than medicine or biology, wrangled a position in the SS Health Department and was granted the rank of lieutenant in the Waffen-SS. There, Gerstein became closely acquainted with the T-4 euthanasia program, in which thousands of German mental patients were killed with poison gas. Indeed, his purpose in joining the SS Health Department was, allegedly, to find out more about the program; Gerstein maintained until his death that he was an inside "mole," or spy, for the Confessing Church. His job involved responsibility for dealing with various poisonous substances as an expert in "health technique." In the summer of 1942 he traveled to Poland, where the mass gassing of Jews in extermination centers had already begun. His job was to demonstrate to Odilo Globocnik and Christian Wirth, two SS officers already in leadership positions in the death camp network, the effectiveness of Zyklon B, a commercial pesticide, in gassing human beings to death. Globocnik and Wirth were using, at that point, diesel exhaust from special engines as the killing agent.

Gerstein visited the Belzec camp in August 1942, where he watched a demonstration of the use of diesel exhaust in the killing process. He compiled a detailed, eyewitness account of the proceedings and spent the next years trying to get the news of the gassings to the outside world in hopes that stopping them would become a high priority of Germany's opponents. In fact, according to Gerstein's own personal report, he first gave the news of Belzec to a Baron von Otter, a Swedish diplomat he happened to meet on the train home from Poland. The Swedish government, as it happened, was fully aware of the exterminations, whether from Otter or some other source. Perhaps fearful, however, of a German invasion of their neutral country, Swedish officials never passed the news on to Allied governments or to international bodies such as the Red Cross. Gerstein also tried to pass on the information to the British government through contacts in the Dutch underground, again to little avail. Even religious leaders failed to act on Gerstein's reports of events at Belzec. The papal representative in Berlin refused to even see him, while Protestant leaders and his friends in the Confessing Church proved to be so intimidated by Nazi terror that they failed to act. Convinced that he had failed, and by then fully aware of the extent of the Third Reich's killing programs, Gerstein committed suicide in a French prison on July 17, 1945. *See also* Final Solution, Vol. 1; resistance movements, Germany; T-4 Program, Vol. 2.

Gisevius, Hans Bernd (1904–1974)

German diplomat and contact man between the German resistance movement and Allied intelligence officers from his post as German vice-consul in Zürich, Switzerland, from 1940 to 1944. Gisevius was born on July 14, 1904. A traditional conservative and supporter of President Paul von Hindenburg and the Prussian officer corps, Gisevius joined the Nazi movement in 1933 along with other members of the Stahlhelm, a right-wing organization made up mostly of police veterans. He was at first an officer in the Gestapo but soon joined the police department in Prussia, the only German state with an independent administration under the Third Reich. From this position he became involved in various plans to overthrow Hitler, none of which amounted to anything.

After World War II started Gisevius joined the Abwehr, the intelligence section of the High Command of the German armed forces, and he was posted to Zürich in 1940 as vice-consul. The Abwehr had emerged as a center of resistance to Nazism within the German armed forces and Gisevius maintained regular contact with such Abwehr conspirators as Hans Oster and Wilhelm Canaris. While in Zürich he had frequent meetings with Allen Dulles, chief of the Office of Strategic Services (OSS), the American intelligence section and forerunner to the Central Intelligence Agency (CIA). Gisevius kept Dulles informed of resistance plots within Germany and served as a liaison between the OSS and German resistance leaders General Ludwig Beck and Carl Goerdeler. In 1944 he managed to survive both interrogation by the Gestapo and Hitler's sweeping vengeance after the July 1944 Plot, which resulted in the deaths of Oster, Canaris, Beck, Goerdeler, and hundreds of others. He escaped to Switzerland in 1944 before the Gestapo could track him down again.

Gisevius, clearly one of the rare "good Germans" in the eyes of the Allies, testified at the 1945–1946 Nuremberg war crimes trials as a special prosecution witness. He spoke against Hermann Göring and on behalf of Wilhelm Frick and Hjalmar Schacht. Soon after, he published his memoirs, titled *To the Bitter End*. The memoirs remained one of the major sources of information about the German resistance movement with which Gisevius was so closely tied. In his book Gisevius also took the German people to task for being unwilling to tell themselves the truth about the actions of Hitler and his regime. He died in Germany in February 1974 after dividing his time among the United States, Berlin, and Switzerland. *See also* Abwehr, Vol. 1; resistance movements, Germany, Vol. 2.

Globke, Hans (1898–1973)

Civil servant and a leading source of the legal justification for the Third Reich's anti-Semitic policies. Globke was born in the Rhineland on September 10, 1898, and in 1925 took a law degree. His first civil service position was as deputy to the police commissioner in the city of Aachen. In 1929 he became an administrative adviser in the Prussian Ministry of the Interior. In both posts he proved to be a loyal servant of the Weimar Republic just as in later years he was a loyal servant of the Third Reich and, somewhat surprisingly, a loyal servant of the postwar Federal Republic of Germany. He never joined the Nazi Party.

Using his legal skills as well as his administrative background, Globke helped write some of the most important legislation produced under the Third Reich. In 1933, for instance, he helped justify Hitler's attempts to rule Germany absolutely by advancing the argument that Germany was in a state of national emergency. He also satisfactorily explained the dissolution of the independent administration of the state of Prussia and, soon after, its reconstruction along Nazi lines. In 1936 Globke wrote, along with Wilhelm Stuckart, an official in the Interior Ministry, a document known as the Commentary on German Race Legislation. The work, based on the Reich Citizenship Law, one of two pieces of racial legislation announced at the 1935 Nuremberg party rally, provided Hitler's regime with a legal basis for the continued persecution of Jews. The authors claimed that German citizenship, and therefore the legal rights of citizenship, would be based on the qualities shared by members of the German Volk, who were by definition different from other peoples. "Alien" peoples, such as Jews, could not hope to attain citizenship in the German Reich, and therefore could not enjoy the civil rights taken for granted by "members" of the German race. The document, in effect, explained why Hitler's regime had the right to deny Jews, and other "aliens," the rights of citizenship, and it became the basis for later, more specific measures passed against Jews. One, put forward by Globke himself, was to require all German Jews to add either "Israel" or "Sarah" to their names for the sake of easy identification by administrators and officials. During World War II Globke's legal pen remained busy, providing further justifications for German oppression and so-called Aryanization measures in the countries Germany occupied during the war.

After the war Globke became a target of both Jewish groups and the Communist government of the German Democratic Republic, or East Germany. The latter tried him in absentia for his actions and sentenced him to life in prison. In democratic West Germany, however, Globke found himself with renewed responsibility. In 1953 Konrad Adenauer, the West German leader, appointed Globke state secretary of the chancellery. Globke stayed in the post until his retirement in 1963; Adenauer refused to accept his many offers of resignation. Globke died in Switzerland on February 13, 1973. *See also* Aryanization, judicial system in the Third Reich, Vol. 1; Reich Citizenship Law, Vol. 2.

Globocnik, Odilo (1904–1945)

SS lieutenant general and head of all SS police operations in the Lublin district of occupied Poland from 1941 to 1943. He played a major part in the mass extermination of European Jews by representatives of the Third Reich.

Globocnik was born in Trieste, a city on the coast of the Adriatic Sea, on April 21, 1904. Trieste was then within the Austro-Hungarian Empire, and Globocnik's background was Croatian. Too young to fight in World War I, he became a construction worker before joining the Austrian Nazi Party in 1933. Aggressive, violent, and amoral, Globocnik quickly became a leader of the Nazis within the Austrian province of Carinthia, and he joined the Austrian SS in 1933. Though Austrian authorities imprisoned him at one point for his pro-Nazi activities, Globocnik continued to rise in importance. He became an intermediary between Adolf Hitler and the Austrian Nazis in the months leading up to the Anschluss, the annexation of Austria by the Third Reich, and soon after the Anschluss was completed he was named Gauleiter of Vienna. Showing a tendency toward reckless greed that was to shadow him in later years, Globocnik took advantage of his post to speculate in foreign currency, a crime in the Nazi regime. He was therefore dismissed as Gauleiter in January 1939. Appreciating his ruthlessness and violent anti-Semitism, however, Heinrich Himmler appointed him SS leader in the Lublin district on November 9, 1939. In that position Globocnik rose to be one of the most powerful German occupation officials in Poland. He was a fundamental cog in Himmler's plan to wrest control of the area away from Hans Frank, the Nazi occupation governor-general.

After Nazi and SS authorities decided that mass extermination was to be the "Final Solution to the Jewish Question," and that most of the gassings would be performed in occupied Poland, Globocnik was named head of the Reinhard Action. One of the two major divisions of the extermination program, the action was named after Himmler's deputy, Reinhard Heydrich, who was assassinated in the spring of 1942. As head of the Reinhard Action, Globocnik established and helped to manage four of the six death camps: Belzec, Majdanek, Sobibor, and Treblinka. At least 1.6 million Jews were killed at these four camps. In other regards Globocnik ruled the Lublin district with an iron fist, intimidating and terrorizing the Polish population with his own private police units made up of ethnic German volunteers. His authority was effectively absolute, since he answered to no one but Himmler, and the SS leader was pleased by the efficiency of the Reinhard Action death camps. By November 1943 they were no longer necessary, and Himmler ordered all but Majdanek closed.

According to his orders, Globocnik was to oversee four separate projects during the Reinhard Action. These were to kill Polish Jews, use slave labor wherever appropriate, take over the land and property of Jews, and appropriate portable wealth such as jewels and precious metals for the purposes of the

SS. In the latter tasks Globocnik, still greedy, acted with great enthusiasm. According to his own reports to Himmler he took from the Jews he executed the equivalent of hundreds of millions of marks. As before in Vienna, however, Globocnik proved to be light-fingered, and even Himmler objected when he appropriated a great deal of the money for himself. Globocnik was dismissed from the Lublin post in early 1944, sent back to Trieste along with his personal army of ethnic Germans, and made SS chief of the Adriatic region.

When World War II ended Globocnik attempted to go into hiding in the Austrian mountains. He was eventually found out, however, and either captured by a British patrol before committing suicide or murdered by partisans. His precise fate is unknown. *See also* extermination camps, Final Solution, General Government, Vol. 1; Reinhard Action, SS, Vol. 2.

Gluecks, Richard (1889–1945)

Inspector of concentration camps during World War II, and a high official in Nazi Germany's attempt to exterminate Europe's Jewish population. Gluecks was born on April 22, 1889, and was therefore almost the exact same age as Adolf Hitler. During World War I he was an artillery officer, and after the war he was a businessman in the Rhineland. He joined the Nazi Party during the 1920s, but his experiences and accomplishments were unremarkable until the mid-1930s, when he began working for the Inspectorate of Concentration Camps under Theodor Eicke, the founder of concentration camp practices. From 1936 to 1940 he was Eicke's chief of staff at the inspectorate's headquarters in Oranienburg near Berlin. One of his responsibilities was training camp administrators. Meanwhile, he also rose to the rank of SS brigadier general.

After a spell training occupation officers in 1940, Gluecks was appointed to replace Eicke, who was being kicked upstairs, as inspector of concentration camps in February 1940, and in time he was promoted to lieutenant general of the Waffen-SS to reflect his new status. As inspector, Gluecks proved to be a highly competent bureaucrat seemingly oblivious to the moral aspects of mass extermination. Within the always evolving SS hierarchy, Gluecks headed Section D of the SS Economic and Administrative Central Office, which was run by Oswald Pohl. Gluecks and Pohl were the men responsible for handing down Hitler and Himmler's orders to the commandants of the individual concentration and extermination camps. In addition, Gluecks played a role in deciding the fate of millions of Jewish deportees: either immediate death or slave labor. He tended to define those who would survive as slaves simply as a percentage of all who arrived at the camps. He also oversaw the extensive medical experimentation facilities at Auschwitz, a camp he founded as a prison and labor center in 1940, as well as the camp's staff of SS doctors. The final fate of Gluecks is unknown. In May 1945 he was in a naval hospital at Flensburg in northern Germany, the site of Admiral Karl Dönitz's brief post-Hitler regime, where he was recovering from shock in the aftermath of an Allied bombing attack. He either committed suicide in the hospital or disappeared, some argued, to be executed by a Jewish vengeance squad in the chaotic months following the end of the war. *See also* Inspectorate of Concentration Camps, Vol. 1; Eicke, Theodor, Vol. 3.

Gobineau, Artur Comte de (1816–1882)

French aristocrat, diplomat, and racial theorist whose major work, *Essay on the Inequality of Human Races*, is thought to have been an important influence on Nazism. Gobineau was born near Paris on July 14, 1816, to an old noble family. Thanks to the support of fellow aristocrat and author Alexis de Tocqueville, he joined the French Foreign Office in 1848 and in later years served in a number of French embassies across Europe in a variety of different posts. He left the foreign service in 1877, moving to Rome and devoting the rest of his life to scholarship.

Essay on the Inequality of Human Races was, however, one of Gobineau's earlier works, published in two parts between 1853 and 1855. It was largely ignored after its publication, but by the end of the century it was well known across Europe and especially popular in Germany; Frenchmen tended not to take it seriously. In the work, Gobineau argued all human civilizations had, knowingly or not, accepted the fact that there was inequality among the races, and had constructed their civilizations accordingly. Moreover, he argued, there were only three races in the world, an idea that remained in place in European thinking for a long time. Those three races were, as Gobineau put it, the white, black, and yellow. Though he acknowledged subdivisions among those three categories, recognizing that particular racial characteristics were stronger or weaker among particular national peoples, he allowed only three races that were, moreover, unequal physically and mentally. The superior race, in Gobineau's view, was the white race, among whose members the Aryan stood at the highest position. The Aryan strain, he argued, predominated in every European nation that had made major contributions to human civilization.

Gobineau also argued that racial degeneration was an inevitable characteristic of human development. The races and their subdivisions, in other words, started out pure but grew weaker over time as the result of race mixing. One reason, he asserted, for the nineteenth-century predominance of European civilization was the fact that European peoples had managed to preserve the relatively purer blood of their highest examples, the Aryans. But when the Aryans allowed their race to be sullied by mixture with inferior races, the decline of European civilization would inevitably begin. Gobineau went on to claim that this process was key to the understanding of history.

Again, Gobineau's ideas were most popular in Germany, although nationalists across Europe and America used them to justify racialist ideas. His book was a best-seller in late-nineteenth-century Germany, where it was read enthusiastically by, among others, Richard Wagner and Houston Stewart Chamberlain. Supporters founded a number of Gobineau societies, and journalists and politicians claimed that the author's ideas were proven by the emergence of the strong and powerful Second German Reich. Chamberlain's *The Foundations of the Nineteenth Century*, which was likely the major intellectual influence on Nazism, was based in Gobineau's ideas, and *Rosenberg's Myth of the Nineteenth Century* as well as Hitler's *Mein Kampf* are full of the assumptions of racial inequality and the need to preserve racial purity that Gobineau's work implied. *See also* racial science, racism, Social Darwinism, Vol. 2; Chamberlain, Houston Stewart, Vol. 3.

Goebbels, Joseph (1897–1945)

Reich minister of public enlightenment and propaganda, Nazi cultural czar, and one of the top officials of the Third Reich. Goebbels's mastery of the techniques of propaganda was one of the major factors allowing the Nazi Party to rise to power, to consolidate its hold over Germany, and to pursue its racial and territorial goals during World War II.

Joseph Goebbels was born in the Rhineland town of Rheydt, not far from the French border, on October 29, 1897. His father was a laborer and his family, devoutly Roman Catholic. As a child he suffered a bout of polio that left him disabled and with a limp for the rest of his life. Educated at Catholic schools, the young Goebbels was rejected from army service during World War I because of his disability. A strong student, he received aid from a Catholic organization to pursue studies in literature and history at the

Universities of Freiburg, Bonn, Würzburg, Cologne, Munich, and Heidelberg. As a doctoral student at Heidelberg he worked with the renowned Jewish scholar Friedrich Gundolf, becoming an expert in European literature. Goebbels, indeed, was the most well-educated of all Nazi leaders in the culture of Europe, and his later propaganda statements and speeches showed his mastery of language, imagery, and allusion.

After finishing his education Goebbels tried to live the life of a literary bohemian, producing a string of mediocre writings. In 1924 he wrote a play entitled *The Wanderer*, which was rejected by a performing company in Frankfurt. He published a novel in 1926 called *Michael: A German Destiny Through the Pages of a Diary*, but it too failed to attract an audience. Meanwhile, Goebbels found an alternative outlet for his intellectual energies and flair for melodrama in the fledgling Nazi Party. He joined it in 1922 and found a mentor in Gregor Strasser, the leader of the northern, left-wing branch of the Nazi Party. In 1925 Strasser named him Nazi Party business manager in the Ruhr region as well as editor of the *National Socialist Letters*, a newsletter jointly published by Gregor Strasser and his brother Otto. Working with the Strassers, Goebbels developed a rather radical outlook, calling for the abolition of capitalism and an alliance between German workers and the Russian Bolsheviks against the bourgeois corruptions of the west. In a northern Nazi manifesto issued in 1926, moreover, he referred to Adolf Hitler as a "petit bourgeois" who had to be thrown out of the Nazi Party for, presumably, standing in the way of a true revolution.

Goebbels's attitude toward Hitler changed remarkably, however, during the Bamberg Conference of March 1926, where Hitler forced a showdown between himself and the Strasser brothers over the leadership and direction of the party. Goebbels went to the conference as an ally of the Strassers but, sometime during Hitler's arguments, he

Joseph Goebbels's expert propagandizing was instrumental to the Nazi hold on Germany.

sensed the future Führer's power. Always the opportunist, he switched loyalties. Hitler, happy at this point to welcome the well-educated Goebbels into a movement that was still largely made up of bully boys with little administrative or organizational skill, made him Gauleiter of Berlin in November 1926. The job was a challenging one, since the Nazi organization in Berlin was small, loosely organized, and beset on all sides in a city that, at that time, was dominated by Social Democrats and Communists. Goebbels, however, proved equal to the job, severing the Berlin party organization from its ties to the Strassers and establishing his own weekly newspaper, *Der Angriff (The Attack)*, to publicize the Hitlerian line. It was also in Berlin that Goebbels began to demonstrate his propaganda skills in both the media and on the streets. He published posters and pamphlets demonizing his opponents, namely Jews, Communists, and the Berlin city government, in obvious and insidious ways. He staged parades, spoke at public meetings, and fomented street brawls. He also developed a fawning admiration for Adolf Hitler, of dubious sincerity, comparing Hitler to Jesus.

While Hitler appreciated Goebbels's attention-getting techniques as well as his over-the-top admiration, other leading Nazis disliked him. Goebbels is thought to have felt overwhelming inadequacy because of his disabled leg, his short stature, and his dark hair, as well as the fact that he had no military experience. Indeed, he was physically the antithesis of the Aryan ideal. Others took advantage of these circumstances in the backstabbing circles of high Nazi Party authority. Goebbels was dubbed "the half-Frenchman, "the little-mouse doctor," and "the scheming dwarf." Goebbels learned not to care, compensating with keen intelligence by building Nazi authority over Germany as well as his own personal power. He understood that, at least on one level, his foes were jealous of his education and intellectual abilities and he used those advantages, shamelessly and brutally, in his own interest.

Goebbels's mastery of propaganda and the manipulation of the public mind played a major part in the Nazi Party's electoral successes in 1932, and after Hitler took power in 1933 Goebbels was named to the cabinet as Reich minister for public enlightenment and propaganda. Along with the more general effort to "coordinate" all aspects of German life into the Nazi regime, Goebbels's post gave him control over all branches of media and cultural life: literature, journalism, film, publishing, radio, music, and the fine and dramatic arts. He took stringent efforts to nazify cultural life by removing Jews, setting strict guidelines for allowable works, and putting artistic and publishing institutions under state control. As ever the master of the symbolic public ritual, Goebbels staged the massive Burning of the Books ceremony on May 10, 1933, in Berlin, destroying hundreds of books by Jews, Marxists, liberals, internationalists, and any others deemed un-German. Meanwhile, he and his wife, Magda, along with their six children—Helga, Hilda, Helmut, Holde, Hedda, and Heide, names chosen to share the first letter of Hitler—became the first family of the Third Reich, since Hitler had neither wife nor child. This status came with some problems, as Magda's first husband had been Jewish and Goebbels proved himself to be a voracious womanizer with a weakness for film actresses. In 1938 Hitler himself had to intervene when Magda threatened to divorce Goebbels over his affair with a Czech actress named Lida Baarova. Nevertheless, Goebbels and family continued to enjoy a close familiarity with the Führer that other top Nazis, such as Hermann Göring and Joachim von Ribbentrop, came to resent.

During the 1930s Goebbels emerged as a major Jew baiter, probably expanding the standard Nazi line rather than expressing any deeply held beliefs. He played a major role in instigating the Kristallnacht pogrom of November 1938 by making an inflammatory speech in Munich that, some alleged, started the riots. During World War II, moreover, Goebbels played an active part in the mass extermination of Jews by personally arranging the deportation of Jews from Berlin as well as intimating the policy of extermination in his public speeches.

The relationship between Goebbels and Hitler grew even closer over the war years. Goebbels took up the task of propping up German morale while also advising Hitler on political and cultural matters. In February 1943, after the Allies announced their demand for unconditional surrender from

Germany, Goebbels took advantage of the moment with a major speech at Berlin's Sportpalast. During the speech, which was nearly a revival of the feverish Nazi enthusiasm of the early war years, Goebbels reminded his listeners that what lay ahead of them, given Allied demands, was either victory or death. He asked them if they wanted total war and the crowd responded hysterically, "Sieg Heil!" As the German war effort collapsed, however, Goebbels was forced to be more creative in his propaganda, on the one hand threatening the people with the imminent arrival of "Asiatic hordes" from the Soviet Union while on the other promising their redemption with science fiction "secret weapons" and "weapons of reprisal." Goebbels played a key role in the crushing of the July 1944 Plot when he convinced a local army major that Hitler had, in fact, survived the assassination attempt. Soon afterward Hitler rewarded him by naming him plenipotentiary for the mobilization of total war, with the responsibility of mustering and motivating the last-ditch efforts of German reserves. The time for miracles, however, was past.

Goebbels joined Hitler in the Berlin Führerbunker in early 1945, where the Führer had chosen to spend his final days. He was the last of the old-line Nazis to remain personally loyal. Using once again his gift for melodrama and his sense of historical perspective, Goebbels helped convince Hitler that his best course was suicide in a final, nihilistic gesture as the Third Reich crumbled around him. In his last will and political testament, Hitler named Goebbels his successor as Reich chancellor but Goebbels, after a final attempt to contact the Russians, decided to commit suicide himself. On May 1, 1945, after an SS doctor administered poison injections to his children, Goebbels had himself and Magda shot by an SS orderly. Trite to the end, he dimmissed his associates with the words "When we depart, let the earth tremble" (Wistrich, 1995). *See also* Ministry of Public Enlightenment and Propaganda, propaganda in the Third Reich, Vol. 2; Goebbels, Goebbels Explains National Socialism; Goebbels, Goebbels's False Optimism in April 1945, Vol. 4.

Goerdeler, Carl (1884–1945)

Lord mayor of the city of Leipzig from 1930 to 1937 and the most important civilian member of the German resistance movement. Goerdeler was born in the town of Schneidemühl in East Prussia on July 31, 1884. His father was a local district judge, and Goerdeler chose to follow in his footsteps by studying law and entering the civil service. He achieved his first important post as deputy mayor of Königsberg in 1922. Soon after becoming lord mayor of Leipzig he was named commissioner of prices under the Weimar government of Chancellor Heinrich Brüning. His early success, historians argue, was the result of important personal connections as well as Goerdeler's commanding, hardworking personality. Moreover, he was a traditional Prussian conservative in his outlook, sympathetic toward the aristocracy and devoted to Protestant Christianity.

Goerdeler remained price commissioner in the early years of the Third Reich, although he resigned in 1935 because the government rejected his proposals for reform. He resigned from his mayor's post in 1937 when, after returning from a trip outside Germany, he returned to Leipzig to find that local Nazis had removed a statue of the Jewish composer Felix Mendelssohn from city hall. At that point he joined the movement to oust Adolf Hitler from power. He took a job as an economic adviser with the firm of Robert Bosch of Stuttgart, whose leader was also opposed to the Nazi regime. In that position he frequently traveled outside Germany and told people of the dangers of the Nazi regime.

As the resistance movement in the German armed forces coalesced in 1938 and 1939 around the Abwehr and General

Ludwig Beck, Goerdeler emerged as the most powerful civilian leader. He had a number of important contacts both within the military and among businessmen inside Germany and out, and was well respected for his administrative talents. Leading conspirators singled him out for important posts in any post-Hitler German government. Nevertheless, Goerdeler remained a conservative Prussian, and he wanted Germany to keep the territory conquered or annexed by the Nazis while hoping that Great Britain and the United States would join post-Nazi Germany in holding back the expansion of the Soviet Union. He even imagined that either Joseph Goebbels or Heinrich Himmler could be induced to join an anti-Hitler coup.

Goerdeler played a major part in planning the July 1944 Plot on Hitler's life, and the conspirators planned for him to be German chancellor in the new government. After the failure of the plot he was arrested by the Gestapo, who found in his living quarters a great deal of evidence incriminating others in the plot. Goerdeler kept lists, for instance, of future cabinet members as well as other documents. Roland Freisler's People's Court sentenced him to death on September 8, 1944; the sentence was carried out on February 2, 1945, when Goerdeler was hanged in Berlin's Plötzensee Prison. *See also* July 1944 Plot, Vol. 1; resistance movements, Germany, Vol. 2; German Resistance Movement, A Vision for a Post-Hitler Germany, Vol. 4.

Göring, Emmy Sonnemann (1893–1973)

Actress who became Hermann Göring's second wife. After working on the stage in Weimar, she met Göring in 1932, a year after his first wife died. They arranged to marry in 1935. Their wedding was one of the great social events of the Third Reich, attended by nobles and notables from across Germany and the rest of Europe. The tall, slim, blond Emmy, who fitted the Aryan ideal of womanhood, became one of the regime's great hostesses, a counterpart to the maternal Magda Goebbels as first lady of the Third Reich. She and Göring had a daughter, Edda, in 1938. For the remainder of the Nazi era she largely remained behind the scenes, nonpolitical but sharing her husband's life of wealth and ostentation, which was acquired partly through plunder and slavery. After World War II she visited Göring in his cell whenever possible, and was one of the people suspected of providing him with the poison capsule with which he killed himself. This was never proved, however, and Emmy never spoke of it. In 1948 she was convicted of being a Nazi fellow traveler by a German court, and served a brief prison term. She was also prevented from pursuing her acting career for five years. In any case, she was unable to revive her career, and spent the rest of her life in Munich with Edda. In 1967 she published a memoir, *By My Husband's Side*, which is unsparing in its praise of Hermann Göring's character and actions and in which she claims that the period during which she knew her husband was the only time she felt truly alive. Emmy Göring died in Munich on June 8, 1973. *See also* women in the Third Reich, Vol. 2; Göring, Hermann; Göring, Karin von Kantzow, Vol. 3.

Göring, Hermann (1893–1946)

Adolf Hitler's designated successor as Führer of the Third Reich and holder of a number of top political, military, and economic offices. Göring was generally accepted as the second most powerful man in Nazi Germany and, aside from Hitler himself, was the most popular Nazi leader among ordinary Germans.

Hermann Göring was born in the town of Rosenheim in Bavaria on January 12, 1893. His father, a judge, had served as a high official in the German colony of Southwest Africa. Embarking on a military career, Göring entered an officer's school in Karlsruhe and, when World War I began, he served as a lieutenant of infantry. Later transferring to the nascent air force, he became one of Germany's most revered fighter aces, allegedly downing twenty-two Allied aircraft and earning numerous decorations as the commander of the famed Richthofen Fighter Squadron. Photographs from the time represent Göring as a romantic war hero, handsome, swashbuckling, and brave.

After World War I, like many young officers, Göring found it difficult to settle into a peacetime existence. After working for a time for Fokker, the airplane manufacturer, he gave in to his wanderlust and moved from Germany to Denmark and then to Sweden, working as an aircraft consultant, show pilot, and cargo carrier. In Sweden he met an older, married noblewoman, Baroness Karin von Kantzow, and married her once her divorce was finalized. The new Karin Göring was well connected in Munich, where their wedding was held in 1922, and it was through her that Göring met Adolf Hitler. The two joined forces. The Nazi Party gave Göring an outlet for his power hunger and energy; Hitler, for his part, was well aware of the prestige that the aristocratic, wealthy war hero would give to the fledgling Nazi movement. He named Göring supreme commander of the SA. During the Beer Hall Putsch of 1923 Göring marched at the forefront and was wounded in the brief skirmish that ended the putsch. Able, nonetheless, to escape, he spent the next four years in exile in Austria, Italy, and Sweden. While recovering from his injuries he became addicted to morphine, a condition that, many argued, changed his appearance and perhaps his personality, and he spent some months under observation in a mental hospital.

Thanks to a general amnesty in 1927, Göring was able to return to Germany. He rejoined the Nazi Party and again quickly and naturally gravitated toward center stage and a leadership role. He was one of the first Nazis to be elected to the Reichstag; from his Berlin base he worked to further Hitler's influence in the capital. When, in elections held on July 31, 1932, the Nazis became the largest political party in Germany, Göring became the president of the Reichstag, playing a major part over the next months in the negotiations that put Hitler in office as chancellor of Germany on January 30, 1933. He joined Hitler in the cabinet as minister without portfolio and served as Reich commissioner for aviation, but his most influential posts, in the early years of the Third Reich, were as president of Prussia and Prussian minister of the interior. Prussia was the largest state in Germany and the only one allowed a measure of independence from the national government during the era of the Third Reich. Moreover, the national capital, Berlin, the center of Germany's administrative and political offices, was in Prussia. As the top Prussian official Göring helped to consolidate the Nazi regime in numerous ways. Thought by some to have been behind the Reichstag fire of February 27, 1933, he certainly used it as an opportunity to ban Communists and Social Democrats from important posts in Prussia as well as limit civil rights and freedom of the press. In addition, as minister of the interior, Göring created the Prussian secret police, which was later transformed into the Gestapo, and established the first concentration camp for political prisoners in Oranienburg, a Berlin suburb. These innovations were later taken over by Heinrich Himmler, Reinhard Heydrich, and the SS, but they remained Göring's creations. Göring was a key figure in the Blood Purge of June 30, 1934, for which he directed police operations, helping Hitler eliminate a number of threats to the Nazi regime, most notably SA chief Ernst Röhm.

Over the next years, as Nazi Germany recovered from the Great Depression and political turmoil of the early 1930s and began to rearm, Göring's responsibilities continued to expand. In March 1935 he was appointed commander in chief of the Luftwaffe, the Third Reich's air force, and he involved himself intimately in the design and testing of new aircraft and the training of combat pilots. In 1936 Hitler appointed him plenipotentiary of the Four-Year Plan, which made him, arguably, the top economic official in the Third Reich, although over the years he had difficulty maintaining his jurisdiction in this regard. The Four-Year Plan was designed to ready Germany for a major war by 1940, and Göring threw himself wholeheartedly into managing the German

Hermann Göring, high-profile Reichsmarschall and commander in chief of the Luftwaffe, inspects his airmen.

economy from the top down. His emphasis, of course, was on heavy industry and rearmament. Always inclined toward self-aggrandizement, Göring took advantage of his position as leader of the war economy to build his own industrial empire, a state-run collection of enterprises known as the Hermann Göring Works. By 1939 it employed over seven hundred thousand people and was worth hundreds of millions of marks, making Göring an extremely wealthy man. Meanwhile, Hitler continued to shower him with offices and honors. As World War II approached Göring was appointed head of the Council for Defense of the Reich and, on September 1, 1939, he was named Hitler's official successor as Führer. After the fall of France in 1940 Göring was promoted to Reichsmarschall, a high military rank, standing above general field marshal, created for him alone.

By the time World War II started Göring had also become the foremost celebrity of the Third Reich, with a lifestyle to match. His two primary residences were a palace in Berlin and a vast hunting estate he named Karinhall after his first wife, who died in 1931 (Göring subsequently married Emmy Sonnemann, an actress). At Karinhall, Göring lived the life of a feudal lord surrounded by modern conveniences. He was fond of dressing in traditional costume, complete with green leather jackets and Robin Hood hats, and taking the role of Reich master of the hunt. He also staged lavish parties for Nazi and foreign dignitaries, hosted by Emmy, the unofficial first lady of the Third Reich, at which Europe's best foods and wines were served. During World War II Göring's agents scoured Europe for great works of art, which were stolen and transferred to one of his homes. He reveled in his power and ostentation, and many ordinary Germans loved him for it. They found him, despite his increasing girth, heroic, charming, and gregarious, uproariously good company over drinks with the common man or cocktails in high society. Many Germans vastly preferred him to the neurotics and misfits who filled other high Nazi posts, such as the sarcastic, caustic Joseph Goebbels, the sadistic pornographer Julius Streicher, the menacing and cold Heinrich Himmler, and even the aloof Hitler, who cultivated the image of a god rather than a man. Göring was an extrovert who loved life and who seemed to be full of human warmth. People often referred to him, even during his war crimes trial at Nuremberg, as "our Hermann."

Despite his lifestyle and image, however, Göring remained a calculating, power-hungry politician, capable of arbitrary and extreme cruelty when it suited his needs. He was never a strong believer in Nazi racial or territorial ideology, but nonetheless worked hard to support Hitler in his aims, certain that this support would increase his own authority. In early 1938, for instance, he helped concoct the scandals that forced the resignations of Generals Werner von Blomberg and Werner Freiherr von Fritsch; Göring hoped that he might take over their military responsibilities. Later that year he played a key role in the annexations of both Austria and Czechoslovakia, threatening in public at one point to bomb Prague, the capital of Czechoslovakia, if the Czechs did not submit. Although he had no history as an ideological anti-Semite, Göring had a hand in the mechanisms of the Holocaust as well. Göring, always on the lookout for economic advantage, devised the notion to fine Germany's Jews one billion marks in the aftermath of the Kristallnacht pogrom of November 1938. He was also a guiding force behind the "Aryanization" of Jewish economic enterprises by turning them over to German owners at robbery prices. On several occasions in these years he warned that Europe's Jews might find themselves subjected to a "final reckoning." Perhaps most damning, in terms of intent if not action, it was Göring who sent a note to Reinhard Heydrich in July 1941 authorizing him to seek a "general solution to the Jewish Question in . . . Europe," (Wistrich 1995).

Like his Führer, Göring proved to be a less effective tactical military commander than politician, basing his decisions on encouraging heroic behavior rather than on sound strategy. As commander in chief of the Luftwaffe, Göring played the key role in preparations for Operation Eagle, the attempt by the Luftwaffe to clear the skies over Great Britain in advance of the German invasion in August or September 1940. In the subsequent Battle of Britain, however, Göring made several major strategic errors, most notably choosing to bomb London rather than finish off Royal Air Force planes and bases, which allowed the British to recover. Göring also failed to effectively counter British radar, ultimately giving up on the effort. The Luftwaffe's failure in the Battle of Britain played a major role in Hitler's decision to give up his plans for the invasion of Britain. At that point, Göring began to lose favor in Hitler's eyes, a development that was compounded when the Luftwaffe failed to save the German forces trapped in Stalingrad in late 1942, despite Göring's airy promises, and when it proved utterly incapable of preventing widespread Allied bombing of Germany beginning early in 1943.

Göring's status continued to drop as the years of the war passed, despite his many honors and Reichsmarschall's rank. Privation and bombing made a continuation of his luxurious lifestyle an impossibility, though he learned to hide the ongoing failures of the Luftwaffe from Hitler. Meanwhile, his jurisdiction in other areas began to wane as the result of challenges from cleverer, more ambitious, or more capable leaders. Albert Speer, minister of armaments and war production, replaced him as the central figure in the war economy, while Heinrich Himmler had long before supplanted him as police leader. Joseph Goebbels responded to Germany's decline with utter subservience to Hitler, which raised his esteem, while Martin Bormann, as he did with almost everyone else, strove to undermine Göring in the Führer's eyes. Göring's final humiliation came in early 1945, when from Bavaria he responded to Hitler's decision to remain in the Berlin Führerbunker with a declaration that he, Göring, understood Hitler to have abdicated his authority and that he, Göring, was ready to step in to replace him. Hearing of this, Hitler was furious, stripping Göring of all his party and military posts and condemning him to death in absentia.

Göring was captured on May 9, 1945, by troops of the American Seventh Army. He was the highest-ranking Nazi to be captured alive by Allied forces. Brought before the International Military Tribunal at Nuremberg in late 1945, along with twenty others, he once again assumed center stage and regained a measure of his old flash and spark. Göring considered himself now the highest-ranking official of the Third Reich, and took charge over the other defendants, dictating an attitude of haughty defiance that most of them rejected or were incapable of. He adopted a pose of self-conscious martyrdom, sure that future generations of Germans would remember him as a national hero. During his testimony, Göring demonstrated his agile intellect as well as his arrogance, verbally sparring with prosecutors. The judges, however, were not impressed, and found no factors that might mitigate Göring's immense and obvious guilt for the crimes of the Third Reich. He was found guilty on all four counts of the indictment and sentenced to death. He was scheduled to be the first to be hanged at the Nuremberg prison on October 16, 1946. Hours before, however, in the late evening of October 15, Hermann Göring committed suicide using a poison capsule he had either concealed or had smuggled into his cell. *See also* Four-Year Plan, Luftwaffe, Vol. 1; Nuremberg trials, Vol. 2; Göring, Göring Commemorates the Days of Struggle, Vol. 4.

Göring, Karin von Kantzow (1889–1931)

First wife of Hermann Göring, Adolf Hitler's second in command, and the source of much of her husband's early prestige as well as of his personal fortune. Karin von Kantzow was born in 1889 into a family of Swedish aristocrats; her father was a career army officer. She suffered from epilepsy, and was involved in an unhappy marriage when she met Göring, who was working as a pilot in Sweden. The two fell in love, and after she secured a divorce, Karin married Göring, who was four years her junior. She apparently acted as a sort of mother figure to him, caring for him during his morphine addiction in the late 1920s. Karin Göring died of tuberculosis on October 17, 1931. In her honor Hermann Göring named his Prussian estate Karinhall. *See also* Karinhall, Vol. 1; Göring, Emmy Sonnemann; Göring, Hermann, Vol. 3.

Greiser, Arthur (1897–1946)

The top Nazi among the ethnic Germans of Danzig in the Polish Corridor and, during World War II, Gauleiter of the Warthegau, the new province the Germans carved out of the western part of Poland. Greiser was born in Poznan, then Posen in East Prussia, on January 22, 1897. During World War I he served as an officer in the German navy and, after the war, as a member of the right-wing Freikorps. He joined the Nazi Party in 1929. In 1930 he joined the SS, where he became an early protégé of Heinrich Himmler. From 1930 to 1939 he was one of the most powerful Nazis in Danzig, the port city that the victors had awarded to Poland at the end of World War I but which was historically German. There he was not only deputy district leader of the Nazi Party but also president of the Danzig Senate.

On October 21, 1939, weeks after the German conquest and partition of Poland, Greiser was named Reich governor, or Gauleiter, of the Warthegau and an SS officer, rising to the level of SS general in 1943. Greiser took an enthusiastic interest in the plans to transform the nature of the population of the Warthegau through forced resettlement and deportation. Jews living in the region were immediately deported to the ghettos next door in the Polish General Government. Non-Jewish Poles, meanwhile, were forced to undergo strict "Aryanization" examinations to see if they might somehow be decreed to be German rather than Polish. Those who failed, and Greiser had far more stringent requirements than other officers, were either deported to the General Government or forced to become servants. To complete this strange circle, thousands of ethnic Germans from the Baltic states of Estonia, Latvia, and Lithuania as well as from the Balkans were resettled in the Warthegau; Greiser often housed them on farms or in apartments deserted by Jews or Poles just a day earlier. Between 1939 and 1943 the German population rose nearly 300 percent.

Greiser was also consistently cruel in his treatment of Poles and Jews, and played a role in the confinement and murder of civilians, the collection of forced laborers, and the deportation of Jews to the extermination camps. After the war he sought to escape to southern Germany but was eventually arrested by American forces and extradited to Poland. The Poles hanged him for his crimes in Poznan on June 20, 1946. *See also* Danzig, ethnic Germans, Vol. 1; resettlement, Warthegau, Vol. 2.

Groener, Wilhelm (1867–1939)

Second in command of the German Imperial Army at the end of World War I and, over the next months, the main contact person between the army and German politicians. He later served the Weimar Republic in several cabinet posts. Groener was born in Ludwigsburg in southwestern Germany on November 22, 1867, and became a career soldier at the age of seventeen. Gravitating toward administrative staff positions rather than field commands, Groener joined the General Staff in 1899, and played a large role in devising deployment tactics using German railroads. During World War I he was promoted to lieutenant colonel and took control of armaments within the war office. He took a brief field command in 1917 after a falling-out with General Erich Ludendorff, his nominal superior, but he returned to a staff post in October 1918 as quartermaster general of the German army, replacing Ludendorff in the post. His only superior in the army was Field Marshal Paul von Hindenburg.

As World War I ended Groener found himself at the center of German politics. He was the man to whom, on November 9, 1918, fell the responsibility of telling Kaiser Wilhelm II, the German emperor, that he no longer could count on the loyalty of his armies and should therefore abdicate. Over the next months he led the demobilization of millions of German troops and worked closely with Friedrich Ebert, the leader of the fledgling Weimar Republic, in settling Germany down. The new republic, as it happened, emerged out of an understanding that the German army would support Ebert, a Socialist politician, if it was given authority to prevent either a civil war or a Communist uprising. To combat communism, both Groener and Ebert agreed that freebooting units of German soldiers, the Freikorps, should be allowed free reign to conduct street warfare, at least temporarily.

Groener also urged that the army support the republic in accepting the Treaty of Versailles, a document that few other officers could stomach but that Groener believed had to be accepted to restore order to Germany. He continued to try to build bridges between the hesitant army and the Weimar government until 1932. From 1920 to 1923 he was minister of communications in the Weimar cabinet, and from 1928 to 1932 he served as minister of defense. He was also minister of the interior in 1931 and 1932. He was a strong anti-Nazi, concerned both by Nazi political ambitions and by the infiltration into the German military of Nazi loyalists. One of Groener's protégés, however, was convinced he could use Adolf Hitler and the Nazis to serve his own ends. This was General Kurt von Schleicher, who had been mentored by Groener and used by Groener as a liaison between the army and the Weimar cabinet in 1932. After Groener banned the SA in April 1932, Schleicher began to turn against him and concoct plans involving Hitler and other Nazi leaders in future cabinets. Groener spoke out against the SA in the Reichstag on May 10, only to find himself taunted and shouted down by Nazis. Disgusted already by Schleicher's betrayal, and sick with diabetes, Groener resigned his posts on May 13. His departure marked the removal of the last, and most well-respected, anti-Nazi at the highest levels of the German government, helping to clear the way to Hitler's seizure of power. Groener died in Bornstedt, near Berlin, on May 3, 1939. *See also* November criminals, Weimar Republic, World War I, Vol. 2; Wilhelm II, Vol. 3.

Grynszpan, Herschel (1921–1940?)

A young Polish Jew whose shooting of a German diplomat in Paris on November 7, 1938, provided the pretext for Kristallnacht (the Night of Broken Glass), a nationwide attack on German Jews which took place mostly the night of November 9. Herschel Grynszpan was what the Nazis called an "Eastern Jew" as opposed to an assimilated German Jew. He was born in the German city of Hanover in 1921 but his father, Zindel, had emigrated from Poland to Germany in 1911. Herschel left school at the age of fifteen and began a wandering life that led him eventually to Paris, though his primary goal was immigration to Palestine. In the fall of 1938 he received a letter from his sister informing him that she and the rest of their family had been deported from Hanover to western Poland. The Nazis, it seemed, had begun an effort to remove Eastern Jews from the Reich; with little notice the Grynszpan family, along with hundreds of others, was simply dumped on the Polish side of the border. The young Grynzspan, who was perhaps mentally unstable, decided to avenge the deportation and unnecessary suffering of his family. On November 7 he took a hidden revolver to the German embassy in Paris, where he was admitted into the office of Undersecretary Ernst vom Rath. Rath, ironically, was an outspoken anti-Nazi then under investigation by the Gestapo. Shouting that vengeance was necessary Grynszpan shot Rath, who died of his wounds two days later.

Adolf Hitler and Joseph Goebbels, among others, heard the news of the shooting in Munich during their annual celebration commemorating the Beer Hall Putsch of 1923. Goebbels's diaries suggest that Hitler promptly approved a major attack on German Jews, and in front of a large crowd of old Nazi fighters the propaganda minister delivered a scathing speech attacking Grynszpan and urging that good Germans avenge his attack. The result was Kristallnacht. Evidence that has recently come to light suggests that the SS and SA were already planning a large attack; the Rath shooting merely provided them with an excuse. Over the next days several hundred German Jews were murdered and thousands of Jewish homes and businesses were sacked while most of the nation's synagogues were burned to the ground. Afterward, twenty thousand Jewish men were marched off to concentration camps while Jewish community leaders were presented with a bill for 1 billion marks, necessary in Nazi logic because the Jews had "caused" the rioting and should pay for the damage.

Herschel Grynszpan, for his part, was arrested and held by the French for the murder of Rath. World War II broke out, however, before he could be tried, and in June 1940 the new Vichy regime extradited Grynszpan to Germany. There Goebbels planned a huge public trial that would provide the Nazis with a new pretext, this time for the war between Germany and France. Grynszpan disappeared while in custody, however, and though rumors persist that he survived the war and lived on in Paris under a new name, he was officially declared dead by a German court in 1960. *See also* Eastern Jews, Kristallnacht, Vol. 1.

Guderian, Heinz (1885–1954)

One of Germany's great tank commanders during World War II and the main German designer of the blitzkrieg strategy, which served the Third Reich well in the first years of the war. Guderian was born in Kulmhof (later Chelmno in Poland) on June 17, 1885. He attended a military academy and served as a junior officer during World War I. During the Weimar era he served in a variety of posts, becoming an expert in field communications. In 1931 he was promoted to lieutenant colonel as well as chief of staff of the Inspectorate of Motorized Troops. There he began to develop his expertise in tank warfare, realizing far earlier than most of his counterparts that tanks, Panzer in German, would play a major role in future ground warfare and that, therefore, strategies should be developed around the effective use of tanks. In 1936 he published a book entitled *Achtung: Panzer! (Attention: Tanks!)* in which he described the potential power of tanks as an organized attack force, using mobile communications equipment allowing commanders to make rapid decisions and adjustments. Adolf Hitler agreed with his tactics, even though old-school officers were hesitant, and Guderian enjoyed rapid promotions as well as a forward position, with his tanks, when German armies rolled into Austria during the Anschluss of March 1938. By 1939 he was a lieutenant general and commander in chief of all Panzer divisions.

The invasions of Poland in September 1939 and France in May 1940 allowed Guderian further opportunites to demonstrate his skills as a tactician and commander. In Poland his tanks quickly dispersed or destroyed Polish infantry, and he was awarded the Knight's Cross in October of 1939. During the invasion of France his Panzer divisions, part of the 19th Armored Corps, were among the first to get through the Ardennes forest in the attempt to split the Allied lines. In fact, between May 10 and May 20, 1940, Guderian was able to move from the German border, through the Ardennes, and between Allied lines to the English Channel coast at Abbeville and Calais. Guderian's rapid advance necessitated the evacuation of most of the British Expeditionary Force from the beaches at Dunkirk, a force that got away only because Hitler ordered Guderian to stop.

Guderian continued his exploits on the eastern front during the invasion of the Soviet Union beginning on June 22, 1941. His tank divisions came within two hundred miles of Moscow in late summer before he was ordered south to join other German armies in the attempt to establish control of southern Russia's rich agricultural and oil-producing regions. Along with General Ewald von Kleist, another tank commander, Guderian's divisions captured four Soviet armies in the fall of 1941. The arrival of the Russian winter, however, rendered rapid tank movements impossible. Guderian tried to make this fact clear to Hitler, but the Führer refused to accept his "defeatist" arguments and, despite his brilliant tactics and impressive accomplishments, Guderian was dismissed from his command in December 1941.

He remained in semiretirement until February 1943, when he was recalled as inspector general of Panzer forces. This began, however, a period of inconsistent support for Hitler and the Nazi regime. In the aftermath of El Alamein and Stalingrad, Guderian was sure that Germany could no longer win the war, and he toyed with plans to remove Hitler from command of the army. He knew of the German resistance movement, which enjoyed the support of a number of generals, but he did not join it despite attempts to recruit him. After the failure of the July 1944 Plot, Guderian found himself once again in Hitler's good graces. He was raised to the post of chief of the General Staff of the High Command of the German armed forces, one of the top positions in the German military, and he publicly denounced the conspirators. He also served on the military honor court, along with Generals Wilhelm Keitel and Gerd von Rundstedt, which tried high-level military officers accused of involvement in the plot. The court sent dozens of top officers to concentration camps and execution grounds after stripping them of their military ranks and honors.

On March 21, 1945, Guderian was dismissed from his posts once again. This time, Hitler was frustrated by Guderian's argument that Germany should seek a peace with the western Allies in hopes that the Third Reich could then devote all its energies to stopping the advance of the Soviet Union in the east. Guderian was captured by American forces on May 10, 1945, but was never seriously considered as a candidate for a war crimes trial.

Guderian spent his remaining years in retirement in Bavaria. In 1951 he published his memoirs, entitled *Erinnerungen eines Soldaten (Remembrances of a Soldier)*, in which he blamed the failures of the German army in World War II on the inept military decisions of Adolf Hitler as well as the yesmen who supported him from their top command positions. He died on May 15, 1954. ***See also*** Barbarossa, Vol. 1; Panzer, Vol. 2; Rommel, Erwin, Vol. 3.

Hacha, Emil (1872–1945)

The last president of Czechoslovakia before it was absorbed into the Third Reich and thereafter a puppet ruler of the Protectorate of Bohemia and Moravia. Hacha was born in Bohemia on July 12, 1872, and became a lawyer and judge before entering politics. In 1925 he was named the first president of the Czechoslovakian Supreme Administrative Court. Perhaps since few others were ready or willing to fill the post, Hacha became president of Czechoslovakia on November 30, 1938, shortly after the nation was forced to give up the Sudetenland in humbling and humiliating fashion at the Munich Conference of late September. He replaced Edouard Benes, one of the nation's founders. Unlike Benes, who had tried to resist Germany's aggressions, Hacha adopted a conciliatory tone toward Adolf Hitler, hoping to preserve what was left of Czechoslovakian national life. By March 1939, however, Hitler cared little who governed Czechoslovakia or what stance they took. He mobilized his forces along the border and prepared for an invasion, claiming that the Czechs continued to oppress Germans living there.

Hacha, along with his foreign minister, Frantisek Chvalkovsky, traveled to Berlin on March 14 to discuss the matter with Hitler. The next day, during their meeting, Hacha tried to convince the Führer that he was willing to subordinate his nation to German desires if it was allowed to remain independent. Hitler responded by insulting Hacha and arguing that the Czech's "belligerent" attitudes were still apparent; therefore, a German invasion was justified. After reminding Hacha that his forces greatly outnumbered the Czech armies, and that he was prepared to level Prague, the capital, Hitler left the room. Hermann Göring and Joachim von Ribbentrop then presented Hacha with a surrender demand, at which point the Czechoslovak leader fainted. He was revived by, in Göring's phrase, "Herr Reich Injection Master" Dr. Theodor Morell, personal physician to Hitler. Upon reviving he signed the document allowing Hitler's armies to march peacefully into Prague and end the independent existence of Czechoslovakia.

During the Nazi occupation Hacha remained, according to Hitler's desires, state president of the Protectorate of Bohemia and Moravia. In reality he was little more than a figurehead, and the true authorities in Prague were the various Reich protectors, who included brutal SS officers such as Reinhard Heydrich and Kurt Daluege. Hacha was imprisoned by Soviet forces after they liberated Czechoslovakia in early 1945. He died in prison in Prague on June 27, 1945. *See also* Bohemia and Moravia, Protectorate of, Vol. 1; Munich Conference, Vol. 2.

Halder, Franz (1884–1972)

Chief of the General Staff of the German army from 1938 to 1942 and very tentative opponent of both Adolf Hitler and the Third Reich's war plans. Franz Halder was born in Würzburg on June 30, 1884. His family had traditionally provided officers for both the Prussian and German armies. During World War I Halder was an officer on the General Staff and in 1919 he joined the Weimar-era Reichswehr. He was promoted steadily to

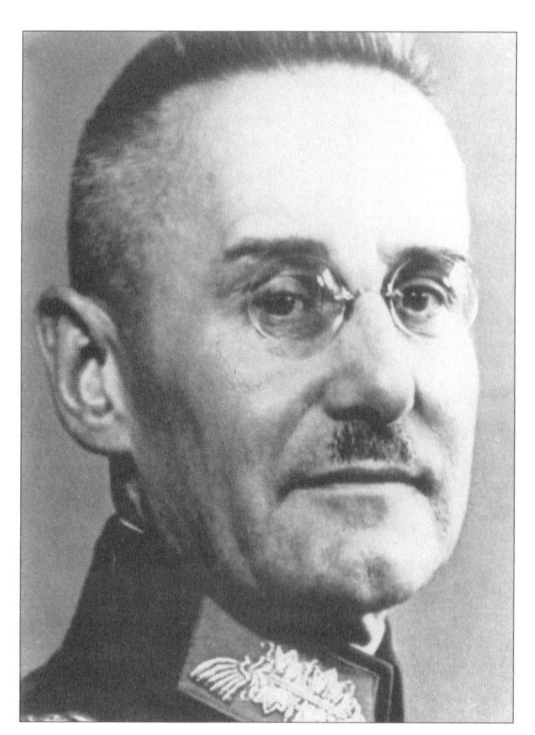

German general Franz Halder (pictured) opposed Hitler's interference in military strategy and was confined in a concentration camp for the last months of World War II.

higher ranks: In 1926 he was appointed senior quartermaster to the Reichswehr, a post he held until 1938; he became a major general in 1935 and a lieutenant general in 1937. After General Ludwig Beck, concerned about Nazi domination of the German army as well as Hitler's war plans, resigned as chief of the General Staff in August 1938, Halder was appointed to replace him.

As a traditional officer, Halder had misgivings about the Nazis and was aware that elements of the officer corps wanted to oust Hitler from power. However, he was hesitant to break the oath of loyalty that he had sworn to Hitler, and refused to take part in any plot that involved an assassination attempt, although in 1938 he indicated that he might support an army takeover of power in order to prevent a large-scale war that, he suspected, Germany would ultimately lose. He severed any true connection with army resisters after the Munich Conference of 1938 forestalled war, at least for a few months, and he seems at least partly to have fallen under Hitler's spell. He played a large role in the army's plans for both Poland, western Europe, and the Soviet Union in 1939, 1940, and 1941 and was extremely pleased by the German military successes of those years.

As the months passed Halder disagreed more and more with Hitler's interference in military affairs and planning. The Führer dismissed him from his post in September 1942, when Halder argued that German forces should not be concentrated in the Russian city of Stalingrad, a city Hitler had declared vital to the German war effort. He spent the next years in retirement. After the July 1944 Plot Halder was arrested, threatened with execution for his past associations, and confined to a concentration camp. He remained there until Germany was defeated; American forces liberated him on April 28, 1945. After the war Halder remained in retirement, publishing a brief memoir that claimed that Hitler's interference with top officers and indifference toward the lives of ordinary German soldiers betrayed the country. He died in the village of Aschau in Bavaria on April 2, 1972. *See also* resistance movements, Germany; Wehrmacht, Vol. 2.

Hanfstaengl, Ernst (Putzi) (1887–1975)

Upper-class Bavarian, global sophisticate with American ties, and an early supporter of Adolf Hitler. Hanfstaengl also served as chief of the Foreign Press Office of the Nazi Party from 1931 to 1937.

Ernst Hanfstaengl was born in Munich on February 2, 1887. His wealthy parents operated an art dealership, and a grandfather and an uncle fought in the American Civil War. As a young man Hanfstaengl attended Harvard University in Cambridge, Massachusetts; he spoke fluent English and was quite comfortable among Americans. From 1905 to 1919 he lived in New York

City, where he was originally supposed to manage the New York branch of the family art business. Reportedly he was disappointed that he could not fight for Germany during World War I. He returned to Munich in 1919, taking up a position among the city's well-to-do cultural circles. Known to his many German and foreign friends as Putzi, Hanfstaengl was a gregarious, humorous companion, refined host, and accomplished pianist.

Hanfstaengl first became aware of Hitler when an American friend who worked at the embassy in Berlin spoke of him. After attending a political meeting where the Nazi leader spoke, Hanfstaengl became an immediate convert. He was one of several early followers who helped make Hitler more respectable to elements of Munich's upper classes through introductions and patronage, and he also put himself to work as a fund-raiser. Hanfstaengl's efforts were instrumental in allowing the Nazi Party to purchase the *Völkischer Beobachter*, the party newspaper, in 1921. In 1923 he took part in the Beer Hall Putsch, and after the effort failed Hitler fled for solace to Hanfstaengl's bungalow in the nearby Alps at Uffing. During Hitler's brief jail term in Munich, Hanfstaengl frequently visited him to help keep his spirits up.

Hanfstaengl remained a part of Hitler's inner circle for years, providing, historians claim, a welcome source of humor and light relief during the so-called Days of Struggle before the Nazis came to power. He was appointed chief of the Foreign Press Office in 1931, where he was encouraged to use his many foreign contacts, as well as his engaging personality, to build support for the Nazi movement. Foreign reporters, indeed, found Hanfstaengl to be one of the few Nazis whose company they enjoyed and whose perspective they could appreciate.

Beginning in 1934 Hanfstaengl began to lose favor among both Hitler and other leading Nazis. His devotion to Nazi ideology seemed insufficient, and rougher, more displeasing figures such as Hermann Göring and Joseph Goebbels resented both his easy, upper-class charm and his access to Hitler. Hanfstaengl partly reacted in kind, referring publicly to Goebbels on one instance as a "pig." Hitler, for his part, began to wonder whether Hanfstaengl might be more interested in financial gain than National Socialist purity, and spent less and less time in the formerly beloved Putzi's company. After hearing rumors in 1937 that rivals were planning to kill him by dropping him from an airplane, Hanfstaengl left Germany. He went first to England and then to the United States, working for a time during World War II as an adviser to the American government on the Third Reich. Following a brief period of internment after the war, Hanfstaengl returned to Munich, where he died on November 6, 1975. *See also* Days of Struggle, Vol. 1; Old Fighters, Vol. 2; Hitler, Adolf, Vol. 3.

Hassell, Ulrich von (1881–1944)

Career diplomat and leading member of the German resistance movement. Ulrich von Hassell was born in Pomerania in eastern Germany on November 12, 1881. His family was a traditional aristocratic family of Prussia, devoted to public service, Protestant Christianity, and social paternalism. He married within his class as well; his wife was the daughter of Grand Admiral Alfred von Tirpitz, founder of the German navy and its chief commander during World War I. After taking a law degree, Hassell joined the Imperial German Foreign Office in 1908, spending much of his career in high-level foreign posts. In 1911 he was named vice-consul in Genoa, Italy. After the interruption of World War I Hassell was, successively, embassy councillor in Rome in 1919 and consul-general in Barcelona, Spain, from 1921 to 1926. He then held ambassadorships in Copenhagen, Denmark, from 1926 to 1930; Belgrade, Yugoslavia, from 1930 to 1932; and Rome from 1932 to 1938. In this last position he was well placed to observe the inner workings of Mussolini's

Fascist regime as well as Hitler's increasing ties to the Fascists.

Hassell, by heritage a strong nationalist, was originally sympathetic toward Nazism. But after Hitler took power he grew increasingly concerned about the Führer's territorial ambitions as well as the breakdown of public order and decency at home. Unable to hide his dislike for the vulgarity, brutality, and shortsightedness of the Nazis, Hassell was forced into retirement in 1938 after Joachim von Ribbentrop, whom Hassell violently disliked, took over as foreign minister. He then joined General Ludwig Beck and politician Carl Goerdeler among the leaders of the German resistance movement. He served as the movement's chief diplomat, traveling widely in his retirement to drum up support for the resistance across Europe. He also tried, after World War II limited his ability to travel, to convince Germany's top generals to commit themselves to the resistance, although prominent figures such as Franz Halder, Walther von Brauchitsch, and Erwin Rommel generally resisted his arguments.

As the years passed Hassell grew increasingly disillusioned about the prospects for success of the resistance. Not only did so many top generals fail to act according to what he believed were Germany's true interests, but foreign diplomats, especially in Great Britain, were uninterested in the resistance's plans for a post-Hitler Germany. Indeed, along with their American allies, British officials persisted in their demand for an unconditional German surrender. Hassell's vision of Germany after the Nazis, however, was virtually impossible for the Allies to sympathize with. It called for, basically, a return to the German borders of 1914, allowing Germany to hang on to its territorial gains in Austria, Czechoslovakia, and Poland. Moreover, Hassell wanted to bring back the Prussian monarchy and, like many resistance leaders (and many Nazis as well), seemed to think that the British and Americans would ultimately join Germany in a war to stop the expansion of Soviet communism.

Hassell learned that he was under observation by the Gestapo as early as April 1942, and he began to reduce his resistance activities. After the failure of the July 1944 Plot, however, Hassell knew that ultimately he would be implicated in the conspiracy and arrested. As it happened Gestapo officials came for him on July 28, 1944, and he received them in his office, calmly and in all likelihood with the distance and disdain of his class. He had already buried his diaries in a chest in his Bavarian garden. Later published, they became one of the main sources of knowledge about the German resistance movement. Hassell, meanwhile, was tried by the People's Court Hitler convened to dispense revenge in the aftermath of the plot. Sentenced to death, he was hanged in Plötzensee Prison in Berlin on September 8, 1944. ***See also*** July 1944 Plot, Vol. 1; resistance movements, Germany, Vol. 2.

Heinkel, Ernst (1888–1958)

German engineer and aircraft designer whose Heinkel-11 planes were the standard German midrange bomber aircraft during World War II. Heinkel was born in Württemberg in western Germany in 1888 and took a degree in mechanical engineering at the University of Stuttgart. He took an early interest in aviation, noting that airplanes rather than helium-filled airships were likely to be the aircraft of the future. During World War I he operated an aircraft factory that produced planes for the Austro-Hungarian army as well as the German navy. In 1922 he opened his first German factory at Warnemünde, in Germany's far north. This business, the Heinkel Aircraft Works, first made seaplanes but then shifted to military aircraft. It played an important part in supplying the Luftwaffe, the Third Reich's air force, with high-quality planes, and in honor of his contributions Heinkel was named a leader of the war economy (Wehrwirtschaftsführer), an honorary position given to industrialists.

Among Heinkel's accomplishments was the production of the world's first jet aircraft, the HE-178, the prototype of which was first successfully tested on August 27, 1939. The more pressing needs of the Luftwaffe for more conventional fighters and bombers during World War II, however, discouraged the development of jet aircraft over the next years.

After the war Heinkel escaped both prosecution and imprisonment, despite the fact that his plants had employed tens of thousands of foreign workers and despite the fact that he was named a fellow traveler by a German denazification court. He returned to the airplane business in the early 1950s, selling his works to the large German firm of Messerschmitt-Bolkow-Blom. He died on January 30, 1958. *See also* Luftwaffe, Vol. 1.

Heisenberg, Werner (1901–1976)

One of the most influential physicists of the twentieth century and one of the few top German scientists to remain in the country during the era of the Third Reich. Heisenberg was born in Würzburg on December 5, 1901. He took a degree in physics at the University of Munich. Recognized as a brilliant scientist early on, he studied closely with Niels Bohr, one of the founders of atomic physics, from 1924 to 1927. He won the Nobel Prize in physics in 1932. From 1927 to 1941 he served as professor at the University of Leipzig, and then from 1941 to 1945 he was both professor of theoretical physics at the University of Berlin and director of the Kaiser Wilhelm Institute for Physics in Berlin. Along with Bohr and other scientific greats such as Albert Einstein and Max Born, Heisenberg's work helped shape a transformation in physics and, some claimed, in humankind's understanding of the universe. Among the ideas Heisenberg is best known for is his "uncertainty principle," which is built around the notion that there are no strict laws of cause and effect that organize the physical universe; rather, the universe can only be understood on the basis of chance and statistical probabilities. He was also one of the founders of quantum mechanics.

Heisenberg was never a Nazi, but chose to stay in Germany rather than go into exile like Einstein, Born, and hundreds of other scientists and intellectuals. Nevertheless he suffered persecution and neglect from Nazi officials. The SS in particular considered him a practitioner of "Jewish physics," and too close an associate of Einstein. Although he enjoyed the personal protection of Heinrich Himmler, who knew that Heisenberg had many supporters among German politicians and diplomats, the late 1930s and the years of war were largely periods of professional stagnation and personal loneliness for the physicist. He tried in vain to maintain the international stature of German physics in the face of the departures of so many great minds as well as official indifference or outright hatred. Only late in the war, when politicians and military strategists realized that German atomic science had fallen behind that of other nations, did Heisenberg once again get support. He subsequently played a role in the German effort to develop atomic weapons, seemingly oblivious to the political or moral implications of the project.

After World War II Heisenberg maintained an international profile. From his post as the director of the Max Planck Institute in Göttingen, he published many papers as well as important books such as *Die Physic der Atomkerne* and *Die Naturbild der Heutigen Physik*. He died in Munich on February 1, 1976. *See also* Braun, Wernher von; Einstein, Albert, Vol. 3.

Helldorf, Wolf Heinrich Graf von (1896–1944)

President of the Berlin police and a major participant in the July 1944 Plot to assassinate Adolf Hitler and overthrow the Nazi government. Helldorf was born in Merseburg in Prussia on October 14, 1896, to a minor aristocratic family. During World War I he served as an officer, despite his youth, and won numerous medals. After the war he took part in right-wing direct political action as a member of the Rossbach Freikorps and also during the 1920 Kapp Putsch. After the putsch failed he went into self-imposed exile in Italy. Returning to Germany in 1924, Helldorf was elected to the Prussian state legislature and, in 1926, joined the Nazi Party. By 1931 he was a general within both the SA and the SS. In 1933, after the Nazis took power, he was elected to the Reichstag as a Nazi deputy and was appointed president of police in Potsdam, a Berlin suburb, where his direct superior was Hermann Göring as Nazi minister for Prussia. He was raised to Berlin police president in 1935, where he remained until 1944.

Helldorf was one of a number of high-level Nazis whose records during the Third Reich were ambiguous. He has been accused, for instance, of vicious anti-Semitism as well as graft and corruption. On the other hand, he heavily criticized the inaction of the Berlin police during the Kristallnacht pogrom of November 1938, claiming that the police should have stopped the attacks and the looting. Like other young aristocrats such as Claus von Stauffenberg or Henning von Tresckow, Helldorf appeared to lose his enthusiasm for the regime as the years passed and as Germany's war effort grew increasingly hopeless. During the July 1944 Plot he made it known to the conspirators that he would control the Berlin police in the hours after Hitler was assassinated, using them to ensure that the post-Hitler regime maintained control of the capital. Like the other conspirators, however, Helldorf was arrested after the plot failed. He was executed on August 15, 1944. *See also* July 1944 Plot, Kapp Putsch, Vol. 1.

Henlein, Konrad (1898–1945)

Former physical education instructor who became leader of the Nazi Party in the Sudeten region of Czechoslovakia and, after its annexation by the Third Reich, the local Gauleiter, or Reich governor. Henlein was born in the village of Maffersdorf in Bohemia on May 6, 1898, to a Czech mother and a German father of lower-middle-class background. After fighting for Austria-Hungary in World War I, which resulted in a period as a prisoner of war in Italy, he worked as a bank clerk. In 1925 he became a physical education teacher at a club for ethnic Germans in the Sudetenland, and in 1931 became leader of the German Gymnastic Union of Czechoslovakia.

Since the Nazi Party was outlawed in Czechoslovakia, Henlein formed and became the leader of an alternative known as the Sudeten German Party. During the 1930s, when Henlein enjoyed huge financial subsidies as well as promises of glory from Adolf Hitler and the German Nazis, the Sudeten German Party became the largest party in Czechoslovakia. Almost from the beginning Henlein's demands were substantial; he wanted autonomy for the Sudeten Germans within a loose national federation. Meanwhile, using German funds, which amounted to fifteen thousand marks a month in addition to less regular gifts, as well as a front organization known as the Sport Abteilung, Germans sympathetic to Nazism infiltrated both Czech politics and numerous cultural and regional associations. Henlein, for his part, began to consider himself a politician of international stature, traveling frequently to Berlin as well as to London, where he convinced British leaders that he had no contact with the Third Reich.

By the spring of 1938 Hitler was ready to proceed with his plans for the territorial expansion of the German Reich. After annexing Austria, his next target was the Sudetenland, and he made it clear that he was willing to use military force if necessary. Henlein confidently increased his demands. In May he issued the so-called Karlsbad Program, which demanded not only autonomy for the Sudeten Germans but the right to live according to "German culture," by which he meant Nazism and even anti-Semitism. After the Munich Conference of September 1938 granted the Third Reich the Sudetenland, Henlein was named Reich commissioner of the region. On May 1 he became Gauleiter. He held, in addition, the posts of Reichstag deputy and, after June 1943, SS lieutenant general. In May 1945 Henlein was captured by American forces. He killed himself soon after in an Allied internment camp. *See also* Karlsbad Program, Vol. 1; Munich Conference, Sudetenland, Vol. 2.

Hess, Rudolf (1894–1987)

Deputy Führer of the Third Reich from 1933 to 1941. Rudolf Hess was born in Alexandria, Egypt, on April 26, 1894. As a young man he went into business but joined the German Imperial Army at the outbreak of World War I. He served as a troop leader in the same regiment as Adolf Hitler, the 16th Bavarian Infantry, and as an air force officer. After the war he settled in Munich, where he attended the university and became involved in extremist right-wing politics by joining the Epp Freikorps. It was as a university student in political science that Hess conceived of the necessity for Germany to expand its territory in the east as a matter of biological and cultural necessity. His thinking along the lines of Germany's need for lebensraum, living space, was to be a major influence on Adolf Hitler. He joined the Nazi Party in January 1920, impressed by Hitler's oratory and charisma. After taking part in the Beer Hall Putsch of 1923 he was arrested and sentenced to seven months in prison alongside the Nazi leader. During their time in Landsberg Prison in Munich Hitler and Hess conceived and wrote *Mein Kampf*. It is generally accepted that Hess took Hitler's dictation, but some have argued that much of the book is, in fact, Hess's work. In any case he certainly made major contributions to those sections of the book having to do with geopolitics as well as Nazi Party structure.

Hess served as Hitler's personal secretary from 1925 to 1932, when the Nazi Party emerged as a national political movement. He was also one of Hitler's closest advisers and confidants. His greatest strength, from Hitler's point of view, was blind obedience and absolute, unquestioning loyalty, characteristics Hess displayed even after World War II. His intelligence was not towering, nor did he possess strong organizational or administrative ability or the initiative to act independently. He appears to have considered Hitler as a sort of father figure, and at times a

Hitler's deputy Rudolf Hess made a mysterious solo flight to Scotland in 1941, apparently to negotiate a peace with Great Britain.

god, the personification of Germanness, and was willing to subordinate his personality entirely to that of the Führer. Hitler, susceptible to such flattering attitudes, rewarded Hess with a wide variety of posts after the Nazi Party took power in 1933. Hess was named deputy Führer of the Nazi Party in April 1933, although the job required little more than introducing Hitler at rallies and speeches, shadowing him wherever he went, and providing an example to Germans of the sort of loyalty required in the totalitarian Third Reich. Hess once claimed, for instance, that Hitler was always right and would always be right. He was also a member of the cabinet as minister without portfolio and served on the ministerial Council for Defense of the Reich. In 1939 Hitler named Hess second in the line of succession to himself as leader of the Third Reich after Hermann Göring.

Believing, presumably, that he was acting in the best interests of Adolf Hitler and the German nation, Hess made one of the most surprising and unexpected moves of any top Nazi during the era of the Third Reich. On May 10, 1941, he flew alone in an appropriated fighter plane from Augsburg to Scotland, where he parachuted to the ground near the estate of the duke of Hamilton, a man he had met during the 1936 Berlin Olympics. Hess apparently wanted to use the duke's contacts with the British government to negotiate a peace between the two warring nations. According to Hess's muddled thinking, still fixed on the notions of racial unity and territorial expansion. he needed to convince the British that Germany's actions in eastern Europe were justified and that, if the British continued to resist the "destiny" of the Third Reich, they would be crushed. By making peace with Germany, however, Britain would be able to maintain its vast overseas empire. The British, however, were having none of it. They simply arrested Hess and imprisoned him as a captive of war. During his wartime internment, Hess's fragile mental balance seemed at times to collapse. Back in Germany, meanwhile, there was do doubt that he had lost his mind. Hitler declared him insane, while Goebbels's propaganda machine blamed his solo flight on delusions and hallucinations arising from World War I injuries.

Rudolf Hess was one of the twenty-one top Nazis brought before the International Military Tribunal at Nuremberg in late 1945. During the trial he appeared to be mildly unhinged, staring vacantly into space with sunken eyes and claiming, in response to prosecutors' questions, that he could not remember anything from the Nazi era. He later admitted that his amnesia was faked. The tribunal found that, despite his neurotic behavior while under the care of the British and his alleged loss of memory, he was competent enough to understand the charges that were brought against him and that he was completely sane before his strange flight to Scotland. Partly for his involvement in secret war preparations in 1938 and 1939, the tribunal found Hess guilty of war crimes and conspiracy to commit war crimes. He was sentenced to life in prison.

Along with six other Nuremberg defendants sentenced to prison terms, Hess was taken to Spandau Prison in Berlin on October 1946, which was under the four-power authority of the United States, Great Britain, France, and the Soviet Union. When Baldur von Schirach and Albert Speer were released after serving their sentences in 1966, Hess was the only prisoner remaining at Spandau. Suggestions that he be released were all vetoed by the Soviets. In the end, Hess spent more than twenty years alone in Spandau, accompanied only by his guards. He died at the age of ninety-three, on August 17, 1987. Some reports claimed that he hanged himself with an electrical cord. In an era of rising neo-Nazism Hess became a martyr, and sympathizers turned his Bavarian home into a shrine for their movement. ***See also*** Hess flight, *Mein Kampf*, Vol. 1; Nuremberg trials, Spandau Prison, Vol. 2;

International Military Tribunal, The Charges Against the Surviving Nazi Leaders, Vol. 4.

Heydrich, Reinhard (1904–1942)

Chief of the Reich Central Security Office (RSHA) and the number two official in the SS. Heydrich, in appearance and demeanor a prototypical Aryan "blond beast," was the chief architect of the Nazis' decision to solve the "Jewish Question" through mass extermination. Top Nazis also considered him a possible successor to Adolf Hitler as Führer of the Third Reich.

Reinhard Heydrich was born on March 7, 1904, in the town of Halle in Saxony, central Germany. His father was a musician who founded the Halle Conservatory; local records suggested he may have been born Jewish, although this was never conclusively proven during the period of Heydrich's greatest notoriety. Too young for service during World War I, Heydrich joined a Freikorps unit in 1919 and became active in extreme nationalist circles. He joined the German navy in March 1922 as a junior officer based in Kiel. One of his mentors in naval intelligence work was Wilhelm Canaris, later Heydrich's rival in the Third Reich's intelligence-gathering circles. Handsome, charming, cultivated, and a bit of a womanizer, Heydrich was court-martialed by the navy in 1931 for seducing the daughter of a Kiel shipyard director and forced to resign his commission. Soon after he joined the Nazi Party and the nascent SS.

In these years the SS was a small force of bodyguards under the authority of the much larger SA. Its chief, Heinrich Himmler, however, had grand ambitions, and one of his goals was to attract men like Heydrich who were young, well educated, and cultivated and who fit the Aryan physical ideal. The blue-eyed Heydrich was tall, slim, and blond. Moreover, he was both athletic— an accomplished swordsman, rider, and pilot —and artistic, a violinist who loved Mozart and Haydn. He also had an officer's background in intelligence work. Heydrich came quickly to Himmler's attention, and by December 1931 was named an SS major. In July 1932 he was promoted to colonel and the chief of the security service (SD) of the SS. The promotions continued to come quickly as Himmler and Heydrich in tandem worked to take control of the various police units in the state of Bavaria. Heydrich became an SS brigadier general in March 1933 and, after he had played a key role in the Blood Purge of June 1934, lieutenant general. By this time he was unquestionably Himmler's chief protégé and the number two man in the SS.

During the mid-1930s Heydrich built the SD into an important, nationwide intelligence-gathering network, seeking young, university graduates to staff it. By nature suspicious, he compiled dossiers on hundreds of high-ranking Nazi officials as well as on so-called enemies of the Reich. In 1936, Heydrich was able to combine his intelligence and security work with police work when he was named head of the Berlin Gestapo as well as the commander of the national Security Police (Sipo). From these leadership positions he became one of the major operatives of the Third Reich's terror state, proving merciless in the arrest and interrogation of political enemies, criminals, and rivals. He was also not averse to using blackmail or cultivating scandals to do the dirty work of the Nazi regime. He played a major part, for instance, in devising the personal and sexual scandals that helped force the resignations of Generals Werner von Blomberg and Werner Freiherr von Fritsch, once Hitler and Hermann Göring decided that was what they wanted, and he was also a key organizer of the Gleiwitz raid, which on August 31, 1939, provided the Nazis with a pretext for the invasion of Poland.

Like many other top Nazis, Heydrich has been the target of a great deal of interest from commentators and historians. Many suspected that the source of his ruthlessness and brutality was a deep-seated insecurity at least partly derived from the constant accusations by other Nazis that he was half-Jewish. He overcompensated, many believed, by being the perfect technician of terror as well as an assertive, authoritarian administrator. Himmler and Hitler, for their part, may have believed that suspicions about Heydrich's background kept him enthusiastically loyal to the Nazi regime and his superiors. Moreover, he was the only top Nazi who truly fit the Aryan physical ideal about which ideologists so often spoke and wrote. Neither Göring, nor Goebbels, nor Hans Frank, nor Hitler or Himmler themselves came close to personifying this ideal. Regardless of the origins of his cruelty and inhumanity, or his absolute lack of moral scruple, Heydrich proved to be the perfect front man for the Third Reich. He was not particularly interested in Nazi ideas or, as such, in Nazi racial and territorial plans. Instead, his goal was the exercise and expansion of power.

Heydrich's opportunities to exercise power grew markedly in 1939, when he was named head of the new Reich Central Security Office (RSHA). The RSHA was an SS organization in which all police and security functions were combined. Although Himmler was still his superior, and Heydrich remained fawningly obsequious and obedient toward him, the younger man now had direct supervision over all police and security functions within both the German Reich and, as World War II commenced, the territories occupied by Germany. One of the main responsibilities of the RSHA was addressing what SS functionaries referred to as the "Jewish Question." Heydrich had begun to take interest in the issue in 1938, seeing it as an opportunity to expand SS jurisdiction. That year, for instance, he asked a young Austrian SD functionary named Adolf Eichmann to return to Vienna to open an SS Office for Jewish Emigration. The operation proved so successful in both facilitating Jewish emigration and making money for the SS (since Jewish property was often bought at low prices or confiscated outright from those trying to escape an increasingly uncertain future) that Heydrich opened a similar office in Berlin. He was also an organizer of the Kristallnacht pogrom of November 1938. After Germany conquered and partitioned Poland in the fall of 1939, it was Heydrich who took the initiative to order the concentration of Poland's huge Jewish population in ghettos. It was also Heydrich's idea to govern the ghettos through Jewish Councils made up of local dignitaries, thus forcing the Jews to take an active part in their own oppression. Meanwhile, RSHA functionaries performed much of the dirty work of rounding up Polish Jews, as well as uncooperative Polish Catholics, and introducing totalitarian terror into Poland. Through his various actions in occupied Poland, Heydrich made it clear to the top leadership in Berlin that he was the man to develop and implement the "Final Solution to the Jewish Question."

On July 31, 1941, after Heydrich spent the first weeks of the German invasion of the Soviet Union flying with the Luftwaffe, he received a directive from Hermann Göring. It authorized him to seek a "complete solution of the Jewish Question in those territories . . . under German occupation" (Shirer, 1960). Göring's letter also used the phrase "final solution." Heydrich, however, was already ahead of him. As part of SS preparations for their role in the Soviet invasion, Himmler had authorized Heydrich to organize special task forces, or Einsatzgruppen, earlier versions of which the SS had used in both Poland and Czechoslovakia. These new Einsatzgruppen, made up of volunteers from various SS police and militarized units, were charged at first with fairly straightforward wartime tasks: rounding up anti-German partisans, fomenting anticommunist rebellion among local peoples, and plundering archives and records offices. According to some accounts, however, Heydrich gave the task forces verbal orders to simply massacre Jewish populations. Between June 1941 and

January 1942 they killed an estimated 1.5 million Soviet Jews by gunfire. Thanks to the work of Heydrich's Einsatzgruppen, massacre came to be accepted as the "Final Solution to the Jewish Question."

In September 1941, Heydrich received a new posting in addition to his others. He was named chief protector of Bohemia and Moravia, meaning a sort of colonial governor over much of what had been Czechoslovakia. Although his time in Prague, the capital, was brief, Heydrich tried to govern the protectorate with a combination of ruthlessness, directed at those who opposed the Nazi occupation, and relative kindness toward the ordinary population in the cynical hope that he would win them over. Meanwhile, he continued to play a key role in the development of the Final Solution: the gassing of Europe's Jews in dedicated extermination camps. In late November 1941 Heydrich invited a number of Nazi bureaucrats to an important conference to be held at a villa in the Berlin suburb of Wannsee. The conference, scheduled for early December, had to be postponed while Nazi leaders digested the entry of the United States into World War II after December 7. It finally took place on January 20, 1942. At the Wannsee Conference, Heydrich informed the relevant functionaries the "Jewish Question" was to be solved through mass extermination, and that the SS would play the central role in implementing and managing the operation. Accompanying him in Wannsee were his protégé Eichmann, now a Gestapo "Jewish expert" in charge of logistics and transportation, and Heinrich Müller, top man in the Gestapo. One of the clear messages of the Wannsee Conference, to those who were there, was that Reinhard Heydrich had found yet another way to increase his importance among the Nazi hierarchy. The murder of Poland's Jews, meanwhile, was code-named Operation Reinhard in recognition of Heydrich's decisive role in the implementation of the extermination plan.

On May 27, 1942, Heydrich, who rode overconfidently around Czechoslovakia in an open car, alone, was ambushed. The attackers were Czech nationalists who were trained in London and parachuted in. Several opened fire on Heydrich's car while another man threw a grenade underneath it. Heydrich was badly wounded and died of his wounds on June 4. He was the only leading Nazi ever successfully assassinated. Heydrich was honored at his funeral by Hitler, Himmler, and his old rival Canaris; meanwhile, Nazi vengeance for the assassination was vast and savage. Over one thousand Czechs were killed in reprisal and an entire village, Lidice, was liquidated even though its inhabitants had nothing to do with Heydrich's death. In addition, several thousand Jews from the nearby camp at Theresienstadt were taken to their deaths in Poland. In his speech at Heydrich's funeral Hitler referred to him, with much justification, as "the man with the iron heart" (Schellenberg, 2000). *See also* Final Solution, Vol. 1; RSHA, SD, Wannsee Conference, Vol. 2; The Wannsee Conference Protocols, Vol. 4.

Himmler, Heinrich (1900–1945)

Reichsführer-SS and for all intents the second most powerful man in the Third Reich after 1938. As chief of all SS operations, including the Gestapo and the militarized Waffen-SS, and as Nazi interior minister from 1943 to 1945, Himmler was a key figure in the maintenance of the Nazi terror state as well as in German military operations. Himmler's racial doctrines and policies were also, arguably, the major force behind the mass extermination of European Jews during World War II.

Heinrich Himmler was born in Munich on October 7, 1900. His background was petit bourgeois, or lower middle class, his father a high school teacher and devout Roman Catholic who had worked for a time as a tutor to the Bavarian royal family. Educated at a high school in the Munich suburb of Landshut, Himmler volunteered for the Bavarian infantry, but he never saw action during World War I. After the war he studied agriculture at a technical college in Munich, and he retained a special interest in agricultural practices even as one of the most powerful men in Nazi Germany. After graduation in 1922 he worked briefly for a fertilizer manufacturer before joining the Nazi Party. Recognizing the educated young man's ambition and abilities, Adolf Hitler made him the business manager of the Nazi Party in Bavaria. He took part in the Beer Hall Putsch of November 1923 as standard-bearer to Ernst Röhm. Afterward he served as an aide to Gregor Strasser, as well as his deputy district leader in Bavaria. Himmler became acting Gauleiter of Lower Bavaria in 1925 and of Upper Bavaria in 1926. He also served as acting propaganda officer.

In 1927 Himmler left the party briefly after marrying Margarete Boden, the daughter of a Prussian landowner who was seven years older than he. He tried his hand as a chicken farmer but proved unsuccessful and returned to the Nazi Party in 1929. Hitler named him the head of a small unit of personal bodyguards known as the Schutzstaffel, or SS. The group was also known as The Black Corps because of its uniforms which sported a lightning bolt insignia.

When Himmler took over the leadership of the SS, which was under the nominal control of the SA, the organization contained only three hundred men. This was a sufficient base, however, for Himmler's ambitions to play a major role in the development of the Nazi state. Himmler proved to be a brilliant political insider, steadily expanding SS jurisdiction over wide areas of German life and consistently outmaneuvering his rivals. Hitler simply considered Himmler's expanding power and authority an example of the leadership principle at work; since Himmler kept winning out over others, he was superior to others, according to Hitler logic, and therefore deserved to grow into a leadership role. As long as the SS remained loyal to the Führer personally and to the Nazi state, Hitler was perfectly happy to see Himmler take on much of the dirty work of terror and totalitarianism.

Himmler's initial goal was to make the SS independent of the SA. To that end he took an elitist approach to recruitment and orientation, in marked contrast to the SA, which accepted all comers. Himmler wanted young university graduates as well as the scions of upper-middle-class, aristocratic, and military families. He set strict guidelines for health, appearance, and background, among other things requiring SS recruits to demonstrate purely Aryan genealogy at least two hundred years back. He also put SS men through rather stringent training in both ideology and obedience. One result was that the SS proved to be a much more streamlined force than the SA, more efficient and much better disciplined. By 1933 its membership had risen to over fifty thousand. Meanwhile, with the assistance of a young protégé, Reinhard Heydrich, Himmler organized a section within the SS known as the SD (Sicherheitsdienst) in 1931. The SD was an intelligence-gathering and security unit; through its offices Himmler and Heydrich compiled dossiers on almost every other top Nazi. Its initial target, however, was Ernst Röhm, Himmler's mentor from the early days of the Nazi struggle who was now the head of the SA.

The turning points for the SS, and for Himmler's role in the Third Reich, came in 1933 and 1934. With Heydrich's help Himmler became the most powerful Nazi official in Bavaria, named Munich police president as well as commander of the secret political police throughout Bavaria in the early months of 1933. In that capacity he established the first true concentration camp, Dachau, near Munich, and staffed it with SS men. By September he was commander of all political police outside the state of Prussia, where Hermann Göring held sway and where the local political police were known as the Gestapo. Outmaneuvering Göring, Himmler was appointed head of the Gestapo in Prussia in April 1934. Soon he combined the force with others throughout Germany, making him Gestapo chief throughout the Third Reich. Meanwhile, Himmler played a major role in the planning and execution of the Blood Purge of June 30, 1934. He prepared a list of enemies of the state targeted for arrest and killing, and SS men carried out most of the murders. Among those killed were Ernst Röhm and Gregor Strasser, potential challengers to Hitler. Soon after, Hitler declared the SS to be an organization independent of SA authority, and it effectively replaced the soon to be moribund SA as the strongest paramilitary wing of the Nazi Pary. Himmler's star continued to rise.

On June 17, 1936, Hitler gave him the title of Reichsführer-SS and control of all police functions within the Third Reich. This included not only the secret state police, or Gestapo, but also the Criminal Police (Kripo), the Security Police (Sipo), and the Order Police (Orpo). Himmler also controlled the growing concentration camp network, staffed with guards now known as members of the Death's Head–SS as well as the militarized bodyguard units under Sepp Dietrich known as the Leibstandarte-SS. This impressive list of responsibilities made Himmler the key figure in the terror state that in those years was infiltrating every corner of German life.

Beginning in 1937 or 1938, Himmler began paying serious attention to racial

Heinrich Himmler inspects an inmate at the Dachau concentration camp. As head of the vast SS, which administered the Nazi extermination camps, Himmler played an integral role in the Nazi plan to murder the Jews of Europe.

ideology and its practical applications. The concentration camps, for instance, which had previously held mostly political prisoners, now became destinations for those determined to be racially unsuitable for "membership" in the German nation. At first Himmler focused his attention not on Jews and Gypsies but on those known as "asocials," who found themselves sent to concentration camps for "rehabilitation." Meanwhile, Himmler also supported attempts to ensure that the future German Reich would be as racially pure as possible, such as the Nuremberg Laws, which, since the SS controlled all police functions, it was his duty to enforce. Himmler was also an enthusiastic eugenicist, reflecting his agricultural background. He believed that a better German could be bred, just like better chickens or pigs could be bred in the barnyard. To accomplish this, on the one hand, eugenicists weeded out those determined to carry some sort of unfortunate "genetic" condition by sterilizing them. On the other hand, and this is where Himmler was most active, healthy and racially pure Germans were encouraged to have large numbers of children. To Himmler's mind, since SS men were the cream of the German race, SS men should father a disproportionate number of children, thus raising the quality and cultural level of the race. SS men who wanted to marry, for example, had to prove that their future brides were as racially pure as they were by obtaining the appropriate certificate from the SS Race and Resettlement Office. As World War II approached, Himmler even proposed that SS men be allowed to take second wives and established Lebensborn, or Fountain of Life, homes, where the children of SS men, legitimate or illegitimate, and their mothers could be cared for at SS expense. Himmler himself had several illegitimate children, although he was hardly the ideal German in appearance, and volunteered to be godfather to all Lebensborn infants. His obsessions with racial purity and human breeding were to be applied, with far more brutal results, in eastern Europe during World War II.

Beyond his growing racial concerns, and his use of the SS to deal with racial matters, Himmler had a broad interest in the occult and in naturopathic medicine, interests which some traced to his wife's influence. His personal preoccupations with such matters inspired other top Nazis to label him a crank. Himmler saw himself, for instance, as the reincarnation of an ancient Germanic king, Henry the Fowler of pre-Christian Saxony, a man who led a terrifying drive to the east to root out Slavic populations. He thought the SS, moreover, constituted the modern version of the medieval Order of Teutonic Knights, which likewise engaged in a drive to the east. Himmler maintained a medieval castle at Wewensburg, where he presided over meetings of SS officials in a vast chamber containing a round table in the effort to connect with this glorious, partly mythical past. In addition Himmler organized the Ancestral Hertiage Research Office to find connections between the Nazi movement and ancient Nordic writing, ritual, and agricultural practices. The SS chief also saw spiritual significance in rural life, again reflecting, perhaps, his agricultural training and interests. He believed that peasants were the "blood spring" of the German race and therefore needed to be nurtured and protected. One reason for the renewed Drive to the East which the Third Reich was to begin in 1938 was to gain more land for German peasants, so that this "blood spring" might flow more fully and freely.

Himmler's authority expanded still further in 1938, as did his obsessions with race. He saw the annexation of Austria as an opportunity to expand SS jurisdiction by providing much of the occupation administration and authority, a pattern that was to continue throughout the occupations of eastern European territories and, to a lesser extent, western Europe. Like Hitler, Himmler was perfectly happy to give his underlings free rein provided they were loyal, consistent, and successful, and one young SS officer, Adolf Eichmann, greatly helped to increase SS interest in the "Jewish Question" by filling an administrative vacuum in Vienna with the new SS Office for Jewish Emigration. Indeed, after Eichmann's success in facilitating the departure of German and Austrian Jews from the Reich, as well as the Kristallnacht pogrom of November 1938, the SS became the key Nazi Party organization in devising policies to address the "Jewish Question." Since the SS was, fundamentally, a police organization with growing administrative responsibilities, the SS saw the "Jewish Question" as a police and administrative problem, requiring practical solutions rather than the random and disorderly anti-Semitism of Kristallnacht.

The beginning of World War II saw Himmler's responsibilities expand even further. By now he had established the Waffen-SS, a huge militarized contingent which was to fight alongside the regular German army, the Wehrmacht. The Waffen-SS was to play a large role in the conquests of western Europe and in the invasion of the Soviet Union in June 1941. Himmler, for his part, saw the Waffen-SS as not only a sort of private SS army but as a way to spread the Nazi racial ideal. He formed units of the Waffen-SS from foreign volunteers judged to be sufficiently "Aryan." Meanwhile, Hitler appointed him, in October 1939, Reich Commissar for the Strengthening of Ethnic Germandom, with responsibility for overseeing the transformation of the population of eastern Europe. The process began in occupied Poland but soon spread to the Soviet Union and other territories, where Himmler asserted himself as the most powerful Nazi authority, challenging party officials such as Hans Frank and Alfred Rosenberg. In its simplest form, Himmler's task was to move Germans into these new territories while either subduing or eliminating the local peoples. Hundreds of thousands of ethnic Germans from across eastern Europe, as well as a few settlers from the German Reich itself, were brought into the territories designated to be parts of the future Greater German Reich. Local people were sometimes protected by becoming "Germanized," which meant passing through a series of tests and physical examinations that varied widely but which might establish someone legally as "German" rather than, say, Czech or Polish. Slavs, which meant in reality Russians or Poles, were to be turned into slave laborers, and no great trouble was to be taken to keep them alive or encourage them to have children. Slavic culture, moreover, was to be destroyed by eliminating the local intelligentsia and dismantling cultural and educational institutions. These measures were quite consistent with Himmler's racial obsessions as well as his desire to install the SS as a sort of new aristocracy in occupied eastern Europe.

With regard to the 8 million Jews who lived in Poland and the western areas of the Soviet Union, Himmler's original notion was to find some way to remove them from the Greater German Reich through emigration, forced or otherwise. Groups of Jews, in fact, were able to leave Germany and the occupied territories almost until the onset of war between Germany and the Soviet Union. The necessities of war, however, made the emigration of Jews impractical, and the SS began to move in the direction of mass murder. Himmler himself seemed to set the tone with apocalyptic speeches he began making in 1940 and 1941, and in early 1941 he made the decision to use gas chambers to kill "excess" prisoners in the German concentration camps. When, under the leadership of Reinhard Heydrich, now Himmler's number two man, special units of SS men began the murder by gunfire of Jews in the occupied areas of the Soviet Union, Himmler accepted the policy as a matter of course. He even made flying visits to some of these Einsatzgruppen, as the special SS task forces were known, reminding them that heartless cruelty toward non-Germans was necessary. When shown an actual shooting action, however, Himmler proved to be somewhat squeamish, becoming, according to his adjutant, SS general Karl Wolff, green in the face and sick to the stomach. Soon after Himmler certainly had a hand in the decision to find, as he put it, a more "humane" way of killing, namely through gas chambers. As it happened, the program to build extermination centers in and around occupied Poland, to massacre first Poland's ghettoized Jews and then Jews brought in from across Europe, and to use a small number of Jews as slave laborers in attached camps was an SS operation approved and sponsored by Himmler. The camps also gave him the opportunity to perform medical experiments using Jews, Slavs, and prisoners of war as guinea pigs. These experiments too were consistent with Himmler's racial and eugenicist obsessions.

Himmler, like many other top Nazis, represented a paradox to many outside observers as well as later historians. He certainly looked like neither an architect of police terror or a racial mass murderer, resembling instead a benign mail clerk or a schoolteacher with his owl eyeglasses and well-groomed mustache. By all accounts he maintained a pleasant, soft-spoken demeanor and demonstrated good manners. Unlike Hermann Göring or Joachim von Ribbentrop, he did not live ostentatiously, nor did he seek to enrich himself personally through theft or plunder (although the SS in general was guilty of huge amounts of both). A British visitor, in fact, once referred to Himmler as the most "normal" man one could imagine. Nevertheless, he remained a racial fanatic and an occultist crank, as well as an effective political infighter. He appeared impassive but frequently suffered from severe headaches and stomach problems, and was a hypochondriac, imagining further ills. He was a cold, efficient bureaucrat of mass terror and death, ruthlessly committed to the Third Reich's racial and territorial goals.

Himmler probably reached the peak of his power in 1943. By that time the extermination and resettlement programs in eastern Europe were well under way. The Waffen-SS had risen to rival the Wehrmacht in size and was in the process of integrating the populations of the occupied areas, when it was not helping to exterminate or enslave them. In the occupied countries the SS played the dominant role, having asserted themselves more definitively than either Nazi Party or military officials and, particularly in eastern Europe, having amassed a huge economic empire. Many of the most powerful officials in the Third Reich—Heinrich Müller, head of the Gestapo; Arthur Nebe, chief of the Criminal Police; Ernst Kaltenbrunner, chief of the Reich Central Security Office after Heydrich's assassination; and Eichmann, the chief logician of the Holocaust—were Himmler's underlings. Himmler himself, meanwhile, continued to assume new responsibilities and honors. In August 1943 he replaced Wilhelm Frick as the minister of the interior, thereby gaining control over German courts and government workers. In the same year Hitler named him the leader of the National Socialist Party. After the July 1944 Plot Hitler even gave him a prominent role in the Wehrmacht as commander in chief of the Reserve Army as well as leader of Army Group Center on the eastern front.

Toward the end of 1944 Himmler began to suspect that the German war effort was hopeless, and he began to prepare himself for, in effect, life after Hitler. He ordered that the gassing of Jews at Auschwitz, the last remaining death camp, be stopped and even that Jews be allowed to receive charitable aid from neutral Sweden. He also sent peace feelers, without Hitler's knowledge, to the Allies via Swedish Red Cross diplomat Count Folke Bernadotte. Apparently hoping that the Allies might consider him a possible postwar German leader, he proposed to surrender German forces to General Dwight D. Eisenhower, the supreme commander of Allied forces in the west, but keep on fighting on the eastern front. Himmler seems not to have understood that there was no possibility Eisenhower would take him seriously. He even wondered whether he might become the head of a Nazi government based in northern Germany that would fight alongside the western Allies. Hitler, learning of Himmler's moves, furiously dismissed Himmler from all of his party posts, accused him of treason, and ordered him arrested.

At the end of the war Himmler made his way to Flensburg in northern Germany, where Hitler's successor, Admiral Karl Dönitz, had set up a rump government. Dönitz, however, wanted nothing to do with the SS chief, who was high on the list of Allied war criminals. On May 21, unsuccessfully disguised as a Gestapo agent, he was arrested by British forces near Bremen, and the British quickly discovered his identity. During a medical examination on May 23, 1945, Himmler killed himself by biting down on a capsule of poison he had hidden in his gums. British medical personnel tried to save him by pumping his stomach, but their efforts proved useless. Like Hitler, Heinrich Himmler managed through death to avoid a reckoning at the hands of his victims and opponents. *See also* Ancestral Heritage Research Office, Final Solution, Lebensborn, Vol. 1; SD, SS, Vol. 2; Himmler, Himmler Claims His Legacy, Vol. 4.

Hindenburg, Oskar von (1883–1960)

Son of President Paul von Hindenburg who worked as a military and political adviser to his father in the months prior to the Nazi seizure of power. Oskar von Hindenburg was born on January 31, 1883, and, like his father, served in the traditional German officer corps. After Paul von Hindenburg was elected president of Weimar Germany in 1925, his son became an informal liaison between the president's office and the army. As the years passed, the already aged president grew to rely on his son more and more for political advice, and Oskar was involved in the 1932 intrigues among Franz von Papen, Kurt von Schleicher, Alfred Hugenberg, and others which eventually resulted in the president's accepting Hitler as chancellor.

According to some accounts, Oskar von Hindenburg was vulnerable to political blackmail because he had engaged in various forms of tax evasion over the transfers of land in East Prussia. Specifically, some suspected that Oskar was guilty of having land that was intended for his father recorded in his name instead in order to avoid inheritance taxes. On January 22, 1933, Oskar met with Hitler in a secret interview. According to rumors Hitler let it be known that, unless Oskar convinced his father to accept him as chancellor, he would make the tax scandal public and work for President von Hindenburg's impeachment on those grounds. Allegedly, this was enough for Oskar to try to convince his father that a Hitler cabinet was acceptable. In any case, the president finally did appoint Hitler as chancellor on January 30. Perhaps in gratitude, or perhaps because of a deal made that January 22, the Hindenburg estates were enlarged substantially, and tax free, some months later.

After his father died in August 1934, Oskar von Hindenburg publicly supported Adolf Hitler's bid to combine the offices of chancellor and president, claiming that the president had always seen Hitler as his successor. Afterward he sank into obscurity and played no further role in the politics of the Third Reich. He died in Bad Harzburg in the Federal Republic of Germany on February 12, 1960. *See also* Eastern Assistance scandal, Vol. 1; Hindenburg, Paul von, Vol. 3.

Hindenburg, Paul von (1847–1934)

German war hero and last president of the Weimar Republic. Hindenburg had the misfortune, as a very old man trying to preserve order in his country, of finding himself forced to accept Adolf Hitler as chancellor of Germany.

(Left to right) Paul von Hindenburg, Kaiser Wilhelm II, and General Erich Ludendorff in a World War I staff meeting. In 1933, as president of the Weimar Republic, Hindenburg appointed Adolf Hitler chancellor of Germany.

Hindenburg was born in Posen, East Prussia, on October 2, 1847, to a respectable family of officers and aristocrats. He joined the Prussian army and served as an officer in the Austro-Prussian War of 1866 as well as the Franco-Prussian War of 1870, both conflicts that helped unify the Second German Reich. Afterward he continued his rise to greater positions of authority, finally retiring as full general and commander of the German Fourth Army in 1911.

His retirement was brief. In August 1914, after World War I began, he was recalled to take command of German forces on the eastern front. There, along with his chief of staff, Erich Ludendorff, he led a number of decisive victories over the Russians. He was promoted to general field marshal in November 1914, and subsequent victories on the eastern front made him the most popular figure in Germany, an old soldier known popularly but respectfully as the "Iron Hindenburg," an echo of the "Iron Chancellor" Otto von Bismarck. In August 1916 he was named supreme commander of German forces by Kaiser Wilhelm II and transferred to the western front. Although he prevented an invasion of Germany, he was unable to pursue attacks into France and, recognizing also the effects of the Allied naval blockade, he recommended that the kaiser abdicate his throne and Germany sue for peace. After leading the German withdrawal following the armistice of November 11, 1918, Hindenburg retired once again to his estates at Neudeck. Allied plans to try him as a war criminal never materialized.

In 1925 Hindenburg found his retirement cut short once again, but this time he was recalled to be a politician rather than a war leader. After Friedrich Ebert, the first president of the Weimar Republic, died in February 1925, elections were held to choose his replacement. Hindenburg agreed to be the candidate of a coalition of right-wing parties. In the runoff election, held in April, he defeated the center-left candidate, Wilhelm Marx, by only one-half million votes. Hindenburg's victory was a surprise not only in Germany but across Europe, where politicians expressed concern that Hindenburg might work to end the Weimar Republic and bring back the Prussian monarchy. The German electorate, though, had a great deal of respect for the old war hero and, acting according to his sense of duty rather than his traditional, monarchist sympathies, Hindenburg pledged to uphold the Weimar Constitution.

After the Great Depression hit Germany in 1929 and 1930, however, Hindenburg found it ever more difficult to uphold his duty, and he came under the influence of a group of political insiders and ambitious officers who hoped to create a more conservative regime, among them Franz von Papen, General Kurt von Schleicher, and his own son, Oskar von Hindenburg. The Weimar Constitution, in Article 48, gave the president the power to rule by decree in the event of an emergency, and Hindenburg was forced to evoke those powers again and again, since a ruling coalition could not be formed. In 1930 he appointed Heinrich Brüning, the leader of the Catholic Center Party, as chancellor. Brüning remained in office until June 1932, issuing decrees in Hindenburg's name while growing increasingly unpopular in the face of growing economic problems as well as increasing violence in the streets between Nazis and Communists.

Hindenburg was reelected president in the regular, seventh-year election held in early 1932. In the April runoff he received a majority of 53 percent of the vote; the remainder was split between Adolf Hitler and the Communist leader Ernst Thälmann. Again, in June, Hindenburg was convinced by his advisers to replace Brüning with the conservative politician Franz von Papen, who tried to staff his cabinet with traditional aristocrats and military officers. Meanwhile, Hindenburg still completely rejected the political ambitions of Nazi Party leader Adolf Hitler, whom he considered little more than an upstart corporal despite his party's popularity at the polls. When, as a result of elections held in July 1932, the Nazis became the largest party in Germany, Hindenburg found himself forced to consider Hitler as a possible cabinet member.

Meanwhile, Papen as well as Schleicher began to devise opposing plans that would allow them to take power while containing, they believed, the Nazis. Schleicher replaced Papen as chancellor, again on Hindenburg's appointment, early in December 1932, but he played his hand badly. He originally tried to construct an unrealistic coalition that stretched across Germany's political spectrum and which would involve Gregor Strasser, not Adolf Hitler, as Nazi leader. When that plan fell apart in January 1933 he proposed a military dictatorship. Hindenburg flatly refused the notion and deposed Schleicher on January 28. Instead, Hindenburg accepted a coalition urged upon him by Papen and Oskar von Hindenburg which would place Hitler in office as chancellor with Papen as vice-chancellor. Opinions vary as to the reasons Hindenburg was finally willing to accept the upstart "Bohemian corporal" as the leader of the German government (in the Weimar system the president was head of state). Some argue that he simply concluded that it was Germany's best hope to avoid street warfare and perhaps a Communist revolution. Others argue that he wanted to stop ruling by decree and instead give power back to the cabinet and Reichstag, believing, like Papen and others, that Hitler could be easily controlled. The least charitable assessment is that Hindenburg had simply grown too old and absentminded to be capable of careful decisions.

After Hitler took office Hindenburg remained president until his death on August 2, 1934, at the age of eighty-eight. He took less and less part in politics, however, choosing to remain instead at Neudeck. Hitler continued to tread lightly with regard to Hindenburg, particularly in hopes of cementing the support of the officer corps; thus he remained respectful toward the president despite his bold moves to destroy democracy and the rule of law. In any case, Hitler knew that in all likelihood the old war hero would not live long. He struck a deal with high-ranking officers in the spring of 1934, ensuring them that he would crush the "leftist" wing of the Nazi Party, led by SA chief Ernst Röhm, if they supported him in his bid to combine the offices of chancellor and president when Hindenburg died.

Hindenburg died at Neudeck on August 2, 1934. Soon after Hitler proclaimed himself the sole leader, or Führer, of the German Reich. Hindenburg was given a military burial with full honors at Tannenberg in East Prussia, where he had enjoyed a great victory over the Russians in 1914. His body was removed from its tomb, however, in 1944 as new Russian armies approached. American forces found it in an obscure vault in April 1945, along with the bodies of two other German heroes, Kaiser Frederick Wilhelm I and Frederick the Great. *See also* Machtergreifung, Pact of the *Deutschland*, Weimar Republic, Vol. 2; Papen, Papen Recounts Hitler's Takeover, Vol. 4.

Hitler, Adolf (1889–1945)

Dictator of the Third Reich and leader of the National Socialist German Workers' Party, or Nazi Party. Rising from obscure lower-class origins, Hitler became one of the great conquerors, as well as one of the great murderers, in world history.

Adolf Hitler was born in the Austrian village of Braunau am Inn, near Linz, on April 20, 1889. His father, Alois Hitler, was a minor customs official and his mother, Klara Poelzl Hitler, Alois's third wife, was twenty-three years younger than her husband. Alois was born under the name Schickelgruber but changed his name to a variation of his uncle's "Hiedler" in 1876. He and Klara had five children but only two, Adolf and a sister, Paula, survived to adulthood. Hitler had an unhappy, discontented childhood, compounded by his tendency to be moody and emotionally unstable. He adored his mother, who was a hard-working, tolerant, complacent woman who, Hitler remembered, spoke of him as her favorite child and indulged his needs, daydreaming, and mood changes. His father, in contrast, had settled into a bitter middle age, having endured the deaths of two wives and numerous children. Alois Hitler drank to excess and ran his household with authoritarian violence; he was known to whip his children and beat his wife. In addition to having to bring his drunken father home on a number of occasions, Hitler recalled that his father constantly embarrassed him and corrected him.

As a boy Hitler's education was uncertain and inconsistent. His mother hoped that he might enter the Roman Catholic Church, but he was expelled from a monastery school for smoking. After his father retired from the customs service and took up real estate speculation and farming, the family moved to a suburb of Linz, where Hitler continued his education. At first a strong student who insisted on being the leader during playground games, Hitler lost interest in his studies as he entered high school. His strongest subject was history, but he devoted little energy to performing well and, in later years, he had little good to say about his education, or about teachers in general. The one teacher he remembered fondly was Leopold Pötsch, a strong German nationalist who wanted German-speaking Austria to break away from the Hapsburg Empire and join Germany. Meanwhile, Hitler had also acquired a companion, August Kubizek, the closest the future Nazi leader ever came to having a boyhood friend. It was to Kubizek that he spoke of his dream to become a painter, a career that til his death in 1903 his father refused to consider.

In October 1907, Hitler moved to Vienna, where he lived a rootless existence. He left behind his mother, who was dying of cancer and supported only by her husband's small civil service pension. The young man's hope was to pursue artistic studies at the Vienna Academy of Fine Arts, but his application was rejected on the grounds that he lacked the proper high school diploma, contributing to his later hatred of educated people and the institutions they ran. Klara Hitler's death in December 1908 left him emotionally devastated, although his inherited pension allowed him to live reasonably comfortably in Vienna for some time. Although in his book *Mein Kampf*, as well as in informal discussions, Hitler remembered his years in Vienna as "five years of misery and woe," recent research suggests that he was not entirely unhappy there and that, contrary to his assertion that Vienna was where he first encountered the "Evil Jew," he often engaged in small business dealings with local Jews, preferring to sell them his copied sketches and posters because they paid him higher prices. After his mother's pension ran out, however, Hitler was destitute, surviving on charity and odd jobs and living in men's shelters.

Most historians agree with the assertion that Hitler began to absorb a sort of ideological German nationalism as well as ideological (as opposed to personal) anti-Semitism during his Vienna years. Among his major influences were Karl Lueger, the mayor of Vienna, who issued outspoken denunciations of the threat represented by what he perceived as Jewish high finance, and Georg Ritter von Schoenerer, a pan-German politician. Hitler also enthusiastically absorbed the ideas of Jörg Lanz von Liebenfels, a former monk who published a journal extolling the virtues of the white, Nordic peoples and the threats to them represented by inferior races. Suffused with ancient Germanic mythology and symbolism, Liebenfels's journal *Ostara* fascinated the young Hitler, who read every issue enthusiastically and discussed its ideas, or rather staged monologues, in Vienna's low-life café society and in his men's hostels. One symbol from *Ostara* which Hitler was to remember was the swastika. Stereotypical anti-Semitism as well as mystical racialism and German nationalism were formative influences, remaining with Hitler for the rest of his life and providing the basis for Nazi ideology. Meanwhile, Hitler also learned to despise communism and liberalism for their weakness, flabbiness, and internationalism.

In May 1913 Hitler moved from Vienna to Munich, the capital of the German state of Bavaria. According to some accounts, he left Austria in order to avoid military service, not because he was a pacifist or coward but because he did not want to fight for the multinational Austro-Hungarian Empire. In any case, after being recalled to Austria in early 1914 for military induction, his services were rejected on the grounds of physical weakness. After World War I began in August 1914, Hitler petitioned the Bavarian royal family and was permitted to join the 16th Bavarian Infantry Regiment. He served with great distinction in the war, fighting on the western front and as an orderly and messenger. He was gravely wounded in 1916 and again in 1918, spending several months in a military hospital recovering from an attack of poison gas. He received the Iron Cross, First Class, in 1918 for single-handedly capturing sixteen enemy soldiers; the decoration was rarely awarded to enlisted men. Like many of his generation, the war experience had a profound effect on Hitler's outlook. He learned of the power, and to his mind the necessity, of violence, and he came to believe that the camaraderie and sacrifice of men at war were spiritually preferable to the bland comfort of liberal, middle-class life.

Hitler chose to remain in the army after the war ended. He was embittered by Germany's defeat, by the growth of communism

Adolf Hitler (front row, far left) with his unit during World War I. Hitler, who served with distinction and was wounded during the war, was deeply embittered by Germany's defeat.

in Germany, and by the humiliation of the Treaty of Versailles, but he still lacked an outlet for his energies and beliefs. Assigned by Reichswehr authorities in Munich to provide them with information on the city's numerous right-wing political groups, Hitler went to a meeting of the so-called German Workers' Party in September 1919. Having grown convinced, especially after the signing of the Treaty of Versailles, that he should enter politics, Hitler decided to join the party. It was certainly nothing special, at this time little more than a drinking club of disaffected war veterans with random grievances against the Weimar Republic. But Hitler decided that the German Workers' Party was the appropriate outlet for his ambitions. He soon discovered, moreover, that he had a gift for oratory as well as for organization.

After leaving the army early in 1920 to devote his full-time energies to the party, Hitler emerged as its leader. Along with its founder, Anton Drexler, he formulated a list of twenty-five points representing the German Workers' Party credo. These included German nationalism, a denial of the possibility that Jews could ever be members of the German nation, and repudiation of the Treaty of Versailles. The codified Twenty-Five Points also addressed the dangers of high finance and big industry, preferring instead that large enterprises be nationalized and German workers be protected. To reflect these ideals, Hitler renamed the party the National Socialist German Workers'

Party, or Nazi Party (after the German pronunciation of the first two syllables of the word "National"). What he had in mind was, it appeared, a true national socialism as opposed to the international socialism that communism advocated. Only a purified German nation, in other words, could unite its people against the various "dangers" that Hitler, illogically, threw into the same pot: international Jewry, communism, liberalism, and big business.

Hitler also infused elements of edgy violence and militarism into the nascent Nazi movement, perhaps learning a trick or two from the Italian Fascist Benito Mussolini. He formed strong-arm squads of street thugs, dressed them in brown uniforms, and placed them under the authority of a freebooting Reichswehr officer and fellow traveler named Ernst Röhm. These units, formed initially to provide security at party meetings, were called storm troopers (SA), or more familiarly, Brownshirts. They were to play a major role in Hitler's rise to power. In addition, Hitler drew on his experience in Vienna and quasi-artistic instincts to create the Nazi symbolism that the world would come to know well: the swastika; the imperial eagle; red, white, and black banners and armbands; and the militaristic "Heil Hitler!" greeting. These strategies, along with Hitler's mesmerizing public speeches, drew increased attention to the Nazi Party and its membership rose markedly. Meanwhile Hitler, who could be extremely charming in the right circumstances, began to cultivate contacts among Munich's high society, which both facilitated fund raising and made him more respectable as a politician. These contacts, among other things, helped him acquire the *Völkischer Beobachter (People's Observer)*, the Nazi newspaper.

By 1923 the Nazi Party had thousands of members and enjoyed the support of a number of powerful people, most notably World War I hero General Erich Ludendorff. Hitler had refined his message and more clearly identified his enemies: Marxists, liberals such as the French and British, the "November criminals" who had "stabbed Germany in the back" by accepting the Treaty of Versailles, and the "Jew," the stereotypical scapegoat who stood for virtually anything Hitler disliked. Hitler now decided to make a strike for power, to start a revolution, while Germany suffered from massive inflation. With Ludendorff's help, he staged the ill-fated Beer Hall Putsch on November 9, 1923. Charging into a Munich beer hall where a political gathering was taking place, and surrounded by uniformed SA men, Hitler fired a pistol into the air, proclaimed the beginning of the National Socialist revolution, and tried to convince Munich's political and military leaders to join him. When they rejected him, he and Ludendorff, along with other Nazi notables such as Röhm, Hermann Göring, Rudolf Hess, and even a very young Heinrich Himmler, staged a march through Munich's streets, hoping to garner mass support. The putsch ended with a firefight at a police barricade, in which sixteen early Nazi martyrs were killed. Hitler was arrested and put on trial for high treason on February 26, 1924.

Defending himself rather than hiring a lawyer, Hitler took advantage of his trial to publicize the Nazi cause and foment his brand of German nationalism. Much of Germany paid attention, and the trial helped turn the Nazi leader into a national political figure, a man prepared to accept heavy sacrifices to defend Germany. The judges, apparently, were impressed as well; although Hitler was found guilty he was given the relatively light sentence of five years' imprisonment. In the end he spent only nine months in jail, enjoying a relatively comfortable imprisonment in Munich's Landsberg fortress. There he received frequent visitors and installed Hess, a loyal follower, in a next-door cell. The two of them concocted the first volume of *Mein Kampf (My Struggle)*, the bible of the Nazi movement. Published initially to slow sales in 1925, *Mein Kampf* became a best-seller as Hitler's star rose. By

1939 it had appeared in eleven languages and sold over 5 million copies, making Hitler a wealthy man. The book itself was a turgid, disorganized discussion of Nazi goals and ideas that few people actually read. It was a crude, Social Darwinist polemic that preached that races were involved in a struggle for existence; in this struggle power was all, above morality, justice, and humanity. Hitler and Hess went beyond this to explicate the ideas that were to form the basis for the Third Reich, begin World War II, and result in the deaths of millions of people. These included the notions that the German race was a master race at risk of weakening through race mixing; the need for Germany to acquire lebensraum, or living space, in eastern Europe; and the idea that Jews, racial aliens, did not belong in the Germanized Europe of the future.

After his release from prison in December 1924, Hitler was at a low ebb, the Nazi Party having been banned. Nevertheless, he returned to political activism with a new strategy. He no longer sought to take control of Germany through violent revolution; this would alienate the army, the aristocracy, and big business, and likely open the nation up to a Communist uprising. Hitler's new tack, which he pursued vigorously from 1925 to 1933, was to rise to power through legal means, to manipulate the Weimar Constitution by building a mass movement while fomenting violence and uncertainty through street warfare so that he could present himself as Germany's savior. In 1926 Hitler outmaneuvered his rivals for party leadership, notably Gregor Strasser, who led the northern, leftist wing of the party, and began to construct a nationwide network of political support. With the help of Göring, Hess, Himmler, and a relatively new recruit, propaganda master and maverick would-be intellectual Joseph Goebbels, the Nazi Party grew slowly but steadily during the late 1920s. In 1928 it won twelve seats in the Weimar Reichstag, the German parliament.

The turning point for Hitler and the Nazi Party came with the onset of the Great Depression in Germany in 1929. The vast unemployment and economic disarray devastated the middle classes, many of whom lost faith in the ability of the Weimar Republic to govern. Weimar politicians unfortunately adjusted to this loss of confidence by governing ineffectively. The coalition of center parties that had held the government together fell apart over economic policy, and Chancellor Heinrich Brüning, using powers granted by the Weimar Constitution, was forced to rule by decree. As the center dropped out of German politics more and more people gravitated toward the extremes: Nazism and communism. Hitler was well placed to take advantage of these circumstances, blaming the depression on Communists, Jews, and liberals while promising to restore Germany's greatness. In addition, he arranged with the nationalist media baron Alfred Hugenberg to publish articles critical of Weimar economic policies, thereby reaching a huge national audience. During this same era, and encouraged by businessmen such as Hugenberg and Fritz Thyssen, industrialists and financiers stepped up their support for Hitler, especially after he assured them that he was not, in fact, a Socialist, and opposed leftist institutions such as labor unions and the nationalization of industries. Many German conservatives came to believe that Hitler represented Germany's best hope against communism and socialism, despite his low-class origins and the political excesses of his followers.

Meanwhile Hitler also took his battle to the streets to build up a following among the German masses. The SA, now numbering in the millions and still led by Ernst Röhm, engaged in countless street battles with Communists and practiced politics through intimidation. It was sometimes joined by a smaller force, Himmler's streamlined SS. Though top politicians saw the SA as a threat to social order, and at one point

President Paul von Hindenburg banned it, Röhm's Brownshirts helped to ensure Hitler's mass following.

In the 1930 elections the Nazi Party received 6 million votes and 107 Reichstag seats, making it the second-largest party in Germany. In 1932, after finally acquiring German citizenship, Hitler ran for president of Germany, opposed in a runoff election by Hindenburg and Ernst Thälmann, the Communist Party candidate. He received well over 13 million votes in the runoff, although Hindenburg was returned to office with an absolute majority of 53 percent of the vote. Hitler's greatest electoral showing took place in elections held in July 1932, when the Nazis became the largest political party in Germany with 230 seats in the Reichstag. Although this was not enough to form a government without a coalition partner, and even though the Nazis suffered a setback in the next elections in November, Hitler now felt confident enough to demand the chancellor's office.

In these years Hitler stabilized his personal life as well. Thanks to the royalties from *Mein Kampf*, as well as the generosity of various benefactors, he established residences in both Munich and the Alpine border region between Bavaria and Austria known as the Obersalzburg. He chose not to marry, claiming that he was married to the Nazi movement but displaying little gift for personal relations in any case. The great love of his life, many argued, was a young, distant relative known as Geli Raubal, over whom Hitler exercised a rather possessive supervision until her suicide, for reasons that remained mysterious, in 1931. Afterward he took Eva Braun as his mistress, finally marrying her hours before their deaths in April 1945. Eva Braun was a former athlete, model, and photographer's assistant whom Hitler had met through Heinrich Hoffman, his official photographer. She proved to be both devoted to Hitler and undemanding, the perfect companion for a man preoccupied with, as he saw it, a great and frightening personal destiny. The exact nature of their relationship was never known; she never bore him any children and rarely appeared with him in public, usually pining away instead in the Obersalzburg. In other respects Hitler had few true acquaintances and no close friends. Potential friends, such as Hoffman or the wealthy Ernst Hanfstaengl, were distanced by personal ambition or alienation and, as noted, Hitler was a solitary brooder rather than a gregarious friend. In the right company, often among wealthy women, he could be charming. But among his entourage, according to their accounts, he was a bore, subjecting them to his endless lectures and commentaries on subjects ranging from racial doctrine to world history to Hollywood cinema.

Hitler finally became chancellor of Germany on January 30, 1933, in the aftermath of a complicated web of political intrigues. His rise to power was perfectly legal under the Weimar Constitution, and he had played almost to perfection his double game of cultivating Germany's traditional conservatives while fomenting mass support through propaganda and intimidation. After being denied the chancellor's office by Hindenburg, who had the authority of approving the appointment, Hitler intrigued with Hugenberg, now head of the German Nationalist People's Party, and Franz von Papen, a conservative politician, to undermine the government of General Kurt von Schleicher, a Hindenburg protégé. Schleicher failed to play his hand effectively, seeking to assemble a coalition that stretched across the political spectrum while splitting the Nazi Party by offering Gregor Strasser, not Hitler, the vice-chancellorship. Strasser refused Schleicher's flirtations and resigned from the party. In January 1933, when Schleicher proposed a military dictatorship, Hindenburg finally decided he had had enough and dismissed Schleicher. Soon after he accepted the Hitler-Papen-Hugenberg coalition, and Hitler, to the surprise of many, became head of the German government.

Papen, Hugenberg, and other conservatives believed that they could control Hitler, but in 1933 and 1934 he undermined them through a variety of political tricks, special measures, "enabling acts" that gave him dictatorial powers, and, when necessary, outright murder. In the process Hitler created a single-party totalitarian state, with himself as the unquestioned leader, or "Führer." The process began with the mysterious Reichstag fire of February 27, 1933. The Nazis blamed it on the Communists and took advantage of the crime to ban the still rather large German Communist Party, giving the Nazis an absolute majority in the shrunken Reichstag and making a coalition unnecessary. Soon after, the Nazi Reichstag gave Hitler special powers to act independently of the German government in reducing civil rights and targeting enemies of the state in the name of national security. Meanwhile, Nazi Party officials infiltrated the German civil service, police, and educational and cultural institutions while Jews, Social Democrats, and Communists were forced out. By the summer of 1933 the Nazi Party was the only party left, all others either having been banned or chosen to dissolve voluntarily.

In 1934 Hitler's main challenges were to secure the support of the traditional officer corps, which was still skeptical of the rule of this low-class World War I corporal from Austria, and to diminish the threat of a "second revolution" from the SA, where Röhm had leadership ambitions of his own. In the spring he arranged with top military officials to deal with Röhm as long as they, in return, supported his bid to combine the offices of chancellor and president upon the death of the aged and ailing Hindenburg. The officers agreed. On June 30, 1934, with the help of both the army and Himmler's SS, Hitler rid himself of Röhm while settling several other old scores with the so-called Blood Purge, an orgy of political murder. Röhm was killed along with Gregor Strasser, Schleicher, and perhaps one hundred others.

Hitler declared to a shocked Germany that these drastic measures were necessary to preserve social peace, and the army backed him up. After Hindenburg died that August, Hitler completed his consolidation of power by declaring himself the sole Führer of the Third German Reich. Meanwhile, the "coordination" of German life by Hitler's regime continued steadily, as the Führer and his underlings took control of almost every corner of German life from the courts to women's groups to education to culture and the arts.

Hitler remained, during these years, committed to the goals of racial purification and territorial expansion he had outlined in *Mein Kampf*. Beginning in 1935 he enjoyed a string of foreign policy successes that put the Third Reich, and the world, on the road to war while cementing his personal authority at home. In 1935, for instance, he repudiated the Treaty of Versailles by enlarging the German army, now known as the Wehrmacht, far beyond the treaty's restrictions and in 1936 marching it into the forbidden Rhineland. Also in 1936 he convinced the British to scrap the treaty's limitations on the German navy. He built up a modern air force, the Luftwaffe, and tested it during the Spanish Civil War. These rearmament measures, moreover, helped provide German workers with full employment while ensuring the support of finance and industry. Meanwhile Hitler pursued alliances with Benito Mussolini's Italy and with Japan. In late 1937 he announced his intention to revive Germany's medieval Drive to the East to top military and diplomatic officials; when some of them expressed reservations, he had them removed. In early 1938 Hitler cemented his control over the German armed forces, every member of which he already demanded swear a personal oath of loyalty to him, by removing sixteen top generals and declaring himself commander in chief of the new High Command of the German armed forces (OKW). Meanwhile, he impressed numerous foreign observers with the efficiency of his state, his apparently seamless popular support, and his restoration of Germany to a position of strength and power in the world.

Hitler had also suffused the Third Reich with the so-called Führer Principle and Führer cult. The first was the notion that effective leadership must come from the top down and must derive from a single individual. This single leader was the personification of the institution he led, and was responsible for both its successes and its failures; indeed, Hitler believed, the success and value of any institution, whether it was the local bicycle club, an infantry unit, or the Third Reich itself, depended on the

Hitler, with Himmler at his side, salutes passing SS troops during the Nazi Party Day ceremonies in Nuremberg in September 1938.

quality of its leader. The Führer cult, on the other hand, was the belief that spread among Germans that Hitler was somehow sent by destiny to redeem them, and many Germans actually came to worship Hitler as their savior. *Mein Kampf* could be found on almost every coffee table and Hitler's picture appeared everywhere. His birthday, April 20, became a national holiday as did January 30, the day he took power. German women by the dozens sent letters and proposals of marriage and motherhood to their "handsome Adolf," while schoolchildren swore oaths of loyalty. Hitler calmly accepted this adoration as both his due and the product of his terrible destiny, and even in his personal life cultivated his image as a man apart. He was a vegetarian who did not drink or smoke, and he indulged in a neurotic hypochondriasis, imagining ailments and surrounding himself with doctors and personal cooks.

Hitler's popularity probably reached its peak in 1938, when his revived Drive to the East enjoyed its first and almost bloodless successes with the Anschluss of Austria and the annexation of the Czech Sudetenland. Until that time most Germans, as well as the rest of the world, had blinded themselves to the dark sides of Hitler's totalitarian system and its racial obsessions: the concentration camps, the increasing anti-Semitic legislation, the persecution of the churches, the eugenic measures that resulted in perhaps one hundred thousand forced sterilizations. Hitler, indeed, managed to keep much of this activity out of public scrutiny until the Kristallnacht pogrom of November 1938 and his increasing war threats and saber rattling in 1939. Even when much of the world was convinced that he was a power-mad dictator when his forces invaded Poland on September 1, 1939, starting World War II, the majority of Germans continued to hold him in high esteem as, over the next two years, the Third Reich enjoyed success after success on the battlefield and Hitler became the master of almost the entire European continent. Poland was defeated in nineteen days, Denmark capitulated on the first day of the German attack, and Norway was beaten within two months. The Netherlands, Belgium, Luxembourg, and even France fell in six weeks in the late spring of 1940. Hitler's only military setback was the failure of the Luftwaffe to successfully clear the way for a German invasion of Great Britain, although this was mitigated by Hitler's belief that the British were not only racial allies but also, thanks to the global British Empire, world conquerors. He hoped the British would one day see the light and join him in his quest to reorder Europe racially and crush communism. With every success Hitler grew more and more confident in his destiny and his abilities, and by 1941 he was less willing than ever to accept the advice, much less the criticism, of others. Meanwhile, SS functionaries under Heinrich Himmler began to implement the darkest aspects of Hitler's racial obsessions in eastern Europe. Poland was partitioned, and millions of Polish Catholics and Jews were forced to move to make way for German settlers, the Jews to specially organized ghettos to await further plans.

As he himself saw it, Hitler's greatest personal challenge began on June 21, 1941, when the Third Reich launched its invasion of the Soviet Union. The war between the two, to Hitler's mind, was a war for racial supremacy as well as national survival. All his ideals and goals, from racial reorganization to the expansion of the German Reich to the destruction of communism, hinged on Germany's ability to defeat the Soviets. Either Germany would succeed in this task, Hitler claimed, or justifiably be destroyed. From the beginning, therefore, the war in the east carried apocalyptic overtones which were passed down from Hitler to his underlings in the SS and Nazi occupation authorities, and even to a certain degree to the regular German army. The SS, however, which had always enlisted the truest Nazi believers, in the east proclaimed itself willing to make the necessary personal "sacrifices" to accomplish Hitler's goals. The result was the Holocaust, the murder of 6 million Jews by gunfire and poison gas, as a matter of "national necessity." In addition the SS played a role in the attempt to transform the gentile populations of Poland and the western Soviet Union into docile slaves, both at home and within the German Reich. These measures continued even after it was apparent that the German war effort in the east was hopeless; Hitler in effect made the decision that his racial goals were more important than his military goals, to the distress of many top officers.

When German forces were stopped at Moscow in December 1941, when they failed to capture Leningrad, and when they were decimated at Stalingrad over the winter of 1942–1943, Hitler's cause in the east was lost. Meanwhile, he had neglected to pay sufficient attention to the American entrance into the war in December 1941, allowing the western Allies to enjoy a string of victories in North Africa and southern Italy. Hitler, to his detriment, saw military efforts in moral rather than strategic terms; if German forces lost, it was because they were badly led, weak, or insufficiently inspired, not because of poor weather, bad supply and communication lines, or the wrong strategy. By early 1943 the Führer, disgusted with most of the efforts of his top officers, took personal control of almost the entire German military effort. His will, however, could not make up for the Russian winter or the seemingly endless supply of Soviet reinforcements. Nor could it make up for the steady Allied bombing attacks that were destroying his armaments factories and transportation networks.

Hitler began his retreat from reality in 1943, accompanied by a steady decline in public appearances. His moodiness, observers reported, had reached extreme forms, and he was prone to fits of anger and hysteria as well as brooding. His health also began to suffer, perhaps partly from the strange ministrations of the quack doctor Theodor Morell, whom Hitler praised but whom Göring joked should be called "Herr Reich Injection Master" because of his tendency to inject the Führer with strange chemical concoctions. Hitler also began to grow increasingly paranoid, distancing himself even from Nazi Old Fighters such as Göring and Wilhelm Frick. As he retreated further and further into paranoid fantasy, management of the Third Reich fell more and more to his underlings, many of whom began to plot their own futures. Albert Speer, minister of armaments and war production, took almost complete control of the German economy while pondering an assassination attempt. Himmler continued to run his dark, murderous SS empire with great efficiency, but by the end of 1944 began pondering peace gestures toward the Allies. Of the old-line Nazis, only Goebbels remained fanatically loyal to Hitler and was rewarded with a number of new posts. Behind the scenes, however, the scheming Martin Bormann and a few others of Hitler's entourage provided the main contact between Hitler and his regime. The Führer himself remained interested only in strictly military leadership.

When he survived the July 20, 1944, attempt on his life, planned by conspirators mostly among the German officer corps, Hitler was once again reminded that he was a man of destiny, and his vengeance for the plot was vast and merciless. He took up the idea that it was not he but the people of Germany who had failed. In January 1945 he retreated, along with his entourage, to the Führerbunker, a vast concrete command center buried beneath the Reichs Chancellery in Berlin. He stayed there until his death on April 30. He intended to leave behind a destroyed continent. For virtually no strategic reason he allowed his forces to devastate the city of Warsaw before they left it, and only the actions of a few unwilling officers saved Paris from the same fate. In Germany, meanwhile, he ordered that what remained of the nation's industrial plant and communications and transport system be destroyed, measures that were already under way from Allied bombings. He, or more often Goebbels, exhorted the German people to superhuman efforts to revive the necessary fighting spirit and save their country, but few Germans could muster the necessary enthusiasm as the Third Reich crumbled around them and they counted their dead.

During his several months in the Führerbunker, Hitler continued his patterns of random orders; criticism of both German and foreign leaders; vague hopes that miracles in weaponry or diplomacy might save him; and endless monologues about race, history, and destiny. All but a few of his oldest comrades deserted him; he condemned both Göring and Himmler to death for alleged betrayals. Bormann and Goebbels remained with him, along with his personal servants, chefs, medical people, and SS guards, who were trained in unquestioning, blind obedience. By April, with Soviet artillery as well as Allied bombs shuddering around the bunker, he decided to kill himself. He staged a desultory birthday celebration on April 20 and then, on April 29, he married Eva Braun. Soon after he dictated his last will and political testament, predicting that Germany would once again rise from its ashes to take its place as the home of the master race, and that he would be remembered as a national hero. He named Grand Admiral Karl Dönitz his successor as head of state, and charged Bormann with delivering the documents to Dönitz. On April 30, while Eva Braun committed suicide by taking poison, Adolf Hitler killed himself with a gunshot to the mouth. According to his orders, SS guards then took their bodies up to the garden of the Reichs Chancellery, doused them with gasoline, and set them afire so that they would not be desecrated by the Soviets. Rumors persisted that Hitler survived, but evidence is clear that he was, indeed, dead on April 30, 1945. *See also* Beer Hall Putsch, Vol. 1; *Mein Kampf*, National Socialist German Workers' Party, Vol. 2; Dietrich, The Personality of the Führer; Hitler, Hitler's Last Will and Political Testament; Hitler, Hitler Implies a Future Jewish Holocaust, Vol. 4.

Hitler, Alois (1837–1903)

Adolf Hitler's father. Alois Hitler was born Alois Schickelgruber in the village of Strones in western Austria on June 7, 1837. His parents were not married, and he took the name of his mother, Anna Marie Schickelgruber, a peasant woman. His father was an itinerant worker named Johann Georg Hiedler, who finally married Anna Marie in 1842. They neglected, however, to register Alois as a now legitimate child, and he continued to be known by the name of Schickelgruber.

After working for a short time as a cobbler's apprentice during his teenage years, Alois Schickelgruber joined the local Austro-Hungarian government as a minor customs official. He remained there for his entire working life. His postings were in various towns in western Austria, including Braunau am Inn, where his son Adolf was born in 1889. While Alois took seriously the life of a minor bureaucrat, and succeeded in raising himself to the lower middle class, he was much less happy in his personal life. He married his first wife, Anna Glasl, in 1864. She was ill for most of their married years, and she died in 1883. Soon after her death Alois married Franziska Matzelberger, a woman who had already been his mistress for a number of years. In fact, the two of them had an illegitimate child of their own. After Franziska died in 1885 Alois married again. His third wife, Klara Poelzl, was a peasant girl who was Alois's second cousin; the couple had to obtain special permission from the local Roman Catholic bishop before they were married. Klara, Adolf Hitler's mother, was twenty-three years younger than Alois. Her grandfather was Johann Nepomuk Hiedler, Alois's uncle, who had mostly raised Alois as a boy. In 1887 Alois changed his name officially to Alois Hitler, a variant of Hiedler.

Adolf Hitler's father, Alois Hitler (left), and mother, Klara Poelzl Hitler (right). The Hitler household was marred by Alois's drunkenness and violence.

Therefore, the son who was born to Alois and Klara on April 20, 1889, was named Adolf Hitler.

Alois Hitler retired in 1895. He spent the next years trying to make money by buying and selling farms and by beekeeping, occupations that kept his young family on the move. He spent much of his free time drinking in local taverns, and young Adolf was forced more than once to retrieve his drunken father and bring him home. Alois Hitler was also a violent husband and father, and both Klara and Adolf suffered numerous beatings. Adolf, for his part, showed a stubborn streak early on and infuriated his father by asserting that he wanted to go into the arts and not follow Alois into a civil service career.

Alois Hitler died on January 3, 1903, in the village of Leonding. He left his wife and two children a small civil service pension. ***See also*** Hitler, Adolf; Hitler, Klara Poelzl, Vol. 3.

Hitler, Klara Poelzl (1860–1908)

Mother of Adolf Hitler. Klara Poelzl was born in the Spital region of Upper Austria on August 20, 1860. At the age of fifteen she went to live with Alois Hitler, a distant relative by marriage. After the death of his second wife Alois decided to take his young ward, Klara, as a third wife. She was already pregnant. The two married on January 7, 1885. The marriage resulted in five children but only two, Adolf, born in 1889, and Paula, born in 1895, survived to adulthood. Klara Hitler's married life was difficult; her husband was twenty-three years older than she and prone to drunkenness and violence. She adored young Adolf though, and the boy returned her adoration.

After Alois Hitler died in 1903, Klara moved with her two children to a suburb of Linz. There she tried to bring the children up on a small civil service pension. Adolf was no help. A brooding dreamer, he had rejected his mother's notion that he should go into the Roman Catholic Church as a monk and made it known that he planned to be an artist instead. Klara could not understand these ambitions, but she worked hard to support the young layabout. Klara Hitler died of cancer in Linz on December 21, 1908. Adolf Hitler, then living in Vienna, was crushed and hurried home for the funeral as well as to ensure the continuation of the pension money. *See also* Hitler, Adolf; Hitler, Alois, Vol. 3.

Hoffman, Heinrich (1885–1957)

The official photographer of the Nazi Party and of Adolf Hitler in particular, Hoffman was a member of Hitler's inner circle of companions and associates from the early days of Hitler's political career. Heinrich Hoffman was born in Fürth on September 12, 1885. His father was a professional photographer, and the young Heinrich expressed an interest in the field as a young boy helping out in his father's studio. During World War I he worked as a photographer with the German army, and in 1919 he published the first of many books, a photographic account of the political upheaval in postwar Bavaria.

Hoffman's familiarity with the political scene in Bavaria and its main city, Munich, led him to meet Hitler in 1920 or 1921. Hitler was then little more than an ambitious politician with single-minded determination and a gift for rabble-rousing, but Hoffman suspected that Hitler might become an important figure. Consequently he found a way into the Nazi leader's inner circle. Over the next years Hoffman provided Hitler with both a change of pace from the rough men who were attracted to the Nazi movement in its early days and an entrance into the more respectable, artistic culture of Munich. Hitler, for instance, became a frequent visitor to the Hoffman family house, where he could enjoy a relaxing, cultivated atmosphere. Moreover, Hoffman introduced Hitler to Winifred Wagner, the daughter-in-law of the composer Richard Wagner and the leading figure behind the annual Wagner festival in Bayreuth, a village near Munich. In later years Hoffman introduced Hitler to an attractive and athletic young woman named Eva Braun, who was working as an assistant in his photography shop. Braun later became Hitler's mistress and, for one day in 1945, his wife. Hoffman's daughter, meanwhile, married Baldur von Schirach, the Hitler Youth leader, although the marriage broke up in the late 1930s.

Hitler would not allow anyone but Hoffman to take his photograph, and Hoffman's pictures of Hitler proved to be one of the Nazi movement's most important propaganda tools. Hoffman depicted Hitler in a variety of poses and performing a variety of acts, and the photographer accompanied the Nazi leader everywhere he went. After 1933, when Hitler was the sole leader of Germany, these photos ranged from determined portraits to shots of a softer Hitler greeting children to pictures of the Führer engaged in such public works as breaking ground for Germany's autobahns, or highways. The standard procedure was for Hitler to personally review proofs before allowing Hoffman to release photographs to the public. In addition to the pictures of Hitler, Hoffman was the official photographer of numerous other aspects of German life under the Third Reich. His photos of the Hitler Youth invariably show young people happily and attractively engaged in outdoor activities, and his pictures of ordinary Germans often showed them enthusiastically working to support the Nazi regime while enjoying the benefits, such as the Strength Through Joy vacations, that the Nazis brought them. In the 1930s, under his own publishing imprint, Hoffman published a number of monographs, including *The Hitler Nobody Knows*, *Germany Awakened*, and *The Brown House*. He even produced a work of propaganda intended for German Americans entitled *See the Heart of Europe!* Hoffman's photographs indeed remain one of the most important records of life during the era of the Third Reich.

These publications, as well as other ventures, helped make Hoffman an extremely wealthy man. He received a portion of the royalties, for example, from published photographs as well as from the many postage stamps that depicted Adolf Hitler. Meanwhile, Hoffman proved to be a loyal Nazi Party member. He served from 1933 as a member of the rubber-stamp Reichstag and was promoted by Hitler personally to a position as professor of the arts. Hitler, for his part, greatly appreciated Hoffman's artistic tastes, which ran toward the comical and vulgar and somewhat lurid.

After the war Hoffman was tried as a war profiteer by the Federal Republic of Germany. He was sentenced to ten years' imprisonment and the loss of almost all of his personal fortune. After serving a reduced sentence of five years, Hoffman was released in 1952. He died in Munich on December 16, 1957. *See also* Braun, Eva; Hitler, Adolf, Vol. 3.

Horthy, Miklos (1868–1957)

Ruler of Hungary under the title of regent from 1920 to 1944. Horthy was born to a family of landed aristocrats in the town of Kenderes in 1868, and as a young man became an officer with the Austro-Hungarian navy. During World War I he proved to be an excellent commander, rising steadily until by the end of the war he was the commander in chief of the Hungarian battle fleet. At war's end, with the dissolution of the empire imminent, the Austrian emperor ordered him to turn over the fleet to the new Yugoslavian governing council. Horthy returned to Budapest, now the capital of independent Hungary, in 1919. He led a successful revolt against Communists who, under Bela Kun, tried to turn the nation into a Bolshevik republic. In March 1920 he named himself regent of Hungary and stayed in that position as a mild authoritarian leader until 1944.

During World War II Horthy was a hesitant ally of the Third Reich, sending forces to aid the German invasions of Yugoslavia in April 1941 and the Soviet Union in June 1941. His interests were mainly territorial, although as an anticommunist he was also unwilling to fight on the side of the Soviets. Hitler often complained that Horthy was uncooperative in military operations. Until 1944 Horthy was able to protect Hungary's population of seven hundred thousand Jews from Adolf Eichmann's deportations, but by the spring of that year Hitler had tired of Horthy's intransigence. He threatened to send in German occupation forces, and before long Eichmann was in Budapest, supervising deportations. The massacre of Hungarian Jews was the last large-scale killing operation of the Holocaust, although it must be mentioned that Horthy as well as a number of international representatives worked hard to save those Jews they could save.

In August 1944 after the collapse of Romania, another hesitant ally, Horthy began peace negotiations with the Allies. Furious, Hitler resorted to blackmail, sending the SS adventurer Otto Skorzeny to kidnap Horthy's son and take over the government. German forces soon occupied Budapest and installed the Hungarian Fascist group the Arrow Cross as a puppet regime for the rest of the war. Horthy, meanwhile, was taken to exile in Germany. He was liberated by American forces in May 1945 and served as a prosecution witness at the Nuremberg trials. Unable to return to Hungary because of the Soviet occupation and subsequent Communist takeover, Horthy entered exile in Portugal. He died there in 1957. *See also* allies of the Third Reich, Arrow Cross, collaboration, Vol. 1.

Höss, Rudolf (1900–1947)

The commandant of the Auschwitz extermination and labor camp complex in southern Poland from 1940 to 1943, and thereafter a deputy in the Reich Inspectorate of Concentration Camps. Rudolf Höss was born in

Baden-Baden in southwestern Germany on November 25, 1900. His background was lower-middle class and Catholic. His father operated a small store and both parents wanted Rudolf to enter the priesthood. After his father died in 1915, however, Rudolf ran away to join the German Imperial Army, where, despite his tender age, he fought with great distinction. At seventeen he was promoted to become the youngest noncommissioned officer in the army. He also won several decorations for bravery.

After World War I Höss continued to fight for right-wing causes as a member of the Rossbach Freikorps, one of the largest of the informal units seeking to protect Germany from communism. In 1923 he was sentenced to prison for his involvement in a political murder, the killing of a high school teacher named Walther Kadow. Kadow, allegedly, had betrayed the Nazi fighter Albert Leo Schlageter to French occupation authorities in western Germany. One of Höss's accomplices in the murder was Martin Bormann, who did not forget Höss's actions in later years.

Höss was released from prison after serving less than five years of a ten-year sentence, and from 1928 to 1934 he was a rural laborer. He joined the Nazi Party and the SS in 1934 and quickly found himself in an official position at Dachau, the first of the concentration camps. A devoted and efficient worker, Höss moved on to Sachsenhausen in 1938 and, in 1940, was promoted to SS captain. He became commandant at Auschwitz on May 1, 1940. At first the camp, located in a swampy area of German-occupied Poland, was designated a camp for eastern prisoners of war. By 1942, however, when top SS officials had decided on mass extermination as their "Final Solution to the Jewish Question," Höss's camp was chosen as one of the main killing centers, located conveniently near railway junctions to both Prague and Vienna.

Höss proved to be an enthusiastic and efficient bureaucratic killer, establishing a system at Auschwitz that was responsible for the deaths of between 1.1 and 2 million people. He was the first to use Zyklon B, a commercial pesticide, in the gas chambers, rather than carbon monoxide exhaust, claiming that it was a humane method of killing, far preferable to shooting and even other gassing methods. He even noted once that he found the gassing process calmed him. Moreover, one of the commandant's overriding concerns was cleanliness and hygiene, and Zyklon B, he found, killed as "cleanly" as he could have wished. SS high officials were so pleased by the operation of Auschwitz that it became, in effect, the model extermination center. Höss too was pleased by his record, noting later in his memoirs that following orders well was what he had been trained to do his entire life. He maintained a house outside the gates of Auschwitz, where according to reports he lived the normal life of a lower-middle-class husband and father.

In November 1943 Höss was kicked upstairs, given a top position with the SS Economic and Administrative Central Office, an agency that operated a number of slave labor centers within the Auschwitz complex. In early 1945, thanks to Bormann's intercession, he was named chief deputy to Richard Gluecks, head of the Inspectorate of Concentration Camps. In the first position he had frequent occasion to return to Auschwitz, where he could admire the system of killing he had had such an influence on. Indeed, the stepped-up operations of Auschwitz in the spring and summer of 1944, when four hundred thousand Hungarian Jews were killed in rapid order in specially renovated facilities, was named the Höss Action in his honor, and he returned to personally oversee the action.

Höss was arrested by British forces in northern Germany on March 2, 1946. He was extradited to Poland, where he was tried for war crimes by a Polish military tribunal. Condemned to death, Höss was hanged right outside his house near the gates of Auschwitz in early April 1947. *See also* Auschwitz, extermination camps, Höss Action, Vol. 1; Höss, A Report from the Auschwitz Commandant, Vol. 4.

Hossbach, Friedrich (1894–1980)

Army general during World War II and, as a junior officer, Adolf Hitler's military adjutant from 1934 to 1938. Hossbach was born in Unna in southern Germany on November 21, 1894, and joined the German Imperial Army just prior to the outbreak of World War I. He served as an officer on the eastern front during the war. Deciding to continue his military service after World War I, Hossbach joined the Weimar-era Reichswehr and was eventually appointed to the War Ministry. In 1934 he was promoted to major and took his post as Hitler's military adjutant. He also became head of the Central Section of the General Staff, an important political position within the Nazi-era Wehrmacht.

Hossbach is best remembered for his participation in an important meeting that took place at the Reichs Chancellery on November 5, 1937, of Hitler and top military leaders. The subject was the Führer's plans for German territorial expansion in Europe and the use of military force if necessary. At the meeting Hitler also made it known that he was prepared to go to war with Great Britain and France. Hossbach took careful minutes at the meeting, which became known as the Hossbach Conference when, at the post–World War II Nuremberg trials, the minutes, known as the Hossbach Memorandum or Hossbach Protocol, were used as evidence of Nazi war aims. The Hossbach Conference also precipitated a change in the nature of military leadership under the Third Reich. Both General Werner von Blomberg, minister of war, and General Werner Freiherr von Fritsch, commander in chief of the army, expressed reservations about Hitler's plans. In early 1938 both were forced to resign from their posts as a result of trumped-up personal scandals. Hossbach himself was fired from his adjutant's post when, contrary to Hitler's orders, he informed Fritsch of the impending scandal.

Hossbach was brought back into the General Staff in 1939, when war loomed. During the war years he served on the eastern front, promoted to lieutenant general in 1942 and general of infantry in 1943. In January 1945 he was promoted yet again to the position of commander of the Fourth Army but was soon after dismissed, again, for acting contrary to Hitler's orders and pulling back his troops from a dubious position. After the Nuremberg Trials, he retired to private life and died on September 10, 1980. *See also* Hossbach Conference, Vol. 1; The Hossbach Memorandum, Vol. 4.

Huber, Kurt (1893–1943)

Professor of philosophy and psychology at the University of Munich and member of the White Rose resistance movement. Huber was born in Switzerland on October 24, 1893. When he was a boy his family moved to southern Germany, and he attended the University of Munich, where he studied philosophy and music. He took a doctoral degree in 1917 and started teaching as a lecturer at the university, becoming a professor in 1926. Although he was interested in the German folk tradition, and tried to set up a department for research into folk songs, he came into conflict with the Nazis, presumably over the interpretation of the German past. Like many professors in Nazi Germany, however, Huber generally kept quiet his reservations about the Hitler regime. This changed in 1942 when he became associated with Hans Scholl, a young medical student and soldier who was the founder of the White Rose, the small group of principled student dissidents whose members included Sophie Scholl, Christoph Probst, and Alexander Morell. Huber encouraged the students in their resistance efforts, becoming a sort of mentor or faculty adviser. He also helped to compose their anti-Nazi leaflets and pamphlets. After the White Rose was exposed by Gestapo informants in February 1943, Huber was condemned to death by a special People's Court along with the Scholls and other members. He was executed by guillotine on July 13, 1943. *See also* White Rose, Vol. 2; Scholl, Hans and Scholl, Sophie, Vol. 3; Student Protest Leaflets: The White Rose, Vol. 4.

Hugenberg, Alfred (1865–1951)

A German media baron of extreme nationalist and expansionist sympathies who, as the head of the German Nationalist People's Party, played an important role in Adolf Hitler's rise to power. Alfred Hugenberg was born in Hanover on June 19, 1865. He was an ardent German nationalist from his youth, and in the 1890s he helped to found the Pan-German League. This organization was dedicated to uniting people defined as ethnic Germans in a larger German Reich, a goal later adopted by Hitler and the Nazis. In support of those efforts Hugenberg moved to East Prussia in 1894, where he attempted to buy up land from local Poles and sell it to resettled Germans. Meanwhile, Hugenberg became a successful businessman and financier, serving with the Prussian Finance Ministry in 1903 and, from 1909 to 1918, as chairman of the board of Krupp Works, one of Germany's largest industrial cartels. He also began to build up a media empire of his own, buying out three publishing houses, an advertising firm, and the controlling interest in UFA, Germany's largest film company. By the mid-1920s Hugenberg was recognized as Germany's leading media magnate. By some accounts he used his media power to influence German public opinion away from the liberalism and international orientation of the Weimar Republic.

Hugenberg also continued to be active in politics. He was elected to the Weimar Reichstag as a member of the German Nationalist People's Party as early as 1920, and he became the chairman of the party in October 1928. Hugenberg's main political supporters were conservatives in both agriculture and big business, although he began to alienate the latter by the early 1930s with his high-handedness. Hugenberg was one of the first national political leaders to realize that Hitler and the Nazis represented a powerful force in German politics. In 1929 his party combined with the Nazis to present a strong opposition to the Young Plan, which reorganized Germany's war reparations payments. In the process Hugenberg opened his media outlets to Nazi propaganda, helping thereby to spread the Nazi message to a wide public. Later, Hugenberg helped form the Harzburg Front, the first major attempt at a right-wing coalition in the Reichstag. It failed, however, when Hitler decided not to join it.

By 1932 the German Nationalist People's Party was dwarfed by both the Nazis and the Communists in terms of its electoral support, and Hugenberg grew increasingly convinced that an alliance with Hitler was necessary for the survival of his party and his right-wing agenda. Over the latter half of the year he entered into various negotiations with Hitler and other conservative leaders, including Franz von Papen, who had defected to the German Nationalist People's Party from the Catholic Center Party, and General Kurt von Schleicher, on whose cabinet Hugenberg served in the last months of 1932. The media baron still hesitated, however, to cede much authority to Hitler, who by this time insisted on being named chancellor of Germany rather than a mere cabinet minister. When Papen finally proposed to President Paul von Hindenburg that a coalition government led by Hitler be formed from the German Nationalist People's Party and the Nazis, Hugenberg finally agreed. He was named minister of economics and agriculture in the new cabinet.

Like Papen and Hindenburg, Hugenberg believed he could control the uneducated, lower-middle-class Adolf Hitler. However, when the German Nationalists drew only 8 percent of the vote in the elections of March 1933, the last free elections before the Nazi dictatorship took hold, Hugenberg lost what little political influence he still retained. The Nazis, for their part, began, to target Hugenberg as a reactionary while SA men publicly harassed German Nationalist People's Party supporters. On June 27, 1933, Hugenberg resigned as leader of the party, which was soon dissolved.

Over the next years, though Hugenberg exercised considerable business acumen, his political importance was nil. He managed to hang on to many of his holdings during the era of the Third Reich; even when he was forced to sell his publishing business in 1943 he in effect exchanged it for other industries. After the war, although he was declared a fellow traveler by a German denazification court, Hugenberg was neither imprisoned nor forced to surrender any of his property. He died in Kukenbruch bei Rinteln in the Rhineland on March 12, 1951. *See also* German Nationalist People's Party, Harzburg Front, Vol. 1; Machtergreifung, Vol. 2.

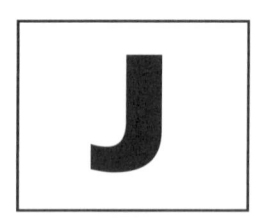

Jeschonnek, Hans (1899–1943)

Chief of staff of the Luftwaffe, the German air force, from 1939 to 1941. Jeschonnek was born in Hohensalza in East Prussia on April 9, 1899. During World War I he served as an officer in the Prussian infantry before joining the German air force. By the late 1930s he was a top official in the Luftwaffe, and he played an important role, along with Erhard Milch and Ernst Udet, in devising operational plans and strategies for Hermann Göring, Nazi air minister. From colonel in 1938, Jeschonnek rose to major general in 1939 to general of fliers and chief of the Luftwaffe leadership staff by 1942. He grew increasingly disillusioned, however, by Göring's unrealistic and high-handed leadership as well as increasingly frustrated by the inability of the Luftwaffe, by 1943, to defend German soil. He committed suicide on August 19, 1943. *See also* Luftwaffe, Vol. 1; Göring, Hermann, Vol. 3.

Jodl, Alfred (1890–1946)

Chief of operations of the High Command of the German armed forces (OKW) during World War II, loyal Nazi general, and Adolf Hitler's most influential military adviser. Jodl was born in Würzburg on May 10, 1890. His family belonged to the traditional German upper class; many of his ancestors and relatives had had distinguished military careers and others were prominent intellectuals and administrators. Alfred Jodl selected a military career and served as an officer during World War I. After the war he joined the General Staff, where he soon became acquainted with the young Adolf Hitler. Prone, according to some accounts, to hero worship, Jodl saw Hitler as a new Napoléon, the potential savior of Germany, and he joined the Nazi Party in 1923.

After the Nazis took power in 1933 Jodl continued his rise within the General Staff. In 1935 he began to play a role in strategic war planning and when the OKW was formed in 1938 he became head of land operations. In April 1939 he was promoted to major general and soon after to chief of operations staff of the OKW, the post that he was to hold to the end of the war. Like his counterpart, OKW chief of staff Wilhelm Keitel, Jodl represented, from Hitler's perspective, a welcome change from such elitist Prussian officers as Ludwig Beck and Werner Freiherr von Fritsch. Jodl, for his part, continued his near hero worship of Hitler, although he was more intelligent than the subservient Keitel and a more careful military adviser. As chief of operations, Jodl personally directed many of the important campaigns of World War II under the guidance of Hitler and Keitel, the major exception being the campaigns on the eastern front. Jodl was promoted to full general in 1944, although by that time his personal influence with Hitler had begun to wane, mostly because Hitler himself took over many of Jodl's operational duties. Nevertheless the general remained an important military adviser, sometimes issuing orders on his own authority rather than Hitler's.

At war's end it was Jodl who officially signed the unconditional surrender documents demanded by the Allies. Signing in the name of the government of Hitler's successor, Grand Admiral Karl Dönitz, Jodl surrendered the German army at Reims in

German general Alfred Jodl arrives in Reims, France, to surrender the German army to the Allies on May 7, 1945.

France on May 7, 1945; the peace took effect officially the next day, as Keitel surrendered in Berlin. Soon after, Jodl was imprisoned, and in November 1945 he was one of the twenty-one top Nazis brought before the International Military Tribunal at Nuremberg. He based his defense on the fact that he was a professional soldier and therefore not in a position to question or disobey the orders of his political and military superior. The tribunal, however, implicated him in some of the Third Reich's worst crimes and found him guilty on all four counts of the Nuremberg indictment. He was hanged along with Hermann Göring, Hans Frank, Keitel, and other Nazi war criminals on October 16, 1946. A German denazification court later found, however, that he restricted himself to operational matters and was not deeply involved in war crimes or crimes against humanity. This court exonerated him posthumously in 1953. *See also* Nuremberg trials, Oberkommando der Wehrmacht, Wehrmacht, Vol. 2; International Military Tribunal, The Charges Against the Surviving Nazi Leaders, Vol. 4.

Kaltenbrunner, Ernst (1903–1946)

Austrian lawyer, police official, and Nazi who, from 1943 to 1945, was chief of the Reich Central Security Office (RSHA), the branch of the SS responsible for, among other matters, concentration camps and all police functions. Kaltenbrunner succeeded Reinhard Heydrich in the position after Heydrich was assassinated in June 1942.

Ernst Kaltenbrunner was born in the Austrian village of Ried im Innkreis, not far from Hitler's birthplace, on October 4, 1903. His family was mostly lower middle class, although both his father and his grandfather had been country lawyers. Like Hitler, Kaltenbrunner went to schools in Linz as a boy, and Adolf Eichmann was one of his childhood acquaintances. He took a law degree from the technical college in Graz in 1926, then returned to Linz to set up a legal practice. Beyond these professional activities Kaltenbrunner was also active in some of the earliest Nazi organizations in Austria, including a National Socialist student group. He also took part in other ethnic-nationalist movements. He officially joined the Austrian Nazi Party, by then a recognized if not entirely legal organization, in 1932. He was attracted early to police work, joining the Austrian equivalent of the SS and providing legal counsel and intelligence to Austrian Nazis. By 1935 his persistence, single-mindedness, and, in all likelihood, imposing appearance (Kaltenbrunner was nearly seven feet tall and carried facial scars from his days as a student) had made him the leader of the Austrian SS. He had also become a target of the Austrian government, which disbarred him and imprisoned him for six months in 1935. After his release from prison Kaltenbrunner worked actively to accomplish the connection, or Anschluss, of Austria to the German Reich. In gratitude for his many services Artur von Seyss-Inquart, the leader of the Austrian Nazis, named him minister for state security in what was to be the last independent government of Austria before 1945.

After the Anschluss was accomplished in March 1938, Kaltenbrunner served the Nazi regime as a member of the Reichstag as well as in a variety of police posts of increasing jurisdiction and responsiblity. By 1941 he was both commander in chief of the SS and lieutenant general of police for much of Austria and the Danube River Valley. In this position he developed an intensive intelligence-gathering network for central and southeastern Europe which in many ways paralleled Heydrich's intelligence efforts in Germany proper. Heinrich Himmler appointed him head of the RSHA on January 30, 1943, much to the surprise of other SS officials, who were unaware of the extensive work of this gigantic Austrian. As head of the RSHA, which was based in Berlin, Kaltenbrunner controlled the Gestapo and the Security Police as well as the concentration camp and extermination camp network in Germany and the occupied territories. He was, therefore, one of the most powerful men in the Third Reich.

Although he lacked Heydrich's personal authority, charisma, and self-discipline, Kaltenbrunner shared his utter brutality. Under his command several million Jews were brought to their deaths in the Polish extermination centers, and he made special efforts to hunt down and collect Jews throughout Europe. In addition, he ordered that prisoners of war be summarily killed and urged locals to kill Allied parachutists. Kaltenbrunner often took a personal interest in killing methods and operations and, in one unusual episode, ordered all French prostitutes to be executed. His fascination with intelligence gathering continued as well. In February 1944 he managed to absorb the Abwehr, the intelligence section of the High Command of the German armed forces, which was led by Admiral Wilhelm Canaris, a man Kaltenbrunner had long considered a personal rival.

Toward the end of 1944 Kaltenbrunner, like his superior, Heinrich Himmler, tried to extend peace feelers by contacting the International Red Cross as well as American diplomat Allen Dulles, the head of the Office of Strategic Services. Neither was interested in his propositions. At war's end he tried to escape to the Austrian Alps but was picked up by American forces. In November 1945 Kaltenbrunner was one of the twenty-one surviving top Nazis brought before the International Military Tribunal at Nuremberg, although a brain hemorrhage suffered on November 18 limited his appearances in court. Like many of the other defendants Kaltenbrunner claimed that he was merely acting under the orders of his superiors, in his case as a government official and policeman. He resented, he claimed, being used as a substitute for Hitler and expressed no remorse for his actions. Kaltenbrunner was found guilty of war crimes and crimes against humanity and hanged at the Nuremberg prison on October 16, 1946. *See also* Nuremberg trials, RSHA, SS, Vol. 2; Heydrich, Reinhard, Vol. 3.

Keitel, Wilhelm (1882–1946)

Chief of staff of the High Command of the German armed forces (OKW) and top military adviser to Adolf Hitler during World War II. His willingness to issue orders involving the regular German armed forces in war crimes, as well as measures against civilian populations, both denigrated the reputation of the military inside and outside Germany and ensured that the Allies considered him a top war criminal.

Wilhelm Keitel was born in the town of Helscherode in central Germany on September 22, 1882. He embarked on a military career as a young man and served as an artillery officer during World War I, suffering a number of wounds. After the war Keitel served briefly as a Freikorps member before returning to the army. After a number of regimental commands Keitel was named chief of the Army Organization Department, a staff post, in 1934. He stayed in the position until 1934. In 1935 he was named head of the Armed Forces Office within the Ministry of War, where a close associate, General Werner von Blomberg, served as war minister. More promotions followed, from major general to lieutenant general in 1936 and to general of artillery in 1937. A loyal Nazi as well as, by this time, a political insider, Keitel was named chief of staff of the new OKW as a result of the shake-up within the German military which took place in early 1938. Blomberg, as well as army commander in chief Werner Freiherr von Fritsch, were forced to resign due to personal scandals. Hitler named himself supreme commander of Germany's armed forces while Keitel was given the top office in the OKW. Although several other generals held technically higher ranks, Keitel enjoyed close access to the Führer and was therefore the most influential military officer in the Third Reich. Keitel returned Hitler's favors by remaining a loyal sycophant throughout the years of World War II. Indeed, Keitel was so unquestioning of Hitler's intentions, and so willing to perform his dirty work, that other top officers called him names ranging from "lackey" to "the nodding ass."

In 1940, after the German defeat of France, Keitel was promoted to field marshal along with a number of other generals. He also enjoyed the honor of negotiating the French surrender terms. Germany's victory over the French was, according to Keitel, due to the fact that Adolf Hitler was the greatest commander in history. Although he tried to dissuade Hitler from launching the invasion of the Soviet Union in June 1941, Keitel became an enthusiastic supporter of the invasion once it was under way. Meanwhile, Keitel also issued instructions that encouraged a variety of atrocities. These included attacks on Poland's intelligentsia in 1939 and 1940 in the effort to destroy Polish culture and the Einsatzgruppen massacres of Jews in the Soviet Union in the summer and fall of 1941. With regard to those massacres, which were largely the work of the SS, Keitel made it clear to army commanders that the SS acted freely on its own authority, independent from the army, and that if the SS did not kill those who had to be killed in the "racial war" between Russia and Germany, the regular armed forces might have to finish the job. Keitel also issued the infamous Night and Fog Decree. This measure, mainly applied in the occupied countries of western Europe, allowed for the arrest and disappearance of those who opposed the German occupation.

On May 8, 1945, Keitel signed the unconditional surrender of Germany's armed forces in Berlin in the name of the government of Hitler's successor, Admiral Karl Dönitz. In November 1945 he was one of twenty-one surviving top Nazis brought before the International Military Tribunal at Nuremberg. During his testimony, as well as in his memoirs, Keitel remained mostly devoted to Adolf Hitler and referred to himself merely as the Führer's loyal cupbearer, although he resented the fact that Hitler had never allowed him to make his own decisions. Convinced of his involvement in atrocities on the eastern front as well as the Night and Fog measures, the tribunal found Keitel guilty of war crimes and crimes against humanity. He was sentenced to death and hanged at the Nuremberg prison on October 16, 1946. *See also* Committee of Three, Vol. 1; Nuremberg trials, Oberkommando der Wehrmacht, Vol. 2; International Military Tribunal, The Charges Against the Surviving Nazi Leaders, Vol. 4.

Keppler, Wilhelm (1882–1960)

Businessman who served as one of the chief contact men between the Nazi hierarchy and German industrialists as well as a financial adviser to top Nazis. Keppler, born in Heidelberg on December 14, 1882, was trained as an engineer. He later held positions with important industrial firms in western Germany. He joined the Nazi Party early and grew acquainted with Heinrich Himmler, who in turn introduced Keppler to Adolf Hitler. Before the Nazis took power in 1933, Keppler was active in raising funds through the so-called Keppler Circle and seeking support for the Nazi movement among his fellow industrialists. He played a key role in convincing many conservative businessmen to support Hitler rather than General Kurt von Schleicher in the political upheaval of late 1932. After the Nazis took power, Keppler became a member of the Reichstag and, in July 1933, he was named Reich commissioner for economic affairs.

In 1935 Keppler joined the SS, and for much of the remainder of the era of the Third Reich he maintained close ties to Heinrich Himmler. He founded, for instance, the Heinrich Himmler Friendship Circle, a cover organization in which businessmen could make contributions to the SS in return for honorary rank and titles. In addition, he played an important role in tying the economies of occupied countries such as Austria and Poland to Germany. He was instrumental in adapting industries in Poland as well as Russia to SS needs during the Nazi occupations of those areas. Beyond these activities Keppler also served as an adviser to Hermann Göring, head of the Four-Year Plan for economic development and, during World War II, as a secretary of state in the German Foreign Office.

At the end of World War II Keppler was imprisoned and in 1949 he was sentenced to ten years by an American war crimes tribunal. He was released, however, in 1951 and died on June 13, 1960. *See also* business in the Third Reich, Heinrich Himmler Friendship Circle, Vol. 1.

Kerrl, Hans (1887–1941)

Loyal Nazi bureaucrat who served from 1935 to 1941 as the Reich minister for church affairs. Kerrl was born in Fallersleben in northern Germany on December 2, 1887. During World War I he served as a lieutenant and received several decorations. Soon after the Nazis took power, Kerrl became Reich commissioner in the Prussian Ministry of Justice, where he took aggressive measures against Jewish lawyers and notaries. In June 1934 Adolf Hitler named him Reich minister without portfolio in the German cabinet until, in July 1935, he became minister for church affairs. In that office Kerrl effectively replaced Reich Bishop Ludwig Müller, who had failed to convince most German Protestants that they should join the German Christian movement, a nazified version of the faith that eliminated all connections between Christianity and Judaism. Kerrl, however, likewise failed to closely tie German Protestantism to the Nazi regime, and his superiors largely gave up the effort. Kerrl died in Berlin in December 1941. *See also* German Christians, Vol. 1; National Reich Church, religion in the Third Reich, Vol. 2.

Kesselring, Albert (1885–1960)

Field marshal in the German air force, the Luftwaffe, and later commander in chief of German troops in Italy and North Africa. Kesselring was born in the town of Marktsheft in Bavaria on November 20, 1885, the son of a minor government official. He joined the German Imperial Army in 1904,

Luftwaffe field marshal Albert Kesselring, pictured greeting airmen, commanded German forces in the Mediterranean and North Africa from December 1941 to March 1945.

and by the onset of World War I he was an artillery officer. During that war he served first with the Bavarian artillery on the western front, than as an officer with the General Staff. With the Weimar-era Reichswehr his career followed a similar pattern: a number of years as a regimental officer and then, after 1932, a staff position and a promotion to brigadier general.

Kesselring was transferred to the Luftwaffe in 1935, and a year later he was appointed chief of the General Staff. His main task was to maintain liaison between the Luftwaffe and the Wehrmacht, the regular army. In 1938, as general of fliers, Kesselring was appointed commander in chief of Air Fleet I. He later led the fleet, as well as others, in the successful German operations against Poland, Belgium, the Netherlands, and France. After the fall of France in the summer of 1940 he was promoted to general field marshal along with Erhard Milch and Hugo Sperrle of the Luftwaffe and eight Wehrmacht generals. In these early western operations Kesselring had directed the devastating bomb attacks on the Dutch city of Rotterdam as well as a number of attacks on southern England during the Battle of Britain. Kesselring's pilots, in fact, inflicted heavy damage on British airfields until his Luftwaffe superior, Hermann Göring, ordered them away to perform militarily inconsequential attacks on London.

Kesselring was commander in chief of German forces in southern Europe, the Mediterranean region, and North Africa from December 1941 to March 1945. Allied opponents considered him among the best of the German officers they were trying to outwit, as Kesselring played a major part in the effective operations of Erwin Rommel's Afrika Korps and in defending northern Italy from Allied advances in 1943 and 1944. Despite heavy losses and supply problems, in fact, Kesselring's leadership may well have delayed the Allied advance through Italy for as much as one year. He could prove a harsh judge, however. In March 1944 he ordered the random shooting of more than three hundred Italians in response to partisan activity against German troops. It was for this incident that a British military tribunal later tried Kesselring as a war criminal.

Kesselring never took part in any resistance movement against Hitler and, indeed, was loyal to the Führer to the end of the war. In search of capable and loyal officers, Hitler reassigned Kesselring to France and the Low Countries in March 1945 to see if he could delay the Allied advance there. By then it was too late, however, and Kesselring's military skill was of little use given the ragtag German army and the lack of supplies. At war's end he was interned by the British, who tried him in Venice for the March 1944 shootings of Italian civilians. He was found guilty and sentenced to death, but in October 1947 the sentence was reduced to ten years' imprisonment. In the end he was released in 1952 because of poor health. Kesselring died in Bad Neuheim on July 16, 1960. *See also* Luftwaffe, Vol. 1; Göring, Hermann; Milch, Erhard, Vol. 3.

Kirdorf, Emil (1847–1938)

Rhineland industrialist and one of the earliest supporters of Nazism from the world of German big business. Kirdorf was born in Mettman in the Rhineland on April 8, 1847. By the time he was thirty he had helped found the Gelsenkircher Mine Works and in later years was instrumental in the construction of two large industrial cartels, the Rhine-Westphalian Coal Syndicate and the United Steel Works. He was also active in right-wing politics. He supported the pan-German movement, which sought to collect all people defined as ethnic Germans in a single large empire, and he dominated the Ruhr Treasury, an organization that made political contributions from funds collected from Rhineland businessmen. He heavily disliked trade unionism, moreover, and was a feared employer.

Kirdorf, by now eighty years of age, joined the Nazi Party in 1927, a fact heavily publicized by Nazi propagandists seeking support among respectable German conservatives. As it happened, however, Kirdorf left the party in 1928 and threw his political support behind the German Nationalist People's Party. He maintained a close relationship with Adolf Hitler nonetheless, and after watching a Hitler speech in 1929 he wrote a note to the Nazi leader acknowledging the importance of the Nazi movement in Germany's rehabilitation. He heartily approved, moreover, of Hitler's opposition to communism and social disorder and was impressed by the Nazi leader's ability to influence ordinary people. Over the next several years Kirdorf employed his personal authority, if not his funds, to convince his fellow industrialists that the Nazi movement did not represent, in fact, a Socialist revolution, and that their interests would remain safe if they supported Hitler. From the other side, Kirdorf helped convince Hitler of the importance of enlisting big businessmen in his efforts. In 1934 Kirdorf rejoined the Nazi Party, which proudly considered his involvement an acknowledgment of the party's respectability among German conservatives. Kirdorf died in Mühlheim in the Ruhr on July 13, 1938. *See also* business in the Third Reich, Days of Struggle, Vol. 1; Flick, Friedrich, Vol. 3.

Kleist, Ewald von (1881–1954)

General field marshal and highly capable commander of tank operations on both the eastern and western fronts during World War II. Kleist was born in Braunfels an der Lein in eastern Germany on August 8, 1881, into a family of traditional Prussian aristocrats with close ties to the family of Field Marshal Paul von Hindenburg, last president of the Weimar Republic. Kleist served as a regimental officer during World War I. After the war he served in the Reichswehr in various appointments, rising to the rank of brigadier general. During the years of the Nazi takeover and consolidation of power Kleist fit the pattern of a Prussian aristocratic officer. From 1932 to 1935 he was commander of a division of cavalry and promoted to lieutenant general. From 1936 to 1939, when he retired, he served as a general of cavalry as well as army commandant of Breslau.

The onset of war, however, brought a quick end to Kleist's retirement. He was recalled to lead an army corps during the invasion of Poland. In 1940, as commander of a tank group, he was among the first to move through the Ardennes in the attempt to outflank French troops and split the Allied armies by moving quickly to the English Channel coast. In April 1941, Kleist led the German force that captured Belgrade during the Nazi invasion of Yugoslavia. Two months later Kleist was at the head of the First Panzer Army during the invasion of the Soviet Union. The force took the city of Kiev in September 1941 and soon after, with Kleist now the head of Army Group A, it led the drive toward the oil fields of the Caucasus. Lack of supplies, notably gasoline, hindered the offensive and in the fall of 1942 Kleist's forces were diverted to support the attack on the city of Stalingrad. Kleist himself, meanwhile, ignored the official directives to treat the peoples of the Soviet Union as subhumans and actively sought the support of many of the Caucasian peoples such as the Azeris and the Ossetians. These peoples, who had little love for either Russia or communism, formed units to help out the Germans, and a number of them ended up in the SS.

After the failure of the Stalingrad offensive Kleist was forced into a long westward retreat. Hitler nevertheless recognized his accomplishments by naming him a general field marshal on January 31, 1943. Over the next months Kleist continued to receive official acknowledgment in the form of decorations, but he also considered joining the resistance movement among German officers. Hitler dismissed Kleist from his commands in mid-1944. After World War II he was captured by British forces and turned over to the Yugoslavs, who tried him as a war criminal in 1948. The field marshal was sentenced to fifteen years' imprisonment but released after only one year and taken to the Soviet Union. He died in a prison camp near Moscow in October 1954. *See also* Barbarossa, Battle of Stalingrad, Vol. 1; Panzer, Vol. 2.

Kluge, Günter Hans (1882–1944)

General field marshal whose military career was marked by marginal successes and indecision. Kluge was born in Posen, now Poznan in Poland, on October 20, 1882. He was an officer in the Prussian army from 1901, and during World War I he served as an officer on the General Staff. After the war, as a member of the Weimar-era Reichswehr, he enjoyed rapid promotions, which continued even after the Nazis took power in 1933. The first challenge to Kluge's steady rise in rank came in 1938, when a number of top officers were forced out in the aftermath of the Blomberg-Fritsch crisis. Kluge, like several others, was forced into retirement. By the summer of 1939, however, with war looming and Germany in need of experienced leaders, he was recalled to duty. He was given command of the Sixth Army, which served with distinction in both Poland and France. In the summer of 1940, after the fall of France, Kluge was promoted to general field marshal along with a number of other top Wehrmacht and Luftwaffe generals.

Kluge had somewhat less success during the invasion of the Soviet Union in 1941. His Fourth Army reached the outskirts of Moscow, but was forced to retreat in the face of a strong Russian counteroffensive. Promoted nonetheless to commander in chief of Army Group Center in December 1941, his armies continued to sputter. Kluge's most notable qualities as a commander were his loyalty to Hitler and his great susceptibility to flattery and to gifts. In October 1942, on the occasion of his sixtieth birthday, Hitler gave Kluge a gift of a quarter of a million marks to be used, partly, to restore his Prussian estate. In July 1944 he was appointed by Hitler to replace Field Marshal von Rundstedt as western commander, but like his predecessor he was unable to prevent the Allied advance.

Like most top officers, Kluge was aware of the resistance movement within the German military, and as one of the top-ranking commanders in the Wehrmacht, Kluge was a prize potential recruit for the conspirators. They tried to get him to join the resistance by letting him know they were aware of and could document Hitler's cash gift. As in other regards, however, Kluge remained noncommittal. He declared himself only willing to support the resistance, particularly the July 1944 Plot, if the attempt was likely to be a success. When he learned that Hitler survived the July 20 bomb, Kluge withdrew his support. He was removed from his commands, however, on August 17, 1944. Those investigating the plot claimed that he should have informed the Nazi hierarchy long before, and Kluge's long string of mediocre military campaigns doomed him as well. Ordered to Berlin, where he feared he might face trial for treason, Kluge killed himself during a road journey in France on August 19, 1944. *See also* Barbarossa, Vol. 1; resistance movements, Germany; Wehrmacht, Vol. 2.

Koch, Erich (1896–1986)

SS lieutenant general and Reich commissar of the Ukraine from 1941 to 1944. Koch was born in Elberfeld in East Prussia on June 19, 1896, and fought as an enlisted soldier during World War I. After the war he worked as a railway clerk. He was an early member of the Nazi Party, joining in 1922. During the early 1920s he was imprisoned by the French for nationalist activities in the Ruhr area. In 1926 he was fired from his railway job for his extremist political activities, although by that time he had become an important Nazi official in the Ruhr. From 1928 Koch was Gauleiter in East Prussia and also served as a Nazi representative, after 1930, in the Prussian state legislature. After the Nazis took power in 1933 Koch became the virtual dictator of East Prussia, holding the rank of overpresident. The state, separated as it was from German proper by the Polish Corridor, was a law unto itself, and Koch was able to institute such policies as collectivization of agriculture and even the marginalization of the SA and SS.

After German forces occupied much of the western Soviet Union in 1941 and 1942, those regions were divided into the two Reichskommissariats of Ostland and the Ukraine. While Alfred Rosenberg held the title of chief of the eastern occupied territories, as they were also known, Koch was named Reich commissar of the Ukraine, and it was he who exercised the true authority there. The Third Reich's long-term plans for the territory were to incorporate it into the Greater German Reich. Part of Koch's responsibility, as local Reich commissar, was to "Germanize" the area in preparation for these plans. Local peoples—Ukrainians, Poles, Belarussians—were to be transformed into a slave labor force and discouraged from reproducing, although some individuals might be "Aryanized" into Germans. Among his first acts was to close all Ukrainian schools, asserting that any education local children might need would be provided by the Germans. Local Jews suffered the same fate as Jews in Poland and elsewhere in the occupied Soviet Union: If they were not shot outright by the Einsatzgruppen, they were sent to the extermination camps in Poland. Koch fully subscribed to the Nazi racial ideology which claimed that Slavs were subhuman, far less valuable than any German, and that Jews had no place in the expanded German Reich. As in much of the rest of the occupied Soviet Union, the Nazi official stance toward local peoples, as enforced by Koch, resulted in a great deal of resistance to Nazi rule as well as widespread partisan activity in the region's vast forests and countryside.

After the Soviet armies swept back through the Ukraine on their way to Germany, Koch retreated to East Prussia. After World War II he managed to hide until 1949, when he was arrested by British security soldiers in Hamburg. In 1950 he was extradited to Poland, where the Polish government, like its Soviet authority, had placed him high on a list of wanted war criminals. After his trial, which finally took place in the late 1950s, Koch was found guilty of the murders of four hundred thousand Poles and sentenced to death. Because of ill health, however, his sentence was reduced to life imprisonment. Koch died in prison in Poland on November 12, 1986. *See also* Reich Commissariat Ukraine, Vol. 2.

Koch, Ilse (1906–1967)

The wife of Karl Koch, the commandant of the Buchenwald concentration camp in Germany. She became known as the Bitch of Buchenwald because of her sadistic behavior toward camp prisoners. Ilse Koch was born in Saxony to a working-class family. In 1936, after working as a librarian she married Karl Koch, an SS lieutenant colonel who was then the commandant of Sachsenhausen. When her husband was transferred to Buchenwald in 1939, she went with him.

Ilse Koch's aggressive actions at Buchenwald became well known, largely due to trial testimony after the war. She had a special horse-riding area built by camp prisoners, for instance, so that she could indulge her favorite hobby to the accompaniment of the Buchenwald orchestra, and frequently rode through the camp whipping prisoners arbitrarily. She also, allegedly, collected gloves, lamp shades, and other items made from the skins of prisoners whom she had had killed, asking once that any prisoners who arrived with interesting tattoos be saved for that purpose.

Karl Koch was tried by the SS in 1944 for using the camp to feather his own nest through theft, the unauthorized use of camp labor, embezzlement, and other offenses. The SS hanged him in 1945, although they found his wife not guilty of accepting stolen goods. In 1947 Ilse Koch was found guilty of murder by an American war crimes tribunal and sentenced to life in prison. She also managed that year to give birth to a son, whom she named Uwe; the father was unknown. The sentence was later commuted by an American occupation official, arousing an international outcry protesting the leniency. In 1949 a West German court tried Ilse Koch for the murder of German citizens, and in 1951 she was found guilty and, again, sentenced to life in prison. She committed suicide on September 1, 1967, using a bedsheet, in her prison cell at Aichach in Bavaria. *See also* Buchenwald, concentration camps, Vol. 1.

Kramer, Josef (1907–1945)

SS official and, in 1944 and 1945, the commandant of the Bergen-Belsen concentration camp, known as Belsen, in northern Germany. After British forces liberated the camp and released reports, photographs, and films of what they found there, Kramer was reviled the world over as the Beast of Belsen.

An early SS recruit, by 1940 Kramer had risen to become the adjutant to Rudolf Höss, who had just taken a position as commandant of Auschwitz, which at that time was merely a prisoner of war camp. He also received training at Mauthausen and Sachsenhausen, earning everywhere a reputation for harshness toward both prisoners and German staff. In 1943, he personally supervised a killing operation at the Natzweiler concentration camp whose victims' skulls were later used in medical experiments. In the spring and summer of 1944 he was commandant at the Birkenau killing center at Auschwitz, where he helped to administer the so-called Höss Action, the double-time massacre of Hungary's Jews.

On December 1, 1944, Kramer was transferred to Belsen as commandant, but he proved completely unequal to the management of a camp that was being filled far beyond capacity. Always the mindless bureaucrat concerned more with proper form filling than keeping people alive, he recorded deaths by the hundreds with the simple entry "typhus." In the last weeks before Belsen was liberated in late April 1945 the camp administration broke down, and Kramer left the prisoners to their own devices and barbarity, resulting in the appalling scene the British found. When the British arrived, the indifferent Kramer was willing to show them around.

During his trial for war crimes Kramer noted that he had no emotional response whatever toward supervising gassings or other actions, which he described in detail. A nearly ideal SS functionary, he simply mentioned that he had been given orders to follow, and followed them as he had been trained to do. Found guilty by a British military tribunal, Kramer was executed in late November 1945. *See also* Bergen-Belsen, concentration camps, Höss Action, Vol. 1.

Krupp von Bohlen und Halbach, Alfred (1907–1967)

The last scion of the famous Krupp family of armaments makers and industrialists in Germany, who took command of the family's holdings in 1943. He was a wide user of slave and prison camp labor.

Alfred Krupp was born in the Ruhr city of Essen, where the Krupp cartel was based, on August 13, 1907. In the tradition of the Krupp dynasty he was brought up to serve the family firm, which had supplied arms to various German governments for several centuries. He joined the board of managing directors in 1936, where he made the most of Krupp's dealings with the government of the Third Reich. By 1939 he was in charge of mining and armaments for Krupp, and his firm supplied the burgeoning Nazi armed forces with huge amounts of munitions and armaments, earning millions in government contracts.

During World War II Alfred Krupp took an active role in the economic exploitation of Europe by the Third Reich and, like earlier Krupp leaders in earlier German regimes, Alfred enjoyed a number of special privileges reflecting the firm's lofty status. The Krupps, for example, transplanted entire factories from the eastern occupied territories into Germany, where they staffed their assembly lines with slave laborers and prisoners of war. He was also allowed to import Jewish laborers from Auschwitz, and to set up a munitions factory at Auschwitz itself. Krupp foreign workers, whether in factories or coal mines, labored under extremely poor conditions, and thousands suffered and died from abuse, neglect, and disease. Alfred Krupp took over sole leadership of the Krupp cartel in 1943 when his father, Gustav, retired from active service. He was soon after made a leader of the war economy, a man whose efforts Nazi leaders considered vital to the German war effort. Meanwhile, on Hitler's orders, the Krupp firm reverted from public ownership, its status since 1903, to a family concern.

In the last two years of World War II Krupp factories, particularly in Essen, were targeted for bombings by Allied planes, and a number of facilities were destroyed or disabled. A devoted Nazi to that point, Krupp began to shift his loyalties, claiming that the Hitler regime owed him compensation for his various losses. In 1945 he was captured by Canadian soldiers and imprisoned. In July 1948 he was found guilty of war crimes by an American military tribunal along with nine of his firm's directors. Krupp was sentenced to twelve years in prison and the loss of his personal fortune. He was released, however, in 1951, the result of an amnesty declared by the American high commissioner John J. McCloy. Both his personal fortune and much of his corporate property were returned to him, and Krupp was once again a going concern. Alfred Krupp was even allowed to take up his position as head of the firm once again in 1953, and the company soon regained its status as one of the largest industrial cartels in Europe, although its focus was now coal mines and steel mills.

Krupp died of heart failure in Essen on July 30, 1967. By that time, however, the Krupp firm, which employed over one hundred thousand workers, was heavily in debt to German banks, to whom it had sold a controlling interest in order to raise the capital to survive. Krupp himself had been forced to give up sole personal control of the firm to the bankers, and so, presumably, the Krupp industrial dynasty was at an end. *See also* business in the Third Reich, Krupp Works, Vol. 1; slave labor, Vol. 2; Krupp von Bohlen und Halbach, Gustav, Vol. 3.

Krupp von Bohlen und Halbach, Gustav (1870–1950)

German industrial magnate who went from being a vocal opponent to a strong supporter of Adolf Hitler and the Nazi regime and whose Krupp industrial empire played a major role in Germany's military effort during World War II. Gustav von Bohlen und Halbach was born in the Netherlands on August 7, 1870, to a family of wealthy bankers. He took a law degree from the University of Heidelberg and started a career with the German Foreign Office, serving in embassies in the United States, China, and the Vatican. In 1906 he married Bertha Krupp, assumed the Krupp name, and became heir to the Krupp industrial dynasty, slowly taking over Krupp factories in Essen, Kiel, Berlin, and other locations throughout Germany.

Until 1933 Gustav Krupp opposed the rise of Nazism, and as late as January 29, 1933, one day before Adolf Hitler took office as chancellor, he warned President Paul von Hindenburg against accepting the upstart Austrian as German leader. Soon after, however, Krupp changed his mind. The occasion was a meeting hosted by the respected economist and financier Hjalmar Schacht held on February 20, 1933. There, Hitler and Hermann Göring convinced a gathering

A 1930 photo of the Krupp von Bohlen und Halbach family includes Bertha and Gustav (seated, second and third from left) and their son Alfred (second from right).

of German industrialists that they were not Socialists and that they would repress any elements of the Nazi movement that professed Socialist sympathies or sought to take control of industry away from industrialists and put it in the hands of workers. Hitler also promised to end the Communist threat to Germany while rebuilding the German army. The latter was a particularly important point to a munitions manufacturer.

Krupp, already the chairman of the Association of German Industry and known worldwide as the German armaments king, was named head of the Adolf Hitler Fund in May 1933. This was a mechanism by which industrialists could make donations to the Nazi Party in return for special favors from the government. Krupp, always aware of the importance of well-placed political contributions, contributed over 10 million marks a year to the fund, and still more to the Heinrich Himmler Friendship Circle, a similar organization designed to raise money for the SS. Meanwhile the Krupp family of firms was able to take great advantage of German rearmament, supplying a great deal of the country's munitions, guns, and tanks and reaping huge sums in government contracts.

During World War II the Krupp cartel, like other German industrial groups, took extensive advantage of slave labor both in Germany and in the areas of eastern Europe occupied by the Third Reich. In the regions around Essen alone, for instance, fifty-seven camps housed up to one hundred thousand slaves in deplorable conditions. The workers included Poles and Russians kidnapped and brought to Germany, Russian prisoners of war, and, from time to time, Jews. The Krupps also built a factory at Auschwitz to exploit the ready supply of cheap, expendable prisoners, who were generally worked to the point of death and then gassed. Later estimates suggested that seventy to eighty thousand workers died in the various camps serving the Krupp industries during the war. Gustav Krupp, meanwhile, turned over the leadership of Krupp to his son and successor, Alfred, in 1943.

After World War II Gustav Krupp was indicted on war crimes but never brought to trial. An American medical board reported that the aging Krupp was growing mentally unstable after suffering a stroke, and that he was unfit to join his son and others in the 1948 trial of Krupp executives. He died in a village near Salzburg on January 16, 1950. *See also* business in the Third Reich, Krupp Works, Vol. 1; slave labor, Vol. 2; Krupp von Bohlen und Halbach, Alfred, Vol. 3.

Kube, Wilhelm (1887–1943)

Nazi governor of Belarus, or White Russia, from July 1941 until his death in September 1943. Despite a strong devotion to Nazism and his approval of early killing actions, Kube stands out as one of the few Nazi Party or SS officials who expressed reservations over the continuing mass extermination of Jews, particularly German-speaking Jews, in occupied Poland and the Soviet Union. Kube was born in Glogau in southeastern Germany in 1887 to a military family. As a young man he studied at the University of Berlin, taking a particular interest in politics and history and becoming a leader in nationalist student movements. After World War I he entered politics, as the general secretary of the right-wing German Nationalist People's Party. In 1924 he was elected to the Reichstag with a new party, the German National Freedom Party. He joined the Nazi Party in 1928, and represented it in both the Reichstag and in the Prussian state legislature. After the Nazis took power Kube was well placed to become a powerful official in Prussia and Hermann Göring, in his role as Prussian state minister, appointed Kube governor of the Brandenburg district, which included Berlin.

Kube's career seemed over in 1936 when he was accused of blackmail, embezzlement, and other offenses by USCHLA, the Nazi Party's internal court, and fired from his positions. In 1940, however, he volunteered for service with the Waffen-SS and Heinrich Himmler, pleased with Kube's political experience and his willingness to serve in the SS at the relatively advanced age of fifty-three, accepted him into the SS as a civil administrator. Kube was named commissar of Belarus in July 1941, and from there reported favorably on the killings of thousands of local Jews in addition to his more mundane duties. Kube differentiated, however, between "Eastern Jews" and those from Germany, claiming that the two were categorically different. He complained to Reinhard Heydrich, who ignored him, as well as to his immediate superior, Heinrich Lohse, about the deportation of German Jews to the ghettos within his jurisdiction. He even took steps to keep Jews of German or ethnic German background alive by, for example, hiring them as servants or in various administrative duties. Kube continued these measures even after strong warnings from superiors such as Alfred Rosenberg, chief of the eastern occupied territories, who threatened to bring him up on charges before an SS tribunal. Beyond differentiating between "Eastern" and "Reich" Jews, Kube also reached a point where he objected to the extreme brutality with which Jews were treated, claiming that harvesting gold fillings from Jews evinced a savagery that reflected poorly on the highly advanced culture of Germany.

On September 22, 1943, Kube was shot to death by a Russian partisan who had gained employment in his household. Perhaps relieved that Kube would not have to be hailed before an SS court, Hitler ordered that he be given an honorable state burial. *See also* Reich Commissariat Ostland, SS, Vol. 2.

Kubizek, August (1889–1971)

Adolf Hitler's closest boyhood friend, whose recollections, published in 1955 as

The Young Hitler I Knew, helped form the early understanding of Hitler's adolescence and young manhood. The two met in 1904 when Kubizek, a craftsman in the Austrian city of Linz, encountered Hitler, then a high school student, at the Linz opera house. Over the next months the two became close friends and roommates. Kubizek later remembered Hitler at that time as an intense, brooding young man. Kubizek left Linz in 1908 to study music at the Vienna Conservatory. There, he rejoined Hitler, who had come to Vienna to study art but was rejected by the Academy of Fine Arts. For a time the two were again roommates, but when Kubizek returned from a summer vacation in the fall of 1908, he found that his friend had moved out of their apartment and not left a forwarding address. Kubizek did not meet Hitler again until 1938, after the Nazi Party had risen to power and his youthful companion had become the dictator of Germany; Hitler made little time for him. Kubizek died in 1971. *See also* Hitler, Adolf, Vol. 3; Kubizek, Hitler Reveals His Dream of Power, Vol. 4.

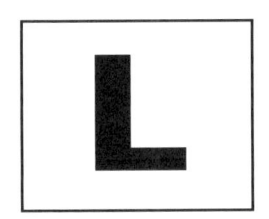

Lammers, Hans (1879–1962)

As head of the Reichs Chancellery, one of Adolf Hitler's top advisers as well as one of the men who controlled personal access to the Nazi leader. Lammers was born into a family of professionals in Lublinitz in eastern Germany on May 27, 1879. He embarked on a career as a public service lawyer after studying at the Universities of Breslau and Heidelberg. His first important post was as a county judge in Beuthen in 1912. After World War I, Lammers moved to Berlin to take up a position with the Interior Ministry as a legal adviser. Moving easily, it seems, from the Weimar Republic to the Third Reich, Lammers, a dedicated, colorless bureaucrat, became head of the Reichs Chancellery in 1933. He stayed in that post until 1945, acting essentially as one of Hitler's several chiefs of staff. The Reichs Chancellery was mostly concerned with matters inside the German government rather than with Nazi Party, military, or SS business. Hitler came to rely on Lammers to handle a great deal of the state business that he had little patience for as well as advice on legal issues. Moreover, Lammers was accepted as one of Hitler's inner circle, spending a great deal of time at Hitler's mountain getaway, the Berghof. In 1937 Lammers joined the Reich cabinet as minister without portfolio, and in 1939 he was named ministerial counsel for defense of the Reich. He was named an honorary SS general in 1940.

Almost inevitably, Lammers was involved in the web of intrigue that surrounded Hitler during World War II, when relationships of power, as well as Hitler's favor, constantly shifted. In 1943 he became one of the so-called Committee of Three, on which Hitler depended to lighten his administrative load but which also took on the role of limiting access to the Nazi leader. The other two were Martin Bormann and General Wilhelm Keitel, rivals of Lammers for the Führer's favor. Lammers, the dogged bureaucrat with a fondness for legal and administrative detail, appeared to lose out to the more clever and deceitful Bormann, and his influence with Hitler waned. In April 1945 Hitler repudiated him entirely, associating him with Hermann Göring, who, with the help of Lammers's legal expertise, had declared Hitler no longer fit to govern and named himself as head of state. Hitler's order to arrest Lammers, however, did not take effect before World War II ended.

Lammers was arrested after the war and put on trial in 1949 by the military tribunal at Nuremberg, now run almost entirely by Americans. He was accused of creating and providing a legal basis for anti-Semitic measures that led to the deaths of hundreds of thousands of Jews. Lammers confessed that he was, indeed, aware of the clearance given to Reinhard Heydrich to implement a "Final Solution to the Jewish Question," but that he never knew what those measures were. He was initially given a sentence of twenty years in prison, which was soon reduced to ten. He was released, however, in 1952. Lammers died in Düsseldorf on

January 4, 1962. *See also* Committee of Three, Vol. 1; Reichs Chancellery, Vol. 2.

Laval, Pierre (1883–1945)

French politician and archcollaborator with the Third Reich as one of the leaders of the Vichy French regime. Laval was born on June 28, 1883, in the the village of Chateldon in the north of France. He studied law at the Universities of Lyon and Paris, taking his degree in 1907. He entered politics as a Socialist in 1914 and served in World War I. In the unstable French politics of the interwar years he was in and out of a number of posts, including minister of public works in 1925 and minister of labor in 1930. He became minister of foreign affairs in 1934, growing notorious for signing an agreement approving the Italian invasion of Ethiopia in 1935, after which he was forced to resign.

Laval returned to the French political scene in 1940, after the French surrender to Germany. He was named both foreign minister and deputy head of state to Marshal Philippe Pétain, the Vichy premier. Convinced early on that a German victory was inevitable, he worked hard to cooperate with Hitler. His constant intrigues, as well as his blind ambition to take over from Pétain, led to his dismissal in December 1940, but he was reinstated in April 1942. After Pétain resigned that month, Hitler, knowing that Laval would be pliable, named him leader of Vichy. Until 1944, when the Allies recaptured France, Laval played a key role in recruiting French workers as laborers for Germany, seeking French soldiers to fight in Hitler's armies, and helping the SS deport French Jews. He also gave the Nazis free rein to plunder the French economy. Like other collaborationists, Laval argued that he was a true patriot, trying to save France from possibilities even worse than the Nazis.

After escaping to Germany in September 1944, and then to Spain, Laval was finally captured in Austria by American forces on July 31, 1945. The Americans turned him over to de Gaulle's Free French government, which tried him for treason. He was found guilty and executed by firing squad on October 15, 1945. *See also* collaboration, Vol. 1; Vichy France, Vol. 2; Pétain, Philippe, Vol. 3.

Leeb, Wilhelm Ritter von (1876–1956)

General field marshal whose early victories in World War II did not prevent Adolf Hitler from forcing him into retirement when Leeb proved less than enthusiastic about the 1941 Russian campaign. Leeb was born in Landsberg, near Munich, on September 5, 1876. His family had a traditional military background. Leeb joined the German Imperial Army in 1905 and during World War I served as a staff officer. Immediately after the war he joined the right-wing Freikorps movement, soon after returning to the army, where he enjoyed steady promotion. By 1929 he was a major general, and in 1934 he was appointed general of artillery as well as commander in chief of the Second Army. Like a number of other top officers he was forced out in 1938 in the backwash of the Blomberg-Fritsch crisis, but found himself recalled soon after as war threatened. In the fall of 1938 Leeb led one of the German armies that marched into Czechoslovakia to take possession of the Sudetenland.

In 1939 Leeb was promoted to full general and commander of Army Group C, although he did not participate in the invasion of Poland. Instead, Army Group C was placed along Germany's border with France, and Leeb's troops directly faced France's vast, and ultimately largely useless, Maginot line defenses. Leeb did not feel that Germany was ready for a major war on either the western or the eastern front, and argued that an attack on Belgium, a neutral country, would be a dishonorable act. Such sentiments were irrelevant to top Nazis and many military leaders, and in any case Leeb participated actively in the German operations against France in the spring and summer of 1940. In July 1940, as a result of a rush of enthusiasm on Hitler's part, Leeb was promoted to general field marshal along with eleven other Wehrmacht and Luftwaffe generals.

In the spring of 1941, Leeb was chosen as commander in chief of Army Group North, one of the three huge armies that were to invade the Soviet Union. Leeb's primary targets were the Baltic states and the major Russian city of Leningrad. Again Leeb argued, to no avail, that Germany was unprepared for such a huge attack. His units moved quickly through the countryside to the outskirts of Leningrad after the attack began, but could not take the city. Hitler ordered a siege, while Leeb wanted his forces to be allowed to retreat from Leningrad in order to shorten supply and defense lines during the brutal northern Russian winter. Finally having had enough of Leeb's resistance, which he perceived as insubordination, Hitler ordered the field marshal into retirement on January 18, 1942. Leeb managed to avoid service for the rest of World War II, and died in the village of Hohenschwangau in Bavaria on April 29, 1956. *See also* Barbarossa, Vol. 1; siege of Leningrad, Vol. 2.

Ley, Robert (1890–1945)

Head of the German Labor Front, the largest Nazi Party organization for civilians. Ley was born on February 15, 1890, in Niederbreidenbach in the Rhineland. He studied chemistry at the Universities of Bonn and Münster and served as a pilot during World War I. He spent the last year of the war as a prisoner of the French after being shot down. After the war he returned to Münster, where he worked as a chemist with the IG Farben conglomerate. In time, however, he was fired for excessive drinking, a problem that continued to plague him in later years.

(Left to right) Hitler, Goebbels, Hess, German Labor Front leader Robert Ley, and Hans Lammers at a Nazi Party gathering in Berlin on January 30, 1941.

Ley joined the Nazi Party in 1924, and thanks to his obsequious loyalty to Adolf Hitler, rose to important party positions. In 1931 he became Gauleiter of the Rhineland, and in 1930 a Nazi member of the Reichstag for Cologne. He also established himself as an anti-Semite and a minor Nazi ideologist in his newspaper, the *Western German Observer (Westdeutscher Beobachter)*, which he filled with vicious articles against Jewish financiers and store owners, sometimes in the attempt to extort money from them. Other targets were bourgeois liberals. As one both educated and willing to perform the dirty work of the Nazi movement, Ley proved useful to his superiors. He was named Reich organization leader in November 1932.

After the Nazis took power Ley hoped to expand his power by becoming the head of the Prussian State Council, but he was blocked in this by Hermann Göring. Soon after, Ley took steps to establish himself as the Third Reich's labor czar by forming, on May 2, 1933, a committee for the protection of German workers. With Hitler's approval, Ley's new group took the lead in coordinating trade unions and other labor groups into the Nazi system, often through intimidation and by imprisoning labor leaders. Within months he had created an umbrella organization, the German Labor Front, designed to look after the interests of German workers. In speeches Ley claimed to be one of them, and wanted to ensure them that they would be respected members of the nation with no need of unions, strikes, or Communist talk about class struggle. The arrival of Hitler, he asserted, meant that the class struggle in Germany was irrelevant.

By 1939 the German Labor Front was the largest civilian organization in Nazi Germany, involving 25 million German workers. Reflecting its size, it also became a huge bureaucracy, with tentacles in every German industry. In many ways it replaced, with a state bureaucracy, the earlier efforts of both labor unions and employers by setting wage rates, controlling hiring and firing, and sponsoring education and social welfare programs such as care for the unemployed and aged. One of Ley's goals was to ensure maximum productivity, and to accomplish this he used both Nazi rhetoric and top-down authoritarianism. German workers, for instance, were told that they were soldiers for the economy while employers and Nazi bureaucrats retained managerial and disciplinary roles.

Ley also helped devise a number of programs to show that workers were being cared for and valued as members of the Third Reich. These included Strength Through Joy, which sponsored recreational activities, cheap vacations, and, by the time World War II began, two large ocean liners. Another was Beauty of Labor, which sent agents out to various workplaces to make sure that employers had made their factory and office environments more pleasant by adding better lighting, potted plants, recreational facilities, or other improvements. One of Ley's crowning glories was the creation of the Volkswagen, the People's Car, allowing him to argue that, unlike workers in other European countries, workers in the Third Reich could own their own automobiles. Though a number of workers participated in the payroll deduction plan that allowed them to save for the car, its factory was shifted to war production in 1939; not only did no German worker drive a Volkswagen, at least until after the war, but no German worker got his money back.

Ley used the vast German Labor Front network, which included banks and insurance companies, as a source of personal wealth as well as personal power. He remained, moreover, an alcoholic and an uncouth hypocrite, largely disliked and ignored by other top Nazis. Nevertheless, he carved out his own niche in the Third Reich's totalitarian system and, thanks to his worship of Hitler, remained an influential figure. During World War II he was put in charge of the Reich housing program and organized new schools known as Order Castles, where future Nazi leaders would be trained. The Order Castles, strange institutions replete with medieval symbolism and discipline, proved highly unpopular.

At war's end Ley was captured by American forces while trying to escape to the Alps. He was to be one of the top Nazis put on trial by the International Military Tribunal at Nuremberg, but he committed suicide in his cell on October 24, 1945. *See also* German Labor Front, Vol. 1; Nuremberg trials, Strength Through Joy, Vol. 2; Ley, Strength Through Joy: Taking Care of the German Worker, Vol. 4.

Liebenfels, Jörg Lanz von (1874–1954)

Right-wing pseudoscientist who claimed to be the founder of Nazi ideology. An Austrian born Adolf Josef Lanz, he self-consciously adopted several versions of the name Jörg Lanz with the aristocratic tag "von Liebenfels." He originally set out for a career in the Roman Catholic Church and studied in a Cistercian monastery for six years. In 1899, however, he was expelled from the order and devoted himself to building what was in effect a religious order dedicated to ethnic Germanism. He called this organization the Order of the Pure Temple. It was based on the idea that the Aryan peoples of Germanic-speaking lands were involved in a perpetual conflict with everyone else, whom he referred to as Chandalas, a description used in India for untouchables, and further subdivided into either "monkey people" or "hobgoblins." Lanz von Liebenfels argued that the Aryans could never improve themselves or human civilization unless these inferior peoples were defeated in a racial crusade. Many of these ideas were published in Lanz von Liebenfels's journal, which he named *Ostara* after the ancient Germanic goddess of beauty. The journal had a wide audience in both Germany and Austria in the first decade of the twentieth century. Back issues of *Ostara*, which was decorated with a variety of symbols including the swastika, were devoured by Adolf Hitler, allegedly, during his years in Vienna from 1907 to 1913, and the young layabout even sought out Lanz von Liebenfels to supply him with more ammunition for his coffeehouse arguments. When, after 1933, Lanz von Liebenfels sought due credit for what he believed was his influence on Hitler and Nazism, the Führer repudiated him and banned his writings. Lanz von Liebenfels died in Austria in 1954. *See also* anti-Semitism, Aryans, Vol. 1; swastika, völkisch state, Vol. 2.

List, Wilhelm (1880–1971)

General field marshal in the Wehrmacht. List was born in Oberkirchberg in western Germany on May 14, 1880. He took up a career in the German Imperial Army, serving as a staff officer during World War I. After the war he fought briefly with the right-wing Freikorps movement before returning to the army. Many of his appointments were administrative rather than field commands. In 1927 he became head of the Army Organization Department in Berlin and in 1930, now promoted to major general, he was named the head of the Reichswehr's infantry school.

After the Nazis took power List continued his steady rise in rank and responsibility. By 1938 he was a lieutenant general and the chief of the German army in Vienna. In 1939, when World War II broke out, he was promoted to full general and stood as the sixth highest ranking officer in the Wehrmacht. List had important commands in the invasions of both Poland and France, and like a number of other top military leaders he was promoted by Adolf Hitler to the rank of general field marshal after the fall of France in the summer of 1940. From June to October 1941 he was the commander in chief of German forces in southeastern Europe, involved in operations and agreements in Bulgaria, Greece, and Yugoslavia. In July 1941 he was named commander of Army

Group A during the German invasion of the Soviet Union. His target was to achieve control of the oil- and agriculture-rich areas of the Caucasus and southern Russia. His failure to do so by September 1942 resulted in his dismissal by a frustrated Hitler. List spent the remainder of the war in retirement. In 1948 he was sentenced to life imprisonment by an American military tribunal for his actions in southeastern Europe and the Soviet Union. He was freed, however, in 1952. List died in Garmisch in southern Germany on June 18, 1971. *See also* List Regiment, Vol. 1.

Lohse, Heinrich (1896–1964)

Reich commissar of the conquered areas the Germans called Ostland: the Baltic states of Latvia, Lithuania, and Estonia, and Belarus (White Russia); all were sites of numerous Nazi atrocities. Lohse was born in Mühlenbarbek in the northern German area of Schleswig-Holstein on September 2, 1896. He was an early member of the Nazi Party in a region that was slow to embrace the movement; Adolf Hitler named him Gauleiter of Schleswig-Holstein in 1925, and over the next years he represented the Nazi Party in the Reichstag. After Hitler took power he became the Nazi governor of Schleswig-Holstein as well as a member of the Prussian State Council and, in 1934, an honorary SA general.

Lohse was appointed the Reich commissar of Ostland in 1941. Together with the Reichskommissariat of Ukraine, the area composed the eastern occupied territories under the overarching authority of Alfred Rosenberg. Rosenberg's influence was minimal, however, and the main challenge to Lohse's authority came not from him but from the SS. Lohse's headquarters were in Riga, and from there he hoped to use local Jewish people as workers in German munitions plants. He was surprised to find that, after the summer of 1941, the SS largely had authority, outside of his jurisdiction, to massacre Jews wholesale. As a Nazi Party official, however, Lohse did not want to question the authority of Reichsführer-SS Heinrich Himmler, and he did little to prevent the extermination of Jews in Ostland, which was one of the first areas to be declared "judenfrei": free of Jews. Among the great massacres in the territory was the liquidation of the large ghetto at Vilna, although many young Jews escaped Vilna and joined Russian and Polish partisans in the nearby forests.

As World War II drew to a close, Lohse managed an escape to the west rather than capture by the Russians or the Poles. In 1948, he was sentenced to ten years' imprisonment by a British war crimes tribunal. He was released in 1951, however, for reasons of ill health, and he returned to live in Schleswig-Holstein. There, thanks to his long years of service in the 1920s and 1930s, he was able to draw a state pension until it was revoked by the West German government. He died in Mühlenbarbeck on February 25, 1964. *See also* Reich Commissariat Ostland, Vilna ghetto uprising, Vol. 2.

Lord Haw Haw (William Joyce) (1906–1946)

An American-born British subject who broadcast pro-Nazi propaganda from Berlin during World War II. William Joyce was born in New York City in 1906 to a family of British heritage. He moved to Ireland at age three and never afterward returned to the United States. He moved to England from Ireland and, in 1933, joined the British Union of Fascists, a small organization led by Sir Oswald Mosley. Finding that the British Union had little appeal among Britons, Joyce left for the Third Reich in 1939, pleased with both Nazi ideas and their image of strength and decisiveness. Nazi authorities used him to deliver propaganda to British forces during the war in statements claiming, for instance, that Germany would inevitably win and that the British should switch to the winning side.

Few Britons took him seriously, dubbing him Lord Haw Haw.

Joyce was arrested by British authorities on May 28, 1945, and tried in London for treason. He was found guilty and sentenced to death. After an appeal failed, he was hanged on January 3, 1946. *See also* Axis Sally, Vol. 3.

Lorenz, Werner (1891–1974)

SS officer and chief of the Ethnic German Intermediary Agency, which played a large role in trying to carry out the Third Reich's goal of transforming the population of eastern Europe in order to make it more German. Lorenz was born in Grünhof in Prussia on October 2, 1891. He came from a wealthy family and never had to work for a living, inheriting both a large agricultural estate and interests in a number of industries; Lorenz carried the air of an aristocratic sophisticate throughout his long involvement with the Nazi movement. He served as a pilot during World War I and with the rightwing Freikorps after the war, soon after turning his energies to the fledgling Nazi Party. He joined the SS in 1931.

Lorenz served as head of the Ethnic German Mittelstelle from 1937 to 1945. The office, a branch of the SS, was designed to tie Germans living outside the Reich to Germany proper. Under Lorenz's authority, and using methods ranging from intelligence gathering to outright subversion, it played a role in a variety of actions, including the annexations of Austria and the Sudetenland. During World War II, the office took charge of the effort to bring German speakers from the Baltic states, Poland, and Russia into the Greater German Reich for resettlement. The transition was rarely smooth; many ethnic Germans were simply uprooted and placed for months in resettlement camps. Reich Germans, for their part, sometimes considered the newcomers foreigners with strange ways. Those ethnic Germans who found themselves, voluntarily or not, in either the SS or the German armed forces rarely were assigned alongside Reich Germans. Lorenz's office was absorbed during the war into the larger Office for the Consolidation of German Nationhood, in which Lorenz himself continued to exercise the bulk of the authority as head of the International Relations Division in the Central SS Office. In 1943 he was named an SS lieutenant general. Perhaps because of the nature of his responsibilities Lorenz remained aloof from many of the atrocities committed by other SS men in eastern Europe; he was charged with bringing Germans in rather than, in whatever way necessary, removing Poles, Jews, or Russians.

In 1948 Lorenz was sentenced to twenty years in prison by an American war crimes tribunal. He was released, however, in 1955. Lorenz died on May 13, 1974. *See also* ethnic Germans, Vol. 1; SS Race and Resettlement Office, Vol. 2.

Ludendorff, Erich (1865–1937)

General in the German Imperial Army, arguably the most powerful man in Germany in the later years of World War I, and one of Adolf Hitler's earliest supporters among Germany's military class. Ludendorff was born in Kruszewnia in what was later Poland on April 9, 1865. He joined the army as a junior officer in 1881, and thanks to his energy, creativity, and assertiveness found himself in increasingly responsible posts, including the head of an organization that helped devise the plans for the German invasion of Belgium and France in 1914. By the time World War I began that year he was a major general and was named quartermaster of the Second Army. After commanding field units in France with great success, Ludendorff was transferred to the eastern front, where Germany was fighting imperial Russia. He was appointed chief of staff to General Paul von Hindenburg, commander of the Eighth Army and later president of the Weimar Republic.

Under Hindenburg, Ludendorff emerged as one of the most powerful men not only

Influential German general and World War I hero Erich Ludendorff (far right) reviews new officers near Berlin in about 1918.

in the German army but in the German state as well. He helped lead German forces to a number of important victories in the east, and in September 1916 he was appointed quartermaster general, with Hindenburg as supreme commander. The two found themselves forced to take a more active role in politics due to the indecisiveness of Germany's politicians and the increasing irrationality of Kaiser Wilhelm II. Ludendorff was instrumental in devising the plan in which the Germans helped Lenin, the leader of the Russian Communists, return to Russia from his Swiss exile in order to guide the Russian Revolution; Ludendorff understood that Lenin would probably take Russia out of World War I. After Lenin's Bolsheviks succeeded in taking over Russia and expressed their desire to make a peace with Germany, Ludendorff helped force the Russians into giving up a great deal of territory in return with the Treaty of Brest-Litovsk, signed in March 1918. In the fall of that year, with German armies unable to break through in the west, he urged Kaiser Wilhelm and the government to sue for peace. In the ensuing upheaval, which ultimately resulted in the downfall of the kaiser, the end of World War I, and the beginning of the Weimar Republic, Ludendorff was removed from his posts. For a short time he lived in exile in Sweden but returned to Germany in February 1919, settling in Munich.

Although he was no longer an officer in the army, Ludendorff still enjoyed a reputation as a strong, nationalist leader, and he took a number of actions to build that reputation further in the years immediately after the war. He took part, for instance, in the right-wing Kapp Putsch of early 1920. He also advocated the repudiation of the Treaty of Versailles, and was one of the driving forces behind the notion that Germany had been "stabbed in the back" by its leaders at the end of the war. As a solution he supported a right-wing revolution based on Germanic nationalism. The young Adolf Hitler, understanding the prestige that Ludendorff would lend to his nascent Nazi Party, took steps to tie the former general to the Nazis. During the Beer Hall Putsch of 1923, in fact, it was Ludendorff who gave the attempted uprising what little credibility it may have had outside the Nazi movement. On the night of November 9, when the putsch began, Ludendorff's arrival in the beer hall turned the crowd the Nazis' way, and on the next day, when Hitler staged a march through the streets of Munich hoping to foment a popular uprising, Ludendorff marched at Hitler's side. Indeed, according to Hitler's plan Ludendorff, not Hitler, would be named the leader of the Nazi Party if the uprising succeeded. When Hitler's march was stopped at a police barricade and firing began, only Ludendorff, not Hitler, Göring, or any of the others, stood his ground; the others flung themselves to the ground and crawled off.

Like Hitler, Ludendorff was arrested and placed on trial for high treason. Unwilling to convict the war hero, however, the judges acquitted him of all charges. While Hitler remained in jail Ludendorff emerged as one of the political leaders of the Nazi Party along with Gregor Strasser. He was elected to the Weimar Reichstag on the Nazi ticket in 1924, remaining there until 1928, and he was the effective commander of the SA. After Hitler was released from prison, however, the two distanced themselves from each other.

In the late 1920s Ludendorff began to develop a bizarre philosophy that blamed all of Germany's troubles on Jews, Freemasons, and "Romanists," by which he meant Roman Catholics. In this he was allegedly guided by his second wife, a psychiatrist named Mathilde von Kemnitz. The two formed a society known as the Tannenberg Group in 1926 to discuss and disseminate information as to how these groups had powers that extended across borders, used secret police, and planned a "Judeo-Masonic World State." Ludendorff claimed that World War I was, in fact, one of their ploys to destroy nations such as Germany. These ideas were even rejected by the Nazis, who found themselves in an uncomfortable position with regard to Ludendorff. He was a hero of the Beer Hall Putsch, one of the greatest events in Nazi history, but he was also increasingly eccentric, his ideas inconsistent with Nazi ideology. Ludendorff, for his part, grew increasingly to distrust Hitler. In 1933 he warned his old comrade Hindenburg, now president of Germany, that Hitler would lead Germany to ruin. Ludendorff died in Tutzing, Bavaria, on December 20, 1937. The Nazis, as they were wont to do in such circumstances, gave him a state funeral with full military honors. *See also* Beer Hall Putsch, Vol. 1; *Total War*, World War I, Vol. 2.

Lueger, Karl (1844–1910)

Austrian politician who used anti-Semitism to attract mass support; he was thought to have been a major influence on the developing ideas of the young Adolf Hitler when the future Führer was a young Viennese vagrant. Lueger was born in Vienna on October 24, 1844. He became a lawyer and entered politics in Vienna in the 1870s, where he helped to found the Christian Social Party, a conservative party interested in restoring Roman Catholic authority and morality. Lueger was elected mayor of Vienna in 1896, using stereotypical descriptions of Jews as financial manipulators and anti-Christians to drum up support among the city's lower classes. The stratagem worked, even though Lueger had no strong history as an anti-Semite, and he continued to vilify Jews publicly until he died in office on March 10, 1910. It is thought that Lueger was one of several early sources from which Hitler absorbed his ideological hatred of Jews based on generalized stereotypes. *See also* anti-Semitism, Vol. 1; Vienna, Vol. 2; Hitler, Adolf, Vol. 3.

Luther, Martin (1895–1945)

A top official in the Third Reich's Foreign Ministry during World War II. He was closely involved in the program to "cleanse" Europe of Jews through mass murder. Luther was born in Berlin on December 16, 1895. During World War II he served as an enlisted man in behind-the-lines posts, and after the war he worked as a laborer in the Berlin area. He joined the Nazi Party in 1933 and went to work for his future boss, Foreign Minister Joachim von Ribbentrop, in 1936 in an agency known as the Ribbentrop Bureau. The bureau was an office within the Nazi Party that depicted itself as the center of foreign policy. From very humble beginnings as an office functionary, Luther rose to be one of Ribbentrop's most trusted underlings. In 1940 Ribbentrop, by now foreign minister, named him to a key post, head of the "Germany" section of the Foreign Office. There Luther had responsibility for maintaining contact between the Foreign Office and other divisions of the Nazi state and bureaucracy, such as the Ministry of the Interior, the Wehrmacht, and the SS.

Over the next three years Luther worked to consolidate his position as a top Nazi official. He often used his contacts with SS leaders Heinrich Himmler and Reinhard Heydrich to go behind Ribbentrop's back in areas of joint jurisdiction, and he built up a cadre of like-minded young Nazis in the hope of ensuring that the Foreign Office would maintain an important role in the Third Reich. In July 1941 he was named undersecretary in the Foreign Ministry, and therefore Ribbentrop's number two man. In January 1942 he represented his ministry at the infamous Wannsee Conference. There, Heydrich made it clear to various officials that mass extermination was to be the "Final Solution to the Jewish Question" and that the SS was in charge of the entire operation. Over the next year Luther proved very cooperative in using the Foreign Office to provide the SS with assistance in deporting the Jews of western and southeastern Europe to the Polish death camps. Like certain other young, highly placed Nazi officials such as Adolf Eichmann, Luther understood that the mass murder program was an opportunity to build his career and reputation. By April 1943 Luther felt confident enough to mount an effort to have Ribbentrop overthrown, understanding that his boss enjoyed little respect among leading Nazis. Ribbentrop, however, learned of Luther's plans in advance and had him taken to the Sachsenhausen concentration camp, where he remained until the last weeks of World War II. He died in a Berlin hospital in May 1945. *See also* Wannsee Conference, Vol. 2; Ribbentrop, Joachim von, Vol. 3.

Lutze, Victor (1890–1943)

The chief of staff of the SA after its former leader, Ernst Röhm, was killed in the Blood Purge of July 30, 1934. Lutze was born in northern Germany on December 28, 1890, and served throughout World War I. He joined the Nazi Party in 1922, becoming a deputy Gauleiter by 1925, a senior leader of the SA by 1928, and a member of the Reichstag in 1930. After the Nazis took power in 1933 he was appointed to the Prussian State Council, to a post as police president of Hanover, and he was also promoted to SA general. Apparently, Lutze was one of the men who confronted Röhm with the various charges that led to his summary execution during the Blood Purge, and Hitler rewarded his loyalty by naming him as the top man in the SA. Under Lutze's leadership, however, and in the face of the more disciplined, aggressive and efficient SS, the SA grew increasingly marginalized, rarely performing more than a ceremonial role. Lutze died in an automobile accident in May 1943. *See also* Blood Purge, Vol. 1; SA, Vol. 2.

Mannerheim, Karl Gustav (1867–1951)

Political and military leader of Finland during the era of the Third Reich. Mannerheim was born in a village near the city of Turku in Finland, not far from the Russian border. When he was a young man his nation was part of the Russian Empire, and Mannerheim fought in the Russian army during the Russo-Japanese War of 1904–1905 and in the early years of World War I. During the Russian Revolution of 1917 he left the country and led the army that prevented a Bolshevik takeover of Finland. Along with other Finnish nationalists, he proclaimed his country's independence in 1919.

After withdrawing from active political life, Mannerheim was recalled by his countrymen to lead their military forces in 1939 when, made confident by the territorial gains that the Nazi-Soviet Pact of August 23 made possible, the Soviets made aggressive moves toward the Finns. Over the winter of 1939–1940, Mannerheim led the Finns in a war against Soviet Russia, surprising the world by devising clever strategies that allowed his tiny country to hold out against the Soviets for several months. During this period the Third Reich observed its peace agreement with the Soviet Union and remained neutral in the conflict. Mannerheim's successes, however, helped to convince German military strategists that they could defeat the Soviet army. Intimations by the French and British that they might send volunteers to help the Finns also suggested to the Germans the necessity of conquering Norway and Denmark.

Despite the staunch defense of his country, Mannerheim was forced to submit to Soviet numerical and material superiority, signing a peace in March 1940 that required him to give up Finnish Karelia. When Germany invaded the Soviet Union in June 1941, Mannerheim allied himself with Hitler in hopes of regaining that territory. Finland remained a military ally of the Third Reich until Mannerheim signed a separate peace with the Soviets in 1944. The Finnish leader categorically refused, however, to cooperate in Nazi wartime atrocities, and he threatened to use the Finnish army to defend his nation's tiny Jewish community against the SS. Mannerheim retired from public life and died in 1951. *See also* allies of the Third Reich, Vol. 1; Russo-Finnish War, Vol. 2.

Manstein, Friedrich Erich von (1887–1973)

One of the top commanders of the Wehrmacht, the regular German army, during World War II. He is most remembered for devising the strategy that allowed German forces to divide their French and British opponents during the invasion of France in May 1940, thus enabling the Third Reich to force a French surrender relatively quickly and easily. Like many top commanders, Manstein also maintained contact with members of the German resistance movement, although in the end he chose to maintain his loyalty to Adolf Hitler and the Nazi regime.

Manstein was born to the son of a German general by the name of Lewinski in November 1887. Both of his parents, however, died soon after he was born, and he was adopted by the Mansteins, a family of Prussian aristocrats. The young Manstein gravitated naturally toward a military career, and became an officer in the German Imperial Army at the age of seventeen. During World War I he served with distinction on both the eastern and the western fronts.

During the era of the Weimar Republic Manstein held various staff and political appointments with the Reichswehr, as the German army was known at that time. He was also promoted regularly. He was a colonel and head of a department in the General Staff by 1933, a major general by 1936, and a lieutenant general by 1938. He also served as chief quartermaster during the late 1930s. As war approached, Manstein was appointed chief of staff to General Ludwig Beck, the commander in chief of the army. After Beck resigned his post out of concern over Adolf Hitler's expansionist plans, Manstein was appointed chief of staff to General Gerd von Rundstedt, who commanded an army group destined for the invasion of Poland. In this position Manstein developed the strategy German forces were to use in France. It involved a blitzkrieg attack through the forests of the Ardennes, which stood in the center of the Allied defenses and which the Allies considered too thick and mountainous for a modern force to pass through effectively. The daring maneuver allowed the Germans to enter France in between the Maginot line defenses to the south and the bulk of the Allied armies, which anticipated a German invasion through Belgium and which were therefore stationed along the French-Belgian border. Manstein himself was sent to lead the infantry corps, which was the first to cross the Seine River in France, an important barrier. In recognition of his successes in France Manstein was promoted to general field marshal and made a general of infantry.

He was then transferred to the eastern front, where the invasion of the Soviet Union loomed as the next military operation to be undertaken by the Third Reich. There, Manstein enjoyed successes with a number of commands. In the initial weeks of the invasion, which began on June 22, 1941, Manstein's 56th Panzer Corps drove quickly through the Baltic regions toward Leningrad, although Hitler chose to besiege the city rather than attempt to take it. In September 1941 Manstein was appointed to the command of the Eleventh Army, which was mobilized along the southeastern front. In this post, which he held until 1944, Manstein enjoyed some of his greatest successes as his army took the Crimea, the important Black Sea town of Sebastopol, and nearly five hundred thousand Russian prisoners.

Manstein was never a devoted Nazi, although he sometimes parroted the party line concerning the necessity for German soldiers to be merciless toward Bolsheviks and even Jews. He remained, however, a devoted military man, concerning himself only with success on the battlefield rather than political or ideological matters. He was first approached by the German resistance movement in 1942. He told them that he might be willing to support them as long as he maintained command of the Eleventh Army and was allowed to take Sebastopol. Once the city was conquered, Manstein declared himself willing to join the resistance, whose guiding light at that moment was his former superior, Ludwig Beck. Manstein insisted, however, on one condition: that the Germans take the Volga River city of Stalingrad. When General Paulus failed at Stalingrad over the winter of 1942–1943, Manstein backed away and reiterated his loyalty to Hitler. He remained convinced that, despite the debacle at Stalingrad, the Germans could defeat the Soviet Union. He helped to reorganize German forces after their retreat from Stalingrad and, for a brief period, revived their thrust into Soviet territory by taking the city of Kharkiv in March 1943. Meanwhile, he repudiated the German resistance movement by, among other things, refusing to accept Major General Henning von Tresckow, a leading member of the resistance, as his chief of staff.

From March 1933 until March 1944, Manstein tried to convince Hitler that he had devised a way to continue the German advance into the Soviet Union. His plan involved a series of strategic retreats, which would both allow German forces to regroup with regular and reliable supplies and reinforcements and encourage the enemy to spread its forces thinly. It was a reasonable strategy that the Führer, however, rejected. On March 24, 1944, by which time Hitler was thoroughly disappointed with most of the Wehrmacht's commanders, Manstein was dismissed from his command. The field marshal spent the last months of the war in retirement at his eastern German estate.

After the war he was arrested by the British, and finally put on trial in Hamburg in 1948 by a British military tribunal. He was accused of encouraging German soldiers to behave ruthlessly toward Soviet civilians in the service of a ruthless ideology that exceeded military conduct. On this charge he was sentenced to a prison term of eighteen years. He was found not guilty, however, of the mass extermination of Jews. In the end Manstein served three years of his sentence, which was first reduced from eighteen to twelve years before, in 1952, he was granted parole for medical reasons. In later years he served as a military adviser to the government of West Germany. He died in a village near Munich on June 10, 1973. *See also* Battle of Stalingrad, blitzkrieg, Vol. 1; Wehrmacht, Vol. 2.

Maurice, Emil (1897–1972)

An early Nazi fighter who served for a time as Adolf Hitler's personal bodyguard. Born in Bavaria in January 1897, he was trained as a clock maker. He was one of the first members of the German Workers' Party, the precursor of the Nazi Party. In 1920, along with a butcher named Ulrich Graf, Maurice organized the Order Troops, whose duty was to protect Hitler and other party leaders as well as project an image of power. Therefore, both he and Graf claimed to be the first Brownshirts, or SA men.

Maurice remained for a number of years within Hitler's inner circle, though other Nazis disliked him for, among other things, his dark skin and French background. He took part in the Beer Hall Putsch of 1923, and later shared Hitler's imprisonment at Landsberg Prison in Munich, where he was the first to take the Nazi leader's dictation of what later became *Mein Kampf*. He also was acquainted with Angela (Geli) Raubal, whom some have called the only woman Hitler ever truly loved. It is rumored that Maurice too was in love with Raubal, and that the conflict of a relationship triangle was a factor in the girl's mysterious suicide in 1931. During the Blood Purge of June 30, 1934, Maurice was one of the Nazi loyalists willing to shoot Hitler's competitors, a task he had undertaken before. In later years he became an SS officer; in 1937, perhaps to remove him from a Nazi inner circle that had grown increasingly sophisticated, Maurice was appointed the head of an organization of Munich craftsmen. He survived World War II relatively peacefully and lived on until February 1972. *See also* Days of Struggle, Vol. 1; Hitler, Adolf; Raubal, Geli, Vol. 3.

Mayer, Helene (1910–1953)

A German women's fencing champion whose high status in the Third Reich was unusual. Born in Offenbach in western Germany in 1910, she was an accomplished athlete, becoming the German fencing champion at the age of fifteen. In 1928 she took a gold medal in the sport at the Amsterdam Olympic Games, and competed in the 1932 Olympics in Los Angeles, moving to California that year to study law. By the time the Nazis took power in 1933 she was a national hero, extolled as such by Nazi propagandists such as Joseph Goebbels, who praised the tall, blond Mayer as the perfect example of German womanhood and encouraged her to return to Germany. Soon, however, it was revealed that Mayer had a Jewish father and grandparents, and therefore, after the Nuremberg Laws of 1935 took effect, she was subjected to a variety of restrictions. She insisted, however, on representing Germany at the 1936 Olympics in Berlin, where she took a silver medal in fencing. German authorities were in fact eager for her Olympic participation, both because of her reputation and skill and because allowing her to compete would seem to show the world that the Nazi regime was not oppressing German Jews. On the podium to accept her medal in clothing bearing the Reich flag and a swastika, she raised her right arm in the Nazi salute, drawing censure from international Jewish organizations. After the Olympics, Mayer returned to the United States, where she continued her studies and her fencing career and became a U.S. citizen. She returned to Germany only in 1952, and died on October 15, 1953. *See also* sports in the Third Reich, women in the Third Reich, Vol. 2.

Meissner, Otto (1880–1953)

A German politician and high-level bureaucrat in the Reichs Chancellery from 1920 to 1945, first under President Friedrich Ebert, then under President Paul von Hindenburg, and finally under Adolf Hitler. He was one of the individuals who helped Hitler come to power in 1933 by convincing Hindenburg to appoint him chancellor of Germany.

Meissner was born in Alsace, along the French-German border, in March 1880. He eventually took a law degree and a job with the German state railways. During World War I he served both in the infantry and in political posts along the eastern front. In 1918 he joined the German Foreign Office and then in 1920 took the post as head of the Reichs Chancellery, where he became a powerful adviser to the powerful. Along with Oskar von Hindenburg, the president's son, Meissner was active behind the scenes in assembling the conservative coalition that Hitler was to head as chancellor beginning January 30, 1933. Hitler decided to keep him on, naming him state secretary and, in 1937, Reich minister. Meissner mostly laid low, however, during the era of the Third Reich, the model of the inconspicuous but steady bureaucrat.

After the war Meissner was acquitted of all charges of war crimes, first by an American military tribunal and then by a German denazification court. He wrote a memoir entitled *State Secretary Under Ebert, Hindenburg, and Hitler*, which was published in 1950. He died in Munich in April 1953. *See also* Machtergreifung, Vol. 2.

Mengele, Josef (1911–1979?)

Perhaps the most infamous of Nazi doctors and the man known as Auschwitz's "Angel of Death." His responsibilities at Auschwitz included conducting the selections separating those to be gassed immediately after arrival from those allowed to survive for

Nazi physician Josef Mengele subjected Auschwitz inmates, including many children, to inhumane medical experiments.

slave labor. He also performed cruel and gruesome experiments using camp inmates, often children, as research subjects.

Josef Mengele was born in Bavaria on March 16, 1911. He moved to Munich in the 1920s to study philosophy. There he discovered the racial ideology of such figures as Alfred Rosenberg, the Nazi philosopher. Rosenberg argued, among other things, that the Aryans were a superior race threatened by the prospect of race mixing with inferior races such as Jews. The notion struck Mengele as correct, and he became a devotee of eugenics and racial science. He took a medical degree from the University of Frankfurt am Main and became a dedicated Nazi.

Mengele's great scientific interest was in finding ways to enrich the German "bloodstock." In 1934 he joined an organization known as the Institute for Hereditary Biology and Race Research, where he conducted research on twins, on the premise that increasing the production of twins, provided they were racially pure, would be one way to maintain the racial health and superiority of the German people. In 1939 he joined the Waffen-SS and served as a medical officer in France and the Soviet Union. In 1943 Heinrich Himmler appointed him chief medical officer at Auschwitz, where his notoriety lay in his life-or-death power at railroad siding selections. With a glance and a gesture Mengele would order a prisoner immediately to the gas chambers or to the barracks for slave labor. On other occasions Mengele could be equally arbitrary and cruel: In one instance he condemned an entire barracks of 750 women prisoners to the gas chambers simply because he was told that the block was infected with lice.

Mengele also took advantage of the flow of prisoners into Auschwitz to continue his experiments on twins, particularly children. He generally selected twins for survival even though as a matter of course children too young to work were executed immediately. The doctor then installed them in a special "children's wing" of the Auschwitz hospital, where he performed numerous experiments on them. These included injecting chemicals in their eyes to make them turn blue and, once, having two children sewn together in order to create a pair of conjoined twins. In an eerie way Mengele seemed fond of children, and often gave his research subjects candy or other rewards if they behaved themselves.

After the war Mengele was initially interned in a British hospital. But using false papers he escaped, first to Rome and then to Buenos Aires, Argentina, using the name Gregorio Gregori. Considered a top Nazi war criminal, for years he managed to elude the various organizations and individuals who never stopped searching for him. These included Interpol; the Israeli Secret Service; the West German government; and Simon Wiesenthal, the independent Nazi hunter. He was spotted on a number of occasions and reported to have become a citizen of Paraguay and to have lived in Brazil. In 1985, after a reward of $50,000 was offered for information about him, witnesses claimed that he had died in a drowning accident in Embu, Brazil, in 1979. A number of forensic scientists sent to Brazil to investigate the skeleton determined that it was probably that of Mengele. *See also* Auschwitz, Vol. 1; medical experiments, selection, Vol. 2.

Milch, Erhard (1892–1972)

A top officer, and part organizer, of the Luftwaffe, the air force of Nazi Germany. Erhard Milch was born in the north German port of Wilhelmshaven on March 30, 1892. His father was a minor naval employee and his mother was Jewish, a fact that caused him surprisingly little trouble in later years. During World War I Milch served in the German air corps. After the war he joined a Freikorps unit and served briefly in a police air squadron. From 1920 to 1933 he worked in civil rather than military aviation with both the Junkers group and Lufthansa, Germany's main civil airline. From 1926 to

1933, in fact, he was chief of finance on Lufthansa's board of directors.

While he worked for Lufthansa, Milch developed an interest in Nazism, and in 1933 he joined the Nazi Party. Hermann Göring, the head of the Reich Air Ministry and the Luftwaffe, named him state secretary of the Air Ministry. He also served as the armaments chief of the Luftwaffe, working closely with manufacturers, industrialists, and financiers. His skill in this area brought him into close contact with Albert Speer, Reich minister for armaments and war production during World War II. Göring knew of Milch's Jewish mother, but the fact did not bother him inordinately since he never shared the doctrinaire anti-Semitism of Adolf Hitler and other Nazis. Bearing out a famous boast he once made that he himself determined who was or was not a Jew, Göring simply Aryanized Milch by having his mother sign a document declaring that she was not, in fact, his mother, and that Erhard was born illegitimate.

Meanwhile, Milch distinguished himself not only with political and organizational achievements but also as a field commander. In 1939 he commanded the Air Fleet V, and later commanded Luftwaffe fleets during the German attacks on Norway and France. He was promoted to general field marshal, along with his Luftwaffe colleagues Albert Kesselring and Hugo Sperrle, on July 19, 1940, for his work in helping to defeat France. From 1941 to 1944 he was the inspector general of the Luftwaffe in addition to several other posts: technical director of the Air Ministry and, after 1942, transportation chief of the German Reich along with Speer. In the later years of World War II Milch, like Speer, tried to convince his superiors to modify the production of aircraft and armaments to better counter the production of the Reich's enemies, but he found that Göring and Hitler lacked his practical perspective.

Milch was arrested after the war and put on trial in 1947 for war crimes, most notably the use of slave labor and the targeting of civilians during air campaigns. The Nuremberg tribunal sentenced him to life in prison, but he was released in 1954. In later years he worked as an industrial adviser in the Ruhr area. He died in Wuppertal in 1972. *See also* Luftwaffe, Vol. 1; Göring, Hermann; Kesselring, Albert, Vol. 3.

Model, Walther von (1891–1945)

One of the few top regular German army commanders whose loyalty to Adolf Hitler was unquestioning and consistent. Model was born to a middle-class family in eastern Germany on January 24, 1891. His father was a music teacher. He embarked, instead, on a military career and served during World War I and the Weimar era in a number of posts. After Hitler took power in 1933, Model became a devoted Nazi. In 1935 he began a rapid rise with his promotion to head of the Technical Department of the General Staff. By the time World War II began he was a major general and a tank commander on the Polish front. He also served in France, where he was promoted first to lieutenant general and then to full general. During the invasion of the Soviet Union, Model was head of Panzer troops and a field commander with both the 3rd Panzer Division and the Ninth Army, which reached the outskirts of Moscow. In June 1944 Hitler promoted him to general field marshal; he had outlasted and outperformed many of his former superiors and, in any case, Hitler preferred him to other top officers, most of whom were elitists or aristocrats who emerged out of the Prussian military tradition. Model's background, however, was far more humble, and he had risen through the ranks through achievements as well as his loyalty to the Führer. Model, in fact, was one of the few men who could object to Hitler's ideas in person without fear of risking offense. As field marshal, Model was returned to the eastern front in the summer of 1944 to see if some way could be found to stop the building Soviet advance.

As the war drew to a close Model continued to outlast his colleagues. On August 17, 1944, he was named head of Army Group West, the top German commander in western Europe. He replaced the dismissed Field Marshal Günter Hans von Kluge, who had enraged Hitler by failing to contain the Allied advance through northern France. During the Battle of the Bulge of December 1944, Model commanded with great distinction and resourcefulness; the initial success of the German offensive was largely due to his shrewd tactics. Model and his forces were surrounded in mid-April 1945 in the Ruhr industrial area of western Germany. Rather than be captured he shot himself on April 21, 1945. *See also* Battle of the Bulge, Vol. 1.

Molotov, Vyacheslav (1890–1986)

Commissar of foreign affairs of the Soviet Union from 1939 to 1949. Molotov was born in Kirov in European Russia in 1890 under the name of Skriabin. After joining the Bolsheviks, Russia's revolutionary Communist Party, in 1906, he changed his name to Molotov, a variation on the Russian word for "hammer." He was a key figure in planning the Bolshevik takeover in October 1917 as well as in the civil war and political intrigues that followed. From 1930 to 1941 he served as the premier of the Soviet Union.

Molotov was named foreign commissar in May 1939. He helped to negotiate the Nazi-Soviet Non-Aggression Pact, also called the Molotov-Ribbentrop Pact, which was announced on August 23, 1939. The pact assured Adolf Hitler that the Soviet Union would not interfere with his planned invasion of Poland; in return the Soviets were promised a large chunk of Polish territory. The agreement also defined the separate spheres of influence that the two nations were to possess in eastern Europe. The pact was from the beginning a temporary expedient for both sides, and Molotov broke off negotiations with his Nazi counterpart, Joachim von Ribbentrop, in late 1940 in response to German moves in Finland and Romania. Over

Soviet foreign minister Vyacheslav Molotov signs the Nazi-Soviet Non-Aggression Pact in August 1939.

the next months he appeared to have a clearer understanding than his leader, Joseph Stalin, that a German invasion was imminent. To ensure that the Soviets would not have to fight a two-front war, Molotov negotiated a nonaggression treaty with Japan, Germany's ally, announced on April 13, 1941.

After the German invasion began on June 21 of that year Molotov played an important role in Soviet efforts during World War II as both foreign commissar and a member of the five-man State Defense Committee, which was to guide both political and military policies. He was the chief Soviet negotiator with the western Allies, appearing at all their major conferences and sometimes acting as a substitute for the overworked or ill Stalin. He traveled to London and Washington, D.C., in May 1942 to secure British and American commitments to send supply convoys to the Soviets. In addition, he wanted to pressure the western Allies into opening a second front against Hitler to take some of the military burden off of his country.

The slowness, from Molotov's perspective, of the opening of this second front (though President Franklin D. Roosevelt of the United States promised it as early as 1942, it did not come until D-Day, June 6, 1944) helped inspire Molotov to once again open up negotiations with Ribbentrop through intermediaries in June 1943. The negotiations came to nothing, however, and the western Allies chose not to make an issue of them. Molotov went on to play important roles at the Yalta and Potsdam Conferences of 1945, where the Soviet Union asserted its lasting presence in eastern Europe. He was also the first Soviet delegate to the United Nations.

After World War II Molotov continued to play a central role in Soviet politics. He served again as commissar for foreign affairs from 1953 to 1956 and held a seat in the Central Committee of the Soviet Communist Party. He fell out of favor, however, in 1957 because of his opposition to Stalin's eventual successor Nikita Khrushchev and he was expelled from the party in 1962. In 1984, however, he was reinstated as a national hero and member in good standing of the party. Molotov died in Moscow on November 8, 1986. *See also* Moscow War Crimes Declaration, Nazi-Soviet Pact, Vol. 2; Stalin, Joseph, Vol. 3.

Moltke, Helmuth James Graf von (1907–1945)

German aristocrat, legal adviser to the Abwehr, the intelligence section of the High Command of the German armed forces (OKW), and a leader of the German resistance movement against Adolf Hitler. Moltke was born in Kreisau in eastern Germany on March 2, 1907. His ancestors included Field Marshal Helmut von Moltke, whose armies had defeated France in 1870, and his family was one of Germany's oldest and most distinguished. His mother was part English and both parents were deeply religious, factors that may have helped to inspire both Christian pacifism and a pro-English outlook in Moltke.

Moltke pursued a career in international law in Berlin in his early twenties, during Germany's Weimar years, while overseeing the management of his family's estate at Kreisau. He opposed the Nazi movement from the beginning as immoral and likely to lead Germany to ruin. His expertise in international law brought him into the Abwehr, which he joined in 1939. The organization was already a center of resistance to Hitler through the opposition of Admiral Wilhelm Canaris and General Hans Oster, two top Abwehr officers. During World War II Moltke used his position, as well as his wide range of contacts across Europe, to resist the Nazi regime in small ways: He helped a number of Jews, prisoners of war, and slave laborers escape the Reich, for instance. He is also credited with a role in helping most of the Jews of Denmark to escape deportation to the Polish death camps by passing word of the impending deportation order to sympathizers in the occupation government in Denmark.

Moltke formed the Kreisau Circle, named for his rural estate though most of its meetings were in Berlin, in 1933. The Kreisau Circle was a sort of discussion group of opponents to Nazism. It remained active until 1943, and many prestigious Germans maintained contact with the group. These included religious leaders, aristocrats, intellectuals, military officers, and, at Moltke's insistence, Socialists and trade union officials. Although active resistance leaders in the military, such as Claus Schenk Graf von Stauffenberg and Henning von Tresckow, had connections to the Kreisau Circle, Moltke's group remained more a forum for high-level discussion than a center of conspiracy. Members focused on what might become of Germany and Europe after the era of Nazism, and expressed hope that once again the notions of Christian charity and the rule of law might be revived in the German fatherland.

Moltke was arrested by the Gestapo in January 1944 for alerting a colleague that he was a target for arrest. He remained in various prisons for a year. After the July 1944 Plot on Hitler's life Moltke was connected with the conspirators, and like thousands of other Germans he was put on trial before the People's Court for, allegedly, betraying the Third Reich. He was not directly implicated in the July Plot but Nazi officials nevertheless condemned him for not informing them of resistance activities. He was hanged in Plötzensee Prison in Berlin on January 23, 1945. *See also* Abwehr, Kreisau Circle, Vol. 1; resistance movements, Germany, Vol. 2.

Morell, Theodor (1890–1948)

A medical quack who served as Adolf Hitler's personal physician. His early medical career consisted of a period as a ship's doctor as well as several years treating venereal diseases and other complaints among Berlin's artistic community. He came to Adolf Hitler's attention in 1935 after curing Hitler's photographer, Heinrich Hoffman, of a bacterial infection using rudimentary antibiotics. Finally convinced of Morell's special skills, Hitler, who suffered from a variety of ailments ranging from digestive problems to fatigue, agreed to see him. Morell's solution was to dose the Führer with vitamins, hormones, and dextrose for a year, using injections. Strangely enough, Hitler was cured, at least in the short term. The treatment gave him a confidence in Morell that was to last for nine years, despite the fact that many others in Hitler's circle ridiculed or hated the doctor. Hermann Göring, for instance, called him "Herr Reich Injection Master" because of his love for magical injections of strange concoctions. Hitler's mistress, Eva Braun, called him a pig, and refused to see him because of his offensive personal habits. Hitler remained loyal, nonetheless, and relied on Morell to inject him with something whenever he was feeling ill or needed to present a strong public image. The injections themselves consisted of a variety of enzymes, antibiotics, and drugs, including amphetamines. More reputable doctors in Hitler's circle, reputable medically if not morally, believed that Morell's cures were in fact making the Führer sicker. Among them was the surgeon Karl Brandt, who played a leading role in the T4 euthanasia program and, in 1944, took over from Morell as Hitler's personal doctor after Morell was dismissed in the aftermath of the July Plot. Morell, meanwhile, had grown wealthy from his contact with the Führer. Using public money, he built factories to produce such cure-alls as Morell Russian Lice Powder, which enjoyed a captive market among the German armed forces. He died near Berlin in May 1948. *See also* Hitler, Adolf; Hoffman, Heinrich, Vol. 3.

Müller, Friedrich Max (1823–1900)

Nineteenth-century German-English scholar whose work familiarized the term "Aryan," although racial thinkers such as the Nazis later misunderstood and corrupted his meaning. Müller was born in the German town of Dessau on December 6, 1823. As a young man he became an expert in both the study of languages and comparative religion while a student at the Universities of Leipzig, Berlin, and Paris. His particular interests were in what European scholars referred to as Orientalism, the study of the Middle East, India, and East Asia, and he specialized particularly in Sanskrit studies, Sanskrit being the ancient religious language of India. In 1846 Müller went to England, where he studied a number of ancient Indian manuscripts held in the offices of the British East India Company as well as at Oxford University. He focused his energies on producing a new translation of the Rig Veda, one of the most ancient of Sanskrit religious texts. In 1856 Müller became both a professor of languages at Oxford University, and, choosing to stay in England, a popular writer and lecturer. He often argued that the evolution of human thought could be understood through the development of language.

Müller began to use the term "Aryan" as a simple improvement on the earlier term "Indo-European." Since the late 1700s, other Orientalists had argued that the Indo-European peoples, who originated in south-central Asia, had dispersed in the second millennium B.C., settling in areas from India westward to the British Isles. In the areas they settled—north India, Iran, Greece, Italy, western Europe—they formed the basis of developing civilizations and, despite wide spans of time and space, Indo-European societies continued to share certain elements in terms of gods, political structures, and values. Müller's fundamental work was in the study of these peoples, for whom he preferred the term "Aryan," which he derived from the Sanskrit word *Arya*. The word translated roughly as "land of the noble." In ancient Sanskrit texts it was one of the names used by people to refer to their north Indian homeland.

Müller's fame as a scholar led to the widespread adoption of the term by racial thinkers, who came to think of Aryans as a race rather than widely dispersed peoples who spoke related languages. These thinkers further manipulated ancient myths and stories from India, Greece, Rome, and Germanic Europe to suggest that the Aryans were a pure and superior race, evincing striking qualities of heroism, energy, and creativity. Müller was outspokenly distressed by this misunderstanding of his ideas, claiming that by Aryan he meant no physical trait whatsoever but simply those who speak an Aryan language. Despite these denials, however, the term stuck, as did the understanding among many that there was such a thing as a superior Aryan race that had lost its purity over the centuries. Adolf Hitler and the Nazis, in later years, took this belief one step further in their attempt to restore the ancient purity of the Germanic branch of the Aryans, and the notion appeared frequently in Nazi writing and policy making. Some Nazis, for instance, objected to the oppression of Gypsies on the grounds that, as migrants originating in India, they were fellow Aryans. A solution was found when others argued that, as their devious behavior and unhealthy appearance (to Nazi eyes) suggested, the Gypsies had been sullied over the centuries by race mixing, and were therefore no longer truly Aryan. Müller died in Oxford, England, on October 28, 1900. *See also* Aryans, Vol. 1.

Müller, Heinrich (1901–?)

SS lieutenant general, head of the Gestapo during World War II, and one of the Nazi officials most directly responsible for carrying out the Third Reich's policy of "cleansing" Europe of Jews through mass extermination. Müller's word alone could, and often did, send thousands of people to the gas chambers of Auschwitz or one of the other death camps. As head of Section IV of the Reich Central Security Office

(RSHA), the Gestapo, from 1939 to 1945, Müller was also the direct superior of logistics and "Jewish" expert Adolf Eichmann.

Heinrich Müller was born in Munich on April 28, 1901. He served with distinction in World War I, earning the Iron Cross, First Class, one of the German army's top honors. He became a policeman in Bavaria after the war and gravitated toward counterintelligence via the investigation of potentially subversive groups. These included the Communists and, ironically, the Nazi Party. In the early 1930s Reinhard Heydrich, the head of the Security Service (SD) of the SS, asked him to join his organization, where he rose quickly to become the chief officer of the Gestapo. He officially joined the Nazi Party in 1939, when the SD reorganized into the larger RSHA, a delay that brought him enemies within the Nazi hierarchy. Nevertheless Heydrich and Heinrich Himmler, SS chief, maintained complete confidence in his ruthlessness, intelligence-gathering ability, and willingness to perform lawless but "necessary" tasks.

As Heydrich's subordinate, Müller was intimately involved in the "Final Solution to the Jewish Question" as soon as it was decided in the fall of 1941. He was one of the officials present at the Wannsee Conference of January 20, 1942, where, along with Heydrich and Eichmann, he informed Nazi Party and political officials of the policy of mass extermination. In subsequent months Müller signed numerous orders sending Jews to the death camps from across Europe: from the ghettos in Poland and occupied Russia, from holding camps such as Theresienstadt, and from the occupied nations of western Europe. At least one hundred thousand deportations could be connected directly to the Gestapo chief. He continually urged Eichmann to find more and more victims, his professional status so closely tied to the mass killing process that he was obliged to find ways to continue and expand it. When, in 1943, the Italians proved less than cooperative in gathering and deporting their Jews, Müller was sent to Rome to find out exactly why so many Italian Jews were being allowed to escape. Toward groups of prisoners other than Jews, such as Allied prisoners of war, Müller was hardly more merciful. In one instance he ordered the immediate shooting of a number of escaped British prisoners of war who were caught by SS policemen. Following the Nazi racial line, he was regularly cruel and arbitrary toward Russian prisoners.

Müller was one of the officials who joined Adolf Hitler in the Berlin Führerbunker in the last months of World War II. There he continued to serve as a police officer and, strangely given the circumstances, sought to be appointed successor to the now-disgraced Heinrich Himmler. He disappeared from the bunker on April 28, 1945, two days before Hitler's suicide. He was never conclusively identified, dead or alive, after that. Some concluded that he was killed by Soviet forces who entered Berlin, and his death was recorded on May 17, 1945, but that has never been confirmed. Later reports claimed that he was alive either in eastern Europe, thanks to contacts with Soviet intelligence officials, or in South America, the destination of many SS war criminals. He remains on lists of wanted Nazi war criminals. *See also* Final Solution, Führerbunker, Gestapo, Vol. 1; Wannsee Conference, Vol. 2; Heydrich, Reinhard, Vol. 3.

Müller, Ludwig (1883–1946)

Protestant pastor and theologian who served for a time as Adolf Hitler's Reich bishop and the head of a nazified Protestant sect known as German Christians. Müller was born in Gütersloh in northern Germany on June 23, 1883. During World War I he served as a military chaplain, and after the war he was a pastor in the naval command in the northern German port of Wilhelmshaven. He first came to Hitler's attention in 1926, when he was assigned to a military district in Königsberg, East Prussia. Müller was already known among German military officers for his strong nationalism and anti-Semitism, topics that figured prominently in his sermons, and General Werner von Blomberg arranged a meeting between the pastor and Hitler. After the Nazis took power in 1933 Hitler made Müller the chief official in the Evangelical Protestant Church, the largest denomination in the Reich. Müller was to head up the "coordination" of Protestantism into the Nazi regime.

In short order Müller became head of the German Christian movement, which claimed that Hitler was a prophet who had come to rescue Germany from the Jewish threat. Moreover, the German Christians recommended that Christian belief and ritual be transformed to reflect Aryan values. The Old Testament of the Bible was to be discarded, as were the teachings of St. Paul. Moreover, German Christians rejected the idea that Jesus of Nazareth had lived and preached as a Jewish reformer. They claimed, instead, that he was a pure Aryan. In July 1933, a German Christian synod held in Wittenberg elected Müller as Reich bishop. In this role he led the struggle between the German Christians, and by extension the Nazi regime, and the new Confessing Church, a Protestant body headed by Martin Niemöller. The Confessing Church repudiated both Müller's nazified theology and the attempt by the Reich bishop to bring the Protestant Church under the authority of the Nazi state. In time, Hitler lost interest in this religious struggle and lost faith in Müller. Müller killed himself in Berlin in March 1946. *See also* German Christians, Vol. 1; religion in the Third Reich, Vol. 2; Hitler, The State Must Dominate the Churches, Vol. 4.

Mussert, Anton (1894–1946)

The leader of the Fascist organization in the Netherlands, which was known as the National Socialist Movement in imitation of German Nazism. Mussert was born in 1894 and was trained as an engineer. He formed the Dutch Nazi movement in the late 1930s, and by the time World War II began he was in regular contact with German Nazis. He hoped, like Vidkun Quisling in Norway, to become head of state after the Germans occupied the Netherlands in 1940. However, as in Norway, the Germans preferred to rule the territory with an occupation governor using SS police, although they maintained Mussert as a figurehead, naming him in 1942 the leader of the Dutch people. After the war, on May 7, 1946, he was hanged as a traitor and collaborator in the Dutch capital, The Hague. *See also* Case Yellow, collaboration, Vol. 1; Rotterdam, bombing of, Vol. 2.

Mussolini, Benito (1883–1945)

Fascist dictator of Italy and Adolf Hitler's closest ally among world leaders. Having taken power in 1922, when Hitler was just beginning his political career, Mussolini provided a model for the young Nazi leader. In later years Mussolini, for his own reasons, supported the Third Reich's territorial moves beginning with the annexation of Austria in 1938 and continuing with the invasion of the Soviet Union in June 1941. Even after Mussolini was ousted from power in 1943 Hitler remained loyal to him, rescuing him from self-imposed exile and installing him as head of German-occupied northern Italy until 1945.

Benito Mussolini was born on July 29, 1883, in the village of Dovia in the Italian province of Forlì. His father was a blacksmith with Socialist leanings and his mother was an extremely devout Catholic. Prior to World War I Mussolini undertook a variety of jobs: elementary schoolteacher, laborer, translator. Once he was even arrested, in Switzerland, as a tramp. A strong Socialist at first, Mussolini became the editor of a Socialist newspaper called *Avanti! (Forward!)* in 1912. He broke with the Italian Socialists, however, in 1914 by arguing that Italy should fight on the side of the western Allies; the Socialists preferred a neutral stance. He fought as an enlisted man from May 1915, the month Italy entered the war, to 1917, when he was wounded.

After the war Mussolini transformed himself into a right-wing politician. He edited a new newspaper known as *Il Popolo d' Italia (The People of Italy)*, in whose pages he began to describe a political philosophy he referred to as fascism. The name was derived from the Latin word *fasces*, an ancient Roman symbol of power. Mussolini wrote that fascism allowed the individual man to transcend the petty problems that beset him by favoring membership in a national community. In fact, Mussolini argued, the individual could only truly find himself within a strong national state. These ideas were attractive to many in postwar Italy, a country beset by political instability and high unemployment, and where thousands of disaffected war veterans thronged the streets. Moreover, Mussolini had before him an example of nationalist action, the 1919 takeover of the Adriatic city of Fiume by Gabriele d'Annunzio, a freelance right-wing politician leading an informal force of Italian patriots. D'Annunzio was ultimately forced to back down by the Italian government, but at a cost; the government now appeared less patriotic than the people it led.

In 1919 Mussolini formed the Fascio di Combattimento (Union of Combat), a right-wing, nationalist political party. It attracted numerous followers, including war veterans, the unemployed, conservative craftsmen and farmers, and young people in search of action. As Hitler later did as leader of the Nazi Party, Mussolini proclaimed that the Fascisti (Fascists) would save Italy from the twin threats of communism and liberal bourgeois decadence. Taking their message to the streets, the Fascists formed groups of fighters known as Blackshirts because of their rudimentary military uniforms. The main targets of the Blackshirts were Communist and Socialist organizations and striking workers. Meanwhile the Italian government, a liberal democracy patterned on the British model, made little effort to deal with either the widespread unemployment or political unrest. Mussolini's strong stance against Communists and Socialists brought him the support of many of Italy's industrialists and financiers, who hoped that, at the very least, he could bring order to Italian life. By 1922 the Fascists had support across Italy and controlled entire areas in the northern part of the country. They had increased their representation in the Italian parliament with each election, and by 1922 held thirty seats. Mussolini reinforced this support through propaganda and the projection of an image of strength, a particularly effective strategy in a country whose politicians appeared weak and indecisive.

In October 1922 thousands of Blackshirts descended on Rome, Italy's capital, on Mussolini's instructions. What the Fascist leader had in mind was a demonstration of power, but what he ended up with was the office of prime minister of Italy, somewhat to his surprise. With fifty thousand Blackshirts in Rome, many Italians feared a government coup, and they hoped that the king of Italy, Victor Emmanuel III, would authorize the use of the Italian army to stop what people had begun to call the "march on Rome." But the king, fearing widespread violence, rejected the call to use the army. In protest, the Italian cabinet resigned, and the king, authorized to do so by the Italian constitution, asked Mussolini to become prime minister. The Fascist leader had been waiting for news of developments in faraway Milan, but the king's call allowed him to board a railway sleeping car south and, with the news cameras rolling, stage his own triumphal march on Rome. He took power on October 29, 1922, as Hitler did on January 30, 1933, through perfectly legal means.

During his first year in office Mussolini enjoyed the ability to rule by decree. He took advantage of the opportunity by appointing Fascists to the cabinet and to civil service posts throughout the country. By 1924, when elections had produced a vast Fascist majority in the Italian parliament, Mussolini was able to abolish competing political parties. He ruled Italy in conjunction with a

Grand Council of twenty fellow Fascists and an inner circle known as the National Directory. He took personal control of the army, navy, and foreign policy. Meanwhile, he continued on a course combining violence and terror with public displays of unity and power. In one instance, in 1924, a leading critic of Mussolini, Socialist politician Giacomo Matteotti, was simply murdered by Blackshirt thugs, who as Mussolini consolidated his power found themselves transformed into a sort of political police. He and his comrades continued to dress in elaborate uniforms, stage parades, hold mass rallies at which political songs were sung, and greet each other with a revived Roman salute, which the Germans modified into the Hitler salute. Meanwhile, Mussolini also transformed himself into a conquering hero by defending Italian national interests during a crisis with Greece over the island of Corfu.

Until about 1935, when many Italians were weary of his regimentation and personal pomposity, Mussolini succeeded in creating a reasonably efficient authoritarian state. He was never, it must be said, a totalitarian dictator comparable to Hitler or Stalin; rather, he tried to maintain social order and ensure prosperity by creating a corporatist state, in which the interests of businessmen, workers, and the government would be coordinated. He also sponsored public works projects which he sometimes turned into public relations opportunities by stripping off his shirt, taking up a hammer or shovel, and joining the workmen, at least as long as the cameras rolled. He tried to ensure that the civil service worked efficiently, and he was famously praised both at home and abroad for "making the trains run on time." In a measure that was later adapted under the Third Reich, Mussolini also began the "dopolavoro" (after-work) movement, which provided Italian workers with organized, state-sponsored leisure activities and educational programs.

Mussolini's foreign policy goal was to revive Italian greatness, and he began moves in that direction with a 1936 invasion of the African kingdom of Ethiopia, commanded by General Pietro Badoglio. The Ethiopians had no chance against the bombers and machine guns of the Italians, and Addis Ababa, the capital, fell within months. Widespread global criticism of this aggression and an attempted League of Nations embargo had little effect beyond forcing Italy and Germany closer together. The event was one of many, in fact, which encouraged not only Mussolini but Adolf Hitler, who realized that neither the League of Nations nor the western Allies of Britain and France would stand in the way of aggressive territorial moves.

Mussolini also sent forces to help the Spanish Fascists under Francisco Franco in that nation's civil war from 1936 to 1939.

In 1939 German Nazi dictator Adolf Hitler (left) and Italian Fascist dictator Benito Mussolini (right) allied their nations under the Pact of Steel.

Again, he found himself brought closer to Hitler by these actions, since the Germans sent even more aid to Franco. In 1938, and despite his own ambitions in Austria, Mussolini informed Hitler that he approved of the Nazi annexation of Austria. Hitler, ecstatic and relieved, proclaimed that he would never forget Mussolini for his support. In 1939 the two nations entered the so-called Pact of Steel, which cemented their alliance. The Italian signatory of the pact was Foreign Minister Galeazzo Ciano, who had married Mussolini's daughter, Edda, in 1930.

As World War II approached, both Mussolini and Ciano realized that Italy lacked the industry or the geographical position to sustain a broad European war and made a number of efforts to maintain the peace. Mussolini was the man who proposed the Munich Conference, which settled the fate of Czechoslovakia on September 30, 1938, and he hoped he might pull off a similar miracle prior to the German invasion of Poland nearly a year later. When his efforts failed and the Germans invaded Poland, he remained neutral, not entering the war on the German side until June 10, 1940. Mussolini proved to be very much the junior partner in the Italian-German alliance, although Hitler maintained his warm friendship toward Il Duce, as Mussolini was known. Most of Italy's military efforts proved feeble; the Germans had to step in in both Yugoslavia and Greece to rescue the Italians, and the force that Mussolini sent to the Soviet Union was annihilated. Much of the Italian army was lost to the western Allies in Tunisia in 1943.

Mussolini was deposed by the Fascist Grand Council, including his son-in-law Ciano, on July 24, 1943, when it was clear that the Allies would soon invade Italy and that Mussolini's alliance with Hitler had failed as had his philosophy of "Believe! Obey! Fight!" The new Italian government, led by Badoglio, imprisoned Il Duce in an isolated mountain region known as Gran Sasso. He was rescued, however, by a small force of Germans led by the SS adventurer Otto Skorzeny, who flew in in gliders. The Germans then installed Mussolini as a puppet dictator in northern Italy, the south having been occupied by the Allies; this short-lived regime was known as the Italian Social Republic but was little more than German-occupied territory. It was also beset by partisans. Mussolini's last meeting with Hitler took place, strangely, on July 20, 1944, the day the German resistance tried to assassinate the Führer. Mussolini had already been scheduled to come that day to the Wolf's Lair, Hitler's eastern headquarters. When Mussolini joined him that afternoon as Hitler recovered his energies, they reiterated their old friendship, and the Führer reminded Il Duce, once again, that Hitler's was a special destiny, as his survival made clear.

Mussolini was captured by Italian partisans in April 1945 near Lake Como, along with other Fascist leaders and Il Duce's mistress, Clara Petacci. Knowing that he was to be killed, Mussolini pulled up his shirt, indicating that he preferred to be shot in the chest. The partisans complied. The next day, April 29, the bodies of Mussolini and Petacci, the latter with her skirt tied properly, were hung by their ankles in a public square in Milan. Mussolini had been a harsh, intolerant dictator, but never a racial murderer believing in his destiny to reorder the population and map of Europe like Hitler, and he continued to have supporters in Italy. *See also* allies of the Third Reich; Axis Powers; Ethiopia, invasion of; fascism, Vol. 1; Göring, Göring Celebrates the German-Italian Alliance, Vol. 4.

Naujocks, Alfred (1911–1960)

SS officer and Nazi adventurer, a man Heinrich Himmler and Reinhard Heydrich called upon for a number of special and sensitive assignments. One of these assignments allowed Naujocks, in later years, to claim to be the man who started World War II.

Alfred Naujocks was born in Kiel in northern Germany on September 11, 1911. He briefly studied engineering but soon found work instead as a welder in the same period of the 1920s when he joined the Nazi movement. Skill in boxing, combined with an engaging personality, gained Naujocks a reputation as a street fighter in the early 1930s, when there were frequent skirmishes between Nazis and Communists. In 1931 Naujocks joined the SS and in 1934 he transferred to the SD. There, Heydrich employed him as a secret agent. In 1933 he reached his highest bureaucratic post as the chief of the foreign office of the SD, where his main responsibilities including forging passports and other documents for SD agents sent on assignments outside Germany.

On the evening of August 31, 1939, Naujocks led the so-called Gleiwitz raid, an operation designed to give the Third Reich an excuse to attack Poland the next morning. The raid, an attack on a German radio station just inside the Polish border between the two countries, was conducted by a small contingent of SD agents dressed in Polish army uniforms. They left behind the body of a concentration camp inmate dressed to look like a station employee; SD planners referred to such victims as "canned goods." The Nazi propaganda machine stood ready to call the raid an act of aggression by Poland, a move that Germany indeed used to justify Germany's invasion, which sparked international declarations of war.

Naujocks reappeared across Europe during the World War II years in exploit after exploit, even after Heydrich dismissed him from the SD for insubordination in 1941. In November 1939, for instance, Naujocks helped kidnap two British secret agents in the town of Venlo near the Dutch-German border; the purpose this time was to find a pretext for the Third Reich to invade the Netherlands, at that point still a neutral country. In 1943 he turned up on the eastern front as a Waffen-SS officer. In 1944, after receiving a battlefield wound, he was assigned to Belgium as an economic official, but he apparently kept his hand in while posted in Belgium by carrying out operations against resistance movements in Denmark. He was allegedly responsible for the murders of several Danes and, as a member of a unit of SS assassins known as Group Peter, he presided over a brief spate of terrorist attacks involving bombings in public places and interrogations of innocent people in Copenhagen.

In October 1944 Naujocks deserted to the Allies, convinced that Nazi Germany was going to lose the war. He was placed in a prison camp, and after the war Allied officials prepared to try him for war crimes. He escaped from the camp before his trial, however, and was never formally charged, even when he reemerged as a semipublic figure in Hamburg in the late 1950s. During the intervening years the actions of Naujocks were the subject of speculation. Some claimed that he worked for the covert organization known as ODESSA (Organisation der Ehemaligen Angehörigen) helping SS men escape to South America via Spain. He also worked as a businesman. Naujocks died in Hamburg in April 1960. *See also* Gleiwitz raid, Vol. 1; Venlo incident, Vol. 2; Skorzeny, Otto, Vol. 3.

Nebe, Arthur (1894–1945?)

The head of the Criminal Police, a division of the Security Service of the SS, from 1933 to 1945, and the chief of one of the Einsatzgruppen, or special action squads, involved in the mass shootings of Jews on the eastern front in 1941. He was also a man who, despite his consistent ruthlessness as a police leader and brutality toward Jews, maintained contact with the German resistance movement and was involved in the July 1944 Plot on Adolf Hitler's life.

Arthur Nebe was born on November 13, 1894. He served in the German army during World War I and afterward joined the police in Berlin. His specialty was criminal investigation. In 1931 he joined the Nazi Party and the SS, and soon after took on the role of liaison between the Nazis and the Berlin police. In April 1933 Kurt Daluege, another SS officer and top Nazi policeman, chose him to be the head of the Criminal Police, or Kripo. Kripo's responsibilities initially were similar to those of criminal police forces in other countries: the investigation of crimes and law enforcement. But Nebe's connections to the SS gave the organization much wider responsibilities, and by the mid-1930s Kripo was one of the main instruments used by the Nazis to establish a police state held together by intimidation and terror.

When the SS police and security divisions were reorganized in 1939 into the Reich Central Security Office (RSHA), Nebe was named head of Section V of the RSHA, which was the Criminal Police. Between June and November 1941, as an SS-Gruppenführer, or lieutenant general, Nebe was the chief of Einzatzgruppe B, which was based in the western Soviet city of Minsk. From there Nebe directed operations resulting in the killings of nearly forty-six thousand Jews from the surrounding regions. Despite the efforts of later apologists to excuse Nebe by asserting that he joined the Einsatzgruppe only to remain close to SS decision makers for resistance purposes, the Kripo leader apparently was an enthusiastic killer. He even took films of killing experiments using poison gas, conducted on the populations of Minsk's mental hospitals. A heavy drinker, Nebe in the end had himself recalled to his duties in Berlin because of illness.

Nebe's connections to the resistance date back to 1938, when regular army officers, led by Ludwig Beck, plotted ways to remove Hitler from power. Nebe, apparently agreed to give the plotters intelligence information regarding the SS. In preparations for the July 1944 Plot, Nebe was again recruited as a strong potential ally who could bring to bear a strong force of policemen to help keep Berlin calm during the transition from Nazi rule to the new regime. After the bomb went off at Hitler's eastern headquarters on July 20, Nebe received a call from Heinrich Himmler directing him to send an investigation team to the site. Soon after, knowing he would be implicated, the police leader escaped to an island in a lake near Berlin. He was given up, however, by an angry former girlfriend, captured, interrogated by Heinrich Müller, the head of the Gestapo, and sent to the Buchenwald concentration camp. His ultimate fate remains unknown. Records suggest that he was executed at Buchenwald on March 21, 1945. Later accounts place him in both northern Italy and with a group of former SS men in Ireland, although those sightings were never verified. *See also* Criminal Police, Einsatzgruppen, July 1944 Plot, Vol. 1; RSHA, SS, Vol. 2.

Neurath, Constantin Freiherr von (1873–1956)

German aristocrat, influential politician, and the first foreign minister of the Third Reich.

Neurath was born in Württemberg in western Germany on February 2, 1873. His father was an official at the court of the king of Württemberg. As a young man Neurath took a law degree and then entered the German foreign service, serving from 1903 to 1908 as vice-consul in London. During World War I he was an embassy official in Constantinople, the capital of Germany's Turkish ally. After the war he was promoted to ambassadorships in Copenhagen, Rome, and London. In 1932 he joined the German cabinet as foreign minister, a post he held until 1938 despite the change of regime from Weimar to the Third Reich. Adolf Hitler approved of him because of his traditional, conservative views and because he gave the new regime a veneer of respectability.

In 1938, after arguing against Hitler's expansionist plans, Neurath was forced out of his post. He was replaced as foreign minister by Joachim von Ribbentrop, who already led a Nazi Party diplomatic organization. Nevertheless, Hitler kept Neurath on for his respectability, and Neurath went along with it though he exercised little power in any of a number of posts. He was, variously, minister without portfolio in the German cabinet, a member of the Council for Reich Defense, an honorary SS general, and, beginning in March 1939, protector of the new German colony of Bohemia and Moravia, which was carved from the former nation of Czechoslovakia. The Führer, however, was unhappy with Neurath's performance in "Aryanizing" the colony, and Neurath proved that he had little stomach for such measures as crushing resistance, enforcing state terror, and oppressing minorities such as Jews. In 1942, after asking to be allowed to step down, Neurath was given a leave of absence and Reinhard Heydrich stepped in as the new protector. Neurath was officially replaced by Hans Frick in August 1943. In the next year Neurath gave tacit approval to the July 1944 Plot, although Gestapo officials never managed to connect the passive aristocrat to the plot directly.

After World War II Neurath was included among the twenty-one top Nazis put on trial by the International Military Tribunal in Nuremberg in the fall of 1945. He was convicted of three of the four charges against him: war crimes, crimes against peace, and crimes against humanity. He was sentenced to fifteen years in Spandau Prison in Berlin, but released for health reasons in 1954. He returned to the region of his birth, where he died on August 15, 1956. *See also* Hossbach Conference, Vol. 1; Nuremberg trials, Vol. 2; Ribbentrop, Joachim von, Vol. 3.

Niemöller, Martin (1882–1984)

Pastor of the Evangelical Lutheran Church, Germany's largest Protestant denomination, and outspoken critic of Nazism who spent many years in prison for his views. Niemöller was born in Lippstadt in western Germany on January 14, 1892. An ardent German nationalist, he spent the years of World War I as a naval officer and U-boat commander. He was awarded the prestigious Pour le Mérite for his heroic service. He was ordained as a Lutheran minister in 1924, working first for a missionary service in Westphalia and then, from 1931 to 1937, as pastor of the Berlin-Dahlem Church, home of one of Germany's wealthiest and most influential Protestant congregations.

A vehement anticommunist and critic of the Weimar Republic as well as a devoted nationalist, Niemöller was at first happy to see Adolf Hitler and the Nazis rise to power, and he himself became a Nazi Party member. He changed his mind, however, when the Nazi regime moved to establish state control of the Protestant churches, as well as nazify Christian belief and ritual, with the German Christian movement under Reich Bishop Ludwig Müller. To defend the traditional Protestant Church, Niemöller founded the Pastors' Emergency League in 1934. Soon after he became one of the leaders of the Confessing Church, a new body that issued the so-called Barmen Declaration in May 1934. In this statement Niemöller and seven thousand other pastors declared that they represented the true Protestant Church in Germany; they rejected the attempt by the Nazi state to dominate the churches and repudiated the move to nazify Christian theology by claiming, for instance, that Jesus was an Aryan rather than a Jew.

Niemöller maintained this opposition from his influential pulpit at the Berlin-Dahlem Church. Adolf Hitler, who originally had praised the pastor for his nationalism, now criticized him intensely, claiming that his sermons were political rather than religious statements. Hitler also resented Niemöller's great popularity among both Protestants and Catholics, which hindered his attempt to "coordinate" Christianity into the Nazi regime. In 1937 the Führer ordered Niemoller's arrest, and on June 27 the pastor, suspecting his fate, preached his final sermon at Berlin-Dahlem, proclaiming obedience to God rather than man. Niemöller was arrested on July 1 and taken to Berlin's Moabit Prison.

In March 1938 Niemöller was tried before a Nazi Special Court, an arm of the Nazi judicial system dealing with enemies of the state. The pastor was found guilty of subversive attacks against the Nazi regime and given the relatively light sentence of seven months in prison and a fine of two thousand marks. On Hitler's orders Niemöller was placed in "protective custody" upon his release, and he spent the remaining seven years of the Third Reich in concentration camps. He was sent first to Sachsenhausen near Berlin, then to Dachau, where his companions included Kurt von Schuschnigg, the former chancellor of Austria, and Princes Philip of Hesse and Frederick of Prussia.

Niemöller was liberated when American forces reached Dachau in May 1945. He soon reemerged as a leader of Germany's Evangelical Lutheran Church, serving as a bishop in Hesse-Nassau. He was also a dedicated pacifist who frequently spoke out against nuclear weaponry and the tensions of the Cold War. After his retirement, he lived in Darmstadt in the Rhineland, where he died on March 6, 1984. *See also* Barmen Declaration, Confessing Church, Vol. 1; religion in the Third Reich, Vol. 2.

Nietzsche, Friedrich (1844–1900)

German philosopher whose work, in a simplified and misunderstood form, was used by the Nazis to justify their ideas and actions. Nietzsche was born in Röcken, Saxony, on October 15, 1844. He came from a line of Lutheran ministers and initially set out to enter the church himself. As a student at the University of Bonn, however, he gave up theology to study modern philosophy and classical languages, particularly ancient Greek. A brilliant scholar, Nietzsche became a professor of classics at the University of Basel in Switzerland in 1868, where he remained until he was forced into early retirement in 1878. He then worked as a

The Nazis distorted the writings of German philosopher Friedrich Nietzsche to justify their racist ideology.

writer, often from a small villa in the mountains of northern Italy. Early in his career, he was a strong admirer of the German nationalist composer Richard Wagner, but he later came to view Wagner's music as bombastic and trivial rather than as a true reflection of the "will to power," his basic philosophical and psychological insight.

Nietzsche argued, in such books as *Beyond Good and Evil* and *The Genealogy of Morals*, that the "will to power" was a basic element of the human personality. Everyone, he claimed, wanted to feel a continually increasing sense of power over his life and circumstances. However, he did not mean that power could be gained by oppressing the weak or showing no mercy toward enemies, as the Nazis understood it; such qualities, in fact, were reflections of fundamental weakness. Instead, the "will to power" was the desire to achieve power over oneself by, for example, sublimating one's energies so as to produce great works of art. He also suggested that those seeking to increase their creativity seek further challenges, strife, and pain to increase their sense of power.

Nietzsche's ideal, in fact an old ideal in certain streams of Western thought, was the Übermensch, the "overman" or "superman," best described in his most well-known book, *Thus Spake Zarathustra*. The "overman" would be "beyond good and evil," beyond the morality preached by priests and the common man, because he was so secure in his own strength. Indeed, he would be able to rise above the "slave morality" that, according to Nietzsche, preached kindness and humility. The Nazis not only considered themselves "overmen" but believed Germans in general constituted a master race and set out to revive a "master morality" of hardness, strength, and discipline. Nietzsche himself, however, did not believe in any such concept as a "master race," and even the "overman" was a philosophical ideal rather than a description of actual figures.

Nietzsche in fact was highly critical of Germans, particularly those Germans who saw their militaristic nation as a strong one, and in one instance referred to Germans as "walking beer barrels." Wagner, he came to believe, was simply a product of the presently "besotted" and "depraved" German spirit. He also wrote, in complete contrast to what Nazi ideologists believed, that France, not Germany, had been the source of much of Europe's culture and creativity. Finally, and on another issue that the Nazis were to make much of, he was highly critical of anti-Semitism, and admired the Jews for their ability to survive centuries of oppression with integrity.

Nietzsche suffered a mental breakdown in 1889 and spent the remainder of his life in a Weimar sanatorium where he died on August 25, 1900. Many of his ideas were publicized in a distorted form by his sister, Elizabeth Förster-Nietzsche, who wanted to capitalize on his fame by connecting his philosophy with völkisch German nationalism. These simplified forms of Nietzsche's philosophy became popular reading among the German World War I generation out of which Hitler came. During the Nazi era, party mythmakers adopted Nietzsche's theory of the "overman" as well as his dislike of Christianity, which he considered a reflection of "slave morality," and twisted them to their own ends. *See also* master race, Wagnerism, Vol. 2.

O

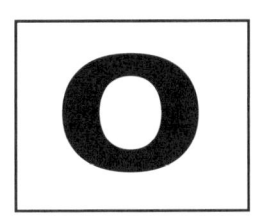

Oberg, Karl (1897–1965)

SS officer and chief of the SS and RSHA in occupied France from 1942 to 1944. Oberg was born in Hamburg on January 27, 1897, and selected a military career. As an officer in World War I he received the Iron Cross, First and Second Class. Of right-wing, nationalist sympathies, Oberg fought with the anticommunist Freikorps in the months after World War I, and during the 1920s he worked as a representative of the Escherich Organization in northern Germany, a body that maintained cordial relations among the Reichswehr, politicians, and nationalist groups.

Oberg joined the Nazi Party and SS in 1932 and worked initially with Reinhard Heydrich's SD. By 1935 Oberg's dedication to security work had raised him to the level of SS colonel, and he was one of Heydrich's chief adjutants. In the late 1930s, however, he returned to the SS proper, and to independent police and military posts. By 1931 he was head of an occupation force in Poland, where he became involved in massacres of Jews and systematic oppression of civilians.

In May 1942, on the personal order of Heinrich Himmler, Oberg was sent to Paris as chief of the local SS and RSHA. He worked, not harmoniously, with military occupation commanders, and his jurisdiction was completely independent of theirs. While in France Oberg took on the job of trying to install a network of state terror comparable to that in other occupied countries and in the German Reich itself. He also enforced anti-Semitic measures and staged military operations against the French resistance. He escaped from France after the Allies liberated Paris in August 1944 and took up a military command in Germany.

Allied forces arrested Oberg in July 1945. He was tried and sentenced to death by an American war crimes tribunal, and then tried by a French court, which also sentenced him to death. The sentence was later reduced, by steps, until he was pardoned by Charles de Gaulle, then the president of France, in 1965. Oberg died on June 3, 1965, in Germany. *See also* RSHA, SD, SS, Vol. 2.

Ohlendorf, Otto (1908–1951)

SS officer, lawyer, economist, and chief of internal police intelligence of the Reich Central Security Office from 1939 to 1945. Ohlendorf was also the commanding officer of Einsatzgruppe D, one of the four mobile killing units that killed up to 1.5 million Jews by shooting on the eastern front during 1941 and early 1942. After the war, Ohlendorf was one of the few top Nazis willing to give evidence of atrocities on the eastern front to Allied war crimes tribunals.

Otto Ohlendorf was born in the village of Hoheneggelsen near the city of Hanover in central Germany on February 4, 1908. He rose to a high position from very humble beginnings: His family were peasant laborers. After graduating from a college preparatory school in Hildesheim, he attended the Universities of Leipzig and Göttingen, where he studied law and economics. An excellent scholar, he originally embarked on an academic career, working at the Institute of World Economy at the University of Kiel. There he specialized in the study of both Nazism and Italian fascism. Devoted to socialism as a young man, Ohlendorf joined the Nazi Party in 1925 and the SS in 1926.

After the Nazis took power in 1933, Ohlendorf remained in academic and bureaucratic positions until 1941. In 1935 he was named to a top position at the Insititute of Applied Economic Science, and soon after joined the SD, the precursor to the RSHA. As an SD officer—he was promoted to major in 1938—Ohlendorf proved skilled in acquiring information through threats and intimidation, although usually he remained behind the scenes while informants and SS policemen performed the dirtier jobs. Compiling reports on what the German people actually thought and believed was one of his responsibilities, but he was often too honest for Heinrich Himmler's taste: Himmler, convinced the Germans were warlike and ruthless, found Ohlendorf too negative and too intellectual when he pointed out that not all Germans favored Hitler's policies. Nevertheless, Ohlendorf's intelligence, ruthlessness, and efficiency as a security officer kept him at the center of SS leadership councils, and when Himmler organized the RSHA in 1939, Ohlendorf was named head of Section III, responsible for internal security.

In early 1941 Reinhard Heydrich, head of the RSHA and Himmler's second in command, organized four Einsatzgruppen, or special assignment units. Their task was to follow the German armed forces as they entered the Soviet Union in the invasion that Hitler was planning. Then, they were to collect intelligence, stir up partisan activity, and, although these orders were not clear until June or July 1941, massacre Jewish civilians. The units were made up of volunteers, and those who offered themselves for the duty tended to be highly ambitious SS men from the various branches of the RSHA and the Waffen-SS. When Ohlendorf volunteered for what was to be his first major stint as a field officer, his position as security chief made him a logical choice to head one of the four special units. Einsatzgruppe D operated behind the German Eleventh Army on the southern part of the invasion front, in the Ukraine and southern Russia. Between June 1941 and June 1942 Ohlendorf organized the murder by shooting of at least ninety thousand Jews in those regions. Here too he tended to leave the tasks of murder and the disposal of bodies to field men. Nonetheless, Ohlendorf proved to be as ruthless and efficient a killer as he was a security chief. He methodically attended to such matters as trying to minimize the psychological impact shooting duty might have on his men: For example, he encouraged his men to shoot simultaneously to reduce their sense of individual responsibility. He was also a pioneer in the use of alternate killing techniques such as gas vans, but complained about their limited capacity.

In June 1942 Ohlendorf returned to his bureaucratic duties and remained at the center of the SS leadership. He served not only as the head of Section III of the RSHA but as an official in the Reich Ministry of Economics, where he gave advice on foreign trade and centralized economic planning. He was promoted to SS lieutenant general in late 1944, a time when many in the SS, including Himmler himself, began contemplating life after Hitler. Ohlendorf apparently encouraged Himmler to surrender independently to the Allies in hopes of maintaining a functioning transitional government in Germany.

After the war Ohlendorf was captured and held for trial by the Allies, whose investigators found him to be a strange combination of cultivated intellectual, efficient bureaucrat, and amoral murderer. He was put on trial in Nuremberg in September 1947 along with other Einsatzgruppen commanders and participants. During his testimony Ohlendorf was honest but unapologetic. He claimed that the massacre of Jews in certain regions was simply necessary to expand Germany's living space. He also compared his killing squads to killers throughout history, including the American politicians and military men who dropped atomic bombs on Japan. In the future, Ohlendorf argued, no one would find anything unique about the actions of the Einsatzgruppen in systematically murdering hundreds of thousands of civilians because of their religion. On April 10, 1948, Ohlendorf was found guilty of various war crimes. He was hanged, along with three other Einsatzgruppen leaders, on June 8, 1951, at Landsberg Prison in Munich. *See also* Einsatzgruppen, gas vans, Vol. 1; Graebe, The Einsatzgruppen in Action, Vol. 4.

Olbricht, Friedrich (1888–1944)

German army officer and important participant in the July 1944 Plot to assassinate Adolf Hitler and replace the Third Reich with a new government. Olbricht was born in Leisnig in Saxony on October 4, 1888. He was a professional soldier his entire life, serving with distinction during Word War I and as an administrative officer to the Reichswehr during the Weimar years. He was promoted rapidly after 1933, again mainly to staff and administrative posts, and came to believe that Hitler's regime would lead Germany to ruin. Moreover, as a devout Roman Catholic, he strongly opposed Nazi oppression. In 1940 Olbricht was named chief of the General Staff of the army High Command and in 1943 chief of staff of the Reserve Army, which was led by General Friedrich Fromm. The Reserve Army consisted of forces stationed throughout the German Reich proper; the Nazis used it as both a means to discourage rebellion and a source of men who might be needed elsewhere, usually on the eastern front.

Olbricht's office was at the Ministry of War on the Bendlerstrasse in Berlin, a most convenient place to observe military operations from the inside as well as build networks of contacts in the resistance movement. Moreover, as chief of staff to Fromm, Olbricht could organize the Reserve Army with an eye toward using this force to support the new government the conspirators hoped to set up after they assassinated Hitler. After an assassination attempt using an airplane bomb failed in 1943, Olbricht worked closely with Lieutenant Colonel Claus Schenk Graf von Stauffenberg in assembling the July 1944 Plot and planning its aftermath. Olbricht's main responsibility during the coup would be to use the Reserve Army to secure control of Berlin in the face of possible resistance from the SS or unwilling units of the armed forces. He set the plan in motion on July 15, 1944, the day for which the assassination was initially planned. When Stauffenberg, who had charged himself with delivering the bomb to Hitler's headquarters, was forced to postpone at the last minute, Olbricht had to come up with a sudden explanation for activating the Reserve Army; he told Fromm that it was simply a surprise training exercise.

On July 20 Stauffenberg's bomb exploded at Hitler's eastern headquarters at Rastenburg in East Prussia. Olbricht's assignment was to arrest Fromm and initiate the takeover of Berlin from his office on the Bendlerstrasse. But he failed to act until Stauffenberg returned to Berlin some three hours later. By then it was too late. Nazi officials knew that the explosion had merely injured Hitler, not killed him, and certain junior officers, as well as Joseph Goebbels, acted quickly to stop the coup. Fromm, who was indeed arrested by Olbricht but soon released by Nazi loyalists, organized a firing squad to kill Olbricht, side by side with Stauffenberg, outside the War Ministry on the evening of July 20. *See also* Bendlerstrasse, July 1944 Plot, Vol. 1; Stauffenberg, Claus Schenk Graf von, Vol. 3.

Oster, Hans (1888–1945)

Officer in the Abwehr, the intelligence arm of the High Command of the German armed forces (OKW), and leader of the German resistance movement. Hans Oster was born in Dresden on August 9, 1888. His father was a Lutheran pastor, and Oster remained a dedicated Christian his entire life. After serving in the German Imperial Army during World War I and in the Reichswehr during the Weimar years, usually in staff positions, he took a post in the Ministry of War in 1933. He was chief of staff to the head of the Abwehr, first Major General Kurt von Bredow and then Admiral Wilhelm Canaris, from 1933 to 1944. In addition he was personally in charge of Section II of the Abwehr, which dealt with administrative and financial matters.

Oster, a traditional conservative, emerged as an active and vocal opponent to Nazism after the unprincipled dismissal of Generals Werner von Blomberg and Werner Freiherr von Fritsch by Hitler in early 1938. He understood, as an intelligence officer, that the move gave the Nazis virtually complete control of the German armed forces, and from that point on he was involved in almost every attempt to overthrow Hitler's regime. His major roles in the resistance movement included maintaining lines of communication among officers, and he also helped turn the Abwehr into a center of resistance. His superior Admiral Canaris, although neither as devoted nor as active as Oster, was persuaded to participate, as was Hans Bernd Gisevius, and Abwehr diplomat. Oster had long resisted the Nazi regime in smaller ways as well. For instance, in 1940 he gave his counterparts in Norway and the Netherlands advance word about Hitler's plans to invade their countries, and devised ways to protect Jews using Abwehr offices outside the German Reich.

Oster was dismissed from the Abwehr in April 1943, partly because of suspicions over his activities, and the Gestapo kept him under surveillance. He was arrested after the failure of the July 1944 Plot on Hitler's life as one of the conspirators, although he had lost most of his power to help the resisters after being released from the Abwehr. Along with Canaris and theologian Dietrich Bonhoeffer, Oster was shot to death at the Flossenbürg concentration camp on April 9, 1945. *See also* Abwehr, Flossenbürg, Vol. 1; resistance movements, Germany, Vol. 2.

Papen, Franz von (1879–1969)

Politician, aristocrat, and one of the men who helped Adolf Hitler legally take power as chancellor of Germany on January 30, 1933. Papen was born in Westphalia on October 29, 1879. His family was part of the traditional Roman Catholic nobility of the region. He originally embarked on a military career, and thanks to his connections and social status, which Papen always relied on more than any personal qualities, became first an officer in a cavalry regiment and, in 1913, a captain on the German Imperial General Staff. During World War I he turned to diplomacy rather than combat and was appointed military attaché to the German embassy in Mexico. In 1916 he left for a similar post in the United States, but the American government expelled him for various intrigues involving German support for a conflict between Mexico and the United States that would distract Americans from World War I in Europe. After returning to Germany he was sent first to a combat unit on the western front, then as a German military adjutant with the Turkish army in Turkey and Palestine.

After the war Papen entered politics a member of the Catholic Center Party He served in the Prussian state legislature from 1920 to 1932. In addition, he became co-owner and chairman of *Germania*, the Catholic Center Party newspaper. In a move typical of the declining aristocracy of Germany in particular and Europe in general, he married the daughter of a wealthy industrialist. The move not only ensured his personal and family fortunes but provided him with contacts and access to Germany's top industrialists and financiers.

Papen's outlook was that of a nineteenth-century aristocrat rather than a twentieth-century popular politician. He believed that men of his class had the right to govern Germany by virtue of their wealth, social position, and experience, and his actions as a politician were guided by this faith in elites. Moreover, Papen was a devout Catholic who wanted to restore the connections between church and state. His fundamental hope was to bring back the Hohenzollern monarchy, whose last emperor, Kaiser Wilhelm II, was forced to abdicate in November 1918. In other regards Papen was a typical aristocrat, impeccable in dress, behavior, and social graces. He belonged to Berlin's Gentlemen's Club (Herrenklub), a group of like-minded men who saw in the liberal Weimar Republic an uncontrolled, undisciplined republicanism. Few politicians, however, took Papen seriously. He seemed too lighthearted, too frivolous, and too much a relic of an earlier era. His main strengths in politics continued to be his status and his connections among the German army, big business, and the Catholic hierarchy. These factions were prepared to accept him as their front man in the effort to transform Weimar Germany back into a conservative, nationalist state dominated by traditional elites, and Papen was willing to take on the role.

In 1932, during presidential elections, Papen switched from the Catholic Center Party to Alfred Hugenberg's German Nationalist People's Party because of his support for President Paul von Hindenburg,

After Hindenburg won the election and took office, he appointed Papen to the office of chancellor of Germany, at least partly on the advice of a close associate, General Kurt von Schleicher. The previous chancellor, Heinrich Brüning, had failed to construct a solid majority in the Reichstag, the German parliament, and many German conservatives had been displeased with his economic measures. In this manner Papen went straight from the Prussian state legislature and the Gentlemen's Club to the head of the German government. During 1932 with the Reichstag in deadlock, the president of Germany ruled the nation by decree according to Article 48 of the Weimar Constitution. With Hindenburg fully behind him, Papen was ready to issue decrees in his name. He appointed a "cabinet of barons" made up largely of aristocrats, which few politicians either in Germany or elsewhere took seriously although it was backed by both the officer corps and big business. Schleicher was named minister of defense. Papen then began to try to impose a more reactionary form of government by closing down, in opposition to the Weimar Constitution, the Social Democratic regime that controlled his old stomping grounds in the Prussian legislature and appointing himself Reich commissioner for Prussia. Meanwhile, Papen also took it upon himself to try to establish control over a new force in German parliamentary politics: Adolf Hitler and the Nazi Party. Over the summer of 1932 he repealed the ban on the SA which Brüning had put in place (on Hindenburg's orders) and called for new national elections to be held in late July. It was in this election that the Nazis reached the peak of their popularity, at least before they took power, by garnering over 37 percent of the vote and becoming the largest single party in the Reichstag.

By the fall of 1932, however, Schleicher had grown increasingly concerned about Papen's reactionary politics as well as his flirtations with Hitler. Like many Germans, Schleicher thought that the Nazis had begun to decline: In the latest election, held November 6, they polled only 32 percent. Schleicher convinced Hindenburg, who as president held the ultimate authority in these matters, to depose Papen, effective December 3. Schleicher was named chancellor in his stead, and the general sought to assemble a cabinet made up of representatives from across the German political spectrum. Rather than deal with Hitler, however, he approached Gregor Strasser, the leader of the northern, liberal wing of the Nazi Party, requesting that he split with Hitler in exchange for a cabinet position and legitimacy for the Nazis.

Papen, meanwhile, began engaging in backroom manipulations of his own, bitter and angry over Schleicher's betrayal and now more than ready to compromise with Hitler. On January 4, 1933, Papen met with Hitler at the home of the Rhineland financier Kurt Freiherr von Schröder. He offered the Nazi leader an interesting proposal designed to outflank Schleicher's tenuous plans for a new government. This was to convince Hindenburg to appoint a new cabinet made up entirely of representatives of the Nazi Party and the German Nationalist Party. Hitler himself would be named chancellor and Papen vice-chancellor. Papen was certain that he could control Hitler, who, from the aristocrat's perspective, was little more than a lower-middle-class rabble-rouser who was no true match for Germany's traditional conservative elites. Hindenburg agreed to the plan, and the joint Hitler-Papen cabinet took power on January 30, 1933.

Papen remained vice-chancellor until the summer of 1934, and provided the new regime with a respectable front as it consolidated its hold on Germany. He increasingly realized, however, that National Socialism represented a dangerous form of social revolution rather than a true return to traditional conservatism. Although he rarely spoke out on such matters, Papen made a speech on June 17, 1934, at the University of Marburg that enraged Hitler. Papen criti-

German vice-chancellor Franz von Papen addresses a meeting of Nazi Brownshirts on February 13, 1933, just two weeks after Hitler took power as chancellor.

cized the excesses of Nazi politicians and the SA and called for a more democratic system based on Christian values, implying that the Hohenzollern monarchy was far preferable to a populist Nazi terror state. Hearing of the speech, Hitler called his vice-chancellor a "worm" and Nazi propagandists returned to their earlier strategy of criticizing traditional aristocrats as threats to the renewal of German culture.

During the Blood Purge, June 30, 1934, Papen was arrested, to his shock and outrage, along with Schleicher and a number of other earlier colleagues, although Hitler's main targets were SA chief Ernst Röhm and Gregor Strasser, who had betrayed the Führer by consorting with Schleicher in December 1932. Papen escaped with his life only at the request of Hermann Göring, who realized that Papen, not Hitler, was a man who could be controlled and manipulated and who could continue to lend the Nazi regime an element of respectability. Within months Papen proved he was willing to serve the Third Reich in a new capacity: He was appointed special minister to the Austrian government and then, in 1936, German ambassador to Austria. While there he helped prepare the way for the Anschluss, the German annexation of Austria. Shortly before German tanks rolled into Austria, on March 10, 1938, he was recalled from his position as ambassador although within months he was appointed Germany's ambassador to Turkey, where he stayed from 1939 to 1944.

Papen was arrested by American forces in the Ruhr in April 1945. In the fall of 1945 he was one of the twenty-one surviving top Nazis brought before the International Military Tribunal at Nuremberg. Like several other defendants Papen was distressed to be included among such men as Göring, Julius Streicher, and Hans Frank. During his testimony he offered an explanation for the excesses of the Third Reich, claiming that "paganism" turned Hitler into a totalitarian and a pathological liar. Although the tribunal denounced him for his intrigues during the Anschluss, Papen was acquitted on all four counts and set free on October 1, 1946. In 1947, however, a German denazification court sentenced him to eight years in prison as a "major offender." He was released on appeal in January 1949 and retired to write his memoirs, which were published in 1952. He died in Obersasbach, in the Black Forest region of southwestern Germany, on May 2, 1969. *See also* Blood Purge, Vol. 1; Machtergreifung, Nuremberg trials, Vol. 2; Papen, Papen Recounts Hitler's Takeover, Vol. 4.

Paulus, Friedrich (1890–1957)

Head of the German Sixth Army during its catastrophic loss at the Battle of Stalingrad over the fall and winter of 1942–1943. Paulus was born in Breitenau in Prussia on September 23, 1890. His father was a civil servant. He joined the German Imperial Army in 1910 and served as a junior officer during World War I. As an officer in the Weimar-era Reichswehr, Paulus rose steadily in rank in a variety of posts, particularly in armored regiments. He was promoted to major general just prior to the beginning of World War II, and during the invasions of Poland, Belgium, and France he served as a staff officer under General Walther von Reichenau. In September 1940 he was appointed senior quartermaster of the High Command of the army, as well as deputy chief of staff to General Franz Halder. He played an important role in planning the German invasion of the Soviet Union, known as Operation Barbarossa, which began on June 22, 1941.

From December 1941 to February 1943 Paulus, now a full general, was head of the Sixth Army, by far his most important field command. On June 28, 1942, he was ordered to take his forces to the city of Stalingrad, a strategic center on the Volga River in southern Russia. His task was to conquer the city and ensure that German forces thereby commanded the Volga crossings. Paulus and his forces reached Stalingrad in mid-October, but they quickly found themselves in a bitter, street-by-street battle. Soon they were further hindered by the onset of the Russian winter. By the end of November a huge Soviet counteroffensive had trapped Paulus's army within the city, and the general's lines of supply were cut off. He asked his superiors in Berlin for aid and reinforcements, but they sent very little. Hermann Göring, commander in chief of the Luftwaffe, pledged to supply Paulus by air, but his airdrops were hardly sufficient for a hungry, cold force that was quickly being decimated by endless waves of Soviet reinforcements. By Christmas 1942 Paulus's men were reduced to eating their horses, while pockets of German soldiers were continually shrinking under the Soviet advance.

Soon after the Soviet encirclement of the Sixth Army in late November, Paulus had asked Hitler for the right to retreat from the city temporarily in order to unite and supply his soldiers. The Führer categorically refused, seeing the Battle of Stalingrad in moral rather than strategic terms. He told Paulus that his forces were to stand and fight, and to sacrifice themselves heroically if necessary, since the fight over Stalingrad, in his view, was a fight for the defense of the western world. To put further pressure on Paulus, Hitler promoted him to field marshal, knowing that no German field marshal had ever surrendered alive to an enemy. He also promoted a number of Paulus's officers to higher rank.

But Paulus knew the battle was lost. By January 31, 1943, the day the Führer's office radioed him with the news that he had been named a field marshal, the Sixth Army had been reduced from a force of over one hundred thousand to fewer than twelve thousand hungry, frostbitten, and downtrodden men. Paulus himself, dirty and unshaven, simply waited in a small, dank bedroom for

Soviet officers to find him. As soon as they did he surrendered the Sixth Army to his Soviet counterpart, Marshal Georgy Zhukov. Hitler, hearing the news, was enraged that Paulus had not committed suicide and that his men had not fought to the death.

Paulus was imprisoned by Soviet officials but released when he agreed to broadcast anti-Nazi propaganda from Moscow. In July 1944, after hearing of the plot to assassinate Hitler and overthrow the Nazi regime, he joined the National Committee for a Free Germany, an organization of German prisoners of war in the Soviet Union that enjoyed official Soviet support. He remained within the Soviet bloc after the war, testifying as a prosecution witness for the Russians at the International Military Tribunal in Nuremberg. He died in the Communist German Democratic Republic in 1957. *See also* Barbarossa, Battle of Stalingrad, Vol. 1.

Pétain, Philippe (1856–1951)

French World War I hero and first president of collaborationist Vichy France. Pétain was born in Cauchy-la-Tour, near Calais, on May 24, 1856. His family were agricultural peasants, but nonetheless he gained entrance to the French military academy at Saint-Cyr, graduating in 1878 as a junior officer. Over the next decades he held a number of staff appointments and, when World War I began, he wore the rank of colonel.

Pétain rose rapidly during World War I, thanks to brilliant leadership in the field. He started the war commanding an infantry regiment but was soon promoted to brigade and then division commander. He became a French national hero when, in February 1916, he stopped the German advance during the Battle of Verdun, a decisive event in the war. Not long after Pétain was promoted to commander in chief of all French armies in the field and, on November 21, 1918, he was raised to marshal of France, a rare honor.

Pétain largely tried to retire from public life after World War I. He served briefly as minister of war in 1934 but was heavily criticized because of his apparent authoritarian and antirepublican sympathies, directed particularly at General Francisco Franco in Spain. He served as French ambassador to Spain, in fact, in 1939 and 1940 before being called back to Paris to serve as deputy premier to Paul Reynaud in May 1940. At that time the French were desperately trying to fend off a German invasion. Pétain was convinced that the French cause was hopeless, and that an ongoing alliance with Great Britain was more a curse than a benefit. Reynaud, who wanted to fight on, was forced to resign on June 16. Pétain, supported by a number of cabinet ministers as well as by the archcollaborationist Pierre Laval, took over as premier and arranged for armistice terms with the ecstatic Hitler. He announced the French surrender on June 26.

Although the armistice arranged for much of France to be directly occupied by German forces, the southern portion of the country was allowed to remain independent. Using emergency powers granted him by the French National Assembly, Pétain set up a new government in the resort town of Vichy in the unoccupied area of France. There, Pétain emerged as both an authoritarian and a collaborationist, although he was far more a French nationalist than Laval, his obsequious hatchet man. As Vichy leader Pétain tried to restore traditional, conservative Catholic culture to France as well as curtail civil rights. Although the Germans occupied Vichy in 1942 when Pétain proved unable to hand over the French Mediterranean fleet, the old war hero retained a great deal of moral authority. Even after his resignation in late 1943 Pétain was still regarded as the true leader of the Vichy regime, though little more than a German puppet. Over the last years of World War II Pétain was involved in the deportation of French Jews, the recruitment of French soldiers to serve alongside the Germans, and by 1944 the use of French laborers in the German Reich. Pétain insisted that such measures were necessary for French survival, claiming in later years that at Vichy he had saved his people as he did at Verdun.

After the Allied landings in France in June 1944, Pétain was taken into exile by the Germans. He returned to France in April 1945, where he was arrested by the new government of General Charles de Gaulle. Placed on trial for treason, Pétain was found guilty and condemned to death, but the sentence was commuted due to his advanced age and ill health. He died in the island fortress of Ile d'Yeu on July 23, 1951. *See also* collaboration, Vol. 1; Vichy France, Vol. 2; Laval, Pierre, Vol. 3.

Pius XI (1857–1939)

Pope of the Roman Catholic Church from 1922 to 1939. Born Achille Ratti near Milan on May 31, 1857, the future pope proved to be an accomplished intellectual and theologian. He took doctorates in philosophy, theology, and law at Rome's Lombard College in 1882, and until 1886 he taught in Milan. From 1888 to 1912 he served as the director of the Ambrosian Library in Milan, after which he became the director of the Vatican Library. He was named papal nuncio, or representative, to Poland in 1918 and archbishop of Lepanto in 1919. In 1921 he was raised to archbishop of Milan and soon after to cardinal. The College of Cardinals elected him Pope Plus XI in 1922.

An extremely skillful diplomat, Pius XI concluded agreements with both the Fascist regime in Italy and Adolf Hitler's regime in Germany. The Lateran Pact of 1929, with the Italian Fascists, ensured that the Catholic Church remained independent of Benito Mussolini's state by establishing the political autonomy of Vatican City. With the assistance of Eugenio Pacelli, his secretary of state and later Pope Pius XII, the pope signed an agreement, the Concordat of 1933, with Hitler, in which the Nazi leader agreed to respect the independence of the Catholic Church in Germany and the individual's right to worship.

Hitler had little intention of observing the Concordat of 1933; before long German Catholics had become targets of SS persecution. On March 14, 1937, Pius XI issued an encyclical, or papal statement, known as "Mit Brennender Sorge," ("With Burning Sorrow"). In it the pope criticized Hitler for betraying the Concordat of 1933 and reminded him that the state could not interfere with the rights of human beings to worship. In addition the encyclical spoke out against the broad injustices and racism of the Nazi regime. Pope Pius XI died in Rome on February 10, 1939. *See also* Concordat of 1933, Vol. 1; "Mit Brennender Sorge," religion in the Third Reich, Vol. 2; Pius XII, Vol. 3.

Pius XII (1876–1958)

Pope of the Roman Catholic Church from 1939 to 1958 and as such a man who has been heavily criticized for keeping silent about Nazi atrocities. The future pope was born Eugenio Pacelli in Rome on March 2, 1876. Educated in theology and ordained as a priest, he served as a professor of ecclesiastical diplomacy in Rome from 1904 to 1914. In 1917 he was named archbishop of Sardis and in 1920 papal nuncio, or representative, to Germany, a position he held until 1929. In 1930 he was made a cardinal and in 1930 a Vatican secretary of state. In that position he worked closely with Pope Pius XI in matters of international diplomacy, and thanks to his experience as nuncio in Germany he became Pius XI's closest adviser in his relations with the Third Reich. Cardinal Pacelli was instrumental, for instance, in drafting the Concordat of 1933 between the Roman Catholic Church and Hitler's Germany.

Cardinal Pacelli was elected to the papacy as Pius XII when Pius XI died in 1939. One school of opinion held that his election satisfied the desire among church leaders for consistency in relations between the Vatican and the Third Reich. In any case, relations with the Third Reich took center stage with the new pope, as they did with all European leaders. He tried to use his position to prevent World War II, but during the war Pius XII maintained a largely neutral stance. Judgments of his behavior vary widely. Some claim that he helped, through secret arrangements, to save tens of thousands of Jews. Others note that he stood silent during the deportations of Jews from Rome and other parts of Italy, citing a letter he wrote to the archbishop of Berlin in 1943 lamenting the fact that, in the current world circumstances, the church could offer nothing but its prayers. He was also criticized for not excommunicating Adolf Hitler. Pius XII died in Rome in 1958. The extent of his knowledge of Nazi atrocities and the morality of his response is debated to the present day. *See also* religion in the Third Reich, Vol. 2; Pius XI, Vol. 3

Pohl, Oswald (1892–1951)

General of the Waffen-SS and head of the SS Economic and Administrative Central Office from 1942 to 1945. In that position he was heavily involved in the operations of the Auschwitz and Majdanek death camps in Poland as well as labor camps and concentration camps throughout the Greater German Reich and the occupied territories. He was born in Duisburg in western Germany on June 30, 1892. During World War I he served in the German navy; as a naval officer in the 1920s he rose to the post of senior paymaster. He joined the Nazi Party in 1926 and the SA in 1929, and in 1934 he left the navy to take the position of chief administrator of the Reich Central Security Office with the rank of SS lieutenant colonel. Pohl's administrative talents had become clear to Heinrich Himmler, who increasingly relied on him to oversee important economic matters for the SS. In June 1939 he became a ministerial director representing the SS in the Ministry of the Interior, and soon after became a member of the Heinrich Himmler Friendship Circle. This organization provided a way for wealthy businessmen to provide money to the SS in exchange for honorary ranks and other benefits, and during World War II it paid for many of the uniforms and supplies of the Waffen-SS.

Pohl was named head of the SS Economic and Administrative Central Office in 1942 and promoted to SS lieutenant general in connection with his new status. In this position he was one of the most important administrators in the wartime Third Reich. Here too, his purpose was mostly to enrich the SS, and Pohl had authority over the economic side of the extermination centers, labor camps, and concentration camps scattered across the territory that Germany occupied, including the Inspectorate of Concentration Camps. Among Pohl's responsibilities was ensuring that the camp network served to make the SS financially independent of the Nazi government. This included making special arrangements with German companies to build factories to take advantage of slave labor in the Polish camps. In addition, Pohl was ordered to consider the victims of the camps themselves as a sort of economic resource. Any valuables they brought with them were appropriated, as were mundane goods like suitcases, shoes, and eyeglasses. Pohl's functionaries even collected human hair and sometimes saw to it that gold and silver false teeth and fillings were removed from corpses. The collected valuables were placed in the so-called Max Heiliger Fund, a special account established by the SS and the Reichsbank, the national bank of Germany.

Pohl avoided arrest at the end of World War II by posing as a farmhand. He was finally uncovered in May 1946 and tried at Nuremberg by an American war crimes tribunal in November 1947. He was found guilty and sentenced to death. The sentence was carried out on June 8, 1951, at Munich's Landsberg Prison. *See also* Max Heiliger Fund, SS Economic and Administrative Central Office, Vol. 2.

Quisling, Vidkun (1887–1945)

Self-proclaimed leader of the Norwegian Fascist Party, Nasjonal Samling (National Union) and would-be dictator of occupied Norway during World War II. Because of his betrayals of Norway to the leaders of the Third Reich, Quisling's name has since become a synonym for "traitor."

Vidkun Quisling was born in Fyresdal in the province of Telemarken on July 18, 1887. He embarked on a military career, graduating from the Norwegian Military Academy in 1911, not long after his country achieved its independence from Sweden. After working for a time under the Norwegian explorer Fridtjof Nansen, Quisling entered politics. He worked in Russia as a delegate to the League of Nations and in 1931 entered the government as foreign minister. A strong anticommunist in a nation that shared a far northern border with the Soviet Union, Quisling founded the Nasjonal Samling in 1933. Although the party never grew to be more than a tiny fringe movement in Norway, Quisling grew increasingly convinced that his country's best hope for survival was through an ideological and military alliance with the Third Reich. In early 1940, with the help of intermediaries in the German navy, Quisling met with Adolf Hitler. He warned the Führer, with some justification, that the British and the French were making plans to occupy Norway to secure transport lines for volunteer forces heading east to fight with the Finns in their war with Russia and to choke off the supply to Germany of Swedish iron ore, much of which was exported from Norwegian ports. The solution that Quisling proposed was that the Third Reich occupy Norway first. Like most others, Hitler found it difficult to take Quisling seriously as a political leader, but events proved that a German occupation of Norway made sense from a strategic standpoint. Consequently, German forces marched into the country on April 9, 1940. The Norwegian government was forced to disband and go into exile in London, and Quisling took advantage of the moment by declaring himself prime minister of Norway. Finding that most Norwegians ignored Quisling, the Germans replaced him on April 15 with Josef Terboven, a Nazi Party official who was named Reich plenipotentiary for Norway. In February 1942 Quisling was restored as a puppet prime minister, but Terboven remained the true authority in the country.

On May 9, 1945, Quisling surrendered to Norwegian police. He was tried for high treason, sentenced to death, and executed by firing squad in Oslo on October 24, 1945. ***See also*** collaboration, Vol. 1; National Union, Weser Exercise, Vol. 2; Terboven, Josef, Vol. 3.

R

Rademacher, Franz (1906–1973)

German Foreign Office official and a major participant in the mass extermination of Jews by the Third Reich. Rademacher was born in Mecklenburg, East Prussia, on February 20, 1906. He chose a legal career, studying at the Universities of Munich and Rostock and becoming a deputy judge in 1932. He officially joined the Nazi Party in March 1933, eventually gravitating toward the Foreign Office. From 1938 to 1940 he served as chargé d'affaires to the German embassy in Montevideo, Uruguay. In May 1940 he returned to Germany, where he handled Jewish affairs in the "Germany" section within the Foreign Office. His superiors were Martin Luther and, ultimately, Joachim von Ribbentrop.

Rademacher was a devoted anti-Semite who truly believed that Jews should be removed from the Greater German Reich that the Nazis hoped to build. Although he was not instrumental in developing the plan for mass extermination, he did put together the so-called Madagascar Plan. This notion, seriously discussed by SS and Foreign Office officials in 1940 and 1941, called for all European Jews to be deported to the Indian Ocean island of Madagascar, off the southeast African coast. When the invasion of the Soviet Union in June 1941 made the Madagascar Plan impractical Rademacher turned his bureaucratic skills to the "Final Solution to the Jewish Question."

Rademacher served mainly as a contact man between the Foreign Office and the SS, which planned and carried out the details of the mass extermination program. He worked closely with Adolf Eichmann, head of the Jewish section of the Gestapo and the man responsible for deportations to the Polish death camps. Rademacher assisted Eichmann in organizing the assembly and deportation of thousands of Jews from across Europe, as his signatures on hundreds of documents makes clear, and he personally ordered massacres on occasion, such as in Belgrade in October 1941.

In April 1943 Rademacher's immediate superior, Martin Luther, was arrested for plotting a coup against Ribbentrop. That was the end of Rademacher's diplomatic career; for the rest of the war he served as a naval officer. For some time after the war Rademacher was largely ignored by occupation officials searching for and prosecuting higher-level Nazi war criminals, but in 1952 he was sentenced to prison for his involvement in the Belgrade massacre. Before his sentence began, however, Rademacher escaped, eventually ending up in Damascus, Syria. The Syrians accused him in 1963 of being a spy for the West and of insulting their government and imprisoned him for two years. He finally returned to Germany in 1966, where he found himself the target of new war crimes trials. He died in the West German capital of Bonn on March 17, 1973, before the latest of the trials could take place. *See also* Final Solution, Vol. 1; Madagascar Plan, Vol. 2; Eichmann, Adolf, Vol. 3.

Raeder, Erich (1876–1960)

Commander in chief of the German navy from 1935 until 1943. Raeder was born in the town of Wandsbeck near Hamburg on April 24, 1876. His background was middle class, but that did not prevent him from building a successful career in the navy, which was not bound, like the German army, to the Prussian aristocratic tradition. Raeder attended the Naval Academy at Kiel in northern Germany and became an officer in 1897. In the ensuing years he served in the Asia-Pacific region and, for a brief time, as an officer on the *Hohenzollern*, the personal yacht of Kaiser Wilhelm II. During World War I Raeder took part in a number of operations, many of them against the British, and was present at the Battle of Jutland, the most important naval engagement of the war. After the Treaty of Versailles limited the size and scope of the German navy, Raeder retreated into the naval archives, where he produced a book on naval warfare. In 1925, however, he returned to active duty as a vice admiral. He was promoted to full admiral and chief of the Naval Command in 1928, holding the post until 1935.

Raeder was not a devoted Nazi, although he admired Adolf Hitler's leadership qualities as well as his strong stance against the expansion of Bolshevism. The Führer, who had little knowledge or understanding of naval operations, named him commander in chief of the navy of the Third Reich in 1935, by which time he was ready to ignore the restrictions of the Treaty of Versailles. As commander in chief Raeder played the major role in building up the navy to compete with the navies of Germany's rivals. Among his efforts were the construction of huge battleships such as the *Graf Spee* and the *Bismarck* and a focus on submarine warfare. Hitler named him grand admiral on April 1, 1939. After World War II began Raeder implemented a policy of unlimited U-boat warfare in the North Sea and Atlantic Ocean, hoping to disable supply and communication lines between Great Britain and North America.

Raeder, however, was cautious in comparison with other Third Reich military leaders. He had opposed, for instance, the reoccupation of the Rhineland in 1936 and advised Hitler against the invasion of the Soviet Union. He was present, however, at

As commander in chief of the German navy until 1943, Admiral Erich Raeder (second from right) is credited with rebuilding the navy to its wartime strength.

the Hossbach Conference of November 1937, where Hitler made it plain that he planned extensive territorial conquests. Unlike other military leaders at the conference, such as Generals Werner von Blomberg and Werner Freiherr von Fritsch, Raeder did not express opposition to Hitler's plans for Austria, Czechoslovakia, and Poland. As he made clear later in a major speech in 1939, Raeder was sympathetic to the idea that such actions were necessary to stop Bolshevism as well as, he now claimed, "international Jewry."

In January 1943 Hitler, unhappy with Raeder's decisions and the performance of the German navy in general, forced the grand admiral to retire. He was replaced as commander in chief of the navy by U-boat admiral Karl Dönitz. He spent the remaining years of the war in retirement and was arrested by Allied forces at war's end. To his surprise, Raeder was one of the twenty-one top Nazis brought before the International Military Tribunal at Nuremberg in the fall of 1941. He fully admitted during his testimony that the Third Reich was guilty of violating the Treaty of Versailles but asserted that it did so as a matter of honor. Raeder was found guilty of crimes against peace, war crimes, and conspiracy and sentenced to life in prison by the Nuremberg tribunal. He was released, however, in 1955 for reasons of ill health. Soon after he published his memoirs, in which he both praised Hitler and justified his own actions on the grounds of restoring Germany's proper place in the world. Raeder died in Kiel on November 6, 1960. *See also* Battle of the Atlantic, Vol. 1; Nuremberg trials, Vol. 2; Dönitz, Karl, Vol. 3.

Raubal, Geli (1908–1931)

Adolf Hitler's niece and, according to many, the only woman he ever truly loved, although opinion varies as to whether this was romantic love or the love of a devoted and overprotective guardian. The mysterious circumstances of her death in 1931 continue to inspire speculation.

Angela Raubal, as Geli was formally and legally known, was born in Linz on June 4, 1908. Her parents were Leo Raubal, a tax official, and Angela Hitler, who was Adolf Hitler's half-sister. Geli was one of three children who were left almost destitute when Leo Raubal died in 1910. For a time Geli lived with Maria Raubal, her aunt, who was a schoolteacher near Linz. In 1917 she moved to Vienna to live with her mother, by then a minor church administrator. Soon after, however, she returned to Linz to attend secondary school, living with relatives. While there she became aware of her uncle Adolf's growing fame as a politician across the German border, and in 1924 she moved with her mother to Munich to keep house for him. There it is said that the young girl developed a small romance with Emil Maurice, Hitler's bodyguard and driver, and that Hitler strongly disapproved of the match.

Beginning in 1928, Geli often accompanied Hitler to various social gatherings, and other members of Hitler's inner circle grew used to seeing her. In 1929 she moved into Hitler's Munich apartment, where she had her own, specially decorated bedroom. In addition, she spent a great deal of time at Berchtesgaden, Hitler's house in the Obersalzburg, the Alpine region along the German-Austrian border, where her mother, Angela, had been brought to manage the household. Hitler's exact relationship with Geli drew speculation even among close party associates (he once spoke of her as his prize possession). He kept her away from people of her own age group, but Geli did manage to sneak away to Vienna from time to time. Meanwhile, she entertained the notion of becoming a popular singer, hoping that her uncle would engineer a successful career for her.

On September 19, 1931, while Adolf Hitler was away in northern Germany, Geli Raubal was found dead in her bedroom in Hitler's Munich apartment. According to servants and police, she had shot herself, dying of suffocation after a bullet punctured her lung. Officials quickly ruled it a suicide, although there was no suicide note. Some attributed her act to remorse and anxiety over her entertainment career, others to an overreaction to her uncle's refusal to allow her to go to Vienna. According to a number of accounts, Hitler was not crushed by her death, failing to attend her funeral in order to go to a Nazi rally. He did, however, leave her Munich bedroom untouched, and American soldiers found it as it was in 1931 when they entered it in 1945. The Nazi leader refused to speak of her after her death and forbade others from speaking of their relationship as well. Father Bernhard Stempfle, one of several people who helped edit *Mein Kampf*, was allegedly shot for speaking too openly of it. Rumors persisted that her death was not a suicide but rather a murder, committed by an enraged Hitler or by Nazi operatives seeking to remove a potential political danger or source of embarrassment to the Nazi leader. *See also* Braun, Eva; Hitler, Adolf; Maurice, Emil, Vol. 3.

Rauschning, Hermann (1887–1982)

One of the few Nazi politicians who turned against Adolf Hitler and became an outspoken critic of the Third Reich. Rauschning was born in West Prussia on August 7, 1887, to a family of minor aristocrats. During World War I he served as a lieutenant in the infantry. After the war he became active in German nationalist movements in eastern Germany, most notably in Danzig, the port city that had been awarded to the revived nation of Poland during postwar negotiations in Paris. Rauschning joined the Nazi Party in 1932, and his work in Danzig brought him to the personal attention of Adolf Hitler. After the local Nazi Party won a majority in local elections in 1933, Rauschning was named president of the Danzig Senate. Since, according to the terms of the postwar agreement, Danzig enjoyed a certain amount of political autonomy under the loose authority of the League of Nations, Rauschning was free to use his influence to expand Nazism in the city. Many longtime Nazis, however, resented both Rauschning's importance in Danzig and the fact that Hitler held him in high regard, and they complained loudly that he was a carpetbagger enjoying political opportunities that should have gone to dedicated "Old Fighters."

By 1935 Rauschning had broken with the Nazis, however, and fled to exile in Switzerland. There he wrote two books, *The Revolution of Nihilism*, published in 1938, and *Hitler Speaks*, published in 1939. Both offered strong criticisms of the Nazi regime as well as warnings that Hitler was insatiably power hungry and might well lead the world into war. He continued to write during the war that indeed followed, and the Nazis banned his books and placed him on a list of foreign enemies who were to be arrested by SS policemen. In 1948 Rauschning moved to the United States, settling as a farmer in Gaston, Oregon. He died in nearby Portland on February 8, 1982. *See also* Danzig, exiles and refugees from the Third Reich, Vol. 1.

Reichenau, Walther von (1884–1942)

Politically astute and cynical German field marshal who, unlike most of his fellow top officers in the Wehrmacht, enjoyed favor in the eyes of Adolf Hitler and other leading Nazis. Reichenau was born in Karlsruhe on October 8, 1884. He joined the German Imperial Army in 1903 and during World War I served as both an artillery officer and on the General Staff. After the war he joined the Reichswehr, where he became, as a major general, head of the Army Chancellery and the Army Supply Office. In 1933 he was appointed chief of staff to the minister of war, General Werner von Blomberg. In this post he took steps to ensure that the army would be strengthened by its ties with the Nazi movement. These included making special arrangements with the SS in 1933 and 1934 that helped to marginalize the SA, which in those years fostered the notion of replacing the Prussian-dominated army with a "people's army" of SA men led by its chief, Ernst Röhm. In the Blood Purge of June 1934, when Röhm and others were killed by Nazi assassins, Reichenau and Blomberg made sure the army simply stood by. Soon afterward, both strongly encouraged their fellow officers to not only support Adolf Hitler and the Nazis but swear a personal oath of loyalty to the Führer. Reichenau reportedly had no great love for Hitler, but seemed to think that he was necessary to inspire the mass support that could stop the spread of communism.

In 1935 Reichenau was promoted to general and posted to Munich, where he enthusiastically supported the emergence of militarized units of SS men. In 1937, despite a lack of field experience and a reputation as a political insider rather than a combat leader, he became head of the Army Group IV and, when World War II broke out, the commander in chief of the Tenth Army. Along with ten other Wehrmacht and Luftwaffe generals, he was promoted to field marshal after the fall of France in 1940.

Reichenau then served as a commander during the invasion of the Soviet Union in the summer of 1941, first as commander in chief of the Sixth Army and then as leader of Army Group South, making him one of the top commanders on the eastern front. He was not enthusiastic about Germany's prospects for inflicting a lasting defeat on Great Britain and France, but on the eastern front he was a ruthless commander who not only wanted to crush Bolshevism but also supported Hitler's racial war against the Jews. He knew of and praised, for instance, the Einsatzgruppen massacres at Babi Yar and other locations. Reichenau died in an airplane crash on January 17, 1942. *See also* Blood Purge, Vol. 1; Wehrmacht, Vol. 2.

Reitsch, Hanna (1912–1979)

German test pilot who set a number of aviation records and an enthusiastic, uncritical supporter of Adolf Hitler who visited the Führer during his last days in his Berlin bunker. Hanna Reitsch was born in Hirschberg in eastern Germany on March 29, 1912. She took early to flying, and gave up an original plan to serve as a flying doctor and missionary in Africa to become a stunt pilot. She set her first record in 1931, at the young age of nineteen, when she flew a glider for five and a half hours, a world record for women. She later extended the record to eleven and a half hours. In 1934 she set the women's altitude world record, and in later years she was the first person to fly across the Alps in a glider and the first to fly a helicopter indoors.

Reitsch was appointed to the German air force, the Luftwaffe, in 1937 on the request of one of its top officers, General Ernst Udet. She became a flight captain and the test pilot of a number of new combat aircraft for the Luftwaffe, including both small jets and huge transports. She also was one of the first to carry out tests involving the V-1 "flying bombs." In 1942 Adolf Hitler, who greatly admired the young flier, awarded her the Iron Cross, First and Second Class, the only woman so honored during the Third Reich. For her part, Reitsch was personally devoted to Hitler and refused to believe the stories of atrocities that surrounded him. She spent the last two years of World War II at the Luftwaffe headquarters of General Robert Ritter von Greim on the steadily disintegrating eastern front.

On April 26, 1945, just four days before Hitler's suicide, Reitsch and Greim flew to Berlin under almost constant Soviet fire to ask Hitler if they could share these final days with him in the Führerbunker. Hitler instead ordered them, on April 29, to leave Berlin and rally what remained of the German air force to continue the fight. Reitsch and Greim made a dangerous escape from Berlin, finally reaching the northern German headquarters of Hitler's successor, Admiral Karl Dönitz. There Reitsch was arrested by Allied forces. She was held in an interrogation center for over a year but finally released by the Americans in 1946.

Several years later Reitsch resumed her life as an intrepid and daring pilot, often competing successfully against men in gliding competitions. She also continued to work as a test pilot, and her adventures took her from Germany to India for a brief spell, then to West Africa, where she established a gliding school in Ghana in 1962. She maintained connections with politicians as well, becoming acquainted in India with both President Jawaharlal Nehru and the young future president Indira Gandhi. In Ghana she was well acquainted with Kwame Nkrumah, an important African independence leader and the president of the country. In her later years she expressed surprise and dismay toward the acts of Hitler and his minions during the Third Reich. Her accomplishments, which included more than forty flying records, remained remarkable and her experience, even under Hitler, might be summed up in the title of her 1951 autobiography: *Flying Is My Life.* Hanna Reitsch died in Frankfurt on August 24, 1979. ***See also*** Luftwaffe, Vol. 1; women in the Third Reich, Vol. 2.

Remer, Otto (1912–1997)

German army major who played a vital role in preventing the July 1944 Plot from overthrowing the government of the Third Reich, and a man who in later years strove to keep the Nazi movement alive. Remer was a devoted officer who was wounded eight times in the early years of World War II and was decorated for bravery by Adolf Hitler personally. On July 20, 1944, when the assassination of Hitler was supposed to coincide with a takeover of Berlin by the German resistance movement, Remer was the commander of the Greater Germany Guard Battalion, a unit of the Home Army designed to defend Berlin in the event of an attempted takeover, which Nazi leaders feared was most likely to come from foreign workers, not from anti-Nazi Germans.

After local conspirators heard that a bomb had gone off at Hitler's eastern headquarters, and presumed that the Führer had been killed, Remer was ordered to seal off the important government buildings in the Wilhelmstrasse and then to take his men to arrest Joseph Goebbels, the highest-ranking Nazi then present in Berlin. Goebbels, however, was able to persuade Remer that Hitler was, in fact, alive and reminded the young officer that he had declared an oath of loyalty to the Nazi leader. To convince Remer, Goebbels even had him speak directly with Hitler on the telephone. Hitler told him to ignore any orders from earlier in the day, to place himself under the authority of Heinrich Himmler, now head of the Home Army, and to take ruthless measures to suppress the attempted coup. Remer's quick actions over the next hours likely assured that the plot would completely fail. He withdrew his forces from the Wilhelmstrasse, took command over all local military units and helped to round up resistance leaders such as Ludwig Beck and Claus Schenk Graf von Stauffenberg. Soon after Hitler promoted him to major general.

After lying low for a few years, Otto Remer emerged as a neo-Nazi in 1950. That year he formed the National Socialist Reich Party, which made a strong showing in elections in Lower Saxony and was disbanded by the Federal Republic of Germany in 1952. Remer himself was sentenced to prison in March 1952 for libel against the German resistance movement of the Third Reich, although he escaped his sentence by going into exile in Egypt. There he called for German support to help the Arabs crush the new threat represented, he argued, by "international Jewry" and the new state of Israel. In the 1980s and 1990s Remer became a symbolic leader of neo-Nazi movements among much younger Germans and also helped to spread the odd idea that the Holocaust never happened. Sentenced to twenty-two months in prison by a German judge in 1992, for "promoting hate, violence, and racism," Remer fled to Spain and died in Marbella on October 4, 1997. *See also* Home Army, July 1944 Plot, Vol. 1; neo-Nazism, Vol. 2.

Ribbentrop, Joachim von (1893–1946)

Foreign minister of the Third Reich from 1938 to 1945. Joachim von Ribbentrop was born in Wesel in western Germany on April 30, 1893. His background was middle class. After studying languages at Metz and Grenoble in Alsace-Lorraine, he worked for four years as a salesman in Canada. He returned to Germany soon after the beginning of World War I and volunteered for active service, serving first on the eastern front and then with the German military representation in Turkey. By the end of the war he had a lieutenant's rank and served as military attaché in Istanbul. At war's end he settled in Berlin and returned to commerce, setting himself up in a business that exported wines and liquors, primarily to Great Britain and France. While in Berlin Ribbentrop proved to be an ambitious social climber. In time he married Anneliese Henckel, the daughter of a German sparkling wine producer, who provided him with access to Berlin's high society as well as a huge house in the ritzy suburb of Dahlem. Ribbentrop also added the aristocratic "von" to his name by arranging to be adopted by a distant relative who had been knighted. These efforts proved useful to him in later years; Adolf Hitler was impressed by Ribbentrop's supposed social connections and sophisticated lifestyle, although other top Nazis recognized him as an ambitious fake.

Ribbentrop joined the Nazi Party in May 1932, and was therefore a latecomer to the movement, another fact that did not endear him to many Nazi "Old Fighters." Hitler, however, liked him and appreciated the fact that the Ribbentrop home was an impressive setting for Nazi conferences in the capital. By 1933 Ribbentrop was an SS colonel, a member of the Reichstag, and Hitler's informal adviser on foreign affairs. The Nazi leader disliked dealing with the tradition-bound German Foreign Office, full as it was with aristocrats. He preferred working with Ribbentrop, who seemed sophisticated and well traveled in Hitler's naive estimation, and who spoke both English and French. The two established the so-called Ribbentrop Bureau as a Nazi Party alternative to the Foreign Office. Ribbentrop became a master sycophant, completely subservient to the whims of his Führer and a shameless flatterer and manipulator. Among the leadership of the Nazi movement Ribbentrop was almost universally disliked: Hermann Göring criticized him, for instance, as a mere wine peddler. Even foreign diplomats recognized that he was in over his head in diplomatic affairs, covering his lack of intelligence and experience with transparent snobbery and arrogance; foreign journalists found him to be a slightly ridiculous figure.

Nazi foreign minister Joachim von Ribbentrop negotiated the Nazi-Soviet Non-Aggression Pact of August 1939.

Nonetheless, Hitler considered him a foreign affairs genius and remained blinded by his flattery.

In the years prior to World War II Ribbentrop played the central role in a number of diplomatic arrangements. In 1935, for instance, he negotiated the Anglo-German Naval Accord, which allowed Germany to build up its navy despite Treaty of Versailles restrictions. The pact was in accordance with Hitler's desire for a rapprochement between the Third Reich and the British, whom he argued were racial allies as well as potential great-power partners. From 1936 to 1938 Ribbentrop pursued this ideal as German ambassador to Great Britain. But London society rejected him and he presented a rather awkward figure; on one occasion he greeted the king of England with the Hitler salute, a gesture that was received in cold silence. Ribbentrop was to remember the slights he received in London. After becoming foreign minister he worked against any potential agreements between the two countries, and indeed helped to convince Hitler that the British could present no obstacle to German ambitions in central and eastern Europe. Meanwhile, having been frustrated in London, Ribbentrop worked hard to establish the so-called Rome-Berlin Axis with agreements in 1936 and 1938.

Ribbentrop was appointed foreign minister of the Third Reich in February 1938, when Constantin Freiherr von Neurath, his predecessor, was forced into retirement after expressing hesitation over Germany's plans for expansion. He then acted as the Führer's main representative in negotiations over Czechoslovakia and Poland, displaying a ready willingness to threaten warfare if discussions did not go Germany's way. Ribbentrop's greatest diplomatic accomplishment, and one of the most decisive events of the era of the Third Reich, was the Nazi-Soviet Pact, also called the Molotov-Ribbentrop Pact, announced on August 23, 1939. The pact guaranteed that the Soviet Union would not intervene should Nazi Germany invade Poland. Since Ribbentrop had also convinced Hitler that the British too would not intervene, the Führer decided the way was clear for the invasion. World War II began just over one week later, on September 1, when Hitler's armies marched into Poland.

During World War II Ribbentrop's influence waned along with the need for diplomacy. He remained, however, an active political infighter, searching for ways to maintain his importance to Hitler by enlarging the jurisdiction of the Foreign Ministry. One way to do so was to enlarge the role of the Foreign Office in the deportation and extermination of European Jews, and Ribbentrop actively sought to get both German allies and occupied countries to turn their Jews over to his compatriots in the SS. When a subordinate, State Secretary Martin Luther, proved more effective in this regard and tried, in addition, to mount a coup against him, Ribbentrop had him imprisoned. Nonetheless Hitler, whose favor was Ribbentrop's only professional asset, paid little attention to the foreign minister in the last months of the war.

At the end of World War II Ribbentrop attempted to hide but was arrested in June 1945 in Hamburg by British forces. He was one of the twenty-one top Nazis brought before the International Military Tribunal at Nuremberg in late 1945, and he was charged on all four counts of the war crimes indictment: conspiracy to commit crimes, crimes against peace, war crimes, and crimes against humanity. His testimony reflected his continued complete subservience to Hitler and otherwise he seemed a ridiculous figure, crying, cringing, and pleading his innocence. He also showed no comprehension of the scope of Nazi crimes or his involvement in them. The tribunal found him guilty on all four counts and sentenced him to death. He was the first of the condemned Nazi leaders to be hanged at Nuremberg on October 16, 1946. ***See also***

Nazi-Soviet Pact, Nuremberg trials, Ribbentrop Bureau, Vol. 2.; International Military Tribunal, The Charges Against the Surviving Nazi Leaders, Vol. 4.

Riefenstahl, Leni (1902–)

Filmmaker whose *Triumph of the Will* and *Olympia* were considered masterpieces, somewhat paradoxically, of both Nazi propaganda and the filmmaking art. Riefenstahl was born in Berlin on August 22, 1902. She entered the arts first as a dancer, trained in ballet with the Russian Ballet as well as other prominent companies and instructors. During the mid-1920s she worked with the great Berlin theatrical producer Max Reinhardt. In 1925 she turned to acting in the movies, becoming closely associated with a filmmaking trend in Weimar Germany which focused on romantic Alpine scenery as the setting for various adventures. Her first movie was *The Holy Mountain*, followed by such films as *The Great Fountain* and *Storms over Mount Blanc*. She formed her own moviemaking company in 1931, and her first production was *The Blue Light*, which she cowrote, directed, and starred in. It won the gold medal at that year's Biennale in Venice, one of Europe's great film festivals. In 1933 she starred with future Luftwaffe general Ernst Udet in *S.O.S. Iceberg.*

Adolf Hitler, a movie lover, was impressed by Riefenstahl's work as both actor and director, and he also admired the tall, athletic, and beautiful young woman as a fine example of German youth and Aryan ideals. In 1933 he appointed Riefenstahl the top filmmaker of the Nazi Party, in charge of making films that would glorify the movement. Her first major work was *Triumph of the Will*, a documentary of the 1934 Nazi Party rally at Nuremberg. Hitler wanted that year's "Party Days," as the rally was known, to be an acknowledgment that he had outlasted such rivals as Ernst Röhm and the recently deceased President Paul von Hindenburg, and that he was now the unchallenged dictator of Germany. Riefenstahl's film was to be the testament to this new state of affairs, and Hitler gave the young moviemaker free rein to organize the rally around her needs. She used a huge staff, including sixteen cameramen and thirty-six strategically placed cameras. Among other preparations, she had special bunkers built beneath speaker's platforms so that she could effectively capture the dynamism of Nazi officials from an angle of deference, gazing up. The final version of the film, released in 1935, begins with Hitler descending from the clouds in an airplane to receive the adulation of the local people and proceeds through meetings of Hitler Youth, firelit rallies, special ceremonies, and hypnotic, repetitive scenes of marches and parades. Many have considered the film the single most effective piece of Nazi propaganda, acknowledging Riefenstahl's innovative and brilliant camerawork, editing, and visual narrative. Like *The Blue Light*, *Triumph of the Will* took first place at the Venice Biennale.

Much pleased by *Triumph of the Will*, Hitler next asked Riefenstahl to make a documentary film of the 1936 Berlin Olympics, which the Führer envisioned as an opportunity to show the world the greatness of both his regime and German athletics. The result was *Olympia*, first shown on Hitler's birthday in 1938. It was released in two parts, known as *Festival of the Nations* and *Festival of Beauty;* like their predecessors, both took the gold medal at Venice. The documentary as a whole, moreover, was recognized as a masterpiece after World War II by the International Olympic Committee, which presented Riefenstahl with a special award in 1948.

After the fall of the Third Reich Riefenstahl faced many questions regarding her political involvement with Nazism as well as her personal relationship with Hitler. In the first regard she claimed to be ignorant, noting that in 1934 there were few measures against Jews and few Germans suspected what Hitler would bring their nation to. She also strongly denied accusations of a romantic relationship with Hitler, charges for which there is no evidence at all, although she did from time to time have to fend off the advances of Joseph Goebbels. Riefenstahl continued to work as a filmmaker and, more notably, a photographer in the years after World War II. She published two photography books on Africa, *The Last of the Nuba* and *The People of Kau*. In 1994 a documentary about her life was released entitled *The Wonderful, Horrible Life of Leni Riefenstahl*. Still a controversial figure, she marked her one hundredth birthday on August 22, 2002, at her home near Munich. *See also* film in the Third Reich, Vol. 1; *Triumph of the Will*, women in the Third Reich, Vol. 2; Braun, Diary Entries, Vol. 4.

Röhm, Ernst (1887–1934)

Chief of staff of the SA and a man whose authority nearly equaled that of Adolf Hitler as a leader of the Nazi Party in its early years. Röhm was born in Munich on November 28, 1887, to a family of civil servants. He embarked on a career as a professional soldier and became an officer just before World War I. He was wounded several times during the war, which was on the whole a period he remembered fondly. Röhm enjoyed the camaraderie of frontline soldiers as well as the violence and risks of combat, later referring to himself as a man who disliked order and peace. After the war Röhm tried to lead the life of a freebooting military man, which was not difficult in the chaos of postwar Bavaria. Although he remained a Reichswehr officer, he also engaged in a variety of extracurricular activities including assembling a secret stock of weapons for use against any left-wing movement that happened to emerge in Bavaria as well as serving in the right-wing, nationalist Freikorps under Franz Xaver Ritter von Epp. Throughout, Röhm tried to keep alive the so-called spirit of the trenches, or the camaraderie and recklessness of the World War I fighting man. He had little taste for politicians or for middle-class order.

Röhm joined the Nazi Party in 1919, having heard Hitler speak and sensing that he was a kindred spirit. The two became close, addressing each other with the familiar German "du" rather than the formal "Sie." Hitler used the address with few others. Over the next several years Röhm proved to be an indispensable asset to the fledgling movement. He maintained important contacts among local Reichswehr officers, but perhaps more importantly, his persona as a swashbuckler and risk taker attracted a number of like-minded young men into the party and the SA, the private army of storm troopers Röhm later led. In these years and again after 1930 Röhm gave the Nazi movement a familiar, popular, down-to-earth appeal that the aloof, socially awkward Hitler was incapable of.

During the Beer Hall Putsch of November 1923 Röhm was assigned the task of taking over Munich's police headquarters, which he accomplished temporarily, and during the march through Munich's streets he stood at Hitler's side. After the failure of the putsch he was arrested, quickly released on probation, and dismissed from the army. For a few years, while the Nazi Party was in disarray if not doomed, he worked as a traveling salesman and a factory hand but was unable to settle comfortably into civilian life. In 1928 he left for Bolivia, where he worked as a military trainer. Hitler, meanwhile, harbored concerns that Röhm's emphasis on militarism and taste for revolutionary upheaval might work against his larger interests. The Beer Hall Putsch had convinced Hitler that the Nazis had to rise to power legally, and probably with the cooperation of traditional, respectable forces in big business and the army. While Röhm languished in either middle-class or Bolivian exile, Hitler was happy to leave leadership of the SA to less charismatic and controversial figures.

The Nazi leader called Röhm back, however, after German elections in September

1930 demonstrated that the Nazi Party had become a force in German politics and that the SA's strong-arm tactics might again be effective. Röhm took command of the SA and enthusiastically built it into a major force in German life. From seventy thousand members in 1930, its membership rose to a half-million by the beginning of 1933. Accepting all comers but mainly attracting the young, the rootless, the unemployed, and the criminally inclined, the SA turned itself into, in effect, one of Germany's major employers during the worst years of the Great Depression, even providing its members with food and a place to sleep. Röhm also provided his followers with a larger purpose: to save Germany from communism. Between 1930 and 1933 the SA fought countless street battles with Communists, and is generally considered to have been victorious in this aspect of the Nazi revolution. But while Röhm played his role to perfection, garnering popular support for Hitler and intimidating opposing politicians, Hitler played an equally dangerous game. He simultaneously employed and disavowed the lawlessness of Röhm's SA in his scheme to achieve respectability among Germany's conservative politicians, industrialists, and officers, who considered the SA an ill-managed pack of low-class rabble-rousers. In 1932 the Nazi leader asked Röhm to respect the ban on the SA ordered by President Paul von Hindenburg. By then Röhm had begun to entertain his own ambitions for the SA and to wonder whether Hitler was in fact a true National Socialist revolutionary.

After the Nazis took power in 1933, Hitler appointed Röhm to his cabinet as minister without portfolio. Since he remained chief of staff of the SA and was now also the head of the Bavarian state government, he was one of the most powerful men in Germany. However, his ambitions began to diverge drastically from Hitler's. Now chancellor, Hitler no longer wanted to foment any sort of people's revolution. Instead he wanted to solidify his authority and stabilize the nation. Röhm, on the other hand, envisioned a sort of soldier's and people's state in which he would be the military leader while Hitler remained the political leader. The SA, he felt, would be the core of a huge national army meant to replace the tradition-bound, elitist Reichswehr. Röhm's ambitions, about which he was very outspoken, alarmed a number of people both inside and outside the Nazi movement. The officer corps, which Hitler considered necessary to his future plans, was shocked by the notion that their forces, with their rich traditions and sense of honor, might by absorbed into a people's army made up of low-class bully boys. Other conservative Germans expressed similar fears, likening Röhm's plans to a Socialist takeover. The SA leader, meanwhile, had made dangerous enemies within the Nazi Party, most notably Hermann Göring and Heinrich Himmler. Göring, who controlled the state of Prussia as well as the Prussian police, wanted no rival to his status as the second man in the Nazi Party while Himmler's streamlined SS saw itself as a far more effective paramilitary force than the flabby, populist SA. Röhm's personal habits alienated many as well; he was an unabashed homosexual, a fact that had always been an open secret among top Nazis, and he enjoyed wild, drunken parties with his entourage of SA men.

Röhm remained in Hitler's inner circle, but by the spring of 1934 the Führer was admitting to himself that the SA leader was a danger to the regime that he was trying to build. In April he made a promise to important military leaders that he would contain Röhm and the SA if they, in return, supported him in his bid to combine the president's and chancellor's office in one. Meanwhile, rumors began to spread that Röhm, perhaps in concert with Gregor Strasser and Kurt von Schleicher, planned a "second revolution" that would allow them to oust Hitler. The rumor was probably false, but it proved to be one of the enduring myths of the Third

Reich. Early in June 1934 Hitler met with Röhm to tell him not to plan a second revolution and to place the SA on leave for one month in July. Soon after Hitler, urged on by Himmler, made the decision to assassinate Röhm. The result was the Blood Purge of June 30, 1934.

That day Hitler, accompanied by an SS bodyguard, left for the resort town of Bad Wiessee, south of Munich. Röhm was there enjoying a brief holiday with some SA comrades and, lacking the capacity for deceit that characterized so many Nazi leaders, had no idea that he was in personal danger. Hitler ordered his old comrade arrested, and Röhm was taken to Munich's Stadelheim Prison. On July 2 Röhm was given the option of suicide when a gun was placed in his cell, but he still refused to believe that he was in mortal danger and did not use it. Soon after he was simply shot by SS guards. The alleged conspirators, Strasser and Schleicher, were also killed in the Blood Purge, as were Schleicher's wife and more than one hundred others with whom Hitler wanted to settle old scores.

After Röhm's murder Joseph Goebbels's propaganda machine went into high gear, justifying the act on the grounds that the SA leader was both a deviant homosexual and a traitor to the German nation. On July 13 Hitler addressed the Reichstag, telling members that the murders of Röhm and the others were necessary to save Germany from revolution and disorder. Military leaders, in accordance with their earlier arrangement, concurred. Over the next years the crippled SA ceased to be a factor in Nazi politics, serving primarily a sentimental and ceremonial role. *See also* Blood Purge, Vol. 1; SA, Vol. 2; Röhm, Germany Needs Simple Soldiers, Vol. 4.

Rommel, Erwin (1891–1944)

German field marshal and highly regarded tank commander known as the Desert Fox because of his exploits with the Afrika Korps in the North African campaigns of 1941 and 1942. Erwin Rommel was born in the town of Heidenheim in southern Germany on November 15, 1891. He joined the German Imperial Army in 1910 and during World War I served as a junior officer in Romania and Italy. He was several times decorated for bravery, awarded the Iron Cross, First Class, and the Pour le Mérite. He remained in the army after the war as an infantry officer and instructor. He came to Adolf Hitler's attention in 1935 and served as a military instructor with the Hitler Youth. The Nazi leader also selected Rommel to be the commander of his personal bodyguard unit. Although he admired Hitler's nationalism and leadership, Rommel never joined the Nazi Party.

Rommel began to earn notoriety as a tank commander during the Third Reich's invasion of western Europe in the spring of 1940. He led the 7th Panzer Division, one of the tank groups that rapidly pushed through the Ardennes into France and proceeded quickly to the English Channel, dividing and isolating the Allied forces. Always at the head of his armies, Rommel was extremely popular with both his superiors and his own men, as well as with Hitler. Even Allied military leaders recognized Rommel's leadership ability and strategic skill, and praised him as a fair, honorable officer.

In 1941 Hitler promoted Rommel to lieutenant general and posted him to Libya in North Africa, where the Germans set out to force the British back into Egypt on the way to taking the port city of Alexandria and the Suez Canal. For over a year Rommel's forces of Germans and Italians, known collectively as the Afrika Korps, were the dominant military force in the region. Rommel, developing a mastery of desert warfare, led the Afrika Korps to victories at El Agheila, Cyrenaica, and Sollum in 1941, and in January 1942 he was promoted to full general. In June 1942 Rommel took the city of Tobruk, which lay within Egyptian territory. It was an important victory over the British, who were forced to leave behind large

German field marshal Erwin Rommel was renowned for his brilliant tank strategy in the North African desert.

amounts of arms and supplies in their retreat to El Alamein, only fifty miles from Alexandria. Rommel was promoted to general field marshal, and the way to Suez seemed clear.

Rommel's string of victories in North Africa led to a number of changes in British leadership in search of an effective response, and in the summer of 1942 a number of factors weighed in the Allies' favor. First, General Bernard Law Montgomery arrived to take command of British forces. Second, the British and their new American allies were able at this point in the war to devote almost all their energies to the North African campaign, as they were fighting the Germans on no other fronts. Finally, Nazi authorities in Berlin failed to provide Rommel with sufficient reinforcements and supplies; their attention was focused on the eastern front and the war with the Soviet Union. When the British attacked from El Alamein in October 1942 the field marshal himself was ill and arrived at the scene of battle too late to influence the outcome. The British victory forced the undersupplied Afrika Korps to begin a long retreat westward across North Africa, which the Desert Fox managed just as skillfully as he had managed earlier offensives. The German effort in the region, however, was doomed when combined British and American landings in November 1942 trapped Rommel between two Allied armies. He was recalled from North Africa in March 1943.

Rommel was then given commands in northern Italy and at the end of 1943 he was named commander in chief of an army group in France as well as inspector of coastal defenses. There he disagreed with his superior, Field Marshal Gerd von Rundstedt, in developing a strategy to counter the expected Allied landings in France: Rommel wanted to prevent any landings in the first place, while Rundstedt wanted to position a huge German force in reserve to push the Allies back into the English Channel. Rommel largely prevailed; when the invasion finally came on D-Day, June 6, 1944, Allied troops faced a variety of defenses placed by Rommel, including heavy artillery, tank units, and millions of land mines. When the Allied landings succeeded nevertheless, and the Allies were able to support their ground troops with virtually unchallenged air superiority, Rommel grew convinced that Germany could not win the war. As early as June 1944 he, along with Rundstedt, tried to convince Hitler to negotiate a peace while Germany's still considerable forces remained largely intact. Hitler, of course, refused to consider the possibility.

By this time Rommel had lost much of his faith in Hitler's leadership ability, and he was also disturbed by the stories of atrocities on the eastern front. He began to listen to the exhortations of fellow officers to join the German resistance movement.

The conspirators hoped to name the popular and internationally respected Rommel to an important post in any post-Hitler government, perhaps even head of state. Rommel never took an active part in the preparations for the July 1944 Plot, however, preferring that Hitler be arrested and publicly tried rather than assassinated. On July 17, in any case, the field marshal was seriously wounded in an Allied air attack, and he was recovering at home near Herrlingen bei Ulm on July 20, the date of the failed attempt. Soon after a conspirator named Caesar von Hofacker, under torture, gave Rommel's name to his interrogators as one of the top officers involved in the plot.

Unlike most of those targeted in Hitler's massive revenge for the July Plot, Rommel was given the opportunity to choose an honorable death rather than a humiliating trial on charges of high treason before Roland Freisler's People's Court. On October 14, 1944, two generals involved in the investigation of the conspiracy came to Herrlingen and informed Rommel that his only options were suicide or trial. Knowing that the sentence of the People's Court was certain death and fearful for his family, Rommel chose to take poison and killed himself that day. Hitler, perhaps grateful that he did not have to place his most popular military man before the People's Court as a traitor, buried Rommel with full military honors. *See also* Afrika Korps, El Alamein, July 1944 Plot, Vol. 1; Panzer, Vol. 2.

Roosevelt, Franklin D. (1882–1945)

President of the United States during the era of the Third Reich. Roosevelt was born in Hyde Park, New York, on January 30, 1882. His parents on both sides, the Roosevelts and Delanos, were wealthy familes of great achievement in the United States, and Franklin Roosevelt grew up within an atmosphere of privilege. He attended Harvard University and Columbia University Law School, graduating in 1907. In 1905 he married Eleanor Roosevelt, a distant cousin. Presiding at the wedding was then-president Theodore Roosevelt, also a distant relative. Roosevelt entered politics in 1910 as a New York state senator. In 1913 President Woodrow Wilson invited him to become assistant secretary of the navy. During the next years, which included American involvement in World War I in 1917 and 1918 as well as the various postwar peace settlements, Roosevelt became an internationally known figure, diplomatic, gregarious, and highly competent. The Democratic Party nominated him for vice president on a ticket with James Cox in the 1920 presidential election, but the two lost handily to Republicans Warren G. Harding and Calvin Coolidge, who, unlike Roosevelt, supported a return to American isolationism and rejected the League of Nations.

In 1921, after joining an investment firm in New York City, Roosevelt suffered a severe attack of polio. The attack left him virtually without the use of his legs for the rest of his life, although their strength waxed and waned with various treatments. Roosevelt, however, did not allow his new disability to deter him from his political activities or ambitions. He made a dramatic appearance at the 1924 Democratic National Convention, inspiring others as a man who had triumphed over personal adversity, and in 1928 he was elected governor of New York. As governor, Roosevelt began to introduce the sorts of measures that, during his presidency, would transform the U.S. government. These included stronger public control of essential utilities as well as, after the Great Depression began in 1929, various public works projects and public welfare and unemployment benefits.

Roosevelt ran for president of the United States in 1932 on the Democratic ticket. During his campaign, in which he visited most of the states of the Union and dispelled any lingering doubts about his disability, Roosevelt promised to protect the common man from the ravages of the Great Depression. He was elected by a landslide. During the first years of his administration he instituted the various New Deal measures that helped to lift America out of the depression as well as change the nature of American politics. He was reelected overwhelmingly in 1936 and again in 1940, becoming the first, and only, U.S. president to serve more than two terms in office.

As the aggressive intentions of the Third Reich in Europe, as well as of Japan in Asia and the Pacific, grew clear by the late 1930s, Roosevelt devoted more and more attention to defense and foreign affairs. Unlike many other American political leaders, he was not an isolationist, and he worked hard to convince Congress to increase the nation's military preparedness. After World War II began with Hitler's invasion of Poland on September 1, 1939, Roosevelt's conviction grew that Great Britain, in particular, must remain free. He began to support the British war effort through a variety of measures, most notably the Lend-Lease program, which in its simplest form supplied his British counterpart, Prime Minister Winston Churchill, with American ships and supplies in exchange for long-term leases of military bases on English soil. On January 6, 1941, in a speech intended to confirm his beliefs as well as send a message to totalitarian and aggressive governments the world over, Roosevelt announced what later became known as the Four Freedoms, to which all people were entitled: freedom of speech, freedom of worship, freedom from want, and freedom from fear. In August 1941, by which time the United States was effectively engaged in a naval war in the Atlantic against the Third Reich, Roosevelt met with Churchill. In the resulting Atlantic Charter they spelled out their war aims, which included a statement that neither nation sought territorial gains.

U.S. president Franklin D. Roosevelt broadcasts a "fireside chat" on April 28, 1935. Roosevelt's direct appeals bolstered American morale during the subsequent war years.

The United States formally entered World War II after the surprise Japanese bomb attack on Pearl Harbor on December 7, 1941. Adolf Hitler declared war on the United States on December 9. Despite his various preparedness measures, which included the first peacetime draft in American history, Roosevelt was ill prepared for a major war, especially in military terms. Nonetheless, the president inspired the American people to work hard and make the necessary personal and material sacrifices to win the conflict. Among the war aims he defined with Churchill and, in time, Joseph Stalin, the leader of the Soviet Union, Roosevelt's priorities were: first, to defeat Germany; to preserve the independence of Great Britain; to support any nation, regardless of its form of government, that was an enemy of the Rome-Berlin-Tokyo Axis; and to turn the United States into the so-called arsenal of democracy. Roosevelt was also a strong anti-imperialist, in contrast to Churchill, and he wanted to diminish the importance of entities such as the British Empire in favor of national self-determination. He hoped to contain the ambitions of the Soviet Union through accommodation and reason, the one area in which many claimed he adopted the wrong strategy.

Roosevelt proved to be a remarkable wartime leader, energetic and vital despite his disability. He inspired the American people through, among other measures, the regular "fireside chats," broadcast on radio, that he began during the 1930s. He also traveled widely to engage in conferences with other Allied leaders, where his vigorous, optimistic view of the future and of foreign affairs contrasted sharply with the power-hungry cynicism of Stalin and the world-weary realism of Churchill. He was a major force behind the formation of the United Nations.

In 1944 Roosevelt won an unprecedented fourth term as president, American voters having overwhelmingly decided that they did not want to switch horses in midstream. By the time of his January 1945 inauguration, however, he was in noticeably ill health. Some commentators have blamed his poor health for what seemed to be the excessive concessions he made to Stalin at a great power conference at Yalta in February; even Roosevelt later confided to Churchill his concern about Stalin's intentions. On April 13, 1945, while the United States was still at war with the Third Reich and with Japan, Franklin D. Roosevelt died of a brain hemorrhage at the family getaway in Warm Springs, Georgia. Much of the world mourned him as one of the greatest of world leaders. *See also* Atlantic Charter, Lend-Lease, Vol. 1; Yalta Conference, Vol. 2; Hitler, Hitler Responds to the Concerns of U.S. President Franklin D. Roosevelt, Vol. 4.

Rosenberg, Alfred (1893–1946)

Unofficial philosopher of Nazism who served as head of foreign affairs for the Nazi Party during World War II as well as chief minister of the eastern occupied territories. Rosenberg was an ethnic German, born in Tallinn, Estonia, to an Estonian mother and Lithuanian father who both had German forebears. Initially a citizen of imperial Russia, he studied engineering and architecture at the Universities of Riga and Moscow. He fled Russia during the Bolshevik Revolution of 1917, settling first in Paris and then in Munich, where he maintained contact with Russian exiles and took up a semimystical form of extreme Germanic nationalism. He was a member of the Thule Society, a nationalist group whose members dabbled in the occult and blamed Germany's problems on Jews, Communists, and Freemasons.

Rosenberg was an early member of the Nazi Party, joining in 1919 and becoming, along with Dietrich Eckart, one of the party's early "intellectuals." His muddled thinking was thought to have had a major effect on the uneducated Hitler, who was impressed by Rosenberg's wide reading, regardless of the fact that the wide reading was in largely obscure and pedantic nationalist tracts rather than the western cultural tradition. In the early years of the Nazi movement Rosenberg joined the ranks of pamphlet authors by producing such works as *The Tracks of the Jew Throughout the Ages*, *The Immorality of the Talmud*, and *The Crime of Freemasonry*. Such works helped give Hitler's fairly unformed ideas a basis in what looked, from the outside and from Hitler's perspective, like serious scholarship. In his writings Rosenberg argued that Allied Freemasons were responsible for World War I, and therefore responsible for Germany's postwar humiliations. He also claimed, in a trite but extremely popular theme of the time, that "international Jewry" was the guiding force behind the Russian Revolution and that, in fact, Jews planned to take over the world through deceit and financial manipulation. Along the same lines, Rosenberg worked to widely publish *Protocols of the Elders of Zion* in the early 1920s. The *Protocols* was a forgery, concocted by the Russian secret police during the czarist era, which alleged that Jewish leaders had met in the 1890s to plot the takeover of European capitals through terrorist attacks. The forgery was widely read and held to be true during the Third Reich.

Rosenberg held a number of important posts in the early years of the Nazi movement, despite the fact that other early leaders considered him an outsider because of his foreign origins, intellectual arrogance, and introverted personality. In 1923 he was named editor of the *Völkischer Beobachter*, the Nazi Party's official newspaper, which provided him with another outlet for his muddled, occult-based nationalism. He also served as deputy leader of the party after the failure of the 1923 Beer Hall Putsch, in which he had taken part, but he proved to be an ineffective politician, unable to fend off more pragmatic rivals such as Julius Streicher. In 1926 he started a monthly magazine entitled *The World Struggle* and in 1929 founded an organization known as the League of Struggle for German Culture. During these years he served as the Nazi movement's main cultural, as opposed to political, propagandist, asserting that there existed truly "German" forms of art, thought, and lifestyle. Finally, he served as Hitler's chief adviser on foreign affairs.

In 1930, the same year he was elected as a Nazi delegate to the Reichstag, Rosenberg published *The Myth of the Twentieth Century*, an ideological and philosophical tome he had been working on for many years. The book was to become, after Hitler's *Mein Kampf*, the second most popular book in the Third Reich and the most systematic attempt to define a National Socialist point of view. It was not an entirely successful attempt; even Nazis criticized Rosenberg's book as turgid and confusing. Nevertheless, the book sold over 1 million copies by 1942 and could be found prominently displayed in the home of any ambitious Nazi.

The Myth of the Twentieth Century was derived in many ways from Houston Stewart Chamberlain's *The Foundations of the Nineteenth Century*. Like Chamberlain, Rosenberg tried to argue that world history was but the history of racial struggle, and that such a thing as a "race-soul" existed, transcending national boundaries. The master race comprised the Nordic peoples of northern Europe, who shared the noble blood of the ancient Aryans of India, Persia, and Greece. Their superiority was demonstrated by values such as honor, freedom, bravery, and nobility, and they were responsible for the political and cultural accomplishments of Europe. Over the centuries, however, according to Rosenberg, the so-called race-soul of the Nordic peoples, and especially the Germans, had become submerged and was in danger of being poisoned through race mixing, or as the author termed it, "psychic bastardization." The "myth" to which Rosenberg referred in his title was the myth of the blood, which was being revived under the symbol of the swastika and, through revolution, would save the world from "racial chaos."

Like all Nazis, Rosenberg targeted Jews as a primary threat to the reawakening of German blood under the swastika symbol, but his main criticism of Judaism was that it was the source of Christianity, to his mind a "race-destroying doctrine." Christianity, he argued, particularly in its Roman Catholic form, must be destroyed. Its focus on human unity and equality under God, as well as its moral precepts of humility and forgiveness, had helped lead the earth into racial chaos by bringing "oriental" ideas into the Germanic world. The Germanic ideals of comradeship and heroism were better reflected by the ancient Nordic gods, such as Wotan, whom Rosenberg felt needed to be revived and whose spirit was reflected in a historical roll call of great Germans stretching from Martin Luther through Frederick the Great, Bismarck, and now Adolf Hitler.

Rosenberg, who tended to be narrow-minded, graceless, and pedantic, was still not well liked by other top Nazis. His book was widely criticized by such men as Baldur von Schirach and Hermann Göring. Moreover, his personality inspired little respect; Goebbels called him a man who became almost a philosopher and almost a statesman but never fully succeeded in anything. Nevertheless Rosenberg remained doggedly loyal to Hitler, who also criticized him in private, and his ruthless ambition prevented him from strong reaction to attacks on his thinking or accomplishments by top Nazis. After the Nazis took power in 1933 he took up a number of posts that kept him on the margins of power and influence but never at the center of policy making. In 1934 Hitler appointed him to the leadership of a committee charged with the ideological education of Nazi Party members, but Goebbels soon replaced him as Nazi cultural czar. Having proven himself an awkward diplomat, Rosenberg was never seriously considered as foreign minister of the Reich, although he remained head of the Nazi Party Foreign Affairs Department until 1945. There his greatest accomplishment was the introduction of Vidkun Quisling, the Norwegian Nazi sympathizer, to German power brokers in December 1939.

During World War II Rosenberg became, in effect, occupied Europe's greatest art thief as the head of two organizations: the Institute for the Investigation of the Jewish Question and the Rosenberg Task Force. The first was ostensibly a think tank but most of its resources were devoted to plundering the libraries, archives, and art collections of European Jews in the name of "research." The second took up the job of looting great works of art from across occupied Europe, notably France, and bringing them to the German Reich with the help of the army. He boasted in his reports that his men had confiscated billions of marks' worth of artworks to enrich the collections of Göring and others.

In July 1941 Hitler appointed Rosenberg to what was to be the latter's most significant administrative post: minister of the eastern occupied territories. These were two occupied colonies, the Reich Commissariats of Ostland (the Baltic countries and Belarus) and the Ukraine, for which Nazi leaders had drastic and brutal plans for racial and economic reorganization that Rosenberg was not entirely privy to. They were the sites of some of the bloodiest massacres of Jews and Russian prisoners of war, and a major source of the Slavic slave labor deported to the German Reich. Although Rosenberg played little part in massacres, and even protested the brutal treatment of occupied peoples, he participated in the roundups of slave workers as well as in the attempt to "Germanize" the area by bringing in ethnic German settlers. As the months passed, however, Rosenberg proved irrelevant to events on the ground as neither field commanders, nor his underlings in the two Reich Commissariats, nor top Nazis such as Heinrich Himmler and

Martin Bormann took him seriously as a policy maker or administrator.

At war's end Rosenberg was tried at Nuremberg by the International Military Tribunal along with twenty other top Nazis. He was found guilty on all four counts of the indictment and condemned to death. Rosenberg was hanged at the Nuremberg prison on the early morning of October 16, 1946. *See also* racial science, Rosenberg Task Force, Vol. 2; Rosenberg, Jews Are, for Now, a Necessary Evil, Vol. 4.

Rudel, Hans-Ulrich (1916–1982)

Fighter pilot who became the most highly decorated military man in the Third Reich during World War II, and a neo-Nazi after the war. Rudel was born in the village of Konradswaldau on July 2, 1916, and attended military school. He joined the Luftwaffe, the Third Reich's air force, in 1938 as an engineering officer in a Stuka contingent. His accomplishments were many and varied during World War II, when he held the rank of group captain. In 1941 he sank two ships, including a battleship, and he was credited with over two thousand five hundred sorties and the destruction of over five hundred tanks, mostly on the eastern front. He was the only recipient of a special decoration, the Knight's Cross with Golden Oak Leaves, Swords and Diamonds, created by Hitler to be awarded to the twelve most worthy Germans after the Axis powers won World War II. He was shot down in Russia in March 1944 and captured, but managed to escape. In February 1945 he was shot down a second time and sustained injuries that resulted in the amputation of a leg.

Rudel went into exile in Argentina after the war. There he became a well-known member of the large German community and he worked to maintain contact between escaped Nazis in Argentina and those who remained in Germany. He returned to Germany in 1951 and became a spokesman for the Socialist Reich Party, a neo-Nazi organization popular in the region of Lower Saxony. He also lent his support to other right-wing nationalist groups. Rudel moved to Brazil in 1956 and to Paraguay shortly afterward, where he continued his right-wing activities. The air force of the postwar Federal Republic of Germany maintained a controversial admiration for the accomplishments of Rudel. After Rudel died in Rosenheim on December 18, 1982, for instance, the air force honored his grave with a low-flying formation of jet fighters. *See also* Luftwaffe, Vol. 1; neo-Nazism, Vol. 2.

Rundstedt, Gerd von (1875–1953)

General field marshal who, from March 1942 to March 1945, was the commander in chief of German forces in western Europe and one of the highest-ranking officers in the Third Reich. Gerd von Rundstedt was born in the town of Aschersleben on December 12, 1875, to a Prussian aristocratic family. He began his military service in the Prussian infantry as an officer in 1893. During World War I he served as a staff officer in Turkey and France. After the war, in the Weimar-era Reichswehr, he enjoyed rapid promotions, serving in both staff and regimental posts. When the Nazis took power in 1933 he was a Generaloberst, or colonel general, and commander of military forces in the Berlin area. Politically aloof and the consummate Prussian officer, Rundstedt became a general of infantry in 1938 and led an army group into the Sudetenland in October of that year. Soon after he retired but, as war approached, he was recalled and named commander in chief of Army Group South, which played a central role in the rapid conquest of Poland in September 1939. In May 1940, as commander in chief of Army Group A, Rundstedt was the top-ranking officer in the armored effort, featuring such tank commanders as Heinz Guderian and Erwin Rommel, which allowed German forces to push through the Ardennes and race to the English Channel.

Hitler ordered Rundstedt, however, to stop in the area of Dunkirk, allowing the British Expeditionary Force to mount its miraculous escape from the nearby beaches. Hitler went on to name Rundstedt the head of the German forces then being assembled to invade Great Britain and promoted him, in July 1940, to general field marshal.

During the June 1941 invasion of the Soviet Union, Rundstedt was again the commander in chief of Army Group South, destined for the Ukraine. His orders were to conquer the Ukraine and southern Russia quickly, including the strategically important city of Rostov, before joining other forces to take Stalingrad and seal off the region under German authority. Rundstedt's forces indeed reached Rostov quickly, but were forced into a tactical retreat in the fall of 1941. Hitler, who never understood the concept of a tactical retreat, disapproved of the move and relieved Rundstedt of his command on December 12, 1941. Soon after, however, the field marshal was again recalled, this time to the post of commander in chief of Army Group West. He remained in that post, except for two brief periods, until March 1945.

One of Rundstedt's primary responsibilities in western Europe was to plan for an Allied invasion. His strategy was to keep at hand a large mobile reserve to expel any Allied troops after they reached the shore. However, on D-Day, June 6, 1944, Rundstedt's reserve was unable to quickly reach the Normandy beaches before Allied troops established themselves, idling instead mostly at the port city of Calais. Rundstedt's attempts to convince Hitler that the war was lost and that the Führer should sue for peace were futile. For his failure to stop the invasion, Rundstedt was removed from his post on July 2, but again he was soon restored.

Rundstedt, like almost all top officers, was aware of the resistance movement within the regular German army. He never joined it, however, despite the fact that he was never a committed Nazi. Citing his age, he argued that the far younger and extremely popular Erwin Rommel, who served under him in France in 1944, should join the resistance instead. After the failure of the July Plot, Rundstedt demonstrated his loyalty to Hitler by heading the military honor court that expelled conspirators from the army before turning them over to the Nazi People's Court for trial. Meanwhile, during the winter of 1944–1945, Rundstedt, back in his position as western commander, organized and led the last German offensive, the Battle of the Bulge.

At war's end Rundstedt was captured by British forces. Despite suspicions of his involvement in war crimes, including illegal treatment of prisoners of war, Rundstedt was never put on trial because of ill health. He died in Hanover on February 24, 1953. *See also* Barbarossa, Battle of the Bulge, D-Day, Vol. 1.

Rust, Bernhard (1883–1945)

As Reich minister of science, education, and popular culture from 1933 to 1945, the highest-ranking education official in Nazi Germany. Bernhard Rust was born in Hanover on September 30, 1883. After high school he studied German, philosophy, languages, and music at several universities, including Munich, Göttingen, and Halle. In 1908 he became a high school science teacher. During World War I he served as an infantry lieutenant. He earned the Iron Cross but also suffered a severe head wound, which was thought to have left him somewhat unstable mentally.

Rust joined the Nazi Party in 1925 and quickly rose to a position of leadership, becoming the Gauleiter of Hanover in 1925. In 1930 he was elected to the Reichstag and also dismissed from his Hanover teaching job for allegedly mistreating a girl student. Adolf Hitler appointed him Prussian minister of science, art, and education in February 1933, and on April 30, 1934, Reich minister of education, with authority over all public educational institutions through the university level. From this post he presided over the transformation of the German educational system in line with Nazi ideology and social goals. The new emphasis was on subjects like nazified German history, the life of Adolf Hitler, physical education, and the false discipline of racial science, which claimed that Jews were a threat to the health of Aryan Germany, among other things. Under Rust, and under the Nazis generally, Germany's educational system went from being one of the world's best to one of its most dubious, and German universities in particular lost a great deal of their former prestige with the exile of hundreds of prominent scholars and scientists, including Albert Einstein, Fritz Haber, and Max Born. Rust also presided over the development of several new educational institutions designed to produce loyal Nazi officials, including the National Political Educational Institutions and the Adolf Hitler Schools.

Rust, always a loyal and fairly unobtrusive official, committed suicide after Germany's defeat in May 1945. *See also* Adolf Hitler Schools, education in the Third Reich, Vol. 1; National Political Training Institutes, Vol. 2.

Sauckel, Fritz (1894–1946)

Plenipotentiary for the mobilization of labor from 1942 to 1945, and in that position one of the Nazi officials most responsible for the widespread use of slave labor in the Third Reich during World War II. Fritz Sauckel was born Ernst Friedrich Christoph Sauckel on October 27, 1894, in Hassfurt in western Germany. His father was a minor postal official and his mother a seamstress. At the age of fifteen he became a merchant seaman with German, Norwegian, and Swedish firms. During World War I he was a prisoner of the French, and after the war he worked as a factory laborer.

Sauckel joined the Nazi Party in 1923 and was therefore ranked among the celebrated "Old Fighters." His loyalty and dependability earned him positions of increasing responsibility within the Nazi movement. In 1925 he became business manager for the party in Thuringia, and he was named Gauleiter of Thuringia in 1937. From 1927 to 1933 he was a member of the Thuringian state legislature. After the Nazis took power Sauckel took a place in the national Reichstag and was appointed governor of Thuringia as well as Gauleiter. In 1939 he was made defense commissioner for the Kassel district. Meanwhile, he married and had ten children, losing two of them to combat during World War II.

On the suggestion of Martin Bormann, Sauckel was named plenipotentiary for labor mobilization in 1942. He was, reportedly, extremely flattered by the honor. His responsibilities were to keep the German military machine operating at the least possible cost to the Nazi state, using German workers if possible but foreigners if Germans were not available. Between 1942 and 1945 Sauckel was responsible for importing between 3 and 5 million foreign workers into the German Reich to work as slaves. Some were prisoners of war, but most were Russians or Poles, kidnapped by German soldiers or by Sauckel's operatives, who were known as "protection squads," and brought hundreds of miles to the west. In Germany they worked in mines and factories, lived in extremely squalid conditions, and died by the thousands of abuse, disease, and neglect. Toward the end of the war, with the eastern front collapsing, Sauckel made new arrangements to import forced laborers from Italy, France, the Netherlands, and Belgium who were doled out to farms and shops as well as factories and mines.

At war's end Sauckel was one of the twenty-one top Nazis tried for war crimes by the International Military Tribunal at Nuremberg in late 1945. He proclaimed that he was just doing his duty, being, as Hitler once told him, a "good soldier" for Germany. He also reported that he was unaware of concentration camps or extermination centers. The evidence against him, however, was unassailable. Sauckel was found guilty of war crimes and crimes against humanity and hanged at the Nuremberg prison on October 16, 1946. *See also* Labor Mobilization Office, Vol. 1; Nuremberg trials, slave labor, Vol. 2; International Military Tribunal, The Charges Against the Surviving Nazi Leaders, Vol. 4.

Sauerbruch, Ferdinand (1875–1951)

A top physician and surgeon whose patients included Adolf Hitler and Joseph Goebbels. Sauerbruch was born in Barmen in Prussia on July 3, 1875. After taking a medical degree he made a distinguished career for himself, with posts including chief surgeon to the German army and head of one of Berlin's top hospitals. In 1933 he signed the list of 960 professors who proclaimed their loyalty to the new Nazi regime. In August 1934 he was the attending physician during the last illness of President Paul von Hindenburg. A devoted Nazi, in later years he operated on a number of high-ranking Nazis, removing a growth, for instance, from Hitler's throat in 1940. In 1943 he saved Lieutenant Colonel Claus Schenk Graf von Stauffenberg, the guiding light of the July 1944 Plot on Hitler's life, after Stauffenberg was seriously wounded in North Africa. Sauerbruch knew of the German resistance movement and counted General Ludwig Beck among his friends, but after the failure of the July Plot he was released by the Gestapo following interrogation. After World War II Sauerbruch was cleared of all charges by an East German denazification court, although the East German government removed him from his various posts. He died in Berlin on July 2, 1951. *See also* Morell, Theodor, Vol. 3.

Schacht, Hjalmar (1877–1970)

Economist, financier, and Reich minister of economics from 1934 to 1937 as well as president of the Reichsbank from 1933 to 1939. Schacht made a substantial contribution to the Nazi rise to power as well as the Third Reich's plan to revitalize the German economy through rearmament.

Hjalmar Schacht was born on January 22, 1877, in the town of Tinglev, later in Denmark but in that era part of the German province of Schleswig. His family was of Danish background. In the 1870s the family immigrated to the United States, but returned to Germany while Schacht was still young, and he completed his secondary education in Kiel before enrolling at the Universities of Munich and Berlin. He originally studied medicine but ultimately took a Ph.D. in economics. The ambitious Schacht built a career in banking, becoming deputy director of the Dresdner Bank in 1908 and a director of the Private National Bank for Germany during World War I. He also worked as an economic adviser during the war for the German occupation government in Belgium.

In 1923 Schacht left banking to take a post with the German government, though he disliked the Weimar regime and preferred right-wing, nationalist politics. He was appointed Reich currency commissioner, with the responsibility of stabilizing the German mark during its era of hyperinflation. He solved the problem by introducing a new currency, the rentenmark, and tying its values to foreign loans and to German land values. After stabilizing the nation's financial system, Schacht was appointed to his first tenure as Reichsbank president in December 1923. There he played an important part in reworking German war reparations payments through negotiations resulting in the Dawes Plan and the Young Plan. He resigned in 1930 over what he thought were excessive concessions by the Weimar government toward the Allies in the final version of the Young Plan.

Always a strong nationalist, and according to some a monarchist, Schacht's increasing alienation from the Weimar regime pushed him closer to right-wing movements. Then, after reading Adolf Hitler's *Mein Kampf* in 1930 and witnessing the growing popularity of the Nazi Party, Schacht decided that Hitler had much more to offer Germany than the Weimar politicians, whom he viewed as indecisive and inept. Over the next years Schacht was involved in a number of efforts to give Hitler a leading part in German politics. In 1931 he joined the Harzburg Front, the first coalition of right-wing politicians to seek Hitler's membership. In late 1932 he encouraged President Paul von Hindenburg to appoint Hitler chancellor of Germany. Meanwhile, Schacht also used his influence with financiers and businessmen to throw their support behind the emerging coalition between the Nazis and the German Nationalist People's Party. Once in power, Hitler appointed Schacht as, once again, president of the Reichsbank and, in 1934, Reich minister of economics.

Hitler himself had little interest in economics, and few Nazis had any training or skill in the discipline. Therefore, Schacht had a fairly free hand to develop economic policy in the early years of the Third Reich. One of his major accomplishments was to free economic activity from Nazi Party control, a move that reassured bankers and industrialists that Hitler's regime was not, in fact, Socialist or revolutionary. Moreover, he took measures to restore Germany to the status of an international economic power with creative exchange and barter programs as well as the creation of available and appealing credit. In May 1935, Hitler appointed him plenipotentiary of the war economy, with the primary responsibility of financing the Nazi military buildup. Schacht's close ties with many German bankers and industrialists, who stood to benefit from government contracts, helped German rearmament proceed rapidly. He also supported massive public works programs.

Despite his many contributions to the economic well-being of the Third Reich, however, Schacht was never a Nazi. Many in Hitler's circle disliked and distrusted him, considering the financier a product of the traditional German conservatism they were trying to replace. Schacht, for his part, disapproved of political "excesses" such as the Blood Purge of June 1934 as well as the increasing hostility toward German Jews. As a traditional conservative with aristocratic values, Schacht was temperamentally and behaviorally different from most leading Nazis, and seemed awkwardly out of place among the publicity seekers, brawlers, and manipulators Hitler surrounded himself with. In 1937 Schacht resigned as economics minister and plenipotentiary of the war economy. Hitler retained him, however, as Reichsbank president and until 1943 as minister without portfolio in the Reich cabinet.

Upset by the Kristallnacht pogrom of November 1938, Schacht negotiated a plan, with Hitler's permission, for the emigration of tens of thousands of German Jews to Great Britain. He entered discussions with London financial and charitable organizations, but in January 1939 he was dismissed as president of the Reichsbank and replaced by the more compliant Walther Funk. The plan came to nothing, and within a few months, to Schacht's distress, World War II began. Schacht did not believe that Germany could maintain a long-term war economy; like other traditional conservatives in the military and aristocracy, he suspected that Germany would lose the war. Despite his continued presence in the cabinet he established contacts with the German

Economist and banker Hjalmar Schacht revived the depressed German economy and facilitated German rearmament.

resistance movement, particularly those participants who were sympathetic toward the restoration of the Hohenzollern monarchy. Although he never took an active part in any resistance activity, or figured strongly in the plans for any post-Hitler regime, Schacht was arrested by the Gestapo the day after the failure of the July 1944 Plot. He spent the remaining months of World War II in concentration camps at Ravensbrück, Flossenbürg, and Dachau, while Gestapo investigators tried unsuccessfully to tie him directly to the assassination plot.

Schacht was one of the twenty-one defendants brought before the International Military Tribunal at Nuremberg in 1945. He remained indignant throughout the trial, surprised to be considered responsible for the atrocities and crimes of the Nazi regime and offended to be named among the likes of Göring, Funk, and Ribbentrop. The tribunal decided that Schacht's participation in German rearmament did not in itself constitute an act of war or a war crime, and he was acquitted, over the protests of the Soviet judge. Soon after, a German denazification court found him guilty of major offenses and sentenced him to eight years' imprisonment, but this decision was reversed on appeal in September 1948. In 1950, a subsequent court cleared Schacht of all possible charges connected to the Third Reich. He reemerged as a powerful financier and economic adviser, as well as an extremely wealthy man, working as a consultant to developing countries around the world and founding a private bank, Schacht and Company, in Düsseldorf in 1954. He published two memoirs, *A Reckoning with Hitler* in 1949 and *Seventy-Six Years of My Life* in 1953. Hjalmar Schacht died in Munich on June 3, 1970. *See also* inflation of 1923, Vol. 1; Nuremberg trials, Reichsbank, Vol. 2; Funk, Walther, Vol. 3.

Schellenburg, Walter (1910–1952)

A top counterintelligence officer who rose to be second in command of the Gestapo, Schellenburg was one of several SS adventurers involved in numerous memorable exploits and negotiations. He was born in Saarbrücken on October 16, 1910, and took a law degree from the University of Bonn. An accomplished and ambitious young man, Schellenburg joined the Nazi Party and the SS in May 1933. He came to the attention of Heinrich Himmler, who named him as his personal aide, and Reinhard Heydrich, who steered him toward counterintelligence. During the annexation of Czechoslovakia, Schellenburg was responsible for organizing the first Einsatzgruppen, special squads of SS men assigned to sensitive tasks. Later, by negotiating with the Wehrmacht, he helped delineate the jurisdiction of Einsatzgruppen during the Soviet invasion, when new special squads of SS men took on the job of shooting to death hundreds of thousands of Soviet Jews. On a rather more mundane level Schellenburg demonstrated his counterintelligence skills during the infamous Venlo incident of November 1939, which the SS staged to create a pretext for the invasion of the Netherlands. Schellenburg's other memorable contributions to Nazi counterintelligence include the creation of a special list of twenty-seven hundred people to be immediately arrested after the Nazi conquest of Great Britain and a special handbook designed to aid Germans in looting and plundering the British Isles while squashing resistance. In July 1940 he was sent to Lisbon to kidnap the duke of Windsor, the abdicated king of England, and the duke's American wife, Wallis Simpson, the duchess of Windsor. The two British royals were on their way to the Bahamas, where the duke was to take up a post as colonial governor. According to Nazi foreign minister Joachim von Ribbentrop, the pair were sympathetic to the Third Reich and might influence a peace or even an alliance between Germany and Great Britain. Schellenburg's mission to Lisbon, however, accomplished nothing, and the episode remains a striking example of the ineptitude and irrationality of the Nazi regime.

In 1940 Schellenburg was promoted to SS major general and until 1942 served as deputy chief of Section VI of the Reich Central Security Office (RSHA), the department responsible for intelligence and secret police activities in the occupied countries. Like Adolf Eichmann, Schellenburg found that his responsibilities increased with the death by assassination of RSHA chief Heydrich in the spring of 1942. He was promoted to chief of Section VI. In 1944, when new RSHA head Ernst Kaltenbrunner abolished the Abwehr and combined the intelligence services of the Gestapo and Wehrmacht, Schellenburg became the head of the new, enlarged organization. For the remainder of the war Schellenburg was the top intelligence officer of the Gestapo, within his jurisdiction second only to Himmler. He continued his intrigues as well, urging Himmler to contact Swedish Red Cross official Count Folke Bernadotte as a possible intermediary in negotiating a German surrender in the west.

After the war Schellenburg was arrested by the Allies and tried in Nuremberg for war crimes. In early 1949 he was found not guilty of direct participation in the massacre of European Jews despite his involvement in the Einsatzgruppen organization. He was, however, convicted of participation in the killing of Russian prisoners of war and sentenced to six years in prison. After his early release in 1950, Schellenburg relocated to Italy, where he died in 1952. *See also* duke of Windsor incident, Gestapo, Vol. 1; Venlo incident, Vol. 2.

Schindler, Oskar (1908–1974)

An ethnic German businessman and Abwehr officer who risked his life and livelihood to save the enslaved Jews who worked in one of his wartime factories and whose actions led to his designation as a Righteous Gentile by the Yad Vashem remembrance authority in Israel. Oskar Schindler was born on April 28, 1908, in the city of Zwittau in the Austro-Hungarian Empire. The various border shifts caused by twentieth-century politics and war have placed the city in the nation of Czechoslovaka in 1918, the Greater German Reich in 1938, Communist Czechoslovakia after World War II, and, as Zvitava, the Czech Republic since 1993. In Schindler's time this city and region were heavily populated by ethnic Germans; Germans themselves referred to the region as the Sudetenland. Schindler was a Sudeten German.

Schindler was born into a prosperous family. His father, Hans, was a successful businessman who owned a factory that produced farm machinery. Schindler grew up expecting a guaranteed job and social position, and the relatively carefree young man was rarely serious about his studies, his work, or rules in general. His mother, Louisa, was a devout Roman Catholic, as were many Austrian and Sudeten Germans, but Schindler himself was no more serious about religion. He married at nineteen; his wife, Emilie, was a strong Catholic whom he had met on a business trip. The marriage was not a particularly successful one, and Schindler harbored some bitterness after Emilie's father refused to provide him with a dowry. Schindler was only periodically serious about fidelity; he had two children outside of marriage although he and Emilie had no children together.

In the wake of the global economic depression of the 1930s, the Schindler family business collapsed, and in the aftermath of pressing financial problems, Schindler's family collapsed too. His father left his mother, who died soon after, and Oskar Schindler was forced to find work to support himself. He eventually became a salesman for a machinery company with business interests in Poland. Skills useful in sales proved to be Schindler's only business skills: establishing contacts, flattering business associates, making deals, and when necessary, overcoming opposition with bribes or kickbacks. Such skills, as it happened, were essential to his later humanitarian efforts.

Schindler saw the annexation of the Sudetenland by the Third Reich in 1938 as a great opportunity for a man like him, although his wife Emilie hated the Nazis. He quickly joined the Nazi Party and, perhaps to avoid military service, took up a post in the Abwehr, the German army's intelligence branch. After the German conquest of Poland in the fall of 1939 Schindler settled in the Polish city of Krakow, which became the capital of occupied Poland. Schindler was well positioned to take advantage of the economic opportunities that presented themselves there. Thanks to his contacts in both the regular German army and the SS, Schindler knew that many businesses would be set up in occupied Poland to produce goods for the German military. He discovered that factory facilities could be purchased cheaply, provided they had been confiscated from Jews. He also learned that labor would be cheap; Poles and Jews were to be collected to provide a slave labor force for the factories. Thanks to his many contacts, his willingness to show important figures a good time in Krakow's nightclubs, and his ability to procure hard-to-find goods—cognac, coffee, chocolate, caviar, cigars—Schindler found it reasonably easy to set himself up as a factory owner. On the outskirts of Krakow Schindler opened a factory to produce enamelware for the German military. It was known as Deutsche Email Fabrik, or Emalia.

The factory employed Jews from Krakow, whose community was ghettoized in March 1941. Among them was Itzhak Stern, a Jewish accountant whom Schindler hired to effectively run the business and select most of the workers. Over the years, and partly due to the efforts of Stern, Schindler appeared to develop a personal relationship with many of his workers. Fully aware of the Nazi policy of mass extermination, and a witness himself to a violent roundup of Krakow Jews in June 1942, Schindler took steps to protect his workers. Besides treating them humanely, he convinced SS officials that they were essential munitions workers, and therefore necessary to the German war effort. Bribes, charm, flattery, and a steady flow of rare luxury goods smoothed his way. Even after the Krakow ghetto was liquidated in March 1943, Schindler was able to protect his Jewish workers, who were essentially the only Jews left in the city. Those not shipped to an extermination camp were relocated to Plaszow, a labor camp commanded by Amon Goeth, an SS officer whose reputation for corruption, brutality, and cynicism was remarkable even among SS men. Finally, in August 1944 the Schindler Jews were moved to Plaszow as well.

Schindler made up his famous list in October 1944, when Plaszow itself was liquidated and shut down. By this time Hitler had ordered that all Jews in Nazi camps, even those earlier deemed to be essential munitions workers, were to be killed. Schindler was forced to bribe Goeth not to kill his Jewish workers, and he made up a list of approximately twelve hundred people who might be "bought" from Goeth and therefore saved from extermination. The scheme worked, and although one trainload of Schindler Jews was temporarily, and almost tragically, rerouted to Auschwitz, they all ended up in a new factory set up in Brinnlitz, near Schindler's boyhood home. There they survived the remaining months of the war pretending, with Schindler's full support, to engage in munitions production but producing no armament through contrived factory problems. Emilie Schindler, still loyal to her husband, proved instrumental in finding enough food to support her husband's charges during this period.

When World War II ended the now-penniless Schindler went on the run, suspecting he would be arrested as a war criminal. Accompanying him were Emilie and eight of the Schindler Jews, who carried a signed letter in Hebrew attesting to Schindler's actions. With other, bigger fish to fry,

however, the Allies did not try Schindler. Rather, he received funds from the American-Jewish Joint Distribution Committee, known as the Joint, as well as from the West German government, the latter indemnifying him for the loss of his property to eastern European Communists. The money enabled him and Emilie to relocate to Argentina, where again he was accompanied by a small contingent of Schindler Jews. He failed, however, in a number of businesses there and squandered his money on luxurious living. By 1958 he was bankrupt and returned to Germany, leaving Emilie behind. Unable to establish himself in business despite other infusions of funds from the Joint, Schindler depended for the rest of his life on the financial support of the Schindler Jews, most of whom had immigrated to Israel. He made frequent visits to Israel, where in 1962 he was named a Righteous Gentile in honor of his rescue of Jews during the Holocaust. Schindler died of liver failure on October 9, 1974, and was buried in Jerusalem. Attending his funeral were a large number of the estimated six thousand Jews who were alive thanks to his actions.
See also Plaszow, Schindler Jews, Vol. 2.

Schirach, Baldur von (1907–1974)

Reich youth leader and, during World War II, Gauleiter of Vienna. Schirach's energy, enthusiasm, and devotion to Adolf Hitler helped attract millions of German young people to the Nazi movement in the 1920s and 1930s.

Baldur von Schirach was born in 1907 in Berlin to an aristocratic family of German and American background. His father served as an officer in the German Imperial Army before resigning to become a theater manager in Weimar and Vienna; Baldur von Schirach was to inherit his father's love of the arts. His mother was an American named Emma Tillou, whose ancestors included two men who had signed the Declaration of Independence. Schirach lived a privileged and pampered life as a young boy and teenager, developing an interest in outdoor activities and adventure in addition to the arts. He joined the Nazi Party in 1924 at the age of seventeen at the University of Munich, where he was a student of German folklore and art history as well as, on Hitler's advice, English history and Egyptology. According to some accounts, he was forced to leave an elite fraternity at the university under suspicious circumstances; the event turned him against his own class and helped send him in search of an outlet for his youthful romanticism and desire for acceptance and adventure. Meanwhile, after reading such works as Houston Stewart Chamberlain's *The Foundations of the Nineteenth Century* and Henry Ford's *The International Jew*, Schirach became a strong anti-Semite. The foundation for such sentiments, however, had already been laid by Schirach's nationalistic schoolteachers.

Almost from the beginning of his Nazi Party membership, Schirach was a member of Hitler's inner circle and an organizer of Nazi youth groups. He also joined the SA. Hitler appreciated Schirach's blind devotion as well as his rejections of aristocracy and the Christian religion. In 1932 Schirach married Henriette Hoffman, the daughter of Hitler's court photographer Heinrich Hoffman, which further cemented his ties to Hitler's entourage. In 1929 he was named head of the National Socialist German Students' League, where he worked hard, with much success, to turn Nazi student movements in universities into the largest organizations of their kind. In 1931 he became youth leader of the Nazi Party, where he was a tireless and enthusiastic organizer as well as a skilled, if rather sentimental, propagandist. Schirach's skills were displayed to their fullest in 1932, when he staged a huge youth rally in the Berlin suburb of Potsdam. The event included a seven-hour parade of more than one hundred thousand young people marching in honor of Hitler. He also was not averse to more direct political action; in early 1933 he led a group of teenage boys into the headquarters of a rival youth organization to intimidate the staff, confiscate documents, and demonstrate that, after the Nazi seizure of power, the group was now obsolete.

On June 1, 1933, Hitler named Schirach youth leader of the German Reich, a post he was to hold until 1940. Over the next years Schirach devoted himself to building up the Hitler Youth, the League of German Girls, and their various subsidiary organizations. By 1936, when Hitler banned all youth organizations not affiliated with the Hitler Youth, Schirach's movement had over 6 million followers, and his efforts played a major role in bringing Nazism into ordinary German homes on an everyday basis. Schirach sought to educate German young people to be devoted to Nazism and to Hitler personally. He drew on various ceremonial rituals, enjoyable activities and outings, and the innate desire to belong in instilling among young people a sense of simple patriotism and obedience. Meanwhile, he was an active writer and poet; as early as the 1920s some had considered him the poet laureate of the Nazi movement. In 1932 he published a book entitled *The Hitler Nobody Knows*, followed by a book of poetry, *The Flags of the Followers*, and a collection of short biographies of Nazi role models entitled *The Pioneers of the Third Reich*. On a more practical level, given his official role, Schirach also wrote *The Hitler Youth* in 1934, in which he claimed that German young people, whose blood was already superior to the blood of others, were being molded into a new master race.

Other top Nazis, however, were slow to accept Schirach as one of their own, particularly as World War II approached. To many of them he seemed soft and effeminate, far from the ideal of the hard German youth he described in his writings and speeches. He also made an easy target for jokes and ridicule as an aristocratic Berliner with a taste for poetry. In 1940 he joined the Wehrmacht as a volunteer, serving as an infantry officer on the western front. Soon after, Hitler removed him from his position as Reich youth leader and assigned him instead to Vienna, where he served as both Nazi Gauleiter and a sort of colonial governor for the remainder of World War II. There he continued to run afoul of Hitler, particularly when he asked the Führer, in person, for better treatment of eastern European peoples and Jews and when he sought to turn Vienna into the cultural center of the Reich. Martin Bormann, who was by then Hitler's most trusted adviser, turned the Nazi dictator against Schirach even further. Nevertheless, Schirach largely toed the Nazi line, approving the deportation of tens of thousands of Jews to the death camps in Poland, and he remained in his post until the end of the war. He gave himself up to American forces after escaping from Vienna ahead of the Soviet Army.

In 1945 Baldur von Schirach was one of the twenty-one top Nazis brought before the International Military Tribunal at Nuremberg. The tribunal found him guilty of crimes against humanity for his participation in the deportation of eastern European Jews and his awareness of the mass exterminations in Poland and Russia. He was sentenced to twenty years in Spandau Prison. During the trial, Schirach was one of the few defendants to outspokenly criticize Hitler, calling him a "millionfold murderer." Schirach served out his sentence and was released from Spandau in 1966. One year later he published a memoir entitled *I Believed in Hitler*, in which he tried to explain the hold that Hitler had on young Germans under the Third Reich. He also recognized his own role in building up the Nazi dictatorship and blamed himself for not doing more to prevent Nazi atrocities. Schirach died on August 8, 1974, in the village of Kröv in southwestern Germany. *See also* Hitler Youth, League of German Girls, Vol. 1; Nuremberg trials, Vienna, Vol. 2; Schirach, The Hitler Youth, Vol. 4.

Schlageter, Albert Leo (1894–1923)

The first martyr to the Nazi movement. Schlageter was born in the village of Schönau in Baden in western Germany in 1894. A decorated lieutenant in World War I, he joined the postwar Freikorps movement as an officer in the Ruhr industrial area, which was occupied by the French. For several years he opposed French authority through a variety of means ranging, allegedly, from sabotage to spying. The French executed him for his crimes on May 26, 1923, after a local German schoolteacher, Walther Kadow, supposedly betrayed him and led him to his arrest.

Though Schlageter was not a member of the Nazi Party, which was at that point active only in and around Munich, Adolf Hitler adopted him as a martyr, citing him as the epitome of the ideal German. Kadow, meanwhile, was killed by a special assassination squad organized by the Freikorps. The squad was thought to include both Martin Bormann, later one of Hitler's closest advisers, and Rudolf Höss, later commandant of Auschwitz. Höss in fact served jail time for his participation in the murder. Schlageter eventually garnered reknown probably unimaginable to him during his lifetime; the Nazis put up a monument in his honor, plays about him were staged, and Germans by the hundreds sang "Albert Leo Schlageter's War Song." ***See also*** Days of Struggle, Freikorps, Vol. 1.

Schleicher, Kurt von (1882–1934)

German army officer and last chancellor of the Weimar Republic, and a figure whose political intrigues helped Adolf Hitler come to power in January 1933. He was born into a traditional officer-class family in Brandenburg, Prussia, on April 7, 1882. He joined the German Imperial Army in 1903 as a junior officer in the 3rd Foot Guards, the same regiment in which Paul von Hindenburg, last president of the Weimar Republic, got his start; Schleicher would remain close to the Hindenburg family. When World War I began he was a captain with the General Staff, where he served until 1918, when he was appointed as adjutant to Quartermaster General Wilhelm Groener at the army's political headquarters in Berlin. Over the next years he became involved in political intrigues by helping to organize both the Freikorps units active around Berlin and the so-called Black Reichswehr, a semisecret military association with aims of overthrowing the Weimar Republic. He was also involved in the negotiations that allowed the German military to covertly train officers in the Soviet Union. In 1926 Schleicher, now a colonel, was appointed chief of a division of the Reichswehr Ministry in the Weimar cabinet.

Schleicher's fortunes rose still further in 1929 when Groener became defense minister. His old mentor promoted Schleicher to

Kurt von Schleicher, the last chancellor of the Weimar Republic, was killed during Hitler's Blood Purge of 1934.

major general and appointed him the top political official in the army as head of the new Reichswehr Ministry Bureau. Over the next several years Schleicher used his position, as well as a close friendship with Oskar von Hindenburg, President Hindenburg's son, to exert a major influence on the course of German politics. For example, Schleicher urged Hindenburg to appoint first Heinrich Brüning and then Franz von Papen to the chancellorship, but also played a role in bringing both of them down. Throughout, Schleicher worked to expand the army's role in the national government and burnish his own prestige and importance.

On December 2, 1932, Schleicher was appointed chancellor of Germany after having served briefly as minister of defense in Papen's cabinet. Like his two predecessors Schleicher exercised the right given the president by the Weimar Constitution to rule by decree. Schleicher's initial goal was to create a government that would provide the Weimar parliament, the Reichstag, with a solid majority. But to do so he needed the support of the Nazi Party. Schleicher devised a plan that, he hoped, would split the Nazi Party while still providing him with enough support to secure the chancellor's office. He spoke with Gregor Strasser, the leader of the leftist-leaning northern wing of the Nazi Party, and offered him the vice-chancellorship as well as the post of chief minister of Prussia. He also sought the support of Ernst Röhm, chief of the powerful SA, promising him that the SA would be incorporated into the Reichswehr and that he, Röhm, would be guaranteed a powerful post. Rather than split the Nazi Party, however, Strasser left it, while Röhm bided his time until it became apparent that Schleicher's plan would fail. Schleicher also offered a deal to Hitler directly, claiming to be ready to support him as chancellor if Schleicher was allowed to remain in the cabinet as head of the Reichswehr.

While Schleicher worked on constructing a coalition that represented nearly all factions in Germany's conflict-ridden social order, Papen was busy with intrigues of his own. He managed to convince a number of important industrialists and landowners that Schleicher's plan was radical to the point of being Socialist. More importantly, he was able to convince President Hindenburg that his own coalition, which would combine the Nazi Party with the German Nationalist People's Party and place Adolf Hitler in office as chancellor, was Germany's best bet to restore order.

After Schleicher failed to put together a Reichstag coalition in January 1933, Hindenburg rejected the general's final plan, which was to install a military dictatorship. On January 28 Schleicher was dismissed from his position and retired from politics as Hitler took office as chancellor and proceeded to build the Nazi dictatorship. On June 30, 1934, Schleicher was killed by Nazi operatives during the so-called Blood Purge, in which Hitler settled a number of old scores. Strasser and Röhm, with whom Schleicher remained in touch, were also killed, as was Schleicher's wife of eighteen months. The murderers claimed that they acted in self-defense, shooting Schleicher and his wife only after the general reached for his own weapon. *See also* Machtergreifung, Weimar Republic, Vol. 2; Hindenburg, Paul von; Hitler, Adolf, Vol. 3.

Schmeling, Max (1905–)

Heavyweight boxer and Germany's most famous athlete during the era of the Third Reich. Schmeling was born in the village of Klein Luckow in Brandenburg on September 28, 1905. After working as a laborer, he moved to Berlin and became a boxer in the mid-1920s. He won the German light heavyweight title in 1926 and the European championship a year later. He proved just as successful after moving up into the heavyweight division, taking the German championship in 1928. Schmeling became heavyweight champion of the world in 1930 by beating the American Jack Sharkey in a bout in New York City. He held the title for two years before falling to Sharkey, in what observers thought was a rather questionable decision, in another New York fight. Joe Jacobs, his manager, famously claimed in a radio broadcast after the decision that "we wuz robbed!" Between 1929 and 1939 Schmeling spent a great deal of time in the United States, which he came to think of almost as a second home, and he was also a very well known figure in late Weimar Germany. In Berlin he moved in high social and cultural circles, where many of his friends and acquaintances were Jews, and he even appeared in movies. In 1933 he married film actress Anny Ondra; they remained married until her death fifty-four years later.

On June 19, 1936, in New York, Schmeling enjoyed his greatest triumph, a twelve-round knockout of Joe Louis, the African American "Brown Bomber" who was considered the best boxer in the world. Coming as it did just before the 1936 Berlin Olympics, Schmeling's victory was seized on by Nazi propagandists as a perfect example of the superiority of the Aryan race, and Schmeling found himself turned into a symbol of Aryan greatness. The boxer, who was very liberal minded, wore the mantle of Nazi hero somewhat uncomfortably, although he later admitted that, for a brief time, he fell under Adolf Hitler's spell like millions of other Germans. Although he never joined the Nazi Party, people around the world thought of him as Hitler's Teutonic dupe. By the time he returned to New York to face Joe Louis a second time, in June 1938, the outside world had grown more aware of what Nazi Germany stood for, and the boxer was vilified. Protesters awaited his ship when he arrived in New York, and he had to be delivered under cover to his hotel. The fight itself was one of the most publicized sporting events of the decade. Yankee Stadium was packed and 70 million Americans, out of a total population of 130 million, tuned in by radio. Louis, whom Americans had turned into a symbol of liberty and freedom despite the fact that, as an African American, he was not allowed into hotels and restaurants in many parts of the country, fought brilliantly. He knocked Schmeling out in just over two minutes. Schmeling's defeat also knocked him off the roll call of Nazi heroes, and he found himself no longer welcome in the company of Hitler or other Third Reich dignitaries. Nonetheless, he won the European heavyweight title again in 1939.

Schmeling's fall from grace was perhaps a relief to Nazi leaders since, again, the boxer was never an enthusiastic Nazi. He refused, even at the height of his success, to give up his Jewish manager, Joe Jacobs, despite being virtually ordered to do so by the Reich Sports Ministry and Joseph Goebbels. In a 1935 bout in Germany, Jacobs even joined Schmeling in the ring after Schmeling won. When the crowd started singing the German national anthem with their arms raised in the Nazi salute, Jacobs, an amused look on his face and a lit cigar in his hand, raised his arm too. Schmeling also refused the Nazi Dagger of Honor, an award that would have given him an honorary officership in the SA. During the Kristallnacht pogrom of November 1938, Schmeling risked his life by hiding the sons of a Jewish friend in his Berlin hotel room.

In 1940 Schmeling was drafted into the Wehrmacht, special permission having been given by Hitler to put him into a paratrooper unit at the rank of private. He took part in the German assault on Crete in May 1941 and was wounded and hospitalized. After he refused to denounce the English army as cruel to a visiting American reporter, Goebbels ordered that Schmeling's name never again appear in print for the duration of the Third Reich. After the war, though he was past the age of forty, he stepped into the ring once again as a professional boxer. He had little success but made enough money to buy a house and set himself up in business as a soft-drink bottler and distributor in a suburb of Hamburg. In his career as a light heavyweight and heavyweight, Schmeling fought seventy bouts, winning fifty-six and drawing four. A frequent visitor to the United States in the years after the war, Schmeling became a close friend of Joe Louis, who spent his last years in poverty and humiliation. When Louis died in 1981, Schmeling arranged to send a large gift to his widow. Noted for his generosity, Schmeling is remembered as a great sportsman in both postwar Germany and the United States, the recipient of numerous awards as well as a place in many top-ten lists of the greatest heavyweight boxers of all time. He published an autobiography, called in English simply *Max Schmeling: An Autobiography*, in 1977. *See also* sports in the Third Reich, Vol. 2.

Schoerner, Ferdinand (1892–1973)

The last general field marshal appointed by Adolf Hitler during World War II. Schoerner was born in Munich in 1892 and took up a military career, where he enjoyed rapid promotion despite his working-class background. He was decorated for bravery during World War I and in 1919 joined the new Reichswehr as a junior officer. In 1923 he helped put down Hitler's Beer Hall Putsch, although he was sympathetic to many of the goals of the Nazi movement. Over the years he developed a strong faith in ideological purity as the source of action, and he became one of the strongest supporters of Hitler among military officers.

Schoerner was a field commander from the early months of World War II, serving as a lieutenant colonel and then as a major general in theaters ranging from Lapland, in Europe's far north, to Greece and the Balkans. He also commanded a tank group on the eastern front, and in April 1944 he was promoted to full general and named commander in chief of Army Group South in the western Soviet Union. He also served as the head of the National Socialist Leadership Staff of the armed forces, where his responsibilities were political and ideological rather than strictly military. By 1944 the eastern front was crumbling, and maintaining military morale and discipline became increasingly difficult. Schoerner took ruthless and brutal steps, including the summary execution of soldiers and officers, to keep his troops in line. He became known, in fact, as "the bloodhound." In early 1945 Hitler promoted him to supreme commander of the German Central Zone, responsible for defending Berlin from the approaching forces of the Soviet Union, which proved to be an impossible task. In his last days, the increasingly out of touch Führer gave Schoerner command of an army group that did not exist and another promotion to general field marshal. Hitler also entrusted Schoerner, as well as Martin Bormann, with delivering his last will and political testament to Grand Admiral Karl Dönitz.

At war's end Schoerner fled to the American zone of occupation in Austria, but the Americans turned him over to the Soviets, who considered Schoerner a top war criminal. He was sentenced to ten years in a Russian prison. After he was released in 1955 he returned to the Federal Republic of Germany. There, he was charged with the murder of hundreds of German soldiers during the last months of World War II. He was finally convicted of manslaughter in 1957 and sentenced to four and a half years in prison. Schoerner died in July 1973 in Munich. *See also* Battle of Berlin, Vol. 1; Wehrmacht, Vol. 2.

Scholl, Hans (1918–1943) and Scholl, Sophie (1921–1943)

Brother and sister leaders of the White Rose, a movement of student resistance to the Third Reich in 1942 and 1943. Hans and Sophie Scholl were born in the Württemberg town of Forchtenburg, where their father was the mayor. They later moved to Ulm. Both members of Hitler Youth organizations as children and teenagers, their sympathies shifted after Hans entered the University of

Munich as a medical student in 1941 and served in the German army on the eastern front, where he witnessed atrocities directed toward civilian populations. By 1942, when Sophie was also a student at the university, Hans had decided, along with two friends, Willi Graf and Alexander Morell, that the Third Reich represented a spiritual and moral breakdown, and that someone had to stand up against it. In this conviction they were supported by a Munich professor of philosophy, Kurt Huber, who found support for their viewpoint in philosophers and writers of the past. Sophie was originally kept out of the discussions of what was to be the White Rose, but she quickly learned of it and insisted on taking part.

From the summer of 1942 to the late winter of 1943, the White Rose developed from an informal discussion group to a loosely organized network of cells in cities across Germany. Its members planned no armed uprising; rather, the Scholls urged their fellows to remind Germans of the evils of the Nazi regime and of the necessity for a renewal of the good side of the "German spirit." The White Rose produced and secretly distributed a number of pamphlets denouncing Nazi atrocities and calling for passive resistance. One pamphlet referred to the massacres of Jews as "a crime not to be compared to any similar one in the history of mankind" (Scholl, 1983). Beyond these activities the Scholls also posted anti-Nazi posters and helped stage the only daylight demonstration in Germany against the Nazis in the history of the Third Reich. They chose the white rose as their symbol to represent a Christian spirit (both Hans and Sophie were devout Catholics) that, through nobility and truth, could triumph over the evils of Nazism.

After dropping leaflets in the courtyard of a Munich University building on February 18, 1943, the Scholls were reported by a building worker who moonlighted as a Gestapo informant. They were immediately arrested and perfunctorily tried by the People's Court, as were Graf, Morell, Huber, and others. All were sentenced to death, and both Hans and Sophie Scholl were executed on February 22 by the guillotine. Sophie Scholl, whose leg had been broken under torture, went proudly to her death, telling a fellow prisoner that she considered herself a martyr whose actions would stir others to act. Hans Scholl showed similar defiance and dignity. *See also* resistance movements, Germany; White Rose, Vol. 2; Student Protest Leaflets: The White Rose; The Verdict of the People's Court on Rebels, Vol. 4.

Scholtz-Klink, Gertrude (1902–1999)

Nazi women's leader and therefore the highest-placed woman in the Third Reich. Gertrude Scholtz-Klink was born Gertrude Treusch on February 9, 1902, in the town of Adelsheim in Baden in southwestern Germany. Her father was a government worker. She dropped out of high school during World War I to devote herself to national service, working for the German Red Cross and in other aid organizations. In 1919 she married Eugen Klink, a teacher and member of the Nazi Party. The two had six children together, two of whom died in childhood. During these years Gertrude's husband urged her to perform support work for the party, tasks that included watching children, cooking, and sewing. Meanwhile, the young woman developed her own attachment to Nazism and took on a more official role. She became the Nazi women's leader in Baden in 1929 and spent the next years actively recruiting support for the Nazi movement among German women. Such support was particularly important in these years, when the Nazis sought to expand their electoral base; simply put, women had the vote. Gertrude Klink made numerous speeches and kept a busy schedule after her husband's death in 1930. She urged German women to adhere to traditional values and tried to convince them that their proper role was as the bulwark of the German household. By the time the

Nazis came to power in 1933 she was also women's leader of Hessen and worked throughout southwestern Germany. She had also remarried: Her new husband was a doctor named Günther Scholtz, and she took the name Gertrude Scholtz-Klink.

In 1933 Scholtz-Klink came to the attention of the national Nazi leadership after her accomplishments in Baden were praised by Robert Wagner, Baden's regional Nazi leader. Officials of the Interior Ministry, under Wilhelm Frick, asked her to be an adviser on women's associations, and she took advantage of the opportunity to close down competing women's groups or incorporate them into Nazi versions. On February 24, 1934, she was appointed Reich women's leader, with authority over all Nazi women's organizations. She also led organizations with a smaller scope, including the Women's League of the German Red Cross and the Women's Bureau of the German Labor Front. Despite these impressive titles, however, she exercised little real authority and had virtually no influence on Nazi policy. The Nazis believed that women, like men, had to learn to serve their nation and their people. The best way for them to do so was as devoted wives, enthusiastic mothers, and the builders of healthy households. Scholtz-Klink, accordingly, was expected to reinforce an old German slogan, "Kinder, Kirche, Kuche" ("Children, Church, Kitchen"), among German women. The measures she urged on women included devoting a period of time to national labor service as well as various incentives disdaining work outside the home in offices or factories. In addition, she served an important ceremonial role, appearing alongside other leading Nazis at party rallies and other meetings. Male leaders expected her to remain docile and uncontroversial as they used her to symbolize German womanhood, and indeed she fitted the physical ideal of the tall, athletic, fair-haired, attractive woman who had borne numerous children to an early Nazi fighter. Scholtz-Klink, meanwhile, remained an energetic servant of the Nazi regime. Between 1933 and 1944 she published more than fifty pamphlets reminding women of their duties. When her husband complained about her long hours of travel and work in 1938, she divorced him, later marrying an SS officer.

Scholtz-Klink fully subscribed to the Nazi ideal of service as well as devotion to Adolf Hitler. During the 1930s, she frequently proclaimed in speeches and at meetings that women, like men, could fight for their race. Their weapons, however, were faithful, selfless motherhood and wooden spoons rather than guns. During World War II she also made it known that women were prepared to not only work in offices and factories but actually take up arms as soldiers if necessary. Hitler, however, avoided her whenever possible, preferring the company of more pliable or glamorous women. Scholtz-Klink complained that she was never able to discuss women's issues with the Führer.

At the end of World War II Scholtz-Klink and her husband went into hiding under a false name in western Germany. They managed to pass through American denazification procedures and remain in hiding until 1948, when her identity was revealed and she was arrested by French occupation authorities. She was sentenced to eighteen months in prison for lying on her denazification questionnaire, but a public outcry led to charges as a major Nazi offender. She was found guilty by a German denazification court at Tübingen, but sentenced only to the eighteen months already served. The West German government, however, prohibited her from any political activity or from engaging in a profession, stripping her also of the right to vote. Nevertheless, Scholtz-Klink remained a devoted and unrepentant Nazi til her death in 1999 and defended her record and ideology under the Third Reich. In 1978 she published a book, *The Woman in the Third Reich*, which combined her speeches and writings from that era with fond reminiscences of Adolf Hitler and explanations of her behavior and attitude. *See also* German Women's Association, Vol. 1; women in the Third Reich, Vol. 2; Scholtz-Klink, An Official Statement from the Reich Women's Leader, Vol. 4.

Schröder, Kurt Freiherr von (1889–1965)

Wealthy Cologne banker who provided early financial support to Adolf Hitler and played a central role in the political intrigues that brought Hitler to power in January 1933. Schröder was born in Hamburg on November 24, 1889. He attended the University of Bonn. During World War I he served as a junior officer with a field unit and later as a captain on the General Staff. After the war he joined the banking house of J.H. Stein, based in Cologne in the Ruhr area, but with branches in Hanover and Berlin. He soon became a partner and built a large personal fortune.

Schröder was an early supporter of the Nazi Party, believing it was Germany's best hope against communism. In the 1920s he joined other financiers and industrialists in founding the Keppler Circle, an organization by which they could donate money to the nascent Nazi movement. In early 1933, through the intermediary Wilhelm Keppler, who had close ties with top Nazis, Schröder arranged for Hitler to meet with Franz von Papen to discuss ways to bring down the government of General Kurt von Schleicher. The meeting between Hitler and Papen, at which they created a coalition of the Nazi Party and the German Nationalist People's Party with Hitler as chancellor and Papen as vice-chancellor, took place at Schröder's house in Cologne on January 4. President Paul von Hindenburg later deposed Schleicher and accepted the coalition, allowing Hitler to become the chancellor of Germany through perfectly legal means on January 30.

After the Nazis took power Schröder found himself well placed to benefit from his longtime support for the movement. Hitler named him president of the Cologne-Aachen Industrial Chamber, and he also took seats on the boards of directors of numerous companies and led the Trade Association of Private Banks. Although he tried to disguise himself as a common soldier after the war, the British found him out and turned him over to a German court. He was tried in 1947 for crimes against humanity, in connection with companies that used slave labor in Germany. He was sentenced to three months in prison and a substantial fine, which was later reduced. Schröder died in Hohenstein, a town in western Germany, in 1965. *See also* Machtergreifung, Vol. 2.

Schuschnigg, Kurt von (1897–1977)

Chancellor of Austria from 1934 until he was deposed and his nation absorbed into the German Reich in the Anschluss of 1938. Schuschnigg was born in Riva, in the Tyrol region of southwestern Austria, on December 14, 1897. His father was an officer in the army of the Austro-Hungarian Empire. After service on the Italian front during World War I, the young Schuschnigg became a lawyer, studying at the Universities of Freiburg and Vienna. He entered politics in the mid-1920s as a member of the conservative Christian Social Party, and in 1927 became the youngest member of the Austrian National Council. A rapid rise through the ranks of power included posts as Austrian minister of justice in 1932, minister of education in 1933, and finally, after Chancellor Engelbert Dollfuss was assassinated by Nazi sympathizers in 1934, chancellor of Austria.

Schuschnigg was politically conservative and a devout Catholic; like Dollfuss, he believed in a strongly centralized, authoritarian state as Austria's best hope, after the breakup of the Austro-Hungarian Empire in 1919, of legitimacy and national survival. During the mid-1930s he managed to control homegrown Fascist movements, but Schuschnigg could not ignore the huge

Austrian chancellor Kurt von Schuschnigg addresses Christian boy scouts in 1935. Schuschnigg opposed the Anschluss, believing that Austrians wished to remain independent.

Third Reich on his western border. In any case, he was something of a pan-German himself, understanding that the much smaller Austria needed recognition and support from his fellow German speakers in Berlin. His survival, however, as well as Austrian independence, depended on his ability to play off Adolf Hitler against Italian dictator Benito Mussolini, who until 1938 entertained his own ambitions with regard to Austria. In 1936 Schuschnigg entered into an agreement with Nazi Germany, in which he agreed to be "friendly" toward the Third Reich as well as define his nation as a "German" one even though he did not subscribe to the Nazis' racial ideology. He also had to allow a few Austrian Nazis into his government.

In early 1938, after Hitler had decided it was time for the Third Reich to begin its territorial expansion and Mussolini had withdrawn his support for an independent Austria, Schuschnigg came under great pressure to allow a Nazi takeover. On February 12, he met with Hitler at Hitler's mountain retreat, the Berghof, where the Führer berated and insulted him, threatening him in the end with a military takeover. Schuschnigg was also forced to accept Artur von Seyss-Inquart, a leader of the Austrian Nazis, as minister of the interior and police commander. As a last resort Schuschnigg declared on March 9 that he would hold a plebiscite, in which he was certain the Austrian people would vote for an independent Austria. The plebiscite was called off, however, as German forces prepared to invade the country. After the Anschluss, in which the Germans entered Austria to find, instead of resistance, an enthusiastic welcome from the local people, Schuschnigg was arrested by the Gestapo; Hitler remained furious over Schuschnigg's unwillingness to turn over his country. In 1941 he was sent to Dachau and spent the remainder of the war in concentration camps.

After the war Schuschnigg moved to the United States, eventually becoming a naturalized citizen and a professor of government at St. Louis University. He published several books recounting his experiences, including *Three Times Austria*, *Austrian Requiem*, and *The Brutal Takeover*. He retired to Austria in 1967 and died there in 1977. ***See also*** Anschluss, Vol. 1.

Schwerin von Krosigk, Lutz Graf (1887–1952)

Minister of finance for the duration of the Third Reich. Schwerin von Krosigk was born in Rathmannsdorff on August 22, 1887, to an aristocratic family. After secondary school in Germany he studied law at Lausanne in Switzerland and at Oxford University in England as a Rhodes scholar. He entered the German civil service in 1910 after completing his required one year's military service. During World War I he returned to the army as a field officer, where he was wounded and decorated for bravery. After the war he rejoined the civil service, first as a government assessor and throughout the 1920s in various other positions of steadily rising rank and responsibility. In 1929 he was named a director in the Reich Ministry of Finance and in June 1932 he became minister of finance in Franz von Papen's cabinet. He would retain the post through two more changes of government and survived even the political and administrative upheavals of the Third Reich.

During the 1930s Schwerin von Krosigk devoted himself to finding ways to pay for German rearmament; in this effort he frequently disagreed with Economics Minister Hjalmar Schacht over specific measures such as the proper creation of credit. The finance minister approved of the Nazi regime's anti-Semitic measures, asserting that German Jews needed to be expelled. When Hitler was succeeded by Grand Admiral Karl Dönitz in May 1945, the loyal and colorless bureaucrat found himself named foreign minister in Dönitz's new and irrelevant cabinet. Arrested and interned by Allied forces after the end of the war, Schwerin von Krosigk was tried for war crimes by an American tribunal in Nuremberg in 1949. He was found guilty and sentenced to ten years in prison, but released in 1951. He died in 1952. ***See also*** Schacht, Hjalmar, Vol. 3.

Seeckt, Hans von (1866–1936)

Commander in chief of the Weimar-era Reichswehr from 1920 to 1926 and the top military officer in Germany during the formative years of the Weimar Republic. He ensured the Reichswehr's loyalty to the Weimar regime by, among other measures, quashing right-wing uprisings such as those planned by the so-called Black Reichswehr and the Nazi Party's Beer Hall Putsch of 1923.

Seeckt was born in Silesia in eastern Germany on April 22, 1866, to an officer-class Prussian family. He joined the German Imperial Army in 1885 and rose rapidly in rank. He spent World War I as a lieutenant colonel in a variety of staff and political positions. In 1916 he was appointed chief of staff to Archduke Charles of Austria and in 1917 he was named chief of staff of the Turkish army. After the war he served on the German delegation at negotiations for the Treaty of Versailles and became commander in chief of the Reichswehr on June 15, 1920. Limited by the treaty to a force of only one hundred thousand men, Seeckt altered the tactics of the Reichswehr to suit a smaller but more mobile force. He also supported the secret training of German air force and tank officers in the Soviet Union.

Seeckt's political sympathies lay with the Prussian-style monarchism he had grown up with, and he had little faith in the

Weimar Republic. He tended therefore to maintain the army's independence from the German government as a sort of state within a state. Nevertheless, he was willing to use force in the service of the government when necessary. On November 9, 1923, informed of Hitler's putsch in Munich, he ordered the local commander, General Otto von Lossow, to put it down. The Nazis had earlier insulted Seeckt as a "lackey" and expressed doubts about his true loyalty to Germany because his wife was Jewish. Not until 1930 did Seeckt become a supporter of Hitler.

Seeckt was forced to retire from his position as commander in chief on October 8, 1926, for committing two errors much disapproved of by the liberals of the Weimar regime. One was to offer Prince Wilhelm of Prussia, a scion of the deposed Hohenzollern monarchy, a military training post. The other was to approve of the old practice of dueling among officers. In 1930 he was elected to the Reichstag, where he stayed until 1932 and expressed sympathies toward Nazi goals. In 1934 and 1935 he worked as a consultant to General Chiang Kai-shek in China, then a German ally. He died in Berlin on December 26, 1936. *See also* Beer Hall Putsch, Black Reichswehr, Vol. 1; Reichswehr, Vol. 2.

Seldte, Franz (1882–1947)

Reich minister of labor from 1933 to 1945. Seldte was born in Magdeburg in Prussia on June 29, 1882. During World War I he served as an infantry officer, receiving the Iron Cross, First and Second Class, but also losing an arm. After the war he founded, along with Theodor Duesterberg, an organization known as the Stahlhelm (Steel Helmet), an association of ex-servicemen devoted to German nationalism and to keeping alive the so-called spirit of the trenches in the face of soft, Weimar-era liberalism. During the 1920s the Stahlhelm rivaled Adolf Hitler's SA as the largest right-wing paramilitary group in Germany. Wearing gray uniforms and staging marches, the members of the Stahlhelm supported a political program that bore many resemblances to Nazism: expanded living space for Germany, repudiation of the Treaty of Versailles, and anticommunism. Hitler, however, wanted no partners in power, and in 1930 he warned both Seldte and Duesterburg that the Stahlhelm would have to defer to his Nazi regime or face drastic consequences. Although Seldte had political ambitions of his own and polled over 2 million votes as a candidate for president of Germany in March 1932, he switched his allegiance to Hitler soon after the election. He served as minister of labor in the cabinet of Franz von Papen and was appointed to the same position in Hitler's first cabinet. Seldte remained labor minister until 1945, but focused his efforts on the government of the semiautonomous state of Prussia as both Prussian state councillor and Prussian labor minister. He also maintained his involvement with veterans' groups. Although Seldte was indicted for war crimes after World War II, he was never brought to trial. He died in the village of Fürth in Bavaria on April 1, 1947. *See also* Stahlhelm, Vol. 2.

Seydlitz, Walter von (1888–1976)

Chief of staff to Field Marshal Friedrich Paulus at Stalingrad and, after his capture by the Soviets, the figurehead of an anti-Nazi organization among German officers sponsored by the Soviet government. Seydlitz was born in Hamburg on August 22, 1888, to an officer-class family. He joined the German Imperial Army in 1908 and served as a junior officer during World War I. During the Weimar era and even after the Nazi takeover, Seydlitz held numerous appointments and enjoyed steady promotions. When World War II began in September 1939 his rank was major general and he commanded a unit during the invasion of France. Though he increasingly, and outspokenly, criticized the Nazi war effort on the eastern front, Seydlitz served his commanders faithfully and enjoyed recognition as an able commander. Before being appointed chief of staff to Paulus, he was promoted to general of infantry as well as commander of the 2nd Army Corps.

Seydlitz, along with the meager remnants of the huge force that had tried to take Stalingrad, was taken prisoner by the Soviets in February 1943. The Russians, who knew of his opposition to the Nazi conduct of the war, put him at the head of the League of German Officers, formed in September 1943 and based in Moscow. Seydlitz's responsibilities included broadcasts in German to troops along the eastern front, encouraging them to overthrow Hitler and end the war. Hitler, for his part, issued a death sentence in absentia on the maverick general. The league expanded rapidly among captured officers and men until July 1944, when the July Plot on Hitler's life failed, convincing the Soviets that the Germans would never rise against Hitler. Seydlitz, despite his anti-Nazi services, remained in Russian prisons until 1955. At that point Seydlitz returned to Germany, where he faced ostracism from fellow surviving officers and had to wait several months before Hitler's death sentence was revoked. He died in Bremen on April 28, 1976.
See also Battle of Stalingrad, Vol. 1.

Seyss-Inquart, Artur von (1892–1946)

Austrian Nazi who played a major role in annexing his nation to the German Reich in the Anschluss of March 1938. Afterward he served as Reich governor of Austria and, during World War II, Reich commissioner of the occupied Netherlands. Seyss-Inquart was born on July 22, 1892, in Iglau, Moravia, then part of the Austro-Hungarian Empire but later in Czechoslovakia. His father was a high school teacher. During World War I he fought in the Austrian army. After the war he settled in Vienna, where he studied law and became convinced that the best hope for Austria, reduced to a small, landlocked nation after World War I, was union with Germany. He joined the Austrian Nazi Party in 1931 to work toward that goal.

Seyss-Inquart joined the Austrian government in May 1937, when Chancellor Kurt von Schuschnigg, who was impressed by Seyss-Inquart's clean-cut demeanor, pleasant personality, and churchgoing habits, made him an Austrian state councillor. Over the next months, however, Seyss-Inquart undermined the chancellor's authority by working, under the direction of Adolf Hitler, for an Anschluss. Through intimidation and the threat of military force, Hitler made Schuschnigg accept Seyss-Inquart as minister of the interior in Austria, with full police powers, on February 16, 1938. Seyss-Inquart used the office to voice his approval of the entry of German forces into his nation. When Schuschnigg was forced to resign as chancellor on May 2, Seyss-Inquart was appointed in his place and therefore presided over the actual entry of the forces of the Third Reich into Austria. On March 3 he passed a law that proclaimed that Austria no longer existed except as a province of the Greater German Reich. Now promoted to SS lieutenant general, Seyss-Inquart remained Reich governor of Austria, or Ostmark as the Nazis called it, until April 1939.

After serving briefly in occupied Poland as the deputy to Governor-General Hans Frank, Seyss-Inquart was appointed Reich commissioner to the occupied Netherlands, a post he held from May 1940 to May 1945. The position made him the top German official in the Netherlands, responsible for pacifying the local population and tying the Dutch economy to that of Germany. He presided over measures including the transport of some 5 million Dutch people to Germany for forced labor and the complete takeover of Dutch agriculture, as well as the Dutch consumer economy, in the service of Germany. He was also instrumental in rounding up the community of some one-hundred-fifty thousand Dutch Jews for deportation to the Polish death camps; those Dutch Jews married to non-Jews were given the choice of sterilization or "resettlement" to the east. Dutch partisans and those who supported them also faced harsh punishments.

At war's end Seyss-Inquart was taken prisoner by Canadian troops. He was one of the twenty-one top Nazis brought before the International Military Tribunal at Nuremberg in late 1945. He was one of the few defendants willing to admit that he shared in the guilt of the Nazi regime. The tribunal convicted him of war crimes, mostly during his period in the Netherlands, and sentenced him to death. He was hanged at the Nuremberg prison on October 16, 1946. *See also* Anschluss, Vol. 1; New Order, Nuremberg trials, Vol. 2.

Skorzeny, Otto (1908–1975)

SS officer and Nazi adventurer who helped a number of Nazis escape from Europe after World War II. Skorzeny was born in Vienna on June 12, 1908. After studying engineering and, allegedly, involving himself in right-wing paramilitary activities, he joined the Austrian Nazi Party in 1930. There he became acquainted with Ernst Kaltenbrunner, later the chief of the Security Service of the SS. He spent most of the 1930s working in the construction business before devoting himself to Nazism after the Anschluss of 1938. Turned down by the Luftwaffe, he joined the SS instead and was posted to Adolf Hitler's bodyguard contingent in 1940. He also served in the militarized Waffen-SS in France and the Soviet Union before an injury in 1942 confined him, for a while, to a desk job. In April 1943 he was given a post in the Reich Central Security Office (RSHA), where his main responsibility was to develop commando strategies that could be used in occupied countries and behind enemy lines.

After a few false starts in Russia and the Middle East, Skorzeny demonstrated his daring and intelligence in a unique mission that took place in late July 1943. Hitler ordered Skorzeny to rescue Italian Fascist dictator Benito Mussolini, who had just been deposed by a new regime and imprisoned by Italian troops in the mountains of central Italy. Skorzeny assembled a small force of troops who piloted gliders to the isolated region where Mussolini was being held. The Italian guards were taken by surprise and Mussolini, who was contemplating suicide, was completely shocked when Skorzeny grabbed him up, pushed him into a small airplane, and flew him into exile in Vienna. Propaganda Minister Joseph Goebbels made the most of the exploit, turning Skorzeny into a daring Nazi hero and, according to Goebbels, the "most dangerous man in Europe" (Whiting, 1998). Skorzeny, who fit the physical ideal of the German hero as an athletic six feet, four inches, and sported a dueling scar on his face, was promoted to SS major general. On July 20, 1944, the day of the attempt to assassinate Hitler and overthrow the Third Reich, Skorzeny, who was on a train to Vienna when he heard of the crisis, returned quickly to Berlin. There he assembled a special SS unit ready to support Hitler, earning him still more praise from the Führer and from Goebbels.

Skorzeny found himself once more at the center of events in October 1944 when Hitler ordered him to kidnap yet another wayward former ally: Hungarian leader Admiral Miklos Horthy. Horthy, who had already been elbowed out by the Nazis and their Hungarian Fascist allies but was still the titular leader of his nation, wanted to sign a separate peace between Hungary and the Soviet Union. This exploit also came off smoothly. In the late fall of 1944 Skorzeny organized another operation in which two thousand English-speaking Germans were dropped behind Allied lines to sew confusion during the Battle of the Bulge. Although the operation inspired major security concerns among the Allies, Skorzeny's men failed to hold any territory long enough for the main German force to arrive and most of them were captured. Skorzeny's final adventure during World War II was to fight under Erich von dem Bach-Zelewski, a brutal SS commander, on the collapsing Polish front.

American troops captured Skorzeny on May 15, 1945, and interned him for two years until a war crimes tribunal acquitted him and set him free. Soon after he was arrested by the Germans but escaped from an internment camp near Darmstadt in July 1948. He then founded the organization known as ODESSA, using the name Robert Steinbacher and funding it with money left over from Nazi businesses and extortion. The purpose of ODESSA was to help Nazis escape possible prosecution in Europe. In 1951 he moved to Madrid, capital of Francisco Franco's Spain, where he began an import-export business that served as a cover for ODESSA. From there he could supply escapees with false identities and funds and help them reach, primarily, South America, although some escapees went to Africa or the Arab Middle East. In addition Skorzeny was active in neo-Nazi groups and maintained contact with groups in Germany that worked for the release of convicted Nazi war criminals. In the late 1950s he bought a horse estate in Ireland and divided his time between this estate, a residence in Madrid, and a house on the Mediterranean island of Mallorca. Skorzeny died in Madrid on July 5, 1975. *See also* ODESSA, Operation Oak, Operation Snatch, Vol. 2; Naujocks, Alfred, Vol. 3.

Smigly-Rydz, Edward (1886–1943)

Military leader and virtual dictator of Poland at the time of the German invasion of his country. Smigly-Rydz rose to a position of military and political importance under the mentorship of Marshal Józef Pilsudski, Poland's first post–World War I leader. The two served together in campaigns against Germany (and under Russian command) during World War I and Smigly-Rydz also aided Pilsudski in the immediate postwar conflict against the new Russian Bolshevik regime. He took power after Pilsudski's death in 1935, holding the titles of marshal and commander in chief. Although Smigly-Rydz's regime was both autocratic and anti-Semitic, he and his fellow Polish officers and aristocrats were strongly anti-German and anti-Soviet, and they pledged to defend their surrounded country.

Smigly-Rydz was unprepared for the German onslaught that began on September 1, 1939. As the Germans launched the most modern offensive then possible, the mechanized blitzkrieg attack, the Poles fell back on a few tanks and aircraft and in some instances tried to counter the German attack with horse cavalry. Polish defenses collapsed within weeks, despite Smigly-Rydz's hope that, by establishing a shrunken defensive line, he could hold out until French and British help arrived. When the Soviets marched into eastern Poland in accordance with the Nazi-Soviet Pact of August 23, Smigly-Rydz realized his cause was hopeless. He escaped to Romania along with his government, returning to Poland to fight in the underground in 1941. The Polish government-in-exile in London, however, repudiated him. Smigly-Rydz is thought to have been killed while fighting the Germans in 1943. *See also* Case White, Vol. 1.

Speer, Albert (1905–1981)

Reich minister of armaments and war production from 1942 to 1945, and the most open and forthcoming of all the top Nazis in the years after World War II. Albert Speer was born in the western German city of Mannheim on March 15, 1905, into an upper-middle-class family. His father was one of the city's top architects. Choosing a career in architecture himself, Speer studied at the Institute of Technology in Karlsruhe and the Universities of Berlin and Munich. In Berlin in 1930 the young architect heard Hitler speak and fell under the spell of the Führer's personal charisma. Although throughout his life Speer claimed to be apolitical, he was not immune to the hope that Hitler could truly save Germany from the ills that had befallen it since the end of World War I, from the threat of communism, and from the weakness of the Weimar Republic. In 1931 he joined the Nazi Party and in 1932 joined the SS, which was on the lookout for young university graduates. The party also began to provide him with an outlet for his professional ambitions. He went to work as an architect for the local Nazi leadership in Berlin and in 1933 he was given the task of arranging a party rally to be held at the Templehof airfield. There, Speer demonstrated innovations he later adapted and expanded at the national Nazi rallies held every year in Nuremberg, including massive flags and banners and special lighting effects. Speer was also credited with devising the endless, spellbinding parades that characterized later rallies. At the 1934 Nuremberg rally he used huge searchlights pointing to the sky to create what one foreign journalist likened to a cathedral of ice. Reportedly, the lights could be seen from one hundred miles away.

Adolf Hitler was very impressed by Speer's work for the rallies and took him under his wing. The Nazi leader considered himself a frustrated architect and was no doubt drawn to Speer's youth and energy as well as his design and organizational skills. He gave him a number of architectural commissions, including the Reichs Chancellery in Berlin. In 1937 Speer was appointed architectural inspector general of the Reich and asked to redesign German cities, notably Berlin, in line with Hitler's plan to make Berlin the showpiece of the future Greater German Reich. Hitler believed that great empires, and great emperors, were remembered for their monumental architecture, citing ancient Egypt and ancient Rome as his models. He wanted the Third Reich to rank with them, memori-

Albert Speer, Hitler's primary architect and minister of armaments and war production.

alized by structures just as impressive as the pyramids or the Roman Forum. In accord with Hitler's vision, Speer designed and built models of huge official buildings and meeting places, stadiums, palaces, and wide boulevards. Most were in a monumental, neoclassical style that other architects considered mediocre, tasteless, or inappropriate, but Hitler was transfixed by them. Few of Speer's conceptions were ever built.

Meanwhile, Hitler showered the young architect with other state and party honors. Speer was given the honorary title of professor, which meant a great deal in Germany, and made a Prussian state councillor.

In 1938 he was named a section leader in the German Labor Front, later heading its Beauty of Labor program. He was elected to the Reichstag in 1941 and held such varied positions as general inspector of water and energy and chief of the Nazi Party technology office.

In February 1942, after Fritz Todt was killed in an airplane accident, Speer was named to replace him as minister of armaments and war production. The appointment came as a great surprise to Nazi insiders such as Hermann Göring, who expected the post himself, and Martin Bormann, who like many others considered Speer essentially an outsider. Nonetheless, over the next few years Speer was as effective at political infighting as he was at organization and logistics. He performed what a number of commentators have referred to as miracles with the German war economy, raising production of essential armaments and equipment despite growing shortages of raw materials and, beginning in 1943, almost continuous Allied bombing attacks. Speer has been credited with keeping the German war effort alive and, in effect, prolonging World War II through his relentless focus on increased production and his industrial innovations. Throughout, he remained oblivious to abuses such as widespread slave labor and the use of prisoners of war as workers. His actions from 1942 to 1945 made him one of the most important and powerful men in the Third Reich, though he was less than forty years old.

The German resistance movement considered Speer a potential sympathizer, but he never seriously contemplated joining the July 1944 Plot. Later he wrote that he considered killing Hitler himself at the beginning of 1945 but was unable to act on the idea. By that time the war was obviously lost, and Speer disagreed wholeheartedly with Hitler's stated belief that since Germany had lost the war, it deserved to be destroyed. In the first months of 1945 he deliberately countermanded Hitler's order to allow Germany's industrial and physical infrastructure to be destroyed, knowing that the nation must have a basis for recovery when the war ended. He even went so far as to tell Hitler, who was then retreating further and further from reality in the Berlin Führerbunker, that the war was lost. The effort, predictably, earned him nothing but a temper tantrum.

After the war, Speer was one of the twenty-one top Nazis tried for war crimes by the International Military Tribunal at Nuremberg in late 1945. He was one of the few defendants, along with Hans Frank and Hans Fritzsche, to admit his guilt and show a substantial degree of remorse. He acknowledged, specifically, that he understood he had committed offenses by using slave labor and by working with SS officials to use concentration camp workers. However, he continued to assert that his activities were technical and economic rather than political. In October 1946 the tribunal found him guilty of war crimes and sentenced him to twenty years in prison, over the objection of the Soviet judge, who wanted him executed.

Speer served out his entire sentence at Spandau Prison in Berlin and was released in October 1966. During his term he had secretly written a memoir, published in 1970 under the title *Inside the Third Reich*, which became an international best-seller. In it, he described not only his own experiences but the inner workings of the Third Reich. According to Speer the Nazi state was not clearly organized and authoritarian but relatively arbitrary and even chaotic, with several competing centers of power guided by top officials such as Göring, Bormann, Himmler, and Goebbels. Thanks to this memoir and to his testimony at Nuremberg, Speer has struck many as the Nazi leader with the greatest integrity and ability, although he remained the ideal technocrat, carrying out his work efficiently and sometimes brilliantly but oblivious to the human costs of his policies. Speer died during a visit to

London on September 1, 1981. *See also* arts and architecture in the Third Reich, Vol. 1; Ministry of Armaments and War Production, Nuremberg rallies, Nuremberg trials, Vol. 2; Speer, Hitler and Germany React to the Start of the War; Speer, A Last Visit to Hitler, Vol. 4.

Speidel, Hans (1897–1984)

German army general and member of the resistance movement who went on to make important contributions to the postwar Federal Republic of Germany. Speidel was born in Metzingen in western Germany on October 28, 1897. He fought as a junior officer during World War I and remained in the army after the war. During World War II he held the rank of general and served in a number of General Staff positions, including chief of staff to the military governor of Paris, General Karl Heinrich von Stuelpnagel. In April 1944, while serving as chief of staff to the Eighth Army on the eastern front, Speidel was called back to France by an old comrade, General Erwin Rommel, to serve as his chief of staff. It was then that Speidel learned of the plot to assassinate Hitler and overthrow the Third Reich, and he worked with Stuelpnagel to persuade Rommel to throw his lot in with the conspirators. Rommel remained hesitant while Speidel and Stuelpnagel drew up a proposed armistice to end the war between the western Allies and the new, post-Hitler government. After the failure of the July Plot Speidel was dismissed from the army and interrogated by the Gestapo. He denied any knowledge of the plot and was declared innocent by the military court of honor convened to judge those conspirators on active duty. He was thus spared the fate that awaited dozens of others, including Stuelpnagel and Rommel.

After the war Speidel took a post as military adviser to Konrad Adenauer, the first leader of the Federal Republic of Germany, and he helped to rebuild the German army as a force allied with the West. From 1955 he was the chief of the Armed Forces Section of the Federal Republic's Defense Ministry. He was also the top German officer in the North Atlantic Treaty Organization (NATO) from 1955 to 1964, serving as NATO commander for central Europe from April 1957 to December 1963. He retired in 1964 to continue a teaching and writing career that began in 1949 with the publication of *Invasion 1944: A Contribution to the Fates of Rommel and the Reich.* In this book he claimed that the German army had been prepared to follow Rommel rather than Hitler and gave an in-depth account of the July Plot. Speidel died at Bad Honnef on November 28, 1984. *See also* Federal Republic of Germany, July 1944 Plot, Vol. 1; Operation Valkyrie, Vol. 2.

Sperrle, Hugo (1885–1953)

General field marshal and one of the top commanders of the Luftwaffe, the Third Reich's air force, during World War II. Sperrle was born in Ludwigsburg in southwestern Germany on February 7, 1885. He joined the army, going to officer's school in 1913, and during World War I he served in the air wing of the German Imperial Army. After the war he also served as an air commander with one of the right-wing Freikorps before returning to the army. By the time the Nazis took power in 1933 Sperrle was a senior officer in the Reichswehr, and in 1934 he was transferred to the nascent Luftwaffe. Dynamic and energetic, he quickly became one of its top officers. In 1936 and 1937, during the Spanish Civil War, he led the Condor Legion, a Luftwaffe contingent sent by Hermann Göring to assist the forces of Generalissimo Francisco Franco. The Condor Legion effectively tested the new strategies of massive bombing and strafing, even of civilian populations, in such Spanish cities as Almería and Guernica. Upon returning to Spain, Sperrle was promoted to general of fliers.

In 1938 Sperrle was named commander of Air Fleet III, based in Munich and one of

Luftwaffe commander Hugo Sperrle played a major role in Hitler's planned invasion of Great Britain.

four German fleets. His planes participated in shows of overwhelming force, during the Czech crisis, and in actual battle, as in France in 1940. In July of that year Sperrle was promoted to general field marshal along with eleven other Luftwaffe and Wehrmacht generals. At the same time he was involved in planning for the invasion of Great Britain, where along with his fellow Luftwaffe field marshals Albert Kesselring and Erhard Milch he tried to convince Hitler and Göring that the Royal Air Force must be completely disabled before Germany could carry out successful bombing attacks. The two top Nazis, however, were unconvinced.

In 1942 Sperrle's air fleet was sent to North Africa to support General Erwin Rommel's ground troops. Afterward he returned to the western front, where he was placed in charge of air defense against the anticipated Allied invasion. Meanwhile, he maintained a luxurious home and headquarters in Paris, where some observers suggested he was in lavishness nearly the equal of Göring. After the war he was tried by an Allied war crimes tribunal but acquitted of all charges. He died in Munich in April 1953. *See also* Luftwaffe, Vol. 1; Operation Eagle, Vol. 2.

Stalin, Joseph (1879–1953)

Dictator of the Soviet Union from 1929 to 1953 and commander in chief of the Soviet military during World War II. Stalin was Adolf Hitler's main political and ideological rival during the era of the Third Reich.

Stalin was born under the name Iosif Vissarionovich Djugashvili in a village near Tbilisi, Georgia, on December 21, 1879. He was therefore not of Russian ethnicity. While studying for the Georgian Orthodox priesthood in Tbilisi he became interested in revolutionary communism, and after being expelled from his seminary, he became active in revolutionary agitation. He became acquainted with Lenin, the leader of the Bolshevik Party, in 1905, and was recognized as an important revolutionary leader in Russia. He also spent a number of years in the czar's prisons or in Siberian exile. He changed his name to Joseph Stalin in 1913, *Stalin* being a variation of the Russian phrase "man of steel."

Stalin played an important role in the Bolshevik takeover of power in October 1917 and in the subsequent civil war, during which the Bolsheviks consolidated their hold on the former Russian Empire and created the Union of Soviet Socialist Republics (USSR, or Soviet Union). In 1922 Stalin was elected chairman of the Central Committee of the Russian Communist Party, where he proved to be an able political infighter. Although Lenin, the leader of the USSR since its inception, grew to dislike the power-hungry and deceitful Stalin, he was unable to remove him. After Lenin died in 1924, Stalin removed his old Bolshevik rivals one by one until, in 1929, he emerged as an absolute dictator.

Between 1929 and 1939 Stalin turned the Soviet Union into a totalitarian dictatorship in many ways comparable to the Third Reich. Dissent was not tolerated, and Stalin used a wide network of secret police, special courts, and political prisons to enforce his will. Moreover, he encouraged a cult that depicted him as the personification of revolutionary ideals. Meanwhile, through a series of so-called Five-Year Plans, Stalin sought to turn the Soviet Union into a major industrial and military power. Among the results was the forced exile of millions of rural families and the deaths of perhaps millions from starvation and abuse, when Stalin tried to "collectivize" agriculture by bringing it under state control. By the mid-1930s Stalin had also adopted a policy of "Russification," a measure that bore some similarities to Hitler's racial ideals. Through Russification, Stalin sought to transform the dozens of different ethnic groups in the Soviet Union into true Russians. He abolished traditional languages and customs and installed strict state control from Moscow, his capital. He also began to entertain territorial ambitions in eastern Europe. Finally, after 1935, Stalin ensured that there was no one left to oppose him by conducting purges in which tens of thousands of potential enemies were simply murdered or sent into exile. Those purged included numerous old Bolsheviks as well as much of the officer corps.

Partly because of the purges, Stalin knew that the Soviet Union was not ready for war with Germany in 1939, although he had watched the growth and aggression of the Third Reich with foreboding. Stalin approved the Nazi-Soviet Pact of August 23, 1939, to buy time and to allow the Soviet Union to absorb a large chunk of Poland, and also because the British and French had refused to enter into defense agreements with him. In the months following the German invasion of Poland, Soviet forces moved into the Baltic states of Latvia, Lithuania, and Estonia as Stalin pursued his territorial objectives. His one setback was the war with Finland in the winter of 1939–1940, which demonstrated to the Germans that the Soviet army was far from formidable.

The German invasion of the Soviet Union on June 21, 1941, caught Stalin completely by surprise. Reports suggest that the news, in effect, paralyzed him for a number of hours. Stalin had failed to prepare the Soviet military to fend off the Germans despite the extra time he had bought with the Nazi-Soviet Pact. Its leading officers were a few old-line Bolsheviks who had survived the purges, and its equipment was out of date. Stalin could merely watch as, over the summer of 1941, German forces swept through the western regions of his vast country, devastating the landscape and massacring millions of people. The Germans, on their part, failed to take advantage of bitterness over Stalin's ruthlessness and Russification policies. Instead of taking advantage of the anti-Russian and anticommunist sentiments of Belarussians, Ukrainians, and others, the Nazis remained committed to their racial goals and oppressed these peoples as members of "subhuman" races.

Stalin managed to survive the initial German onslaught. He brought in a younger officer, Marshal Georgy Zhukov, to direct Russian defenses, and Zhukov turned the Germans away from Moscow in December 1941. Stalin also relied on his country's vastness and brutal winters, moving much of his industry to the east of Moscow and allowing the Germans to languish in the devastated west. Over the next several years Stalin, who had named himself premier of the Soviet Union (a mere formality) as well as marshal of the Soviet Union, played an important role in military strategy, including the decisive victory at Stalingrad in early 1943. Although he is not thought to have devised specific operations, he approved plans among those presented by

Zhukov and other officers and, consistent with his old habits, he kept officers in line through intimidation and uncertainty over their status. He also proved merciless in recruiting soldiers from across the marginally Russified Soviet Union and tossing them in waves into the German lines. By 1944 the Soviet army had begun sweeping westward and in April 1945 it was Stalin's forces that conquered Hitler's capital of Berlin.

Beyond ensuring the revival of the Soviet Union in what he referred to as the Great Nationalist War, Stalin also played a key role in devising overall Allied policy. Although he relied on convoys of war materials from the western Allies, he did not hesitate to badger and intimidate his counterparts, Winston Churchill of Great Britain and Franklin D. Roosevelt of the United States. He continually urged them to open a second front in order to lift some of the military burden from the Soviets, and threatened on a number of occasions to sign a separate peace with Germany if he did not get his way. Churchill was generally reluctant to cooperate with him, but Roosevelt believed that Stalin could be reasoned with and sought to accommodate him, realizing that Allied victory over the Third Reich depended on Soviet efforts.

At war's end, and despite promises to hold free elections, Stalin set up Communist dictatorships throughout eastern Europe, a task largely accomplished by 1948 and made easier by the presence of huge Soviet armies. He also refused to grant independence to the Baltic states. In a sense, Stalin largely accomplished what the Nazis had always warned of: the expansion of communism westward into Europe. His intransigence there, as well as his lingering fear of another invasion from the west, was an important factor in the onset of the Cold War. Joseph Stalin remained the dictator of the Soviet Union, setting the model for totalitarian communism the world over, until he died of a brain hemorrhage in Moscow on March 5, 1953. *See also* Barbarossa, Battle of Stalingrad, Bolsheviks, Vol. 1; Nazi-Soviet Pact, Yalta Conference, Vol. 2.

Stangl, Franz (1908–1971)

Commandant of Treblinka, one of the six extermination centers the Nazis established in and near occupied Poland. Stangl was born in Altmünster, Austria, on March 26, 1908, into a working-class family. He joined the Austrian police in 1931, where he gravitated toward political work. According to reports he joined the Austrian Nazi Party secretly in 1936. After Austria was annexed by the Third Reich in 1938, Stangl's police unit was absorbed into the SS, which had jurisdiction over all police functions.

Stangl first became involved with the extermination measures of the SS in November 1940, when he was apppointed police superintendent of one of the T-4 Program euthanasia centers. The facility, Schloss-Hartheim in western Austria, was also one of the centers used to murder political prisoners in early 1941 as part of Heinrich Himmler's effort to reduce the concentration camp population. In March 1942, now in Poland, Stangl was placed in charge of the Sobibor death camp by Odilo Globocnik, an Austrian who served as SS police commander in the region. Stangl remained at Sobibor for six months, during which time perhaps one hundred thousand Jews were murdered.

In September 1942 Stangl was transferred to Treblinka, a much larger camp located not far from Warsaw. There he proved to be an effective organizer and administrator of mass extermination, earning the respect of both his superiors and his men. Unlike other camp commandants who were either brutal sadists or mindless bureaucrats, Stangl was friendly, amiable, and always well mannered and well dressed. He considered his work a profession that should be performed well, and he later claimed that he had little sympathy for the hundreds of thousands of Jews gassed to death under his command. They were, he suggested, passive and weak, allowing anything to happen to them without offering any resistance, a somewhat ironic comment given that many of those killed at Treblinka while Stangl was there were the Jews of the Warsaw ghetto.

After a small revolt at Treblinka in August 1943, which influenced Himmler's decision to close the camp, Stangl was transferred to Yugoslavia to fight against local partisans. He held the rank of SS captain. Soon after he went to Italy to supervise Italian workers engaged in German war projects. At the end of World War II he was captured by the Americans, who were not yet aware of Treblinka and Sobibor, and briefly imprisoned for his activities against Yugoslav and Italian partisans. In time he was extradited to Austria, where, still able to hide his actions in Poland, he escaped from a minimum-security prison in 1947. Making his way to Rome with a comrade from Sobibor, Gustav Wagner, he escaped to Damascus in Syria. There, joined by his family, he worked as a mechanical engineer until 1951, when he moved to Brazil. In Brazil, where Stangl continued to use his own name in contrast to most other escaped Nazis, he worked as an engineer in a Volkswagen factory. By 1961, however, the Austrian government had placed him on a list of wanted war criminals and issued a warrant for his arrest. He was located by Simon Wiesenthal, the Israeli Nazi hunter, and arrested in Brazil in February 1967. Stangl was extradited to the Federal Republic of Germany, where he was put on trial for complicity in the murder of nearly a million Jews at Sobibor and Treblinka. Found guilty, he was sentenced to life imprisonment (the Federal Republic did not use the death penalty). He died in prison in Düsseldorf on June 28, 1971. *See also* extermination camps, Vol. 1; Treblinka, Vol. 2.

Stark, Johannes (1874–1957)

Nobel Prize–winning physicist and anti-Semitic Nazi who, in contrast to the wave of leading scientists and intellectuals forced into exile during the Third Reich, remained in Germany in high scientific posts throughout the era. Johannes Stark was born in Schickenhof, Bavaria, on April 15, 1874, into a landowning middle-class family. He studied physics, mathematics, and chemistry, earning a doctorate at the University of Munich followed by advanced professorships at technical institutes in Hanover, Aachen, and Würzburg. He corresponded with physicist Albert Einstein during this period regarding photoelectric and quantum theory; Stark's own scientific work focused on electromagnetism and spectroscopic analysis. In 1919 he was awarded the Nobel Prize in physics for his discovery of the splitting of spectral lines in an electric field.

In 1922 Stark published a controversial book, *The Present Crisis in German Physics*, which contained a scathing attack on Einstein and the theory of relativity and bitter criticism of Niels Bohr and the quantum theory. He was forced from his position at Würzburg for advancing the position that true German science was based on racial "objectivity" while flawed "Jewish" science such as Einstein's was based on opinion. Stark's nationalism and anti-Semitism intensified during the rise of the Third Reich. He began making speeches that reflected Adolf Hitler's racial theories, joined the Nazi Party in 1930, and tried to apply Fascist principles to physics, arguing, for example, that theoretical physics was of less value than applied physics, which served the state by improving industry and arms production.

When Hitler took power in 1933 he appointed Stark head of the German Research Association and president of the Physico-Technical Institute, from which Jewish scientists were soon dismissed and replaced, with Stark's approval, by certified "ethnic Germans." Stark held the posts till 1939, when he retired to his private laboratory in Upper Bavaria, maintaining his support of Hitler and continuing to argue against quantum theory in the face of mounting evidence to the contrary. After World War II he was arrested and sentenced by a German denazification court in 1947 to four years' hard labor. He died on June 21, 1957. *See also* Einstein, Albert, Vol. 3.

Stauffenberg, Claus Schenk Graf von (1907–1944)

The central figure in the July 1944 Plot to assassinate Hitler and replace the Third Reich with a new regime. Stauffenberg was born on his family's estate in Greifenstein, Upper Franconia, on November 15, 1907. His family had a rich military and aristocratic heritage; two of his forebears had been generals in the German wars of liberation against Napoléon in the early nineteenth century, and his father was privy chamberlain to the Wittelsbach king of Bavaria. Stauffenberg's education and upbringing were typical of young men of his class; he developed a taste for literature, the arts, and philosophy as well as sports and riding. He was also strikingly handsome, an admirable companion, and a devout Roman Catholic. He joined the German army as a junior officer in 1926, serving with a venerable Bavarian cavalry regiment.

Early in his career Stauffenberg was a strong German nationalist who believed that Germany, historically a great nation, must achieve that status again. Like others of his class he was sympathetic toward monarchism and traditional privilege, but he was not, at first, opposed to Nazism. He took a post with the War Academy in Berlin in 1936 and, two years later, joined the General Staff. He also served in the field, as staff officer with a tank division during the invasion of Poland in 1939 and the invasion of France in 1940. Meanwhile, he had begun to suspect that Nazism was the wrong way to preserve Germany and that Adolf Hitler, especially, was a force for evil. This sense began to grow in the aftermath of the nationwide attack on German Jews in November 1938 known as Kristallnacht. It became a firm conviction in 1941 and 1942, when Stauffenberg served as a staff officer on the eastern front. There one of his responsibilities was the rounding up of Russian prisoners of war for use as slave workers in Germany, and there he became aware of the wholesale slaughter of Jewish and Russian civilians. These experiences led him to join the German resistance movement and altered his political stance in the direction of socialism.

Stauffenberg, the well-known and connected aristocrat, made contact with several branches of the German resistance after committing himself to opposing Hitler. While serving on the eastern front he met Henning von Tresckow, the leader of the resistance among younger German army officers. He also learned of the centers of resistance organized around General Ludwig Beck and the politician Carl Goerdeler, who had been considering various schemes against Hitler since 1938 and 1939. Finally, through his cousin Peter Graf Yorck von Wartenburg, he knew of the Kreisau Circle, the rebellious intellectual center of the resistance. Stauffenberg was likely influenced by all three sources: Tresckow had the energy and drive that he shared; Beck, Goerdeler, and other older officers and diplomats had the necessary authority and connections; and the Kreisau Circle helped Stauffenberg find the moral justification necessary for a putsch against Hitler. He came to understand that, at the very least, the resistance had to make a gesture against the Nazis to show both the world and the verdict of history that not all Germans were willing participants in the Third Reich's plans and atrocities. The German resistance now set out to assassinate Hitler, overthrow his regime and replace it with another, and make a peace with the Allies that would allow the nation to preserve its honor.

In April 1943 Stauffenberg was gravely wounded while serving as an operations officer with a tank division in North Africa. He lost his left eye and for days was in danger of full blindness. He also lost his right hand, part of his left hand, and part of his left leg. He was treated at a Munich hospital by Dr. Ferdinand Sauerbruch, one of Germany's most renowned physicians. Reportedly, while recovering from his injuries Stauffenberg decided to devote his entire energy to overthrowing Hitler and rescuing Germany from, in his mind, the evil that had befallen it. His single-mindedness, as well as his integrity and sense that resistance to the Nazis was not only a political but a moral necessity, put him at the forefront of what was to be the July Plot.

When he was able to return to active service, Stauffenberg was posted to Berlin as chief of staff to General Friedrich Olbricht, who was the deputy commander of the Reserve Army as well as a member of the resistance. This assignment proved essential to the plan that the resistance was to codename "Valkyrie," which called for not only the assassination of Hitler but the neutralization of the SS and Gestapo by Reserve Army troops.

In June 1944 he was promoted to lieutenant colonel and named chief of staff to General Friedrich Fromm. Fromm was the commander in chief of the Reserve Army but blew hot and cold on the resistance plot. Nevertheless, Stauffenberg's position as Fromm's chief of staff provided him with easy entry to Hitler's military conferences on the eastern front on the pretext of determining Reserve Army reinforcements. He proclaimed himself willing to plant the bomb that would kill Hitler and, it was hoped, others. The conspirators originally planned to kill Hitler, Göring, and Himmler with a single blast, but a meeting on July 2, which all three were supposed to attend, was cancelled. A second attempt was called off on July 15. Finally Stauffenberg decided to try to kill Hitler alone. If the conspirators continued to delay, as they had since 1938, the Allies, whose forces had landed in France a month earlier, might advance so close to victory that they might not be willing to negotiate with a post-Hitler regime.

German resistance member Claus Schenk Graf von Stauffenberg led the unsuccessful July 1944 plot to assassinate Hitler and topple the Nazi regime.

Hence, on July 20, 1944, Stauffenberg set off for Hitler's eastern military headquarters, the so-called Wolf's Lair at Rastenburg, East Prussia, ready to assassinate the Führer of the Third Reich. He carried a briefcase containing a bomb, which he was to position as close to Hitler as possible and detonate from a safe distance. Meanwhile, conspirators in Berlin were poised to take over government buildings and deal with any counterresistance as soon as they received word of the successful assassination. Stauffenberg followed the plan, setting off the bomb and hastily flying back to Berlin, certain that his bomb had killed Hitler. There he learned that Hitler had been merely injured by the blast and that his fellow conspirators had failed to act with the same decisiveness that he had shown. Lines of communication and authority were uninterrupted, Hitler's men immediately began the search for conspirators, and Stauffenberg's boss, General Fromm, renounced the resistance movement altogether. Fromm had Stauffenberg and several other conspirators arrested that very day. He subjected them to a summary court-martial intended, no doubt, to convince Hitler that Fromm had had nothing to do with the plot. Early in the evening of July 20 Stauffenberg was found guilty by Fromm's drumhead judges, taken downstairs to the courtyard of the War Ministry, and shot to death in the glare of automobile headlights. *See also* July 1944 Plot, Vol. 1; Operation Valkyrie; resistance movements, Germany, Vol. 2; Tresckow, Henning von, Vol. 3; Hitler, Hitler Promises Revenge for the July 1944 Plot, Vol. 4.

Stieff, Helmuth (1901–1944)

German army officer and a key participant in plots to assassinate Adolf Hitler. Stieff was born in Deutsch-Eylau, East Prussia, on June 6, 1901. He joined the German Imperial Army in 1917, at the age of sixteen, and served briefly in an artillery unit during World War I. He remained in the army after the war and became an officer in 1922. After the Nazis took power he worked with the General Staff. In 1942, at the rank of colonel, he was made head of the organizational branch of the High Command of the German armed forces (OKW).

Stieff was involved in plans to kill Hitler as early as September 1943, when he declared himself willing to place a bomb at Hitler's military headquarters at Rastenburg in East Prussia. Although he ultimately backed out, a few experimental explosives he had placed in a water tower at Rastenburg detonated, prompting Hitler to launch an investigation. Stieff later worked with Lieutenant Colonel Claus Schenk Graf von Stauffenberg, preparing for the July 1944 Plot. He assembled Stauffenberg's bomb and the two men flew to Rastenburg on the same plane. Stieff was arrested at Rastenburg soon after the bomb exploded. After a brutal Gestapo interrogation and a humiliating session before the specially convened People's Court, he was condemned to death for high treason. Along with several others Stieff was hanged by piano wire from a meat hook at Berlin's Plötzensee Prison on August 8, 1944. *See also* July 1944 Plot, Vol. 1; Rastenburg, Vol. 2; Stauffenberg, Claus Schenk Graf von, Vol. 3; Hitler, Hitler Promises Revenge for the July 1944 Plot, Vol. 4.

Stinnes, Hugo (1870–1924)

German industrialist who was an early financial supporter of the Nazi Party. Stinnes was born in Mühlheim on February 2, 1870. As a young man he began to build what became a huge industrial empire. By World War I it included coal mines, shipping lines, iron and steel plants, and a large stake in one of Germany's major energy suppliers. He also bought newspapers, whose editorial tones he modified to suit his conservative, nationalist views. During World War I his companies played a major role in sustaining Germany's war effort. He was a member of the Weimar Reichstag from 1920 until his death in 1924, representing the conservative German Nationalist People's Party. He also funneled a great deal of money to the fledgling Nazi Party in those years.

After the death of the senior Stinnes, the industrial empire was taken over by his sons, notably Hugo Stinnes Jr., who was born in 1897. Although financial difficulties forced a reorganization of the conglomerate in 1925, the Stinnes family still controlled huge enterprises. During the era of the Third Reich its businesses included coal mines, engineering concerns, shipping, and chemical plants. Although many suspect that the Stinnes conglomerate employed foreign workers and prison workers during World War II, investigators could never directly link Hugo Stinnes Jr. with Nazi atrocities.

Strasser, Gregor (1892–1934)

Adolf Hitler's top rival for leadership of the Nazi Party during its formative years. Along with his brother, Otto Strasser, he was the guiding force behind the northern wing of the party, which took seriously the "Socialist" aspects of the Nazi program. Gregor Strasser was born in the Bavarian village of Geisefeld on May 31, 1892. During World War I he fought with an artillery regiment, eventually achieving the rank of lieutenant. After the war he fought with the right-wing Freikorps in Bavaria, where he met Heinrich Himmler and established connections with General Erich Ludendorff. He also joined the Nazi Party and took a position as an SA squadron leader. During the Beer Hall Putsch of 1923 he was tasked with leading a contingent of SA men from the town of Landshut, where he maintained a pharmacist's shop, to Munich, where they joined the main group of rebels under Ludendorff and Hitler. After the putsch failed he was briefly jailed. In 1924, after his release from Munich's Landsberg Prison, where Hitler was also held, Strasser became cochairman of the Nazi Party along with Ludendorff. He continued to build a substantial base of support as a dedicated and decisive organizer, a convincing speaker, and a canny politician. He also took steps to marginalize possible rivals such as Hermann Esser, Hermann Göring, and Ernst Röhm.

From 1924 on Strasser was a full-time politician. Using money he made from selling his shop, he started two publications, first a Nazi newspaper entitled the *Berlin Worker's Newspaper*, edited by Otto Strasser, and second the *National Socialist Letters*, which was aimed at Nazi officials and intended for the making and explanation of policy. He called in a rootless would-be intellectual named Joseph Goebbels to help with the *Letters*. Beyond these regular publications the Strasser brothers started a publishing company, Struggle Publishers, which was based in Berlin. Meanwhile, Strasser was elected as a Nazi delegate to the Bavarian state legislature, giving him the time and freedom to travel widely to drum up support for his version of National Socialism. This interpretation was extremely different from the National Socialism that emerged under the Third Reich. Strasser argued, for example, that the capitalist system was one of Germany's greatest dangers, and that any Nazi state would have to take over both the banks and large industries in the interests of German workers. He also advocated an alliance with the Russian Communists as well as anti-imperialist forces throughout the world in seeking to overthrow western democracy and liberalism as well as capitalism. Strasser, moreover, strongly disapproved of Hitler's inclination to seek support among Germany's aristocrats, military officers, and industrialists, and he believed that his rival was far too unstable and unpredictable to be a viable political leader. Conflicts between the two rivals for Nazi leadership reached their first climax at a party conference held in February 1926 in Bamberg. Both Strasser brothers strongly defended their left-wing principles, but were forced to acquiesce to Hitler's demand that he remain the sole leader of the Nazi movement. Gregor Strasser found himself betrayed there by the nimble-minded Goebbels, who switched his allegiance to Hitler sometime during the conference. Nevertheless, the two Nazi chieftains reached an uneasy peace; while Hitler remained the party's overall Führer, Strasser was named Reich propaganda leader.

The struggle between Strasser and Hitler came to a head in the second half of 1932, just before the Nazi takeover of power. In the effort to increase his support among important political insiders and conservatives such as Franz von Papen and Alfred Hugenberg, Hitler had made it known that he would try to contain the left wing of the Nazi Party, led now not only by Gregor Strasser but by SA leader Ernst Röhm, whom Strasser disliked. Meanwhile, a number of politicians, most notably Kurt von Schleicher, turned to Strasser as a more palatable leader of the Nazi Party than Hitler. In December 1932 Schleicher, at that point German chancellor, offered Strasser a proposition: If he was willing to split the Nazi Party, he might become vice-chancellor as well as prime minister of Prussia. Strasser was somewhat sympathetic, since Schleicher's proposed coalition government was broad-based and seemed to offer a great deal to German workers. He did not, however, want to split the Nazi Party. Hitler learned of Schleicher's proposal and angrily accused Strasser of trying to stab him in the back. Strasser responded in kind, resigned all of his Nazi Party positions, and left for a family vacation in Italy. One month later, on January 30, 1933, Hitler took power as chancellor of Germany.

Strasser never rejoined the Nazi Party, taking work as a consultant with a chemical company. Hitler never asked him to become a member of the new government and replaced him with Rudolf Hess as the new political leader of the Nazi Party. The new chieftain of the left wing of the Nazi Party, to the extent that it existed, was Ernst Röhm, always more of a rabble-rouser and military leader than a politician. Although some reports allege that Strasser maintained contact with both Röhm and the ousted Kurt von Schleicher over the next months, he seems to have led a quiet life. Hitler nursed his grudge, however. On June 30, 1934, Strasser was one of the prime targets of the so-called Blood Purge, when Hitler rid himself once and for all of the danger of a leftist "second revolution" and settled some old scores. Strasser was arrested by the Gestapo and shot to death through the window of his prison cell. *See also* Bamberg Conference, Blood Purge, Vol. 1; Machtergreifung, Vol. 2; Strasser, Otto, Vol. 3.

Strasser, Otto (1897–1974)

A leader of the leftist wing of the Nazi Party in its early years along with his older brother Gregor Strasser. Otto Strasser was born in the southern German town of Windsheim on September 10, 1897. As a young man he studied law and joined the Social Democratic Party (SPD). The SPD strongly stood for the interests of German workers but was opposed to revolutionary communism. He switched to the Nazi Party in 1925, in which his brother had emerged as a leader, professing strong faith in the "socialist" aspects of the program of the National Socialist Party. Otto Strasser picked up the same tune, opposing Germany's aristocracy and big business, and claiming that the economy should be planned and managed by the state. In addition to his party activities he became the editor of the *Berlin Worker's Newspaper*, begun by his brother, and helped found Struggle Publishers, also with Gregor Strasser.

Otto Strasser was a more doctrinaire Socialist than his brother, less a politician than a thinker and writer, and by 1927 he had become a major target of Adolf Hitler's criticism. Hitler considered Strasser a Bolshevik and arranged to buy out the *Berlin Worker's Newspaper* and close it down. In May 1930, Hitler and Strasser had a final confrontation. The Führer demanded that Strasser submit to party discipline and devote his talents to spreading Nazi ideology. Strasser refused, and on July 4, 1930, he was expelled from the Nazi Party. Soon after he formed a splinter party known as the Union of Revolutionary National Socialists, or the Black Front. It failed to attract support among the German electorate, however, and he left for exile in Prague, Czechoslovakia.

During the 1930s Strasser remained an outspoken opponent of Hitler's ideology as well as a proponent of his own version of National Socialism. His initial efforts were published in a newspaper in Prague known as *The German Revolution*. Although he remained devoted to Socialist economic ideals, Strasser also professed a strong faith in ethnic German nationalism and anti-Semitism. He blamed Jews, in fact, along with Freemasons and Roman Catholic politicians, for subverting German nationhood. After Hitler took power he published a number of books highly critical of the Third Reich. These included *What Motivates Hitler?*, *The Construction of German*

Socialism, and *Hitler and I*. A fourth book, published in 1935 and entitled *The German St. Bartholomew's Night*, compared the Blood Purge of 1934, in which other rivals to Hitler, including his brother Gregor Strasser, were murdered, to a political and religious massacre in sixteenth-century France.

Otto Strasser spent the years of World War II in Switzerland and Canada, remaining in the latter country until 1955, when he returned to Germany. He remained an active writer, commenting on World War II, and the Nazi regime, and promoting a vision of a Europe united around Christian and National Socialist ideals. He also remained an outspoken anti-Semite. Strasser died in Munich on August 27, 1974. ***See also*** Black Front, Vol. 1; Strasser, Gregor, Vol. 3; Strasser, A Participant Remembers the Beer Hall Putsch of 1923, Vol. 4.

Streicher, Julius (1885–1946)

Nazi Old Fighter, Gauleiter of Franconia, and perhaps the most notorious anti-Semite in the Third Reich. Streicher was born in the Bavarian village of Fleinhausen on February 12, 1885. Like Streicher himself in later years, his father was a schoolteacher. He joined the German Imperial Army before World War I, provoking great criticism for bad behavior. During the war itself, however, he fought with distinction, was promoted to lieutenant, and was decorated for bravery. After the war he moved to Nuremberg, the capital of Franconia, and became an elementary school teacher. He also became involved in right-wing politics.

In 1919 Streicher formed a political party based almost entirely on blaming Jews for the nation's problems. In 1921 he transferred the entire membership of his party to Adolf Hitler's National Socialist German Worker's Party, becoming himself one of Hitler's closest comrades. In 1925 he was named Gauleiter of Franconia, with offices in Nuremberg, and in 1929 he was elected to the Nazi delegation to the Bavarian state legislature. He had been dismissed from his teaching position in 1928 for overenthusiastically bringing his political views into the classroom. He required his students, for instance, to start the day with a rousing "Heil Hitler!" Streicher also traveled widely through his district, making speeches and drumming up support for the Nazi movement. Streicher's greatest fame, however, came from the weekly newspaper he founded in 1923 and continued to edit until 1945, *Der Stürmer* (roughly, *The Storm Trooper*). The paper became one of the most notorious Nazi publications, attracting attention both within Germany and worldwide for its violent anti-Semitism, crude language, and pornography. In its pages Streicher himself and other authors criticized Jews as well as those Germans deemed insufficiently anti-Semitic, and long before the Nuremberg Laws of 1935 he called for banning Jews from public places. In cartoons, Jewish caricatures were drawn leering obscenely at nuns and "good German girls," as well as hoarding wealth away from starving Germans. The paper even printed lists of Jewish professionals and merchants so that readers would know whom to avoid. Over the years *Der Stürmer* became extremely popular throughout Germany. By 1937 its circulation had reached five hundred thousand, helped along by streetside display cases, a relatively new innovation in newspaper sales. Adolf Hitler approved of Streicher's methods, although he understood that they alienated large numbers of people. He felt that Streicher's crude anti-Semitism was a powerful influence particularly on ordinary Germans. Streicher, for his part, claimed that *Der Stürmer*, probably falsely, was the only newspaper Hitler ever read cover to cover.

Meanwhile, Streicher continued to enjoy Hitler's favor and indulgence. In 1933 Streicher was named head of a committee organized within the Nazi Party to combat Jewish propaganda. He also became a member of the national Reichstag and an SA general.

Julius Streicher (front row, fourth from left) poses with other members of the fledgling Nazi Party in 1922. Streicher published the virulently anti-Semitic Der Stürmer.

Streicher also grew wealthy in the years before World War II. The basis of his wealth was his extremely popular newspaper, but he expanded his financial empire to include ten other newspapers. He also took great advantage of the "Aryanization" program of the late 1930s in which Jewish properties and businesses were appropriated by Nazi authorities for pittances and then turned over to German businessmen.

In the end, however, Streicher's wealth, notoriety, and friendship with Hitler did not make up for his repellent personality and corrupt, psychopathic behavior. He had strange sexual habits and obsessions and was known for whipping prisoners and ruling Nuremberg through intimidation. His accusations and taunts were directed against top Nazis as well as Jews; he derided Hermann Göring, for instance, for his supposed impotence and spread stories that one of Göring's daughters was the result of artificial insemination. By 1939 numerous Nazi officials complained to Hitler about Streicher's abusive, irrational behavior and Hitler responded, in 1940, by banning him from public speaking. Göring, meanwhile, mounted an investigation into Streicher's personal habits and business dealings, which resulted in Streicher being stripped of his Nazi Party posts, including Gauleiter of Franconia.

For the remainder of the era of the Third Reich, however, Streicher continued to publish *Der Stürmer*. Although its circulation dropped substantially, it remained fairly popular and its editorial tone remained virulently anti-Semitic. The paper was unusual in that it mentioned, publicly and approvingly, the extermination actions taking place against Jews in occupied Poland and the Soviet Union. In late 1945, Streicher was among the twenty-one top Nazis brought before the International Military Tribunal convened in his former fiefdom of Nuremberg. Although the tribunal was unable to connect Streicher with crimes against peace or even war crimes, he was found guilty of crimes against humanity for continually inciting Germans to murder Jews during World War II. The tribunal sentenced him to death. During his trial Streicher showed no remorse whatsoever, and as he approached the gallows set up at the Nuremberg prison on October 16, 1946, he denounced the proceedings as a "Jewish festival" (Purimfest). His last words were "Heil Hitler!" *See also* anti-Semitism, Vol. 1; Nuremberg trials, Old Fighters, *Der Stürmer*, Vol. 2; International Military Tribunal, The Charges Against the Surviving Nazi Leaders, Vol. 4.

Stroop, Jürgen (1895–1951)

SS officer who crushed the Jewish uprising in the Warsaw ghetto in April and May 1942. Stroop was born Josef Stroop in Detmold, Germany, in 1895, changing his name to Jürgen in 1941. He was brought up in a lower-middle-class family and fought as an enlisted man in World War I. After the Nazis took power he became an SS policeman, rising to the level of SS major general by 1939. He was ideologically devoted to the Nazi movement, believing fully in anti-Semitism, territorial expansion, and racial purification. Early in World War II Stroop was stationed in the occupied territories of eastern Europe, where he was involved in efforts to subdue local civilian populations rather than strictly military duties.

In early 1943 Stroop was called to Warsaw from his base in Lemberg. He was assigned the task of "pacifying" the Warsaw ghetto, where in mid-January groups of Jews had mounted armed resistance to Nazi efforts to conduct deportations in the process of "liquidating" the ghetto. His forces, which included SS units, a few Wehrmacht contingents, and Polish and Ukrainian auxiliaries, moved into the ghetto on April 19, where they too faced stiff resistance. Stroop had anticipated subduing and emptying the ghetto within a few days and expressed surprise at the Jewish fighters' stubborn guerrilla warfare tactics. For the next twenty-seven days he waged a building-by-building battle that ultimately cleared and virtually razed the ghetto. On May 16, after dynamiting the great Tlomatskie synagogue in a symbolic gesture (the synagogue stood outside the ghetto walls), Stroop cabled his SS superiors in Berlin with the message: "The Jewish quarter in Warsaw is no more" (Shirer, 1960). He later compiled an extensive report detailing his efforts in Warsaw, including daily communications and photographs of Jews surrendering from their bunkers. The report was later published under the title *The Stroop Report* in postwar Poland and West Germany.

After his "success" in Warsaw, Stroop was awarded the Iron Cross, First Class, and sent to Greece, where he served as an SS police commander, returning to his duties of controlling the populations of occupied countries. After the war he was arrested and interned. An American tribunal meeting at Dachau and charged with trying SS war criminals found him guilty of shooting prisoners of war in Greece and sentenced him to death. Soon after, he was extradited to Poland, where he was hanged as a war criminal on September 8, 1951. *See also* Warsaw ghetto uprising, Vol. 2.

Stuckart, Wilhelm (1902–1953)

Jurist and official in the Third Reich's Interior Ministry who helped devise the Nuremberg Laws, as well as other measures, in the attempt to give Nazi anti-Semitism a basis in law. Stuckart was born in Wiesbaden on November 16, 1902. He studied law at the Universities of Munich and Frankfurt and, during the early 1920s, took part in Freikorps efforts against the French occupation of the Ruhr. The French imprisoned him twice. Stuckart joined the Nazi Party in 1922 and became one of its earliest legal advisers. He also entered government service, serving for a time as a judge in Wiesbaden (before he was dismissed because of his Nazism) and as acting mayor of Stettin in Prussia. After the Nazis took power he became an official in the Prussian Ministry of

Education as well as a Prussian state councillor. In March 1935 he took up the post of secretary of state in the Interior Ministry, where he devoted his efforts to exploring the legal aspects of racial ideology.

Stuckart was one of the authors of the two Nuremberg Laws, announced by Hitler at the Nazi Party rally in Nuremberg in September 1935. These two measures denied Jews their rights of German citizenship and made "race mixing" a crime. Later measures that gradually took away the individual rights of German Jews were based on the Nuremberg Laws. Stuckart's argument, explained in a book assembled with a colleague, Hans Globke, and entitled *Commentary on German Racial Legislation*, was that the Third Reich was the realization of the German Volk, or ethnic community. Therefore it was impossible for those not ethnically German to be members of the German Volk and, by extension, citizens of the Third Reich. Stuckart also involved himself in discussions over the various categories of Mischlinge, or persons of mixed parentage.

During World War II Stuckart continued to use legal categories to justify Nazi racial measures, particulary in the occupied territories in eastern Europe. He was the logical representative of the Interior Ministry at the infamous Wannsee Conference of January 1942, where Reinhard Heydrich made it plain that, under SS authority, mass extermination was to be the "Final Solution to the Jewish Question." There, Stuckart voiced concerns over what was to be done with the Mischlinge, since to kill them would be to shed valuable German, in addition to useless Jewish, blood. Although the question was not settled definitively at Wannsee, Stuckart did proclaim himself willing to settle for the sterilization of those with mixed parentage. Stuckart was also appointed to an honorary SS generalship during the war and became head of the SS Commission for the Protection of German Blood.

Stuckart was arrested in 1945 by Allied occupation authorities and interned until his trial in 1949 by an American war crimes tribunal. The tribunal was unable to definitively connect Stuckart to wartime atrocities, and was in effect forced to accept his bald assertion that he knew nothing of deportations or exterminations. He was sentenced to the four years already served and released in 1949. Stuckart was killed in an automobile accident near Hanover in December 1953. Some reports suggest that the accident was actually the work of a gang bent on revenge for Nazi crimes. ***See also*** judicial system in the Third Reich, Vol. 1; Mischlinge, Nuremberg Laws, Wannsee Conference, Vol. 2; The Nuremberg Laws, Vol. 4.

Stuelpnagel, Karl Heinrich von (1886–1944)

Military governor of occupied France and an important participant in the July 1944 Plot on Adolf Hitler's life. Stuelpnagel was born in Darmstadt on January 2, 1886, to a traditional military family; his cousin Otto was a fellow army and occupation officer. Although as a traditional officer trained in philosophy and service Stuelpnagel was opposed to the Nazi movement, he served his nation and his army diligently. From November 1938 to June 1940 he was quartermaster general with the General Staff of the Wehrmacht. He also headed up the German-French commission charged with devising the armistice between the two countries in June 1940. During the invasion of the Soviet Union he commanded the Seventeenth Army. In March 1942 he was called back to Paris to take over from Otto von Stuelpnagel as military governor of occupied France.

Stuelpnagel considered Adolf Hitler and the Nazis a blight on Germany's honor and history, and was involved in plots against him as early as 1939. During the planning for the July Plot, he was given the task of arresting German occupation officers in France and turning local regular military forces over to the conspirators. Under his command, in fact, nearly twelve hundred Gestapo and SS men were detained in

France early on July 20. When he received word that the plot had failed, he destroyed his papers and calmly waited for his arrest. After being told by General Wilhelm Keitel to return to Berlin by air, he set out by car. Along the way, shortly after leaving Paris, he tried to kill himself, unsuccessfully. Gravely wounded by a self-inflicted gunshot wound to the face and throat, Stuelpnagel was taken to Berlin. He was hanged in Plötzensee Prison on August 30, 1944. *See also* July 1944 Plot, Vol. 1; resistance movements, Germany, Vol. 2.

Stuelpnagel, Otto von (1878–1948)

Military governor of occupied France from 1940 to 1942. Stuelpnagel was born in Berlin on June 16, 1878, to a traditional Prussian officer-class family. He joined the German Imperial Army as a junior officer in 1898, and during World War I he acquired a reputation for brutality and even criminal behavior. He remained in the army after World War I and allegedly joined a group of officers interested in mounting a coup against the Weimar Republic. A supporter of the Nazi movement, he was called out of retirement in the late 1930s and named general of infantry.

In October 1940 he was named military governor of occupied France, occupying the post until February 1942, when he was replaced by his cousin Karl Heinrich von Stuelpnagel. Otto von Stuelpnagel, who set up his headquarters in a chateau outside Paris, imposed a harsh occupation by any measure, employing curfews, random punishments, public humiliation, and deportations to Germany, and ordering extreme reprisals for French underground activity. In one instance, the killing of a German officer resulted in the murder of twenty-two French hostages. In another, dozens of imprisoned Jews and Communists were killed in reprisal for underground attacks. After leaving Paris, Stuelpnagel retired to Germany After the war he was captured by Allied forces and turned over to the French for trial. He hanged himself in a Paris prison on February 6, 1948, before his trial could begin. *See also* Stuelpnagel, Karl Heinrich von, Vol. 3.

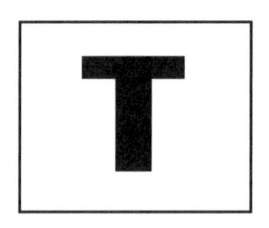

Terboven, Josef (1898–1945)

Reich commissioner for occupied Norway during World War II. Terboven was born in Essen on May 23, 1898. He served as a junior officer during the latter part of World War I, relocating to Munich after the war and working as a bank clerk. He joined the Nazi Party in 1928 and took a position with the SA. Over the next years Terboven acquired the attention and approval of Adolf Hitler, who attended his wedding in 1934. In 1933 Terboven was appointed to the Prussian state council and to the position of Gauleiter of Essen. In 1935 he became the chief Nazi Party official, or "overpresident," of the Rhine province.

After the Germans invaded Norway in April 1940, the Norwegian collaborator Vidkun Quisling named himself prime minister of the new, pro-Nazi regime. Hitler, however, distrusted Quisling, and on April 24 he named Terboven Reich commissioner for Norway. Since the country had not yet been fully conquered, and since Norway's harbors and natural resources were vital to the Third Reich's war effort, General Wilhelm Keitel argued that control of Norway should remain with the army. Hitler overrode him and placed Terboven, now an SA general, in the post. For the next five years Terboven ruled Norway with a cruel hand, dealing harshly with resistance fighters and their sympathizers as well as with Norwegian civilians who questioned German authority. He was responsible for rounding up much of the nation's small Jewish community and deporting them to Germany, and he presided over the takeover of the Norwegian economy by the Nazis. Terboven reportedly committed suicide in Oslo in May 1945. *See also* Weser Exercise, Vol. 2; Quisling, Vidkun, Vol. 3.

Thälmann, Ernst (1886–1944)

Leader of the German Communist Party (KPD) in the years prior to the establishment of the Third Reich. Thälmann was born in Hamburg on April 16, 1886, into a working-class family. He was employed as a transport worker in Hamburg, politically a predominantly left-leaning city, and he joined the Social Democratic Party (SPD) in 1903. Soon after he became active in the city's trade unions. During World War I, when the SPD splintered, Thälmann allied himself to the Independent Social Democratic Party, which opposed the German war effort. He switched to the new German Communist Party, part of the Communist International, in 1919 and quickly rose to a position of leadership. He became a member of the party's central committee in 1921 and a KPD delegate to the Weimar Reichstag in 1924. Sympathetic to the Bolshevik regime in Russia, Thälmann supported an abortive Communist uprising in Hamburg in 1923, and as a Reichstag delegate tried to ensure that the KPD worked in concert with Moscow, not always successfully. He emerged as an international Communist leader as well, serving in high posts with the Communist International in the vague effort to foment international revolution under guidance from Moscow.

During the early 1930s Thälmann was one of Adolf Hitler's greatest political enemies. As early as 1926 the Communist politician had sponsored Communist street

Ernst Thälmann (foreground), head of the German Communist Party, was arrested as an enemy of the Nazi state and killed in Buchenwald in 1944.

gangs ready to do battle with Hitler's SA and SS. By 1931 Thälmann was working hard to accomplish the overthrow of the Weimar regime, and he never grasped the danger that the Nazis represented to his movement or the growing support among German workers for the Nazi Party. In presidential elections held in March 1932, Thälmann received nearly 5 million votes to Hitler's 11.5 million (the winner was Paul von Hindenburg, who received well over 18 million votes), but almost until the Nazi takeover Thälmann considered the Social Democrats his greatest threat. Hitler, in contrast, considered communism one of the major threats to the new Germany he hoped to build, and Thälmann was placed high on his list of political foes. After the Reichstag fire of February 27,

1933, which Hitler blamed on the Communists, Thälmann was arrested as an enemy of the state. He spent the next ten years in the Nazi prison and concentration camp system and was killed in Buchenwald on August 28, 1944. *See also* German Communist Party, Vol. 1; Machtergreifung, Reichstag fire, Vol. 2.

Thierack, Otto Georg (1889–1946)

President of the Berlin People's Court from 1936 to 1942 and, from 1942 to 1945, Reich minister of justice. Thierack's legal opinions helped Nazi leaders justify measures ranging from granting Adolf Hitler absolute power to forcing prisoners of war to perform slave labor to allowing the SS to indiscriminately murder those deemed to be "asocial." Thierack was born in the town of Würzen in eastern Germany on April 19, 1889. He studied at the Universities of Marburg and Leipzig and earned a law degree just prior to World War I. During the war he served as a junior officer, then returned to Leipzig, where he became a public prosecutor. He joined the Nazi Party in the early 1920s and served with the Nazi lawyers' league.

After the Nazis took power in 1933 Thierack's star rose quickly. He was named minister of justice for Saxony in 1933 and in 1935 was appointed to the German Supreme Court. From 1936 to 1942 he presided over the People's Court in Berlin, a special court that met irregularly and in private to deal with Germans who were determined to be disloyal or traitorous to the Third Reich. In 1942 Thierack, by now an honorary SS general, was appointed Reich minister of justice, the highest legal office in Nazi Germany. In that capacity he worked closely with Hitler and his advisers to expand the Nazi system of justice, which rendered earlier law irrelevant. In addition to providing the legal basis for Hitler's absolute authority over all Germans, Thierack concerned himself intently with Nazi racial goals. Top officials such as Goebbels and Himmler looked to him to provide the legal justification for the use of slave laborers (who were expected to be worked to death) as well as the deportation and abuse of prisoners. Thierack also supported Nazi racial measures in eastern Europe by arguing, for instance, that it was much more sensible to allow the peoples of the region to die (usually at the hands of the SS) than keep them for years in prisons. At war's end Thierack was arrested and interned by Allied forces but hanged himself, on October 16, 1946, before he could be brought to trial for war crimes. *See also* judicial system in the Third Reich, Vol. 1; People's Court, Vol. 2.

Thyssen, Fritz (1873–1951)

Leading German industrialist and one of the top financial backers of Adolf Hitler and the Nazi Party until, in the late 1930s, he started to distance himself from the regime. Thyssen was born in Mühlheim in the Ruhr on November 9, 1873. His father, August Thyssen, was one of the wealthiest men in imperial Germany and a devout Roman Catholic. Fritz Thyssen shared his father's Catholicism but, after World War I and the Treaty of Versailles, lent his political support to extreme German nationalism. He was a strong opponent, for example, of the French occupation on the Ruhr in the years immediately after the war and donated large sums of money to antioccupation efforts. His efforts resulted in an inconclusive court-martial at the hands of the French.

In 1923 Thyssen heard Hitler speak and was very impressed by the Nazi leader's ability to sway an audience as well as what appeared to be the discipline of his followers. He made a substantial donation of one hundred thousand marks to the party. Subsequent conversations with Hitler convinced the industrialist that the Nazis were Germany's best bet to prevent the spread of communism; according to Thyssen, Hitler intimated that he was interested in a revival of the monarchy rather than a totalitarian dictatorship. Thyssen had little faith in democracy, arguing that it could never work in Germany, and a highly conservative, traditional system of government was much more to his liking. Over the next decade Thyssen continued to contribute money to the Nazi movement and was one of its chief financial backers. Meanwhile along with his father he helped found Germany's largest steel conglomerate, the United Steel Works, and became the head of the International Steel Society.

Thyssen joined the Nazi Party formally in December 1931, an era when traditional German conservatives, epitomized by Alfred Hugenberg's German Nationalist People's Party, were tying themselves to the Nazis. Over the next months Thyssen used his contacts and influence among Rhineland industrialists to provide further financial and political backing for Hitler.

After the Nazis took power in 1933 Thyssen became, for a time, a Nazi official. He was appointed to the Prussian state council, the Reichstag, as well as to the chairmanship of a Nazi think tank for economic research. By 1935, however, the industrialist and heir to his family's huge fortune began to suspect that he had been misled by Adolf Hitler. He had always been unhappy with the regime's anti-Catholicism, but now began to question the growing oppression of Jews in addition to the top-down emphasis on rearmament, although such measures were good for his businesses. He was also struck by the incompetence or corruption of many of the top officials in the Nazi state, including Labor Front leader Robert Ley. After the Kristallnacht pogrom of November 1938, which shocked him deeply, he resigned as a Prussian state councillor and spoke out against war in the Reichstag. When Hitler's alliance with the Communist Soviet Union was announced on August 23, 1939, Thyssen decided he had seen enough. He left for exile in Switzerland, writing Hitler a letter that explained his decision and his disillusionment with the Nazi movement. Hitler responded to the letter by ousting Thyssen from the Nazi Party, stripping him of his German citizenship, and appropriating his property.

During World War II Thyssen was captured in France by officials of the collaborationist Vichy regime. Along with his wife, he was turned over to the Germans, and the two spent the remaining war years in concentration camps. After the war he regained much of his family fortune but chose exile in Argentina to life in a devastated, defeated Germany. He died in Buenos Aires on February 8, 1951. *See also* business in the Third Reich, IG Farben, Vol. 1; Flick, Friedrich; Keppler, Wilhelm, Vol. 3.

Todt, Fritz (1891–1942)

Technocrat, SS officer, and Reich minister of armaments from 1940 to 1942. The son of a local industrialist, Todt was born in Pforzheim in southwestern Germany on September 4, 1891. He embarked on a career as an engineer but World War I interrupted his studies at a technical institute in Munich. During the war he served as a field soldier and technical observer. After the war he completed his studies at an institute in Karlsruhe and then took a job as a civil engineer.

Todt joined the Nazi Party on January 5, 1922. Rising fairly quickly, and gravitating toward the SS, where young technocrats and intellectuals were welcomed, he was appointed to Heinrich Himmler's staff at the rank of SS colonel in 1931. After the Nazis took power he was named inspector general of German roads. From this relatively humble base Todt steadily expanded his responsibilities until he was the most important engineer in the Third Reich. He put together a large, loosely organized construction group known as the Todt Organization, which played the major role in the Third Reich's construction projects. Among the most noteworthy were the autobahns, Germany's network of highways, and the so-called western wall (or Siegfried line), a system of defenses. Meanwhile, he also took charge of power plants and water transportation. As war approached and the importance of roads, defenses, and communications lines grew, the Todt Organization was given free rein to use labor from virtually any source, including forced labor from concentration camps.

Todt was named Reich minister of armaments in March 1940. He continued to enjoy the favor and appreciation of Adolf Hitler despite disagreements with other top Nazis; until his death, in fact, he tried to remain aloof from politics and simply attend to his technical tasks. He was also named head of the Nazi Office for Technology. As minister of armaments Todt's responsibilities expanded to include the construction of western defenses known as the Atlantic Wall and a network of U-boat pens along the Atlantic Ocean and English Channel. He was also ordered to build a road network across occupied Europe and reorganize the Soviet railway system in coordination with the German one. As the months passed Todt began to believe that the military campaign in the Soviet Union was hopeless, but he remained a loyal Nazi technocrat. He died in an airplane crash in East Prussia on February 8, 1942. Most of his offices and responsibilites were transferred to the young, untested Albert Speer. *See also* Atlantic Wall, autobahns, Vol. 1; Todt Organization, Vol. 2.

Tojo, Hideki (1884–1948)

Army general who served as prime minister of Japan during most of World War II, and who in Allied propaganda ranked with Adolf Hitler and Benito Mussolini as leaders of enemy states, although unlike his counterparts he was not a totalitarian dictator. Tojo was born in the Japanese capital of Tokyo in 1884. A career officer, he achieved prominence in the 1930s as the chief of staff to the Kwantung army, the Japanese army of occupation in Manchuria. Like a number of other Japanese officers, Tojo believed that military needs should outweigh political or cultural considerations, and that the Japanese should not hesitate to use military force to ensure access to vital raw materials. As he grew more prominent in Japan, top-level Japanese decision making increasingly followed this line. He played a key role in instigating the so-called Second Chinese-Japanese War (1937–1945), which clearly signaled to the western Allies that Japan harbored aggressive intentions.

In 1940 Tojo was appointed minister of war under Prime Minister Prince Fumimaro Konoye, who favored peaceful negotiation over militarism. He helped to formulate the Tripartite Pact, a defensive agreement that cemented the alliance among the so-called Axis Powers: Japan, the Third Reich, and Fascist Italy. In October Konoye was forced to resign over the refusal of Tojo and other militarist officers to withdraw from China as well as their desire to occupy French Indochina (later Vietnam, Laos, and Cambodia). Tojo replaced him, ready to respond to American and British embargoes of essential raw materials, especially oil, with acts of war. When talks with American diplomats proved fruitless, he ordered the surprise bombing attack on Pearl Habor, Hawaii, on December 7, 1941, which brought the United States into World War II. Although he was seeking a pretext anyway, Adolf Hitler cited the Tripartite Pact when he declared war on the United States on December 9.

For the next three years Tojo served not only as prime minister but also as minister of war and chief of staff of the army. He was therefore responsible for all Japanese military and political decisions. He enjoyed a large measure of public support in 1942, when Japanese victories were frequent, but his popularity waned when, in 1943, the tide of war turned against him. Tojo resigned from his posts on July 18, 1944, when American forces captured the Pacific Ocean island of Saipan. After unsuccessfully attempting suicide after the Japanese surrender in August 1945, Tojo was arrested by Allied forces as a war criminal. He was one of seven Japanese war criminals sentenced to death and was hanged on December 23, 1948. *See also* allies of the Third Reich, Axis Powers, Vol. 1; Pearl Harbor, Vol. 2.

Tresckow, Henning von (1901–1944)

German army general and leader of the resistance movement. Tresckow was born into a Prussian military family in Magdeburg on January 10, 1901. After working on a family agricultural estate and in the stock market he joined the Weimar-era Reichswehr in 1924. Like many of his class and background, Tresckow initially sympathized with the Nazi Party's desire to repudiate the Treaty of Versailles and restore Germany's high status among nations. He served with distinction in the early battles of World War II, fighting as a staff officer with an infantry division in Poland and France. He was promoted to major general after the invasion of the Soviet Union in the summer of 1941, where he served as chief of staff to General Fedor von Bock in Army Group Center. While serving in the east he came to the conclusion that the German effort against Soviet Russia was hopeless, that the Nazi regime would lead his nation to ruin, and that the assassination of Hitler was necessary. Tresckow made it plain that he himself was willing to kill the Führer, and began to plan independent assassination attempts as early as late 1942. He tried to persuade Bock and other top officers on the eastern front to join him, but only a few younger officers committed themselves. His strongest supporter was his aide, Fabian von Schlabrendorff, a fellow young aristocrat.

Tresckow's first attempt on Hitler's life took place on March 13, 1943, when he planted a bomb on an airplane returning Hitler to Germany from Smolensk in Russia. The bomb failed to go off and Tresckow was forced to quickly disarm the device himself. Undeterred, Tresckow continued to explore other avenues by which he could get close enough to Hitler to kill him. By the end of 1943 he had also established contact with Lieutenant Colonel Claus Schenk Graf von Stauffenberg, a key figure in the resistance movement and the designated assassin during the July 1944 Plot. Tresckow was forced to languish in his post on the eastern front while the July Plot developed under Stauffenberg's guidance. He tried on a number of occasions to have himself transferred to the staff of General Friedrich Erich von Manstein, which would have given him regular access to Hitler at military conferences, but Manstein refused to take him on. Nevertheless, Tresckow played a central role in the July Plot by committing the army in the east to supporting a new, post-Hitler regime.

When news of the failure of the July Plot reached him, Tresckow decided to commit suicide rather than risk implicating others under torture. His final statement to Schlabrendorff became well known in postwar Germany. In it, Tresckow reassured his young friend that they had acted correctly in trying to rid Germany of the Hitler regime. He hoped that the conspirators' gesture would restore a shred of his nation's honor. Finally, he asserted that "the worth of a man is certain only if he is prepared to sacrifice his life for what he believes" (Wistrich, 1995). On July 21, 1944, Tresckow marched to the front lines and fired a weapon to draw fire. When none came he killed himself with a hand grenade. *See also* Operation Flash; resistance movements, Germany, Vol. 2.

Troost, Paul Ludwig (1878–1934)

Adolf Hitler's favorite architect until his death in 1934. Troost was born in Wuppertal in western Germany on August 17, 1878. He was a forerunner of modernism in architecture, favoring simple lines and minimal ornamentation. He became affiliated with the Nazi movement in 1930 when Hitler, expressing admiration for Troost's simple, classical style, gave him a commission to redesign the so-called Brown House, the Nazi Party headquarters in Munich. In later

A large-scale model of Munich's House of German Art, designed by German architect and Hitler favorite Paul Ludwig Troost.

years Troost received commissions to design the Berlin Reichs Chancellery and the House of German Art. The latter, constructed in Munich after his death, became the center of Nazi painting. Hitler, who thought of himself as an architect whose talents and ideas had gone unappreciated in his youth, seemed to genuinely enjoy his frequent meetings with Troost. Troost died of illness on March 23, 1934, remembered by Hitler as both a great architect and a great German. He was replaced as the unofficial architect of the Third Reich by the young Albert Speer. *See also* arts and architecture in the Third Reich, House of German Art, Vol. 1; Speer, Albert, Vol. 3.

Trott zu Solz, Adam von (1909–1944)

Official in the German Foreign Office and the Abwehr, the intelligence section of the High Command of the German armed forces (OKW). He was an important figure in the German resistance movement. Trott zu Solz was born in the Berlin suburb of Potsdam on August 9, 1909. His family were German aristocrats who had provided their nation with diplomats and civil servants for generations. His father had served as minister of education in Prussia. His mother's family was half-American and included John Jay, the first chief justice of the Supreme Court, among its forebears. During his youth Trott zu Solz studied at Oxford University as a Rhodes scholar; friends he made there proved to be important contacts in Great Britain for the resistance movement. He completed his legal studies in Germany and worked as a lawyer and scholar before joining the German Foreign Office in 1939.

Trott zu Solz believed in a strong Germany, but he was opposed to Adolf Hitler and the Nazi regime. Even before the onset of World War II he had emerged as one of the leaders of the ideological resistance to Hitler, at least among young aristocrats. His sympathies were largely based in a strong Christian faith and on what he perceived as the insults to individual dignity and human decency represented by Hitler's totalitarian regime. He also hoped to prevent a war between Germany and Great Britain. In 1938 he made a diplomatic visit to Washington, D.C., to sound out sympathy for anti-Hitler Germans. In June 1939 he went under official cover to England, where he met with both Prime Minister Neville Chamberlain and Foreign Secretary Lord Halifax. He reported back that Germany should remove its forces from Bohemia and Moravia if the Nazis wanted to preserve the peace. Hitler ignored the advice.

During World War II Trott zu Solz continued his diplomatic activities on behalf of the resistance. The British, however, and in time the Americans, hesitated to take him seriously, unsure if he was a double agent and opposed to his position that Germany should be allowed to retain Hitler's territorial acquisitions. Moreover, on at least one occasion he asserted that the resistance might seek a deal with the Soviets if they failed to get one from the western Allies.

After the failure of the July 1944 Plot, Trott zu Solz was swept up in Hitler's wide net of vengeance. He was arrested by the Gestapo and tried by the People's Court for high treason against the German Reich. Condemned to death, he was hanged in Berlin's Plötzensee Prison on August 26, 1944. *See also* Kreisau Circle, Vol. 1; Moltke, Helmuth James Graf von, Vol. 3.

Truman, Harry S. (1884–1972)

President of the United States at the end of World War II. Truman was born in Lamar, Missouri, on May 8, 1884. After failing to gain entrance to the U.S. Military Academy at West Point, he attended a local business college before going into business for himself, unsuccessfully. During the latter months of World War I he served as a lieutenant with an infantry company, and he remained in the army reserves after the war.

Truman entered Missouri politics in 1922 and became a U.S. senator from that state in 1934. In the Senate he paid particular attention to waste and fraud in government spending, as chair of the Interstate Commerce Commission, where he gained a reputation as being tough but honest and fair. In 1940, when American defense spending was on the rise, Truman turned his attention to waste and corruption in that sector, forming the Committee to Investigate the National Defense Program, or the Truman Committee. Over the next years it helped to streamline war production and save the U.S. government billions of dollars.

At the 1944 Democratic National Convention, Truman was accepted as a compromise running mate to President Franklin D. Roosevelt, who was running for his fourth term of office. Truman's national reputation for honesty helped greatly. He had served only eighty-three days as vice president, however, when Eleanor Roosevelt, the president's wife, informed him on April 13, 1945, that Franklin Roosevelt had died.

When Truman took office, the Third Reich had been almost entirely defeated. On April 30 Adolf Hitler committed suicide and on May 8 Germany surrendered unconditionally to the Allies. Truman proclaimed May 8 Victory in Europe Day, VE Day. In July, Truman left for Germany for a conference in the Berlin suburb of Potsdam with Joseph Stalin, premier of the Soviet Union, and Clement Attlee, like himself a successor to a wartime leader as the new prime minister of Great Britain. Partly because two of the Big Three, as the Allied leaders were known, were new, the Potsdam Conference accomplished little more than to confirm what had already been decided at earlier meetings among Stalin, Roosevelt, and Winston Churchill. While at Potsdam, Truman received the news that American scientists had successfully tested an atomic bomb. He quickly gave the order to use such a bomb to end the war with Japan. One was dropped on Hiroshima on August 6, and a second on Nagasaki on August 9. Japan finally agreed to unconditional surrender terms on August 14, and World War II finally ended on August 15 with what Truman proclaimed to be Victory in Japan Day, VJ Day.

Truman was reelected president, to many Americans' surprise, in 1948, and was succeeded by the war hero Dwight D. Eisenhower and his Republican Administration in January 1953. As president Truman presided over the beginning of the Cold War, when West Germany went from being an enemy to an ally and the Soviet Union, from an ally to an enemy. Truman died in retirement in Independence, Missouri, on December 26, 1972. *See also* Potsdam Conference, Vol. 2.

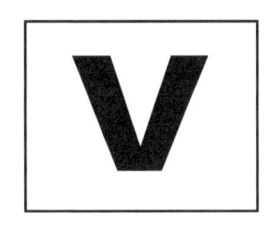

van der Lubbe, Marinus (1909–1934)

Dutch vagrant who was found guilty, deservedly or not, of setting the infamous Reichstag fire of February 1933, an event that greatly helped the Nazis consolidate power in Germany. Marinus van der Lubbe was born in Leyden on January 13, 1909. He worked occasionally as a bricklayer and expressed a vague interest in Socialist and anarchist politics, but he spent much of his time simply wandering from place to place. In 1933 he was in Berlin, living mostly in homeless shelters and thought to be mentally unstable or deficient.

On February 27, 1933, when the Reichstag fire took place, van der Lubbe was found inside the burning building by police, babbling and partially undressed. He later confessed to the police, who were newly under the authority of Hermann Göring, that he alone had set the rather complicated blaze. The confession worked to the advantage of the Nazis, who claimed that van der Lubbe carried a Communist Party identification card and spread the rumor that the fire was a signal to begin a Communist uprising in Germany. The event allowed the new chancellor, Adolf Hitler, to proclaim a state of emergency and suspend a variety of democratic rights and freedoms. He also took advantage of the circumstances to ban the German Communist Party (KPD), giving the Nazis an absolute majority in the shrunken Reichstag.

The arrests of other German Communists, including the head of the KPD, Ernst Torgler, proved unfruitful to police investigators, and van der Lubbe was put on trial by the Leipzig Supreme Court at the end of 1933. He was found guilty of arson and treason and sentenced to death, the Nazis having passed a special law justifying his execution. Van der Lubbe was executed by guillotine in Leipzig on January 10, 1934. The Nazis refused to return his body to his family in the Netherlands.

Van der Lubbe's true involvement in the Reichstag fire has never been conclusively determined. Although he admitted he acted alone, a confession backed up by the policemen who interrogated him during their trial testimony, certain factors made the notion that the Dutchman acted alone seem unlikely. For instance, the fire was determined to have been started by materials placed throughout the building; one location was directly connected to Göring's offices. Moreover, the Dutchman was found to be partially blind, and many felt that he was not mentally capable of either conceiving of or carrying out such a plan by himself. Finally, during the trial itself, van der Lubbe was barely coherent and could not recall what he had supposedly admitted to police investigators, leading some to think the Nazis had drugged the poor man and used him as a dupe from the very beginning. ***See also*** Reichstag fire, Vol. 2.

Wagner, Richard (1813–1883)

German composer and writer. His operas, many of which were based on themes from ancient or medieval Germanic mythology, served as the sound track at Nazi Party rallies and other events, and he was Adolf Hitler's favorite composer. Nazi ideologists also found in his German nationalism and occasional anti-Semitism justification for their own agenda.

Wagner was born in Leipzig on May 22, 1813, and studied conducting at the local university. In 1833 he accepted his first important position as conductor of the Magdeburg Opera. His first operas were written in traditional styles but with the composition of *The Flying Dutchman* (1841) and *Lohengrin* (1848), he began to find his own voice and build a reputation as one of the nineteenth century's greatest musicians. Unlike many other opera composers, Wagner wrote his own texts, or librettos, his goal being not simply musical entertainment but rather transcendent music-dramas. He believed his works should be built on grand themes, and that his music should reflect those themes. His greatest works include, in addition to the above two, *Tristan and Isolde* (1859) and the four-opera cycle *Der Ring des Nibelungen* (1854–1874). The Ring closes with the *Götterdämmerung*, or *Twilight of the Gods*, in which the ancient Germanic god Wotan destroys his own kingdom of Valhalla in a massive spectacle of fire.

Wagner's operas reached a peak of popularity not only in Germany but across Europe in the 1870s and 1880s. By that time, and perhaps also for professional reasons, he had transformed himself into an ardent German nationalist. He believed that his music was a true reflection of the German spirit, perfected and purified, the proper cure for an increasingly cosmopolitan age. He explained these ideas in a wide variety of writings and polemics, which combined with his music-dramas to inspire a spiritual and artistic movement known as Wagnerism. Wagnerism was, broadly defined, the faith that a return to artistic purity would help save European civilization from the triviality of liberal, commercial civilization, which was often identified as being overly Jewish. Wagnerism's greatest shrine was in the Bavarian city of Bayreuth, where, with the help of Bavarian king Ludwig II, Wagner built a theater to house an annual festival of music-drama beginning in 1876.

In addition to his ideological German nationalism (Wagner was no militarist), the composer adopted a sort of ideological anti-Semitism late in his career. He was a critic not so much of Jews as of what he perceived as the Jewish spirit. In contrast to the German spirit, the Jewish spirit was vague, fantastical, trivial, and deceitful, and Wagner criticized composers of Jewish background, such as Meyerbeer and Mendelssohn, for making music to make money rather than to evince the essential truths and higher yearnings of humanity. Wagner joined a number of European thinkers who conflated being Jewish with being somehow unspiritual, materialistic, and with reflecting the "lower" qualities of human life.

The composer died in Venice on February 13, 1883. Bayreuth remained a Wagnerian shrine, presided over by his widow, Cosima Wagner. It attracted a young Englishman named Houston Stewart Chamberlain, who married the composer's daughter Eva and wrote *The Foundations of the Nineteenth Century*, one of the intellectual bases of Nazism. Hitler, who worshiped Wagner's music, started going to the Bayreuth festival in the early 1920s, and became well acquainted with Winifred Wagner, the wife of the composer's son, Siegfried. Hitler once mentioned that he was overwhelmed by emotion the first time he entered Villa Wahnfried, the family's Bayreuth estate. Nazism and Bayreuth proved to be a natural match, much to the denigration of Richard Wagner's historical reputation. After Winifred took over as the mistress of Bayreuth upon the deaths of Cosima and Siegfried in 1930, the town became a shrine to the Nazi version of German nationalism as well as to the composer's music-dramas; indeed, Winifred and Hitler were so close that rumors spread that they planned to marry. The Bayreuth festival, for its part, took its place as one of the great holidays of the Nazi calendar, while Wagner's rich, dramatic music could be regularly heard on the radio, in concert halls, and at various Nazi gatherings. *See also* Bayreuth, Vol. 1; music in the Third Reich, Wagnerism, Vol. 2; Wagner, Winifred, Vol. 3.

Wagner, Winifred (1897–1980)

British-born daughter-in-law of the German composer Richard Wagner, and the leading figure at the annual Bayreuth festival during the era of the Third Reich. Wagner was also one of Adolf Hitler's earliest supporters among Bavarian high society. Born in 1897 in Hastings in southern England as Winifred Williams, she moved to Germany at the age of eight after both of her parents died. She was adopted by a distant relative, Karl Klindworth. A musician and loyal Wagnerian, Klindworth took her in 1914 to Bayreuth, a village in Bavaria where Richard Wagner had established an annual operatic festival. There she met Siegfried Wagner, the composer's son, who was twenty-eight years her senior. The two married in 1915.

Adolf Hitler was himself a lover of Wagner's music, seeing it as a reflection of the greatness of the Germanic spirit (as the composer himself had claimed). In 1923 he met Winifred Wagner, and the two became close friends. Winifred's affection helped make the young Nazi leader more respectable among Munich's social and cultural elite, and she remained supportive of Hitler to the end of her life. While Hitler was in prison after the Beer Hall Putsch, she sent him care packages, and after he was freed Hitler was a regular visitor to Bayreuth for the festival, where he also enjoyed the hospitality of Villa Wahnfried, the Wagners' palatial estate. In 1930 both Siegfried Wagner and his mother, Cosima, the composer's wife, died. Winifred Wagner found herself the leading member of the family and the hostess of Bayreuth, while Hitler turned into a sort of surrogate father to her children. Rumors circulated that the two planned to marry.

During the era of the Third Reich, the music of Richard Wagner provided a frequent sound track, and Winifred turned the Bayreuth festival into a Nazi event, one of the highlights of the Nazi calendar. Hitler returned the favor by subsidizing the festival and exempting it from taxation. He continued to attend the festival every year and continued to enjoy the company of Winifred, whom he praised as one of the great examples of German womanhood.

After World War II Winifred Wagner was forced to give up control of the Bayreuth festival, and she entered into an unrepentant retirement, not speaking of her beliefs or experiences publicly until the 1970s. Then, she reiterated her love for Hitler as well as her agreement with his political views. She died in Uberlingen on March 5, 1980. *See also* Bayreuth, Vol. 1; Chamberlain, Houston Stewart; Hitler, Adolf, Vol. 3.

Wallenberg, Raoul (1912–1947?)

Swedish businessman and diplomat who strove heroically and at the last hour to save the Jews of Hungary from the Third Reich's Final Solution. His efforts saved tens of thousands of lives.

Wallenberg was born on August 4, 1912, to an upper-class Swedish family of bankers, diplomats, and politicians. He studied architecture in Sweden and at the University of Michigan but, unable to find related work, entered commerce instead, first in South Africa and then, in 1936, in Haifa. While in Haifa, then part of the British Palestinian Mandate, and later Israel, Wallenberg came in contact with German Jews who had escaped the Third Reich. After returning to Sweden he set up an import-export firm with Koloman Lauer, a Hungarian Jew who had settled in the country. As a leading international executive, as well as a typically cosmopolitan Swede, Wallenberg traveled frequently to Hungary over the next years and became familiar with the tangled bureaucracy of Hungary's ally, Nazi Germany.

By 1944 the world was aware of what was happening to Europe's Jews in the Nazi death camps. Miklos Horthy, the Hungarian head of state, had managed to protect his nation's seven hundred thousand Jews up to that time but in the spring of 1944, when he made it clear that he wanted a separate peace with the Allies, Hitler sent in German occupation forces. Accompanying them was SS lieutenant colonel Adolf Eichmann, charged with the task of deporting Hungary's Jews to Auschwitz. An international effort began to save them.

In June 1944 Wallenberg was appointed a special secretary to the Swedish legation in Budapest, and he arrived in Hungary in July. By that time Eichmann's enthusiastic efforts had resulted in the deportations of some four hundred thousand of Hungary's Jews. Wallenberg took it upon himself to try to save as many of the rest as he could. He demanded, and was granted, special powers by the Swedish king and government to act independently of diplomatic procedure and protocol, and set to work. Among several desperate tactics, Wallenberg came up with a special "protective pass" decorated with the colors and emblems of the Swedish crown and filled with the forged signatures of top officials. He knew, from his long experience, that Nazi officials and their Hungarian underlings were impressed by official-looking documents. He wheedled and cajoled Hungarian officials to produce thousands of these passes, and distributed them to Jews. Meanwhile, he was able to convince Hungarians that Jews should not be required to wear the yellow Star of David armband in public. Even after Horthy was deposed by the Germans in August 1944 for seeking peace with the Allies, Wallenberg continued his efforts. One new innovation was "Swedish houses." Using whatever funds he could muster, Wallen-

Swedish diplomat Raoul Wallenberg (shown in this passport photo) saved the lives of tens of thousands of Hungarian Jews.

berg acquired or rented property across Budapest. He hung the Swedish flag out front and declared the houses to be sovereign Swedish territory where Jews could take refuge. Other diplomatic legations followed his example, and thereby some fifteen thousand Jews were saved. Later, Wallenberg set up a special office to raise money to support surviving Jews.

One of Wallenberg's great accomplishments was simply to buy time until the Soviet armies could arrive in Budapest, which they did by November 1944. The Swede now found himself, however, in the position of having to explain his actions to suspicious Soviet authorities. Apparently, they could not understand why he would go to all that trouble to save Jews, and they wondered if he was a spy for the western Allies or, strangely, a German sympathizer. Along with a Swiss diplomat who had also helped Hungarian Jews survive, Wallenberg was arrested by Soviet security police and taken to Moscow. His ultimate fate is unknown; the Soviets claimed he died in custody, peacefully, in 1947. *See also* Höss Action, Vol. 1; Eichmann, Adolf, Vol. 3.

Warlimont, Walther (1894–1976)

Army general who played an important role in tying the leadership of the German armed forces to Adolf Hitler's regime. Warlimont was born in Osnabrück on October 3, 1894, to a middle-class family. He joined the German Imperial Army in 1913 and served as a junior officer during World War I. After the war he continued his career with the Weimar-era Reichswehr and, after 1935, with Hitler's Wehrmacht. He was an important German envoy to the Spanish Fascists under Generalissimo Francisco Franco during the Spanish Civil War (1936–1939), leading a contingent of German volunteers and acting as the official representative of the Third Reich's Ministry of War. As an official in the War Ministry in 1937 with the military rank of colonel, Warlimont devised a plan to reorganize the German army so that it would have a single commander in chief as well as a single General Staff. Hitler saw Warlimont's directive, known as the Warlimont Memorandum, and approved it. Among the advantages of the plan, from the perspectives of both Warlimont and Hitler, was that it would reduce the influence of the traditional Prussian officer class, many members of which were only marginally loyal to the Nazi regime. Warlimont, as a man of middle-class background, had reason to want to diminish the status of these officer-aristocrats. Over the next months Hitler created the High Command of the German armed forces (OKW) using Warlimont's plan as a basic guide. Warlimont himself was named deputy to General Alfred Jodl, another officer of middle-class background who became the head of the Operations Staff of the OKW. He also became head of the national defense unit of the OKW. During World War II Warlimont enjoyed regular promotions though he served in a staff and political capacity rather than as a field officer. He was promoted to major general in 1940, lieutenant general in 1942, and general of artillery in 1944. Warlimont and Jodl were the main contributors to the Nazi plan for the invasion of the Soviet Union. On July 20, 1944, Warlimont was injured by the bomb placed by Claus Schenk Graf von Stauffenberg to assassinate Hitler.

At war's end Warlimont was arrested and interned. In 1948 an American war crimes tribunal sentenced him to life in prison for war crimes. The sentence was later reduced. He was released from Munich's Landsberg Prison in 1957 and died in Upper Bavaria on October 9, 1976. *See also* Oberkommando der Wehrmacht, Warlimont Memorandum, Vol. 2.

Weiszäcker, Ernst Freiherr von (1882–1951)

Official in the Foreign Ministry of the Third Reich and ambassador to the Vatican. A member of an aristocratic family, Weiszäcker was born in Stuttgart on May 12, 1882, and served as an officer in the German Imperial Navy during World War I. He joined the German Foreign Office in 1920 and, until 1945, served as a loyal official to both the Weimar Republic and the Third Reich. Prior to the Nazi rise to power he was appointed ambassador to Norway and, from 1933 to 1936, served as ambassador to Switzerland. He also joined the Nazi Party and in time took up an honorary officer's rank in the SS. In 1937 he was appointed a ministerial director in the Foreign Office and, under Joachim von Ribbentrop from 1938 to 1943, chief state secretary. From 1943 to 1945 he was the Third Reich's ambassador to the Vatican, and at war's end he was given sanctuary in Rome by church officials. He was ultimately arrested by Allied forces, however, and in 1949 he was convicted of complicity in Nazi war crimes by an American tribunal at Nuremberg. He was sentenced to five years' imprisonment, although he was released in 1950 following a general amnesty. In his memoirs, published in 1950, Weiszäcker claimed that he was never a devoted Nazi despite his many years of loyal service to Hitler's regime. He died in Lindau, near Berlin, on August 4, 1951.

Wessel, Horst (1907–1930)

SA trooper who wrote the "Horst Wessel Song" (also known as "Hold High the Banners"), which became the most popular Nazi marching song. He was also turned into a martyr of the first order by Joseph Goebbels's propaganda office despite a dubious background among Berlin's lowlife. Wessel was born in Bielefeld on September 9, 1907, and moved to Berlin as a young man. He joined the Nazi Party and the SA in 1926. Fancying himself a musician, and hopeful of building an SA band, he composed the "Horst Wessel Song" in 1928.

Wessel was killed in February 1930 as the result of an apparent lover's quarrel. He had taken up with a prostitute who allegedly had connections with Berlin's Communist underworld. When he died in a fight against Communist thugs, who opposed not only his politics but his relationship with the young prostitute, he became an ideal candidate for martyrdom. Goebbels's propaganda machine sprang into action, and the young storm trooper was depicted as a victim of the Nazi struggle against communism. His song was one of the most popular and well known of the Third Reich and his life, embellished far beyond reality, became the subject of plays and films. *See also* "Horst Wessel Song," Vol. 1; songs of the Third Reich, Vol. 2; Songs of the Third Reich, Vol. 4.

Wiedemann, Fritz (1891–1970)

Adolf Hitler's commanding officer during World War I and, under the Third Reich, an important adviser to the Führer and foreign diplomat. Weidemann was born in Augsburg on August 15, 1891. He joined the army as a young man and entered World War I as a lieutenant. He rose to be the commanding officer of the 17th Bavarian Infantry Regiment, in which Adolf Hitler was one of his enlisted men, serving as a courier. After the war Wiedemann left the army and became a farmer in rural Bavaria. He joined the Nazi Party in 1934. Hitler remembered his former commander fondly, and called on Wiedemann as a personal adviser and adjutant to the Führer. By 1938 Wiedemann was a sort of unofficial foreign envoy for the Nazi leader, representing him in Vienna and London. He was also given the rank of SA brigadier general. In 1939 Wiedemann was assigned to be German consul-general in San Francisco until he was expelled from the United States in June 1941. He spent the remainder of the war years as consul-general in Tientsin, China, which was under Japanese authority.

After World War II Wiedemann was arrested by American forces. He was a witness during the Nuremberg war crimes trials, and was sentenced to eighteen months in prison. After serving out his sentence he returned once again to rural life in Bavaria and died in 1970. *See also* Hitler, Adolf, Vol. 3.

Wiesel, Elie (1928–)

Romanian-Jewish survivor of the Holocaust who became one of the most well known bearers of witness of the experience of the Third Reich's death camps. Wiesel was born in Sighet, Romania, in 1928. He, his family, and other nearby Jewish families managed to survive the massacre of Romanian Jews that took place in 1941, but in 1944 they were all sent to Auschwitz. Elie Wiesel was of the age generally selected for slave labor and he survived Auschwitz, although his immediate family did not. Toward the end of the war he was sent to Buchenwald in Germany.

After the liberation of Buchenwald, Wiesel moved to Paris, where he studied philosophy and worked as a journalist. He published his first Holocaust memoir, *Night*, in 1958. It proved to be a timely reminder to a world whose memory of the Holocaust seemed to be fading, and it was one of the first popular accounts of the true nature of life in the camps. Wiesel later published two novels of camp life, *Dawn* and *The Accident*, as well as other memoirs. In 1976, by then a citizen of the United States, he was named professor of humanities at Boston University. In 1980 he was named head of the American Holocaust Memorial Council and in 1986 he was awarded the Nobel Peace Prize. *See also* Auschwitz, extermination camps, Vol. 1; Levi, Working in a Factory at Auschwitz, Vol. 4.

Wiesenthal, Simon (1908–)

Polish-Jewish survivor of the Holocaust and the most active hunter of escaped Nazi war criminals in the years after World War II. Wiesenthal was born near Lwow in 1908 and studied to be an engineer and architect. He spent most of World War II as a slave laborer in more than a dozen Nazi camps, and he lost almost all his relatives to the Third Reich's "Final Solution to the Jewish Question." At the end of World War II he helped the U.S. Army in Austria in its search for escaped war criminals, later working for the American intelligence agency, the Office of Strategic Services. In 1947 he opened a small office in Linz, Austria, where he gathered documentation on hundreds of escaped Nazis. He also traveled widely to seek out and identify those on his lists. Among his most famous finds was Adolf Eichmann, one of the architects of the Final Solution, whom Wiesenthal located in Argentina. He passed this information to the government of Israel, which arranged to kidnap Eichmann and bring him to Jerusalem for trial. In 1961, the same year as the Eichmann trial, Wiesenthal opened a larger office in Vienna. It was known as the Jewish Documentation Center, and over the years it compiled dossiers on more than twenty thousand wanted war criminals. In addition the center collected an archive on the Holocaust in general. Wiesenthal himself was personally responsible for the arrest of over one thousand Nazi war criminals, working closely with authorities in Austria, Israel, and the Federal Republic of Germany. He also served as the head of the Federation of the Jewish Victims of the Nazi Regime. *See also* concentration camps, Eichmann trial, Vol. 1; Office of Strategic Services, Vol. 2.

Wilhelm II (1859–1941)

The Hohenzollern kaiser, or emperor, of Germany from 1888 to 1918. Grandson of Wilhelm I, he succeeded his father, Friedrich III, who ruled only three months before dying of cancer. As kaiser, Wilhelm II proved to be ambitious and impetuous. He rejected the advice of the Iron Chancellor, Otto von Bismarck, who had been the power behind his grandfather's throne for twenty-five years, and who had built alliances that maintained a precarious balance of power in Europe. Bismarck resigned in 1890, and Wilhelm turned to asserting the divine rights of the monarchy and Germany's rightful "place in the sun" among the great powers of the world. He supported Germany's efforts to acquire a colonial empire and to match or surpass the munitions and naval capacity of Great Britain and other powers. He was also sympathetic toward any notion that Germans were somehow culturally or racially superior to other peoples. For instance, he hailed Houston Stewart Chamberlain's *The Foundations of the Nineteenth Century.*

Although Kaiser Wilhelm loved military pageantry and generally wore uniforms, he was not in favor of starting World War I, as many have held. He in fact was fond of the British, and his maternal grandmother was Queen Victoria. Nevertheless, once the war started he pursued it vigorously, if not always wisely. With the German army unraveling and the threat of a Communist revolution growing, generals and government officials convinced him to abdicate on November 9, 1918. He spent the remainder of his life in comfortable exile in Doorn, the Netherlands, observing in bemusement the growth of Nazism in his home country. During the Third Reich, although a number of important Germans remained monarchists, and even some Nazis were sympathetic toward the monarchy, there was never any serious attempt to restore either Kaiser Wilhelm II or one of his sons to the throne; Adolf Hitler hated the Hohenzollerns. *See also* Second German Reich, World War I, Vol. 2.

Wirth, Christian (1885–1944)

SS officer who played a major part in establishing and managing the Polish death camps, where the Third Reich carried out its plan to exterminate Europe's Jewish population. Wirth was born in Oberbalzheim in western Germany on November 24, 1885. During World War I he served with great distinction as a noncommissioned officer on the western front, receiving the Military Cross, one of Germany's highest honors. After the war he worked as a builder before becoming a policeman in Württemberg, where he acquired a reputation for brutality. During the Third Reich all German police functions were folded into the SS, and by the late 1930s Wirth found himself an officer in the SS Criminal Police (Kripo).

At the end of 1939 Wirth was assigned to the T-4 Program, the plan hatched by Philip Bouhler at the Führer Chancellery to administer the "mercy killing," or euthanasia, of Germany's mentally ill. His first posting was at the Grafeneck Psychiatric Hospital. Later, Wirth moved to a similar facility known as Brandenburg an der Havel. There, as chief of administration, he helped perform the first gassings of victims of the Third Reich—Germans who had been declared incurably insane. It was Bouhler's idea to use gas chambers disguised as baths complete with false showerheads. By mid-1940, when the T-4 Program was under way across Germany, Wirth served as an inspector of the euthanasia centers and therefore, according to Nazi logic, an expert in the logistics of murdering people in gas chambers.

Wirth transferred this "expertise" to Poland in the summer of 1941, after Bouhler made the decision to set up a euthanasia center in Lublin in occupied Poland (the center was never built). When top SS officials made the decision, sometime in the summer or fall of 1941, to massacre Europe's Jews in gas chambers, Wirth was an obvious choice to help establish the camps and their procedures. In December 1941, with the help of a number of guards and other functionaries he brought from the German euthanasia centers, Wirth began to murder Jews in the death camp at Chelmno. In 1942 and 1943 he was charged, along with local SS police leader Odilo Globocnik, with administering the so-called Reinhard Action death camps: Belzec, Sobibor, and Treblinka. Over 2 million people were killed at these camps by the end of 1943.

Wirth, for his part, made major contributions to death camp procedures, such as the use of Jewish slaves, or Sonderkommando, to clean the transports and gas chambers. He also maintained his reputation for extreme brutality, even among SS men.

After the Belzec camp was closed in the fall of 1943, Wirth was transferred to military duty in Yugoslavia and promoted to SS major. He died on May 26, 1944, the victim of either Yugoslav partisans or a Jewish gang bent on revenge. *See also* euthanasia, Final Solution, Vol. 1; T-4 Program, Vol. 2.

Wisliceny, Dieter (1911–1948)

SS officer who served as deputy to Adolf Eichmann, one of the top officials involved in the "Final Solution to the Jewish Question." Wisliceny himself helped to organize the deportations of Jews from Slovakia, Greece, and Hungary. Wisliceny was born in Regulowken in East Prussia on January 13, 1911. The son of a prosperous farmer, he initially set out to be a theology student, but dropped out of his studies. He joined the Nazi Party in 1931 and the SS in 1934, where he soon became a member of the SD, the Security Service of the SS, where he first worked with Eichmann and was for a brief period Eichmann's superior.

After the Anschluss of 1938 Wisliceny joined Eichmann's Office for Jewish Emigration in Vienna, where he acquired a reputation as an expert in "Jewish affairs." From 1940 to 1942 he served as an adviser on Jewish matters to the German representation in Bratislava, the capital of Slovakia, which was a puppet state of the Third Reich during Word War II. Since Slovakia was not one of the occupied territories and not therefore under Nazi authority, he had to negotiate with local officials to arrange the deportation of Jews. In the process he proved himself willing to be bought, in one instance accepting a huge sum of money from local Jewish leaders in exchange for delaying deportations. In 1943 and 1944 Wisliceny served in a similar capacity in Greece, where he helped to arrange the deportation to Auschwitz of the large, wealthy, and cultured community of Jews in the city of Salonika. From March 1944 he was in the Hungarian capital of Budapest, where both he and Eichmann engaged in extensive bargaining over Jews. As before, and unlike Eichmann, he proved himself susceptible to bribes and flattery, although such measures failed to save more than a few Jews.

At war's end Wisliceny was arrested by the Allies and served as a prosecution witness during the Nuremberg war crimes trials. His testimony included some of the first detailed accounts of what went on during the Holocaust. Afterward he was turned over to Czechoslovakia, where, on February 27, 1948, in Bratislava, he was hanged for his participation in the murder of thousands of people. *See also* Final Solution, Vol. 1; Office for Jewish Emigration, Vol. 2; Eichmann, Adolf, Vol. 3; Eichmann and Less, Eichmann Remembers, Vol. 4.

Witzleben, Erwin von (1881–1944)

General field marshal in the German army and a leading member of the resistance against Adolf Hitler. Witzleben was born on December 4, 1881, in Breslau and began his service to the German military as an officer in 1901. During Word War I he led units on the western front, and he enjoyed steady promotions as an officer in the Weimer-era Reichswehr. When the Nazis took power in 1933 he was named commander of the Berlin military district, and in 1935 commander in chief of the Third Army. Beginning in 1938 he was one of the top officers searching for a way to throw Hitler and the Nazis out of power, taking part in the planning of several resistance plots. Nevertheless, when World War II began Witzleben continued to lead his forces well and with honor. After commanding the First Army into France he was promoted to general field marshal, along with eleven other

German general Erwin von Witzleben was involved in numerous resistance plots, including the failed July 1944 assassination attempt.

Wehrmacht and Luftwaffe generals, in July 1940. Before being retired by Hitler in 1941 he was named supreme commander of Army Group West.

Witzleben remained in contact with the resistance movement after his forced retirement, and the conspirators planned to make him commander in chief of the Wehrmacht after they assassinated Hitler and toppled the Nazi regime. He was arrested by the Gestapo on July 21, 1944, the day after the assassination plot failed. Over the next weeks, facing the People's Court as a beaten and humiliated old man, Witzleben was found guilty of high treason against the Third Reich. He was hanged by piano wire from a meat hook at Plötzensee Prison in Berlin on August 8, 1944. *See also* July 1944 Plot, Vol. 1; resistance movements, Germany, Vol. 2; Hitler, Hitler Promises Revenge for the July 1944 Plot, Vol. 4.

Wolff, Karl (1900–1984)

SS officer who served as personal adjutant to Heinrich Himmler and SS commander in occupied northern Italy from September 1943. Wolff was born in Darmstadt in western Germany on May 13, 1900, into an upper-middle-class, professional family. During World War I he served as a junior officer and from late 1918 to 1920 he joined a right-wing Freikorps unit in Hesse. During the 1920s he built up an advertising business in Munich after working in other business enterprises. He joined the Nazi Party and the SS in 1931, and he began to devote his full-time energies to the SS in 1933.

Wolff rose rapidly in the SS hierarchy, becoming one of its top officials. From March to June 1933 he was SS adjutant to the Bavarian governor Franz Xaver Ritter von Epp, and in July he was appointed personal adjutant to Reichsführer-SS Heinrich Himmler. By the time World War II began he was one of Himmler's top advisers, particularly when Reinhard Heydrich left to devote himself to the so-called Protectorate of Bohemia and Moravia. In addition, Wolff acted as the main liaison between Himmler and Adolf Hitler. His rank rose along with his responsibilities, and by 1942 he was both an SS lieutenant general and a colonel general of the Waffen-SS as well as the recipient of numerous Nazi Party and political decorations. Wolff accompanied Himmler on a number of his trips to Poland and the eastern front, where evidence suggests he was not only aware of but played a role in ordering deportations and executions of Jews and partisans.

In September 1943, after Benito Mussolini had been deposed as the Fascist dictator of Italy and the Allies had occupied the southern portion of the Italian peninsula, German forces occupied northern Italy and named Mussolini their local puppet ruler. Wolff was sent to Italy as German military governor and representative of the government of the Third Reich. There he played an important part in forestalling the progress of Allied armies as well as containing Italian partisans, although under his leadership hundreds of Italian Jews, who had been previously protected by the Italian government and people, were deported to Auschwitz. In February 1945 he made contact through intermediaries with Allen Dulles, the head of the American Office of Strategic Services, who was stationed in Zürich. He made it known to Dulles that he was prepared to make a deal to surrender German forces in Italy. After negotiations, the Allies accepted.

After the war he was not arrested by the Allies, partly because of his help in hastening the end of the war but also because he was willing to testify for the prosecution during the Nuremberg war crimes trials. A German court, however, gave him a brief prison sentence, of which he served only one week. Over the next years the sophisticated, articulate, and able Wolff built up a successful advertising business in Cologne. He published his memoirs in 1961, however, which brought him once again to the attention of West German officials seeking to prosecute Nazi war crimes. He was arrested on January 18, 1962, and charged with participation in the Holocaust as well as complicity in the murder of partisans. Although he denied the charges, the Munich court in which he was tried found him guilty. He was sentenced to fifteen years' imprisonment in September 1964 but released, due to mitigating circumstances, in 1971. Wolff later appeared in a documentary on the Third Reich in which he was very plainspoken about his experiences as Hitler's adjutant and claimed that he joined the SS convinced that it was little other than the Nazi equivalent to the elite forces that had existed in imperial Germany. Wolff died in Rosenheim on July 15, 1984. *See also* SS, Vol. 2; Himmler, Heinrich, Vol. 3.

Yorck von Wartenburg, Peter Graf (1903–1944)

German aristocrat and prominent member of the resistance movement against Adolf Hitler and Nazism. Yorck von Wartenburg was born in the village of Klein Oels in eastern Germany on November 17, 1903. His family were respected aristocrats whose members included great Prussian generals and officials. After studying law at the Universities of Breslau and Bonn, he joined the German civil service, rising to the post of senior government councillor. When World War II began he served briefly as a field officer but from 1942 he worked for the War Economy Office.

Yorck von Wartenburg was one of the founding members of the Kreisau Circle, a group organized around ideological opposition to the Nazis and their plans for Europe. The Kreisau Circle was mainly a forum for discussion and planning for Germany's future, however, rather than a center of active resistance plots. These practical plots generally developed in military circles, among whom the young aristocrat had many acquaintances, including Claus Schenk Graf von Stauffenberg, the leading light of the July 1944 Plot. Yorck von Wartenburg based his opposition to the Nazi regime on moral and religious grounds, as did most others in the Kreisau Circle, claiming that the Third Reich was fundamentally wrong in requiring individuals to pledge their devotion to the state and its leader rather than to God and their own consciences.

On July 20, 1944, Yorck von Wartenburg was present in the Berlin War Ministry offices, where he waited for the news that Hitler had been assassinated and the conspirators were ready to take over the government. Instead, he was one of the first to be arrested when the plot fell apart. At his People's Court trial he refused to be cowed or humiliated by the prosecutors, and soon afterward made it known to his wife that he hoped his death might in some small way make up for the guilt of Germany under the Third Reich. Yorck von Wartenburg was hanged at Berlin's Plötzensee Prison on August 8, 1944. *See also* Kreisau Circle, Vol. 1; resistance movements, Germany, Vol. 2.

Zeitzler, Kurt (1895–1963)

Chief of the General Staff of the High Command of the German armed forces (OKW) from September 1942 to July 1944, and in that position one of Adolf Hitler's top military advisers during the critical months of World War II. Zeitzler was born in Cossmar-Luckau in Prussia on June 9, 1895. Although his father was a minister he decided on a career in the army. He served as an infantry officer during World War I and continued his career in the Weimar-era Reichswehr and in the early years of the Third Reich, where he proved to be a very capable planner and administrator, in tune with the requirements and possibilities of modern tank warfare. In the first years of World War II Zeitzler served as both a staff and field officer. He served as chief of staff of the Twelfth Army during the Polish campaign and then as chief of staff of the 1st Panzer Group and Army Group D in western Europe. In the latter post he ranked as a major general.

Hitler was impressed by Zeitzler's leadership skills and creativity as well as, probably, his youth and energy in comparison with other top Wehrmacht officers. In September 1942 the Führer named Zeitzler chief of the General Staff of the OKW, succeeding Franz Halder, whose advice on the eastern front had disappointed Hitler. Hitler hoped that Zeitzler unlike Halder, would not question his military decisions. However, like many others, Zeitzler advised Hitler to allow General Friedrich Paulus's Sixth Army to retreat from Stalingrad in the fall of 1942, understanding that the situation was impossible. Hitler rejected the advice, unable to comprehend the value of a strategic retreat. In later months, however, Zeitzler was able to convince the Führer to allow strategic retreats from Moscow and Leningrad.

As the eastern front collapsed in late 1943 and early 1944 with the failures of operations around Kursk and Crimea, Zeitzler grew increasingly distressed by Hitler's monomaniacal leadership. He asked to be allowed to resign several times. Hitler refused, although he allowed the general to go on sick leave. On July 20, 1944, Zeitzler retired from the army, ostensibly for reasons of poor health. Hitler officially removed him from army rolls on January 31, 1945, meaning that he no longer had the right to wear a uniform or enjoy other benefits. Zeitzler lived in retirement til his death in a small Bavarian village on September 25, 1963. ***See also*** Battle of Stalingrad, Vol. 1; Operation Citadel, Vol. 2.

INDEX

Abetz, Otto, 7
Abwehr, 28, 40, 72–73, 158, 173
Accident, The (Wiesel), 257
Achtung: Panzer! (Guderian), 87
Adenauer, Konrad, 74, 227
Adolf Hitler Fund, 138
Afrika Korps, 132, 194
Amann, Max, 7–8
American-Jewish Joint Distribution Committee, 210
Der Angriff (The Assault) (newspaper), 78
Annalen der Physik (journal), 49
Anne Frank: Diary of a Young Girl (Anne Frank), 58
Anschluss, 18, 116, 218, 219
   role of Seyss-Inquart in, 222
anti-Semitism
   Globke and, 73–74
   Houston Chamberlain and, 29, 199
   Rosenberg and, 199–200
   Streicher and, 237
   see also racism
Army of the Future, The (de Gaulle), 36
Arrow Cross, 121
art
   of occupied countries, plunder of, 200
Article 48, of Weimar Constitution, 26
Aryan
   Friedrich Müller and popularization of term, 159, 160
Aryanization, 74
   of Danzig, 56
   of Ukraine, 135
Atlantic Charter, 197
Auf Gut Deutsch (In Good German) (newspaper), 44
Auschwitz, 121, 122
Austria
   German annexation of. *See* Anschluss
   Schuschnigg and, 218–19
Axis Sally. *See* Gillars, Mildred, 8
Axmann, Artur, 22

Baarova, Lida, 78
Bach-Zelewski, Erich, 9
Badoglio, Pietro, 10, 164
Baeck, Leo, 10–11
Baltic states
   Einsatzgruppen activities in, 9
   Reich commissar of, 146
   Rosenberg as minister of, 200–201
   Soviet invasion of, 229
Barbie, Klaus, 11
Barmen Declaration, 168–69
Barth, Karl, 11–12

Beck, Ludwig, 12–13, 19, 23, 66, 73, 92, 126, 152
Beer Hall Putsch, 50, 95, 111, 149
   Gregor Strasser and, 235
   Röhm and, 192
Benes, Edouard, 13–14, 89
Bergen-Belsen, 136
Bernadotte, Folke, 14
Best, Werner, 14–15
Beyond Good and Evil (Nietzsche), 170
Bismarck, Otto von, 15–16, 257
Black Reichswehr, 212, 220
Blitzkrieg, 87
Blomberg, Werner von, 16–18, 23
Blomberg-Fritsch crisis, 64–65, 97, 142, 174
blood and soil, 35
Blood Purge, 17, 38, 64, 97, 114, 153, 187, 213
   Göring's role in, 81
   Gregor Strasser and, 236
   Röhm and, 193–94
Blue Light, The (film), 191
Bock, Fedor von, 18, 247
Boden, Margarete, 100
Bohemia and Moravia, Protectorate of, 89
Boleshevik Revolution
   Stalin's role in, 228
Bonhoeffer, Dietrich, 18–19, 174
Bormann, Martin, 19–22
   in Committee of Three, 141
Bouhler, Philip, 22–23, 258
Brandt, Karl, 159
Brauchitsch, Walther von, 23–24, 64
Braun, Eva, 24–25, 55, 56, 113
Braun, Gretl, 55
Braun, Wernher von, 25–26
Brest-Litovsk, Treaty of, 148
Britain, Battle of, 71, 84
   Sperrle and planning of, 228
Brüning, Heinrich, 26–27, 79, 112
Buch, Gerda, 20
Buchenwald
   Ilse Koch and, 135
Bulge, Battle of the, 39
Bürckel, Joseph, 48
By My Husband's Side (Emmy Göring), 80

Canaris, Wilhelm, 19, 28, 97, 158, 174
Catholic Center Party, 26
Chamberlain, Houston Stewart, 28–29, 199, 253
Chamberlain, Neville, 29–30
Chelmno, 258
Chiang Kai-shek, 221
Churchill, Randolph, 30
Churchill, Winston, 30–32, 197
   Stalin and, 230
Chvalkovsky, Frantisek, 89

Ciano, Galeazzo, 32–33, 165
Clauberg, Karl, 33
collaboration, with Third Reich
    in Vichy France, 141
Commentary on German Racial Legislation
    (Stuckart and Globke), 240
Commentary on German Rassengesetzubung, 73
Committee of Three, 141
Concordat of 1933, 54, 180
Condor Legion, 227
Confessing Church, 19, 71–72, 168
Criminal Police (Kripo), 101, 167
Curtain Falls, The (Bernadotte), 14
Czechoslovakia, 60
    founding of, 13
    see also Bohemia and Moravia, Protectorate of

Dachau, 100
    Eicke as commandant of, 48
Daladier, Edouard, 34
Daluege, Kurt, 34–35
d'Annunzio, Fiume, 163
Danzig, 186
    "Aryanization" of, 56
Darré, Walther, 35–36
Dawn (Wiesel), 257
Death's Head–SS (Totenkopfverbände), 48
Defense Political Office, 51
de Gaulle, Charles, 36–38
Denmark, 14
Dietrich, Joseph (Sepp), 38–39
Dietrich, Otto, 39–40
DNVP. *See* German Nationalist People's Party
Dohnanyi, Hans von, 40
Dönitz, Karl
    as head of navy, 185
    as Hitler's successor, 40–42
Dora-Mittelbau, 25
Drexler, Anton, 42–43, 110
Duesterberg, Theodor, 221
duke of Windsor incident, 207–208
Dulles, Allen, 129
Dunkirk evacuation, 202

Ebert, Friedrich, 44, 86, 107
Eckart, Dietrich, 44–45, 198
education
    Reich minister of, 202–203
Edward VIII (duke of Windsor)
    plot to kidnap, 207–208
Eichmann, Adolf, 45–46, 48
    trial of, 47
Eicke, Theodor, 48–49, 75
Einsatzgruppen (Special Assignment Groups),
    98–99, 103
    in Soviet Union, 167, 172
Einstein, Albert, 49–50, 231
Eisenhower, Dwight D., 104–105
El Alamein, battles of, 195
elections, of 1932, 243

Enabling Act, 62
Epp, Franz Xaver Ritter von, 50–51, 192
*Erinnerungen eines Soldaten (Rememberances
    of a Soldier)* (Guderian), 88
Essay on the Inequality of Race (Gobineau), 75, 76
Esser, Hermann, 51–52
Ethnic German Mittelstelle, 147
ethnic Germans (Volksdeutscher), 147
extermination policy
    Eichmann and, 46
    Globocnik and, 74–75

Falkenhorst, Nikolaus von, 53
Faulhaber, Michael von, 53–54
Feder, Gottfried, 54–55
Fegelein, Hermann, 55–56
"Final Solution to the Jewish Question," 61
    Heinrich Müller and, 161
    Rademacher and, 183
Finland, 151
    Soviet invasion of, 229
Five-Year Plans, Soviet, 229
Flick, Friedrich, 56
Forster, Albert, 56–57
Foundations of the Nineteenth Century, The
    (Houston Chamberlain), 29, 199, 253, 258
Four Freedoms, 197
Four-Year Plan, 67
    Göring and, 82–83
France
    Bismarck's war with, 16
    occupied, 171, 241
    surrender of, to Germany, 129–30
    see also Vichy France
Franco, Francisco, 57, 164, 227
Frank, Anne, 58–59
Frank, Hans, 59–60
Frank, Karl-Hermann, 60
Freikorps, 34
Freisler, Roland, 60–61
French National Committee of Liberation, 36
Frick, Wilhelm, 61–63, 104
Fritsch, Werner Freiherr von, 63–65, 126
Fritzsche, Hans, 65–66
Fromm, Erich, 66–67
Fromm, Friedrich, 173, 233
Führer Chancellery, 21, 22, 23
Führer cult, 116
Führer Principle, 115
Funk, Walther, 67–68
Furtwängler, Wilhelm, 68–69

Galen, Clemens August Graf von, 70–71
Galland, Adolf, 71
Genealogy of Morals, The (Nietzsche), 170
George VI (king of England), 31
German Christians, 161, 162
German Communist Party, 242
German Labor Front, 143, 144, 226
German Nationalist People's Party (DNVP)

coalition with Nazi Party, 124, 218
German Society for the Abolition of Interest Slavery, 54
German St. Bartholomew's Night, The (Otto Strasser), 237
German Workers' Party, 42
  renaming of, 110
Germany
  postwar, 74, 227
  see also Second German Reich; Third Reich
Gerstein, Kurt, 71–72
Gestapo, 92, 160, 207
  Himmler and, 101
Gillars, Mildred (Axis Sally), 8
Giraud, Henri, 37
Gisevius, Hans Bernd, 72–73
Glasl, Anna, 118
Gleiwitz raid, 166
Globke, Hans, 73–74, 240
Globocnik, Odilo, 72, 74–75, 230
Gluecks, Richard, 49, 75, 122
Gobineau, Artur Comte de, 75–76
Goebbels, Joseph, 8, 21, 200
  Blood Purge and, 194
  early life of, 76–77
  relationship with Hitler, 78–79
Goebbels, Magda, 78
Goerdeler, Carl, 54, 73, 79–80, 92, 232
Göring, Emmy Sonnemann, 80
Göring, Hermann, 17–18, 35, 71, 82–84, 156, 238
  lifestyle of, 80–81, 83
  at Munich Conference, 89
Göring, Karen von Kantzow, 81, 84–85
Götterdämmerung (Twilight of the Gods) (Richard Wagner), 252
Great Depression, 112
Greiser, Arthur, 85
Groener, Wilhelm, 85–86
Grühn, Eva, 17–18
Grynszpan, Herschel, 86–87
Guderian, Heinz, 87–88

Hacha, Emil, 89
Halder, Franz, 89–90
Hanfstaengl, Ernst (Putzi), 90–91, 113
Harrer, Karl, 42
Harzberg Front, 124
Hassell, Ulrich von, 91–92
Heinkel, Ernst, 92–93
Heinrich Himmler Friendship Circle, 130, 138, 181
Heisenberg, Werner, 93
Helldorf, Wolf Heinrich Graf von, 18, 93–94
Henlein, Konrad, 94–95
Henry the Fowler, 102
Hess, Rudolf, 21, 95–97
Heydrich, Reinhard, 97–99
  assassination of, 99
  as commander of Einsatzgruppen, 98–99
  as head of Reich Central Security Office, 98
  Protectorate of Bohemia and Moravia and, 99

Hiedler, Johann Georg, 118
Hiedler, Johann Nepomuk, 118
Himmler, Heinrich, 21, 55, 63, 101, 103–105, 139
  early life of, 99–100
  racial ideas of, 102
Hindemith, Paul, 69
Hindenburg, Oskar von, 105, 107
Hindenburg, Paul von, 64, 105–108
  allows coalition with Hitler, 218
  appoints Hitler as chancellor, 105, 107
  death of, 17, 108
Hitler, Adolf
  assassination attempts on, 234, 247
    see also July 1944 Plot
  Beer Hall Putsch and, 111
  birthplace of, 108
  Blood Purge and, 114
  bodyguard of, 153
  Drive to the East and, 114, 116
  early life of, 108–109
  early political activity of, 50, 110–11
  final days of, 117–18
  joins German Workers' Party, 110–11
  in Landsberg Prison, 111–12
  personal physician of, 159
  photographer of, 120–21
  relationship with Geli Raubal, 185
  relationship with Goebbels, 78–79
  rise to power of, 27, 112–13
  Soviet invasion and, 116–17
  in Vienna, 109
  in World War I, 109, 256
Hitler, Alois, 108, 118–19
Hitler, Angela, 185
Hitler, Klara Poelzl, 108, 118, 119–20
Hitler Speaks (Rauschning), 186
Hitler Youth, 211
Hitler Youth, The (Schirach), 211
Hoffmann, Heinrich, 24, 113, 120–21
"Horst Wessel Song," 256
Horthy, Miklos, 121, 223, 254
Höss, Rudolf, 121–23, 136
Hossbach, Friedrich, 123
Hossbach Conference, 64, 123, 185
Huber, Kurt, 123–24
Hugenberg, Alfred, 65, 112, 124–25
Hungary
  Jews of, 121
  Wallenberg and, 254–55

Illustrierter Beobachter (Illustrated Observer) (newspaper), 52
Inside the Third Reich (Speer), 226
Inspectorate of Concentration Camps, 75
Inspectorate of Motorized Troops, 87
"interest slavery," 54
Invasion 1944: A Contribution to the Fates of Rommel and the Reich (Speidel), 227
Italy
  occupied, under Wolff, 260–61

rise of Mussolini in, 163

Jacobs, Joe, 214
Japan
    surrender of, 250
    Tojo and, 246
Jeschonnek, Hans, 126
"Jewish Question." *See* "Final Solution to the Jewish Question"
Jews
    Hungarian
        killing of, 121
        Wallenberg and, 254–55
    see also anti-Semitism; Schindler Jews
Jodl, Alfred, 126–27
Jones, Jennie, 30
Joyce, William (Lord Haw Haw), 146–47
Juan Carlos (king of Spain), 57
July 1944 Plot, 70, 88
    Beck and, 13
    Canaris and, 28
    Goerdeler and, 80
    Helldorf and, 93, 94
    Karl Stuelpnagel and, 240
    Kluge and, 134
    Nebe and, 167
    Olbricht and, 173
    Remer and, 188
    Rommel and, 196
    Stauffenberg and, 232, 233–34
    Stieff and, 234

Kadow, Walther, 20, 122, 212
Kaltenbrunner, Ernst, 104, 128–29, 223
Kantzow, Karin von. *See* Göring, Karin von Kantzow
Karlsbad Program, 94–95
    see also Sudetenland
Keitel, Wilhelm, 126, 129–30
    in Committee of Three, 141
Kemnitz, Mathilde von, 149
Kempka, Erich, 22
Keppler, William, 130–31
Keppler Circle, 130, 218
Kerrl, Hans, 131
Kesselring, Albert von, 131–32, 156, 228
Khrushchev, Nikita, 158
Kirdorf, Emil, 132–33
Kleist, Ewald von, 133–34
Klindworth, Karl, 253
Klink, Eugen, 216
Kluge, Günter Hans, 134
Koch, Erich, 134–35
Koch, Ilse, 135–36
Kramer, Josef, 136
Kreisau Circle, 159, 262
Kristallnacht (Night of Broken Glass), 54, 86, 87, 98, 245
Krupp von Bohlen und Halbach, Alfred, 136–37
Krupp von Bohlen und Halbach, Gustav, 137–39

Kube, Wilhelm, 139
Kubizek, August, 108–109, 139–40
Kun, Bela, 121

Lammers, Hans, 141–42
Lateran Pact (1929), 180
Laval, Pierre, 142
Law for the Restoration of the Civil Service, 62
League of German Girls (Bund Deutscher Mädel), 211
Lebensborn (Fountain of Life), 102
Lebensraum, 95
Leeb, Wilhelm Ritter von, 142–43
Lenard, Philipp, 49
Lend-Lease Act (1941), 32, 197
Lenin, Vladimir
    view on Stalin, 228–29
Leo Baeck Institute, 11
Letter from Rome, The (Barth), 12
Ley, Robert, 143–45, 245
Liebenfels, Jörg Lanz von, 145
List, Wilhelm, 145–46
Lohse, Heinrich, 146
Lord Haw Haw. *See* Joyce, William
Lorenz, Werner, 147
Lossow, Otto von, 221
Louis, Joe, 214, 215
Ludendorff, Erich, 86, 147–49
Lueger, Karl, 149–50
Luftwaffe, 71, 92, 93, 126, 131, 155, 156, 187, 201, 227–28
    Göring as head of, 81–82, 84
Luther, Martin, 150, 183
Lutze, Victor, 150

Madagascar Plan, 183
Mannerheim, Karl Gustav, 151
Manstein, Friedrich Erich von, 151–53
Marx, Wilhelm, 107
Masaryk, Tomas, 13
Matteotti, Giacomo, 164
Matzelberger, Franziska, 118
Maurice, Emil, 153, 185
Max Heiliger Fund, 68, 181
Mayer, Helene, 153–54
McCloy, John, 56
medical experiments, 33, 155
Mein Kampf (Hitler), 111–12
    original title of, 7
Meissner, Otto, 154
Mengele, Josef, 154–55
Milch, Erhard, 126, 155–56, 228
Ministry of Armaments and War Production, 67
Ministry of Public Enlightenment and Propaganda, 39–40
"Mit Brennender Sorge" ("With Burning Sorrow"), 54, 180
Model, Walther von, 156–57
Molotov-Ribbentrop Non-Aggression Pact. *See* Nazi-Soviet Non-Aggression Pact

Moltke, Helmuth James Graf von, 158–59
Morell, Theodor, 89, 159
Mosley, Sir Oswald, 146
Müller, Friedrich Max, 159–60
Müller, Heinrich, 104, 160–61
Müller, Ludwig, 131, 161–62, 168
Munich Agreement, 34
Munich Conference
    Mussolini and, 89, 165
Mussert, Anton Adriaan, 162
Mussolini, Benito, 32–33, 162–65
    Austria and, 219
    German rescue of, 223
My Political Awakening (Drexler), 43
Myth of the Twentieth Century (Rosenberg), 199

National Socialist German Workers' Party (NSDAP)
    coalition with DNVP, 218
    electoral support of, 113
    founders of, 51
    rise in membership of, 111
National Socialist Letters (pamphlets), 235
Naujocks, Alfred, 166–67
navy, German, 183
    see also U-boats
Nazi-Soviet Non-Aggression Pact, 157, 190
    Stalin and, 229
Nebe, Arthur, 104, 167
Netherlands
    Fascist movement in, 162
    under German occupation, 222–23
    pretext for German invasion of, 166
Neurath, Constantin von, 167–68, 190
Niemöller, Martin, 168–69
Nietzsche, Friedrich, 169–70
Night (Wiesel), 257
Nkrumah, Kwame, 188
Norway
    Quisling and, 182
    under Terboven, 242
November criminals, 44
Nuremberg Laws, 62, 239, 240
    see also Reich Citizenship Law
Nuremberg rallies
    Speer and, 225

Oberg, Karl, 171
Oberkommando der Wehrmacht (OKW), 88, 126, 263
    Hitler becomes head of, 114
    intelligence section of. *See* Abwehr
    Warlimont and creation of, 255
ODESSA, 47, 224
Office for Jewish Emigration, 45–46, 103, 259
Ohlendorf, Otto, 171–72
OKW. *See* Oberkommando der Wehrmacht
Olbricht, Friedrich, 66, 173
Olympia (film), 191
Olympic Games (1936), 154
Ondra, Anny, 214

Order Castles, 145
Ostara (Liebenfels), 145
Oster, Hans, 40, 158, 173–74
Ostland. *See* Baltic states
Otter, Baron von, 72

Pacelli, Eugenio. *See* Pius XII
Pact of Steel, 32, 165
Panzer, 133, 152
Papen, Franz von, 27, 107, 175, 178
    criticism of Nazis by, 176–77
    and Nazi-DNVP coalition, 176, 218
Party Chancellery, 21
Paulus, Friedrich, 152, 178–79, 221
Pearl Harbor attack, 198
People's Court, 60, 61, 244
Pétain, Philippe, 34, 179–80
Pilsudski, Józef, 224
Pius XI, 53, 180
Pius XII, 180–81
Poelzl, Klara. *See* Hitler, Klara Poelzl
Pohl, Oswald, 181
Poland
    Greiser and "Aryanization" of, 85
    under Hans Frank, 59–60
    pretext for German invasion of, 166
    Smigly-Rydz and, 224
Pötsch, Leopold, 108
Potsdam Conference, 250
Present Crisis in German Physics, The (Stark), 231
propaganda
    Otto Dietrich and, 39–40
    in radio, 8, 65, 146
Protestant Christianity
    Confessing Church and, 19
Protocols of the Elders of Zion, 199

Quisling, Vidkun, 182, 200, 242

racism
    Friedrich Müller and, 159–60
    Gobineau and, 75–76
    Houston Chamberlain and, 29
Rademacher, Franz, 183
radio
    Fritzsche and, 65–66
    propaganda in, 8, 65, 146
Raeder, Erich, 183–85
Rath, Ernst vom, 87
Raubal, Angela (Geli), 24, 113, 153, 185–86
Raubal, Leo, 185
Raubal, Maria, 185
Rauschning, Hermann, 186
Reich Association of German Newspaper Publishers, 7
Reich Association of the German Press, 40
Reich Broadcasting Corporation, 67
Reich Central Representation of German Jews, 10–11
Reich Central Security Office (RSHA), 14, 97, 98, 171, 208, 223

Kaltenbrunner as head of, 128–29
    section IV of. *See* Gestapo
    section V of. *See* Criminal Police
Reich Chamber of Culture, 67
Reich Citizenship Law, 73
Reich Commissar for the Strengthening of Ethnic Germandom, 103
Reichenau, Walther von, 186–87
Reich Ministry of Economics, 172
    Hjalmar Schacht as head of, 205, 206
Reich Press Chamber, 7
Reichsbank, 67, 205
Reichs Chancellery, 21, 141, 154
Reichstag fire, 251
Reichswehr, 220
    see also Black Reichswehr
Reinhardt Action, 74
Reinhardt Action camps, 258
    see also Sobibor; Treblinka
Reitsch, Hanna, 187–88
religion
    of Nazism, 131
    see also German Christians
Remer, Otto, 188–89
resistance movements
    in German military, 79–80, 221, 222, 227, 232, 247, 248, 249, 259, 260
    in Germany, 12–13, 18, 40, 72, 91–92, 123, 158–59, 173, 174, 262
Revolution of Nihilism (Rauschning), 186
Reynaud, Paul, 34
Ribbentrop, Joachim von, 7, 168, 189–91
    Nazi-Soviet Pact and, 157, 190
    Pacts of Steel and, 32
    surrender of Czechoslavakia and, 89
Ribbentrop Bureau, 150, 189
Riefenstahl, Leni, 191–92
Der Ring des Nibelungen (Richard Wagner), 252
Röhm, Ernst, 39, 50, 100, 108, 112, 192–94
    trial of Sepp Dietrich for murder of, 39
    see also Blood Purge
Roman Catholic Church, 53–54
Rommel, Erwin, 132, 194–95
    July 1944 Plot and, 196
Roosevelt, Franklin D., 158, 197
    early life of, 196
    Stalin and, 230
    as wartime leader, 198
Rosenberg, Alfred, 139, 198–201
Rossbach Freikorps, 94, 122
Rudel, Hans-Ulrich, 201
Rundstedt, Gerd von, 152, 195, 201–202
Russification, 229
Russo-Finnish War (1939–1940), 229
Rust, Bernard, 202–203

SA (Sturmabteilung), 51, 150
    banning of, 86
    in Hitler's rise to power, 111, 112–13
Sauckel, Fritz, 204

Sauerbruch, Ferdinand, 205, 233
Schacht, Hjalmar von, 55, 67, 137, 205–207, 220
Schellenberg, Walter, 207–208
Schickelgruber, Anna Marie, 118
Schindler, Emilie, 209
Schindler, Oskar, 208–10
Schindler Jews (Schindlerjuden), 209
Schirach, Baldur von, 200, 210–11
Schlageter, Albert Leo, 20, 212
Schleicher, Kurt von, 86, 113, 176, 212–13
Schmeling, Max, 213–15
Schmidt, Charlotte, 23
Schmidt, Hans, 64
Schoenberg, Arnold, 69
Schoerner, Ferdinand, 215
Scholl, Hans, 123, 215–16
Scholl, Sophie, 123, 215–16
Scholtz, Günther, 217
Scholtz-Klink, Gertrude, 216–18
Schröder, Kurt Freiherr von, 218
Schuschnigg, Kurt von, 218–20, 222
Schwerin von Krosigk, Lutz Graf, 220
SD (Sicherheitdienst), 45
    Himmler and, 100
Second German Reich, 15
Security Police (Sipo), 101
Seeckt, Hans von, 220–21
Seldte, Franz, 221
Seydlitz, Walter von, 221–22
Seyss-Inquart, Artur von, 222–23
Sharkey, Jack, 213, 214
Skorzeny, Otto, 121, 223–24
slave labor
    Saukel and, 204
        Flick's use of, 56
    at Krupp's factories, 137, 138
Smigly-Rydz, Edward, 224
Sobibor, 230
Social Democratic Party, 44, 236
    banning of, 62
Sonderkommando, 259
Soviet Union
    German invasion of, 116–17, 133, 145–46, 152, 187, 202
    German occupation of, 135
    rise of Stalin in, 228–29
Spain
    under Franco, 57
Spanish Civil War, 227
Speer, Albert, 21, 67, 224, 226
    Berlin plans of, 225
Speidel, Hans, 227
Sperrle, Hugo, 156, 227–28
SS (Schutzstaffel)
    Economic and Administrative Central Office of, 181
    Himmler and, 34, 100
Stahlhelm, 221
Stalin, Joseph, 158, 198, 228–30

Stalingrad, Battle of, 178, 263
Stangl, Franz, 230–31
Stark, Johannes, 49, 231–32
Stauffenberg, Claus von, 66, 173, 232–34
Stempfle, Bernard, 186
Stern, Itzhak, 209
Stieff, Helmuth, 234
Stinnes, Hugo, 234
Strasser, Gregor, 51, 77, 112, 113, 176, 234–36
Strasser, Otto, 77, 236–37
Streicher, Julius, 52, 83, 237–39
Strength Through Joy (Kraft durch Freude), 144
Stroop, Jürgen, 239
Stuckart, Wilhelm, 73, 239–40
Stuelpnagel, Karl Heinrich von, 227, 240–41
Stuelpnagel, Otto von, 241
Der Stürmer (The Storm Trooper) (Nazi newspaper), 237, 238
Sudeten German Party, 94
Sudetenland, 94

Tannenberg Group, 149
Terboven, Josef, 53, 242
T-4 Program, 23, 70, 159, 230, 258
Thälmann, Ernst, 113, 242–44
Thierack, Otto Georg, 61, 244
Third Reich
    agriculture ministry of, 35–36
    business in, 130
    racial theories of, 73–74
    radio in, 65–66
    religion in, 131, 161, 162
Thule Society, 42
Thus Spake Zarathustra (Nietzsche), 170
Thyssen, Fritz, 112, 244–45
Tirpitz, Alfred von, 91
Todt, Fritz, 67, 226, 245–46
Todt Organization, 245–46
Tojo, Hideki, 246–47
To the Bitter End (Gisevius), 73
Treblinka, 230
Tresckow, Henning von, 152, 232, 247
Triumph of the Will (film), 191
Troost, Paul Ludwig, 247–48
Trott zu Solz, Adam von, 248–49
Truman, Harry S., 249–50
Twenty-Five Points program, 43, 55, 110

U-boats, 41
    Raeder and, 184
Udet, Ernst, 126, 187
Ukraine, 134
    German occupation of, 135
    Rosenberg as minister of, 200–201

Van der Lubbe, Marinus, 251

Vatican City
    pact with Italian Fascists on, 180
    Reich ambassador to, 255, 256
Versailles, Treaty of, 86
    German violations of, 114
Vichy France, 7, 34, 142
    condemnation of de Gaulle by, 37
    Pétain and, 179–80
Victor Emmanuel II, 163
Völkischer Beobachter (People's Observer) (newspaper), 7, 17, 22, 45, 50, 91, 199
Volkssturm, 22
Volkswagen, 144
V-1 and V-2 rockets, 25

Waffen-SS, 9, 38, 103, 172
Wagner, Richard, 252–53
Wagner, Siegfried, 253
Wagner, Winifred, 253
Wallenberg, Raoul, 254–55
Wannsee Conference, 61, 161
war economy (Wehrwirtschaft), 56, 92
Warlimont, Walther, 255
Warsaw ghetto
    uprising in, 239
Wehrmacht, 18, 63, 89, 123, 134, 142–43, 145, 151, 152, 186
    see also Oberkommando der Wehrmacht
Weimar Constitution, 112
    Article 48 of, 26
Weizsäcker, Ernst Freiherr von, 255–56
Wessel, Horst, 256
Westdeutscher Beobachter (Western German Observer) (newspaper), 144
White Rose rebellion, 61, 123–24, 215, 216
Wiedemann, Fritz, 256
Wiesel, Elie, 257
Wiesenthal, Simon, 47, 231, 257
Wilhelm II, 16, 29, 257
    abdication of, 86, 258
Wirth, Christian, 72, 258–59
Wisliceny, Dieter, 259
Witzleben, Erwin von, 259–60
Wolff, Karl, 104, 260–61
wolf packs, 41
women
    Nazi view on role of, 216, 217
Women in the Third Reich, The (Scholtz-Klink), 217–18
World Crisis (Winston Churchill), 31

Yorck von Wartenburg, Peter Graf, 262

Zeitzler, Kurt, 263
Zhukov, Georgy, 229
Zyklon B, 122

PICTURE CREDITS

Cover photo: Mary Evans/Weimar Archive
Estelle Bechoefer, courtesy of United States Holocaust Memorial Museum Photo Archives, 115
© Bettmann/CORBIS, 37, 68
© CORBIS, 50, 63, 131, 248
Franklin D. Roosevelt Library, 197
Hulton/Archive by Getty Images, 10, 16, 20, 41, 58, 138, 143, 148, 169, 177, 184, 189, 206, 219, 233, 243, 260
Library of Congress, 31, 119, 157
National Archives, 24, 82, 90, 95, 106, 110, 127, 164, 195, 212, 225, 228
Simon Wiesenthal Center Archives, 77, 101
State Museum of Auschwitz-Birkenau, courtesy of United States Holocaust Memorial Museum Photo Archives, 154
Courtesy of United States Holocaust Memorial Museum Photo Archives, 46, 238, 254

ABOUT THE AUTHOR

Jeff T. Hay received a Ph.D. in European history from the University of California, San Diego, and now teaches European and world history, including a course on the Holocaust, at San Diego State University. He is the editor of a number of historical anthologies, including Greenhaven's *The Renaissance* and *Europe Rules the World*. He lives in Del Mar, California.

ABOUT THE CONSULTING EDITOR

Christopher R. Browning is Frank Porter Graham Professor of History at the University of North Carolina, Chapel Hill. He holds a Ph.D. from the University of Wisconsin, Madison, and an honorary doctorate from Hebrew Union College. A distinguished historian of the Holocaust, he delivered the George Macaulay Trevelyan Lectures at Cambridge University in 1999. He is the author of six books on the subject, including *Ordinary Men: Reserve Police Battalion 101 and the Final Solution in Poland* (1992), and is currently writing a two-volume study of Nazi Jewish policy during World War II as part of Yad Vashem's multivolume comprehensive history of the Holocaust.